LIBERATING LIFE

LIBERATING LIFE

Contemporary Approaches to Ecological Theology

Edited by
Charles Birch
William Eakin
Jay B. McDaniel

ORBIS BOOKS

Maryknoll, New York 10545

The Catholic Foreign Mission Society of America (Maryknoll) recruits and trains people for overseas missionary service. Through Orbis Books Maryknoll aims to foster the international dialogue that is essential to mission. The books published, however, reflect the opinions of their authors and are not meant to represent the official position of the society.

Copyright © 1990 Orbis Books
Published by Orbis Books, Maryknoll, New York 10545
All rights reserved
Printed in the United States of America

Library of Congress Cataloging-in-Publication Data

Liberating life : contemporary approaches to ecological theology /
   edited by Charles Birch, William Eakin, Jay McDaniel.
      p.   cm.
   ISBN 0-88344-689-8
   1. Nature—Religious aspects—Christianity.   2. Human ecology—
Religious aspects—Christianity.   I. Birch, Charles.   II. Eakin.
William.   III. McDaniel, Jay B. (Jay Byrd), 1949-
BT695.5.L52   1990
261.8′362—dc20
                                        90-36469
                                           CIP

Because God's love itself is subject to no bounds and excludes nothing from its embrace, there is no creature's interest that is not also God's interest and, therefore, necessarily included in the redeeming love of God.

>—Schubert Ogden
>Perkins Theological Seminary
>Dallas, Texas

If we work for the poor and the penguins simultaneously, we can hope for a better common present and future.

>—M. Swaminathan
>President of the Indian National
>Academy of Sciences

Contents

Acknowledgments   ix

Introduction   1
 Charles Birch, William Eakin, and Jay B. McDaniel

PART 1
RESOURCES FROM SCRIPTURE AND TRADITION   7

1. Biblical Views of Nature   9
 John Austin Baker

2. Covenant and Creation   27
 Wesley Granberg-Michaelson

3. New Testament Foundations for Understanding the Creation   37
 Paulos Mar Gregorios

4. A Sacramental Approach to Environmental Issues   46
 John Habgood

PART 2
NEW ETHICAL HORIZONS   55

5. Christian Obligation for the Liberation of Nature   57
 Charles Birch

6. Christianity and Animal Rights: The Challenge and Promise   73
 Tom Regan

7. Ecofeminism, Reverence for Life, and Feminist Theological
   Ethics   88
 Lois K. Daly

PART 3
VOICES FROM AFRICA, ASIA, AND LATIN AMERICA   109

8. Latin America and the Need for a Life-Liberating Theology   111
 Ingemar Hedström

9. The Effects on Korea of Un-Ecological Theology   125
   Jong-Sun Noh

10. Community of Life: Ecological Theology in African Perspective   137
    Harvey Sindima

PART 4
NEW SENSIBILITIES   149

11. The Spirituality of the Earth   151
    Thomas Berry

12. Religious and Cosmic Homelessness: Some Environmental
    Implications   159
    John F. Haught

13. Chance, Purpose, and the Order of Nature   182
    Charles Birch

14. Imaging a Theology of Nature: The World as God's Body   201
    Sallie McFague

15. Revisioning God and the Self: Lessons from Buddhism   228
    Jay B. McDaniel

PART 5
NEW DIRECTIONS FOR THE CHURCH   259

Afterword. The Role of Theology of Nature in the Church   261
    John B. Cobb, Jr.

Appendix. Liberating Life: A Report to the World Council
    of Churches   273

Authors   291

Acknowledgments

The editors wish to express their special thanks to the sub-unit on Church and Society of the World Council of Churches, and to all those involved in the conference at Annecy, France (see p. 5 and Appendix pp. 273-90).

In addition, we wish to express our gratitude to the editors, publishers, and authors who have made possible the inclusion of some of the following essays, specifically William B. Eerdmans Publishing Company for permission to reprint an essay from the book *Tending the Garden* by Paulos Mar Gregorios, and Ingemar Hedström (and the Department of Ecumenical Research, San Jose, Costa Rica) for the rights to excerpts from his books *Somos Parte de un Gran Equilibrio: La Crisis Ecológica en Centro América* and *Volverán las Golondrinas: La Reintegración de la Creación desde una Perspectiva Latinoamericana*. Our thanks to Kathlyn Smith for her translations of these excerpts. We are pleased to include with the author's permission John Austin Baker's "Biblical Views of Nature," which appeared originally in *Anticipation*, 25 (January 1979), pp. 40-46.

The editors extend thanks to Hendrix College for the support it gave this project through a faculty grant and to the individuals of Computer Services at Hendrix College who spent long hours with the computer versions of this book. The editors also are indebted to the Marshall T. Steel Center for the Study of Religion and Philosophy for its general support and for making this project possible at all. Thanks as well to Blaize Stewart for his assistance in manuscript preparation, to Laura Eakin and Kathy McDaniel for their understanding and support, and to Cathy Goodwin for her continuous, invaluable help and good cheer.

Introduction

Charles Birch, William Eakin, and Jay B. McDaniel

Prompted by liberation theologies, Christians rightly see that God is present in the suffering and struggles of the poor and powerless and that authentic Christian life is one of solidarity with the victimized. While the victimized are, of course, other people, they are also fellow animals subjected to cruel treatment in factory farms and scientific laboratories; endangered and extinct species whose habitats have been disrupted by injurious economic practices; and the earth itself, with its shrinking forests, eroded topsoils, encroaching deserts, contaminated waterways, polluted atmosphere, and depleted ozone layer. The "principalities and powers" that oppress the poor also oppress the earth and other living beings. In light of this widespread abuse of life and environment the theme of liberation must itself be extended to include the earth and other living creatures. As liberation theologies enter the twenty-first century, such extension, we believe, is a next step in liberation thinking.

This book consists of essays written by authors committed to this next step. Not all are "liberation theologians," though all have been shaped by, and are in agreement with, the concerns for justice that characterize liberation theologies. Rather all are, in their own ways, "ecological theologians," though they might use other names. They are theologians for whom peace and justice include an unmitigated concern for the well-being of people, particularly the poor, but also a concern for peace with the earth and justice for other living beings. They are troubled by that neglect of plants, animals, and the earth which, despite many biblical emphases to the contrary, has characterized much modern Christian thinking. Their essays are attempts to articulate from their own different points of view the theological foundations for a life-liberating theology and ethic.

In gathering these essays together we have identified a new, emerging consensus among Christian theologians. The consensus is that an anthropocentric ethic, understood as an emphasis on human well-being at the expense of the earth and other living beings, must be replaced by an ethic of respect for life and environment. We think it quite significant that theologians with different perspectives and backgrounds are moved by this common concern. Because they are individually shaped by perspectives as

1

diverse as Latin American liberation theology, Korean *Minjung* theology, African theology, Orthodox theology, Anglican theology, Roman Catholic theology, feminist theology, and process theology, their agreement on the need for a life-liberating orientation is striking. It is as if life itself has cried out for freedom from human exploitation, and they, in different contexts, have heard it. The purpose of this volume is to introduce readers to this emerging consensus, to show how it can be advanced by a variety of Christian traditions, and to add to its momentum.

JUSTICE AND SUSTAINABILITY

An additional purpose of the volume is to show that concerns for ecological sustainability and justice for the human oppressed are often closely linked. This is important because justice and respect for the integrity of creation are sometimes seen, wrongly we believe, as *alternative* human concerns. Those who emphasize human justice sometimes see ecological sustainability as the cry of those who benefit from the present structures of society and who want to distance themselves from the abuses of power within it.

In our view justice and sustainability must ultimately be united into a single vision of life-giving hope. Although the principles of justice and sustainability may be in tension in the structures of present society, social justice and ecological sustainability ultimately require one another. There can be no justice without sustainability and no sustainability without justice. A society that seeks only justice without regard to the consequences of its behavior for the ecological future cannot be just. But it is equally true that a society which abandons concern for justice rides roughshod over the concerns of the poor and the powerless as well as the environment on which the continuance of life depends.

For example, an emphasis on human justice alone, without any concern for the rest of creation, can lead to the promotion of unlimited economic growth—the ever-increasing production and consumption of material goods—as the sole objective of public policy. Of course, a concern for increased production and consumption can be and is a legitimate concern for countries suffering from poverty. But such a concern needs to be complemented by other concerns, including concerns to respect the earth and the rural communities that are closely bound to the earth. An absolute emphasis on economic growth, even in the name of justice, has led in many countries to the development of urban centers for the rich surrounded by ghettos of the poor. The poor have been driven off the land from which they derived a living to make room for agribusiness or deforestation, often being forced into slums in the big cities. The promoters of such programs often argue that their creation of wealth and the wealthy provide both jobs and wealth for the poor. Their formula is as simple as it is deceptive: wealth creates jobs. But it has not worked this way.

There are many reasons why the single-minded pursuit of wealth does not lead to justice. On a global scale there is one centrally important reason. The carrying capacity of the earth is limited for people just as is the carrying capacity of a pasture for sheep; exceed the capacity of such a pasture and the farm deteriorates. There are limits to the resources of the earth and the capacity of the earth to cope with pollution of its waters and atmosphere. All around us are signs that the carrying capacity of the earth for people—whatever the exact capacity happens to be—is now being exceeded. The result is the devastation of the environment.

Furthermore, such limits imply what is known as the "impossibility theorem." This theorem states that the high rate of consumption and pollution of the rich nations would be impossible for all the peoples of the earth. This poses starkly a real problem of justice. Can those of us who live in the rich world morally justify a way of living which is impossible for the rest? We, the editors of this volume, think not.

If it is the case that the carrying capacity of the earth would be exceeded when everyone in the world was as rich as present Americans and Japanese, then either (a) a small proportion of the people in the world can be rich and a large proportion poor (as at present), or (b) the rich must reduce *their* rate of consumption and pollution in order that the poor may increase their rates of consumption. But economic systems the world over operate as though the problems of injustice will be solved by letting everyone, rich and poor, gain in wealth as fast as they can.

In light of the limits to the carrying capacity of the earth and the current emphasis on economic growth as the solution to the problems of injustice, we come face-to-face with the reality that justice and ecological sustainability require each other.

To work for these objectives at a global level is to encounter huge problems. The existence of nation-states makes it difficult to find global solutions at all. But we shall be driven to fight through the difficulties just as nations are beginning to do in seeking solutions to the problems of the greenhouse effect and the depletion of the ozone layer. The burning of Brazilian forests not only drives Indians from their livelihood but puts an unbearable load on the polluted upper atmosphere; it is a global as well as a local problem. The rich world both within Brazil and outside that nation may be required, in the names of both justice and ecological sustainability, to call a halt to such burning and to subsidize some less destructive way of development.

The plight of the poor who are driven to live in the great delta regions such as the Ganges in Bangladesh may in the long run depend upon the rich nations. With some regularity these areas of the earth are plagued by devastating floods. If, as predicted, the greenhouse effect due to pollution of the atmosphere causes a rise in sea level, these people will be among the first to suffer—even more than at present. The reversing of this situation is not a matter of local action. It must be global.

Throughout the world vast areas have been rendered unfit for habitation by plants and animals native to those regions and are now becoming unfit for human habitation as well. Unsuitable practices of land-use have reduced the ability of ecological systems to support human life throughout the third world. In addition, high-risk technologies have resulted in accidents such as those at Bhopal and Chernobyl. In the latter case more than 100,000 people were evacuated and an area of up to 2600 square kilometers was rendered uninhabitable.

The degradation of agricultural land is the most widespread threat to human habitability worldwide. In some cases, natural disasters are worsened by human activity. Desertification, for example, has irreparably damaged millions of hectares of once productive land and made environmental refugees out of millions of sub-Saharan farmers in this decade alone. While more land is rendered uninhabitable each year, more people are added to the world's population than ever before. Furthermore, most of these people are added to areas already in advanced stages of environmental degradation.

Ever since the beginning of the industrial revolution many have tended to regard the world as a factory for the exclusive use of human beings. We have done this with little regard for the life-support systems that make our life possible and for the intrinsic value of those creatures who share the planet with us. It is incumbent upon us to find better ways of managing the environment and to find new sorts of ethics that include all living creatures. Without this, the vision of the liberation of life will be no more than an idle dream.

The good news is that small groups of people around the globe have seen the writing on the wall and are organizing themselves into action groups for the liberation of life. Some are operating at the political level in so-called green parties. Others concern themselves with critical local problems. In Brazil many Christian base communities, with a total of three million members, work with the poor and the oppressed environment that makes them poorer. In Indonesia, six hundred independent development groups work on environmental protection alone. In India, there are similarly some twelve thousand groups working for more appropriate development. These are but a few examples of many more given by Alan Durning in a study of grass-roots movements throughout the world. Whether these scattered beginnings rise in a global groundswell depends upon how many more individuals commit their creativity and energy to the challenge, to new vision and responsible action. As Durning concludes, "The inescapable lesson for each of us is distilled in the words of Angeles Serrano, a grandmother and community activist from Manila's Leveriza slum: 'Act, act, act. You just can't watch'" (Durning 1988, 55).

This book is written by and for those who can't just watch. It is intended as a resource for envisioning new, responsible ways of thinking that can assist us in becoming responsible citizens of the planet.

ORIGINS OF ESSAYS

Before concluding this introduction, a word about the origins of some of these essays is in order. Some (Noh, Cobb, Regan, Haught, McFague, Daly, Birch, McDaniel) were first delivered at a consultation on ecological theology held in Annecy, France, on 10-15 September, 1988, and organized through the sub-unit on Church and Society of the World Council of Churches. This consultation was attended by fourteen persons whose fields included science, theology, philosophy, and ethics. The group was both international and ecumenical in character, including as it did Protestants of diverse denominations and Roman Catholics (though unavoidably no Orthodox members). In order to widen still further the scope of this book contributions were solicited from others representing Anglican, Orthodox, and Latin American perspectives.

Most of the papers delivered at the consultation were circulated in advance of the meeting at Annecy and were discussed in four days of plenary sessions chaired by Jay McDaniel and Charles Birch. Most of the papers in this book were revised in light of these discussions. The remaining two days of the consultation were spent in drafting the report. This was done in three working groups who came together for a final plenary session to produce the final report and recommendations. The report and recommendations were presented to a working committee of the sub-unit of Church and Society of the World Council of Churches in Tambov, Russia, immediately after the consultation in Annecy. This committee took appropriate action on each of the recommendations. We are grateful to the World Council of Churches for allowing us to include the final report and recommendations as an appendix to this volume.

Even with regard to the essays originating at Annecy, France, the following collection of documents is much more than an ecumenical document or an in-house report to the World Council of Churches. It is a resource for the transformation of our thought about and action toward that community which includes not only human beings but other living beings and the earth itself. We hope it serves that end.

WORKS CITED

Durning, Alan B. "Action at the Grassroots: Fighting Poverty and Environmental Decline." *Worldwatch Paper*. Washington, D.C.: Worldwatch Institute, 1988.

PART 1

Resources from Scripture and Tradition

Almost thirty years ago the historian Lynn White, Jr., published an essay indicting the Western Christian tradition for its destructive attitudes toward nature. It was called "The Historic Roots of Our Ecologic Crisis," and it appeared in the prestigious periodical Science (155, 1967, 1203-7). It has since been reprinted often in numerous anthologies, sometimes to the chagrin of Christians who disagree with White's claims. According to White, Western Christians have tended to view nature as merely a means to human ends, merely a resource for human use; as a consequence, they bear "a huge burden of guilt" for the ecological crises to which their societies have subjected much of the earth. White calls upon Christians to recover some of the minority voices in their own tradition—that of Francis of Assisi, for example—in order to move toward a more ecologically sensitive future.

White's claims have not gone unchallenged. Respondents have pointed out that the Christian heritage is much more complex and nuanced than his claims warrant, both in its theology and in its practices; and that the causes of our modern environmental crises have as much to do with cultural, economic, and political forces independent of Christianity as with Christian habits of thought. Still, White's claims have rightly challenged those of us in Christian communities to look anew at our heritages, including scripture, with ecologically sensitized eyes. Are our traditions ecologically bankrupt? The essays in this section show that at least some of our traditions can be employed in service to, rather than destruction of, life on earth. The individual essays written by John Austin Baker, Wesley Granberg-Michaelson, and Paulos Mar Gregorios show how certain biblical perspectives can assist in the cultivation of an ecologically sensitive Christianity; and the essay by John Habgood shows how a sacramental perspective, characteristic of many post-biblical traditions, can enrich our appreciation of the earth and guide us toward sane, humane use of various technologies.

Biblical Views of Nature

John Austin Baker

One or two remarks by way of preamble may be helpful in preventing misunderstandings. This paper is descriptive and interpretative; it is an attempt to convey my understanding of the views of nature found in the biblical writers. It is not intended to draw normative conclusions for our own attitude to nature or our treatment of it. It is, therefore, primarily a religio-historical essay, not one in "biblical theology." The most I have allowed myself by way of contemporary application is to comment at various points on which of our current attitudes and policies seem compatible with the biblical view under consideration, and which do not. Secondly, I have called the paper "Biblical Views of Nature" because I do not believe there is any one view held by the whole range of biblical writers. Any single view which incorporated all their various insights, assuming such a synthesis could be made, would be a theological construct of our day, not something properly called biblical. This is not to say, of course, that there are not themes and beliefs which the biblical writers share in their approach to nature, but the differences are as important as the common assumptions.

Ecological theologies that are shaped by biblical materials require a thorough analysis of the various views of nature held by biblical writers. This essay offers that analysis. It was written more than a decade ago, when theologians in different parts of the world were first realizing the depths of the crisis inflicted upon earth by human exploitation. It appeared in the World Council of Churches' publication *Anticipation* (No. 25, January 1979, 40-46).

Ten years later the essay is even more timely. Acknowledging the diversity of biblical perspectives on nature, Bishop Baker shows how the Bible combines concerns for creation with concerns for the transformation and redemption of the world, and how both sets of concerns have profound implications for an understanding of nature. However contemporary ecological theologians appropriate or repent of the various views of nature in the Christian scriptures, an analysis such as this is indispensable for ecologically sensitive vision.

Again, however, I have allowed myself to draw attention to some of these common (or majority) assumptions, since these can be helpful in any attempt to compare biblical views with those from other sources.

The writers of the Hebrew Scriptures, unlike ourselves, did not have an immense stock of universal or semi-abstract terms. While this limited them in some directions — philosophy and metaphysics, for example — it also saved them from a certain woolliness of thought to which we are peculiarly liable. Thus, the lack of a word corresponding to our term was in some respects a handicap: but it also safeguarded them against lumping together things that have no obvious business together and against being taken in by such phrases as "communing with nature," or "nature, red in tooth and claw." What they saw when they looked around them was not some undifferentiated global category but particular things — mountains, seas, rivers, crawling animals, oak trees, birds, the sun and moon, and so on. Their nearest approach to an all-embracing word for their environment was *'erets*, the earth. The title *Friends of the Earth* they might have understood; *naturelover* would have required some explanation.

How far are humans involved in nature, and how far have they distanced themselves from it? The basic elements of this question can be found scattered in the Hebrew Scriptures. Humanity is part of the panorama of nature. Psalm 104 places humanity with great artistry in the context of all the other teeming life of the earth. If the human is the final figure to be painted in, and therefore in some sense special or climactic, this is very much understated (v. 23). In the same way, in the older creation story (J) in Genesis 2:4b-25, both man and the animals are formed out of the soil. Here, in a strange fashion, the original fusion of supposed fact and faith-image, after an interim period of being dismissed by the religious mind as purely symbolic and crudely so, becomes in our day once again the vivid symbol for a faith-interpretation of literal fact. Genesis does not go as far as the following quotation, but the germ of the idea is there:

> My body was originally formed from an ovum and a sperm in my mother's body, and this ovum and sperm were formed of matter which came into the bloodstream of my father and mother from the world outside. I am formed of the matter of the universe and am linked through it to the remotest stars in time and space. My body has passed through all the stages of evolution through which matter has passed over millions of years. I have been present when matter was first formed into atoms and molecules, when the living cell appeared. I have passed through every stage from protoplasm to fish and animal and man. If I could know myself, I would know matter and life, animal and man, since all are contained within me (Griffiths, 35).

Nevertheless, even this older creation story is concerned predominantly to stress the distinctness of man from the rest of creation. Birds and beasts may share a material origin with man, and even a divine artificer, but they are not adequate companions and partners for him (v. 20). Only another human being, formed out of his own living substance, can be that (vv. 21-23). It is this unique kinship, so the story claims, which explains the all-surpassing force of the bond between man and woman (v. 24). The superiority of man to the animals is further emphasized by the incident of man's naming of all the living creatures. This act has two important implications. First, to give a name to some other being is to claim and exercise sovereignty over it. So a parent names his newborn child, an overlord his vassal (2 Kgs 24:17). True, man gives a name to his wife at her first creation (Gn 2:23), implying the male hegemony characteristic of the biblical world, and reasserts his authority over her, in accordance with God's judicial verdict after their joint offense, by giving her a new name (3:20). But the first of these two names, the generic *woman* (*'iššā*), emphasizes that woman is the only creature who belongs in the same category as *man* (*'iš*).

Second, there is the strong conviction of the whole ancient world that a true name expresses the nature and controls the destiny of its owner (cf. Gn 35:16-18, for example). By giving animals the truly appropriate name for each (Gn 2:19), Adam proves that he has insight into their true nature. This at once puts him on a different plane from them. He is a creature nearer to God than they, for he shares some at least of the insight which enabled God to create them in the first place. So the giving of names to the animals by man is a sign of actual superiority and legitimate authority over them on his part—not the absolute superiority and authority that belong to God alone, but real nevertheless, even if relative. By this act of sovereignty Adam proves that none of these other creatures is a "helper fit for him" (vv. 18, 20); and paradoxically the act of naming by which he claims authority over his wife is also a recognition of her essential equality with him. That this is the correct reading of the story is confirmed by the divine sentence passed on Adam and Eve for their offense in eating of the fruit of the tree of the knowledge of good and evil. Because man has rebelled against his proper overlord, God, his own subjects are to rebel against him. The tillage of the earth was once within his strength and its fruits were all beneficial (2:15); now it is to yield less, and that only to unremitting labor, and some of its produce will be worthless for human consumption (3:17-19). Similarly, the woman who upset the order of things by persuading her husband to disobedience loses the relationship of a free subordinate partner and becomes his servant, driven by a compulsive attachment (3:16). In all this, too, it is possible to discern the traits of kingship in the portrait of man, expressed not only through the naming ritual but also in the ancient cultic symbolism of the tending and watering of the tree of life, a sacral duty of the king.

In the later creation narrative (P) in Genesis 1:1-2:4a, man's supremacy is spelt out categorically, though here, be it noted, the sub-plot of male superiority to the female is eliminated. This is not to be taken as implying equality of the sexes in the writer's mind, merely that in the context of the relation of man to nature, all human beings share in the distinctive superiority of their species in the created order. In this story man's supremacy is given technical theological expression, peculiar to this writer and his school. Man is "in (God's) image" and "after (his) likeness" (Gn 1:26-27). The exact meaning of this phrase has been endlessly debated. There may be influence from the Egyptian formula, according to which the pharaoh is the "image of Amun-Re," in which case there are viceregal overtones, made explicit in v. 28. But the Hebrew and Egyptian phrases are not truly parallel. Much more certain is the implication that man is the nearest visible pointer to what God looks like (cf. Ez 1:26). The interesting question is: How far is this similarity thought to go below the surface into the realm of understanding and character? To some degree it must do, since it is improbable that any writer would make God give even a shadow of his own unique likeness to a creature that had nothing in common with him; and this common-sense conclusion is confirmed by the fact that God entrusts to man dominion over his new and wonderful earth and its other inhabitants.

The major difference between this creation story and the older one, so far as our present subject is concerned, is that in Genesis 1 the theme of a common material origin for man and animals is suppressed altogether. The writer seems to have held a view, instanced elsewhere in the ancient world, that the earth and the sea themselves "brought forth" their various inhabitants (vv. 20-21, 24-25), but he has combined this with safeguards against any divinization of earth or sea by insisting simultaneously that in fact God himself "created" (v. 21) and "made" (v. 25) the creatures these primordial entities generated. The resultant picture is that all animal life was produced either by the earth or the sea as a result of God's creative edict and operation. There is a very careful gradation upward from the production of plant life (vv. 11-12), where God issues the creative fiat, "Let the earth put forth vegetation, . . ." but is not said to have "made" or "created" what is put forth. The writer seems to be saying that animal life, whether on land or in the sea, is more marvelous than mere plant life, and, although issuing from the womb of the earth and from the waters, required a special operation of God to bring it about. Then in the case of man we take yet another step upward. Here the divine edict and activity are everything; no intermediate creative source is named. Man is presented as created by God directly, and the question whether he too came from the earth is at least passed over in silence. It is possible that Psalm 139:15 draws on a myth that man was "earth-born." If such a view was current, then the writer of Genesis 1 has deliberately snubbed it. As for the fact that God is said both to "create" (v. 27) and to "make" (v. 26) man, there do not to the present writer seem to be solid grounds for finding here two distinct theological concepts. As is well-known, the verb *bara'*, "create," is found in the Hebrew Scriptures only with God as subject. The significance of this is hard to assess. The word is used only by the Priestly Writer,

Deuteronomy, Jeremiah, Second and Third Isaiah, Amos, Psalms, Malachi, and Koheleth. With the exception of Koheleth, who is late and therefore drawing on an already established usage, all these sources are strongly priestly in character (the Amos instance comes in a formal hymnic doxology which may or may not be the prophet's own work). Since the Hebrew Scriptures are, to all intents and purposes, the only Hebrew literature of their period that we possess, it is precarious to argue from evidence that *bara'* was an exclusively theological *terminus technicus* with no secular use. Etymologically it has been linked with an ancient South Arabian verb meaning "to build," and with a verb in the dialect of Socotra meaning "to bear, bring forth." The absence of more standard ANE parallels suggests that it might have been a fairly esoteric word, entering Hebrew through a specialized channel of some antiquity. (There may just be some significance in the fact that *Levi*, the priestly gentilic, is also, in one view, related to a South Arabian word for a cultic official.) On balance, the most likely view seems to be that *bara'* simply means "to build" or "construct," but that it came into the Hebrew as part of the sacral vocabulary of priestly circles and may already at its importation have had by convention an exclusive link with the deity. What we are not justified in doing on the basis of known usage is to read into *bara'* anywhere in the Hebrew Scriptures later metaphysical understandings of the idea of creation, such as *creatio ex nihilo*, which is not the sense of Genesis 1:1f. and is indeed not found in Jewish religious writing until 2 Maccabees 7:28, where there is undoubted Hellenistic influence. In the end, therefore, there is no reason to see any substantial difference of meaning between "create" and "make" in Genesis 1. The collocation of the two words at the end of the Priestly creation story (Gn 2:3) is a sonorous full close for the stylistic effect. Nevertheless, with regard to our main point it seems clear that by stressing the direct divine activity involved in the making of man, and by omitting any reference to physical stuff out of which man is formed, this writer is intentionally minimizing that which is common to man and the rest of the animal world. The only common bond is the theological one: both are the works of God and created to fulfill the particular purposes he has in mind for them.

It is clear, however, that humanity's purpose and role is a unique one. Man in Genesis 1 occupies much the same high place in the scheme of things as he does in Psalm 8: "Yet thou hast made him little less than God, and dost crown him with glory and honour. Thou hast given him dominion over the works of thy hands; thou hast put all things under his feet, all sheep and oxen, and also the beasts of the field, the birds of the air, and the fish of the sea, whatever passes along the paths of the sea" (vv. 5-8). To our ears such words sound very like the most blatant human imperialism toward the rest of nature, as does the divine commission to man in Genesis 1:28; and in modern times they may have fostered such an attitude and been used as a divine "exploiters' charter" to justify it. But what in their biblical context did they originally imply?

One connection of this type of language is with the institution of kingship. Under the influence of Mesopotamian models, even quite petty kings in the ANE seem to have used cosmic iconography to express their status and authority. Solomon's throne, with six steps and a curved back (1 Kgs 10:18-20), symbolized universal dominion; and the embroidery on the collar of the later high priests, which was probably zodiacal and signified the whole cosmos, was almost certainly taken over from royal robes of earlier times (cf. Wis 18:24a). "Kingship came down from heaven," the ANE believed, and part of the mystique of kingship was that every king was God's viceregent on earth. One of a king's most important duties was to ensure fertility and prosperity by his obedience to the gods and by his observance of the yearly rituals. We can trace thinking of this kind at many points in the Hebrew Scriptures; for example, in the famine sent on Israel for the wickedness of Ahab (1 Kgs 17:1); or conversely, in a text like Psalm 72, where unimaginable abundance is to be a mark of the reign of the ideal ruler. The conditions pictured in this psalm — for example, the king's worldwide sovereignty (v. 8) — certainly never obtained in any actual reign; but the psalm is nonetheless not just a dream of an indefinite future. Verse 1 refers to an actual king; it is a prayer, perhaps used at the coronation, that the vision painted in the psalm may come true in *this* king's reign. Primarily, therefore, the "man" and "son of man" of Psalm 8 is also the king, whose sacred office endows him with the resources of divine power not just over his human subjects but over all other creatures within his domain; and it is only his sins which cause this power to be withheld. Later this correlation between righteousness and prosperity was to be democratized, and the magical element confined to the direct action of God; in the final versions of Deuteronomy, for example, the responsibility for righteousness is laid on all Israelites equally, and abundance is God's reward for this. But there is also another line of development, which continues to use the figure of the individual ruler. As hopes set on actual rulers are falsified, so longing grows more intense for a ruler who will measure up to God's standards. Under such a king all the anomalies of man and nature will be ironed out, and harmony and abundance will reign. The most famous instance of this hope in Hebrew Scriptures is Isaiah 11:1-9.

By a common feature of human mythical thinking, however, paradise in the end time is thought of as the recreation of a primeval paradise at the dawn of creation, the lost "golden age." Thus we find a small but significant detail common to both Genesis 1 and the eschatological vision of Isaiah 11: the vegetarianism of the creation. Animals eat grass and man eats grains and fruits (cf. Gn 1:29-30 and Is 11:6-7). It is not possible to decide for certain whether the prophetic vision of the end time is consciously drawing upon paradisal traditions of the *Urzeit*, or whether a passage like Genesis 1 owes something to the prophetic imagery. Both no doubt derive along their respective routes from a long, complex, and interwoven traditional history. (Awareness of a link between the eschatological fulfillment and the primal paradise story shows in the words of Isaiah 65:25, "and the snake [shall eat] dust," a reapplication of Isaiah 11:6f.) What we can say is that the basic assumptions of the Israelite view of history work out in two very different shapings of the whole historical sequence in the priestly and prophetic perspectives. Both are acutely aware of human sin and the disruption it has imported into the whole created order. The prophet, however, is interested primarily in the resolution of this discord in the new age God is going to inaugurate, the world in which righteousness is going to be achieved and peace and well-being reign. The priest sees God's goal as something much more immediately manageable; namely a world where life is regulated by the God-given law, and any margin of failure is covered by cultic atonement. Consequently, though recognizing the imperfections of the present, he does not look for any radical reformation of it. The time — which must be a reality at some point — when God's ideals are fully realized is in the primal past. Then all things were "good, very good" (Gn 1:31). The future which the prophetic vision desiderates, and the past, which the priestly theodicy presupposes, are, therefore, inevitably very close to one another in character; both speak of a way the world ought to be, but is not. And both link this ideal condition with the right exercise of kingship, either that of the perfect Israelite ruler or of the human species in its cosmic vocation. But the "dominion" promised to man in Genesis 1 or Psalm 8, and the government expected of the ideal Davidic ruler in Isaiah 11, are poles apart from the kind of right to egotistical exploitation that the words superficially suggest to our ears. They are in essence a perfect obedience to the will of God, which respects the divine order in nature and is rewarded by nature's recognition of man as the greatest of God's creatures and its provision of a sufficiency of food for all flesh (cf. Ps 145:15f.). If this vision has anything to say to our present situation, it is certainly not to ratify the extermination of species or the ruthless greed that exhausts precious natural resources for short-term profit. On the other hand, it would be overly simple to claim the Hebrew Scriptures in support of our modern study of animal life or the work of environmental conservation, since it is clear that neither priest not prophet thought the order of nature as we now see it to reflect God's intentions, either original or ultimate, for it.

We referred just now to the general Israelite assumption that human sin was the factor that had disrupted the cosmic order. The Torah expresses in a number of ways the idea that man declined drastically from the standards of the golden age. The story of Cain and Abel (Gn 4) is one; the decline in the normal length of human life, another (cf. Gn 5 with 10:10-26 and 47:9). (This later feature is another link with the late prophetic vision of restoration in Isaiah 65:17-25, already mentioned, where some improvement in longevity to a norm of 100 years is promised: v. 20.) Another mark of decline of more direct relevance to our present subject, is the change in the divine laws of life after the flood. The new start for the human race, embodied in Noah and his family, is marked by a divine covenant, modeled ultimately on the treaties imposed unilaterally in some ANE empires by suzerains on their vassals, consisting of promises by the overlord and obligations laid upon his subjects. The promise is that never again will God destroy all living things by a flood (Gn 9:8-17; the older version of the story has the same promise, though not in covenant form: 8:21-22). It is interesting and important that this covenant is made not just with man but with all living creatures (five times repeated: 9:10, 12, 15, 16, 17) and indeed with the earth itself (9:13). The new laws of life (9:1-7) replace the ordinances established at the creation and modify them in significant respects. No longer is man's food to be fruit and grains only: "Every moving thing that lives shall be food for you; and as I gave you green plants, I give you everything" (9:3). (This license is qualified for Israel later, when they are granted the higher insight, denied to the nations, of the distinction between "clean" and "unclean" animals. Christianity's rejection of this distinction is thus of great symbolic importance for her universal mission.) The flood and the subsequent new start for the world are thus used as an opportunity to switch from the theoretic "golden age" to the conditions actually obtaining; and one of the saddest features of this change is the degradation of relations between humans and animals from their first created beauty. The language of Genesis 9:1-2, when compared with the phrasing of 1:28f., betrays at once the poignancy of the writer's feelings: "The fear of you and the dread of you shall be upon every beast of the earth, and upon every bird of the air, upon everything that creeps on the ground and all the fish of the sea; into your hand they are delivered." The language is that normally used of a conqueror slaughtering a routed army or sacking a fallen city. Man has become the enemy of all living things.

The Hebrew Scriptures, then, do nothing to justify the charge that they bless an exploitative, humanly self-centered attitude to nature. They recognize man's preying on nature as a fact, but characterize that fact as a mark of man's decline from the first perfect intentions of God for him or as a defect to be eradicated in God's perfect future. This is in tune with another notable feature of the Hebrew Scriptures, namely that they are permeated with what we can only call an affectionate and admiring approach to nature. We have already noted the supreme example of this in Psalm 104, but instances are to be found in other psalms that are not, as is that one, modeled on already existing foreign poetry (cf. Pss 19:1-6; 65:10-13; 84:3; 136; 148). The same attitude is particularly evident in the wisdom literature, with its many similes from observation of animals, weather, plant life, and so on. We also find a kindred spirit in some of the prophets, where the faithful obedience of nonhuman creatures to the divine will is contrasted with the faithfulness and perversity of men: "Even the stork in the heavens knows her times; and the turtledove, swallow, and crane keep the time of their coming; but my people know not the ordinance of the Lord" (Jer 8:7). This admiration of nature finds its climax in the book of Job, where the wonders of the natural order are used for a didactic purpose unique to the Bible, and possibly in all ancient literature: to make the point that humanity's whole attitude to the created order is wrong, because it is totally egoistic, totally anthropocentric. If humans were to stop even for a moment to consider the universe as it actually is, they would see that by far the greater part of it has no relevance to them at all. If God created Behemoth and Leviathan, it assuredly was not for humanity's benefit (chaps. 40-41); it must have been for some purpose opaque to humans, who can think only in terms of themselves and their situation. Such creatures glorify God in their existence according to rules far beyond our ken; God made them and delights in them for their own sake, not for some ulterior usefulness to us as human beings. The same point is made in a rather different way by drawing Job's attention to the seemingly idiotic behavior of certain animals such as the ostrich (39:13-18) or to the apparent pointlessness of certain phenomena, such as the brief spring rains, which cause a short-lived carpet of tiny flowers to appear in the desert (38:26-27). Why have flowers where there is no one to admire them? Man did not arrange any of these; if it had been left to him, he never would have done! But God did arrange them. We are left to draw our own conclusions either that God is daft, or perhaps that we with our purely human-conditioned "wisdom" take far too narrow and short-sighted a view to reach any genuine understanding of reality. This is not to say that a sound and sensible way of dealing with nature is not a part of the wisdom appropriate to humans, and as such itself a gift of God (cf. Isa 28:23-29). Not only is this accepted; it is in fact one particular application of a more general principle developed in the Hebrew Scriptures, which is of some importance for our subject. This is the principle that by observing the way in which nature functions we can arrive at *moral* guidance for human life. In the Hebrew Scriptures this is not taken beyond the most obvious instances; for example, the world is made in such a way that the lazy are likely to starve, and therefore it is wrong to be lazy. But significantly, such conduct is held to be wrong not just in a pragmatic sense but also in a theological one. For, as with everything else in the Hebrew Scriptures, such thinking has an extra dimension, the omni-relevant fact of God. Since it was the wisdom of God that made the world, God must have had some purpose in every detail of its ordering and must therefore have intended laziness to be dangerous. Hence diligent and sensible work can be said to be something God both commands and commends, and sloth something God condemns. There are, then, in the Hebrew Scriptures elements to justify a pragmatic, science-based ethic, at least in some such general terms as these: What by observation we discover really to work best, both for man and for other creatures, is something that loyalty to God requires us to put into practice. Even the point about what is best for other creatures, which may seem very modern, is not without foundation in Hebrew Scriptures in such passages as the law against taking the hen-bird as well as the eggs from the nest (Deut 22:6), or this saying from Proverbs: "A righteous man has regard for the life of his beast"

(12:10), where, be it noted, the quality that makes a man considerate of his working animals is not prudence or good business sense but "righteousness," a point all the more significant when we remember that in the Hebrew Scriptures one of the marks of righteousness is not mere even-handedness but active favor to the weak and deprived.

One reason why the attitude in the Hebrew Scriptures to nature is more sympathetic and comprehensible to us than that of some other ancient people is that for a good many of the writers of the Hebrew Scriptures, though not all, nature had been, to use a modern term, substantially *demythologized*. An example may clarify the point. In the Ugaritic texts of the mid-second millennium occurs the following passage: "If thou smite Lotan, the serpent slant, Destroy the serpent tortuous, Shalyat of the seven heads . . ." The name Lotan is the Canaanite equivalent of one that appears many centuries later in the Hebrew Scriptures, and to which we have already referred, namely Leviathan, who is also a sea-monster. In the Hebrew Scriptures, Leviathan plays a number of roles. In Psalm 74 he is, as in Ugarit, many-headed, and also an enemy of God. (By the process known as historicization his destruction is linked with the Israelites' crossing of the Red Sea at their Exodus from Egypt. A similar association of the killing of the sea-monster with the Exodus occurs in Isaiah 51:9-10, but here the monster's name is Rahab, a mocking name in the Isaiah tradition for Egypt, cf. Is 30:7.) In Isaiah 27:1 we have mention of "Leviathan the fleeing serpent, Leviathan the twisting serpent," another very close parallel to the Ugaritic text, but here the monster symbolizes cosmic evil, to be overthrown by God at the eschaton. In striking contrast to both these uses of the Leviathan figure, however, are Psalm 104 and Job 41. In Psalm 104 Leviathan is a pet with whom God enjoys playing in his leisure moments (v. 26); in Job he is the greatest of all God's creatures, "king over all the sons of pride," and is cited simply to crush the anthropocentric conceit of Job. If we try to date these passages, we find no steady theological trend. A majority vote of scholarly opinion would probably give this sequence: Psalm 104 — Psalm 74 — Isaiah 51 — Job 41 — Isaiah 27. In other words, running side by side we have the sea as something evil and something good, and the monster as a supernatural evil being, a symbol of anti-God forces, and a magnificent testimony to God's wisdom and power.

The theological background to this ongoing activity of demythologizing that developed in certain quarters in Israel may be analyzed very crudely and briefly as follows. The basic premise of Israel's faith is that her God is stronger than anything or anyone, and for this to be so, she found, it was necessary for God to be radically distanced from natural phenomena. Other nations in the ANE had advanced, it is true, well beyond the stage of a simple-minded identification of gods with natural forces or objects. But they were trapped in the morass of polytheism; one of the reasons for this was that the traditional associations of various deities with particular phenomena — the sun, the moon, the stars, storms, vegetation, the sea, and so on—meant that the obvious multiplicity of nature kept getting in the way of their struggles to apprehend the unity of the divine. By a kind of inspired bigotry the Jews, however, succeeded where all others failed. By holding fast to the thesis that God was supreme, in the teeth of all those disasters such as exile and persecution, which seemed to prove the contrary, they found themselves forced to treat everything—nature, humanity, and history—as subordinate to God, indeed as God's instruments, even when the uses to which God put them proved morally inscrutable. This has two very important consequences for the attitude of the Hebrew Scriptures to nature. First, nature is progressively depersonalized and demythologized: "Who makest the winds thy messengers, fire and flame thy ministers" (Ps 104:4). It is no longer the manifestation of supernatural beings but now for the first time actually merits the name nature, though, as we have said, the Hebrew language did not have that concept at its disposal. The climax of this process in the Hebrew Scriptures is the book of Ecclesiastes (Koheleth), which our own outlook on the world finds remarkably sympathetic. Second, following on from this, humans lose their numinous dread of nature. Nature can still frighten them, but only by virtue of being stronger than they in a natural way, from which they may need God to rescue them, but which they recognize as being in principle a strength they can understand and in many cases do something about.

We may summarize the main points emerging from the utterances of the Hebrew Scriptures about nature as follows:

(a) For the writers of the Hebrew Scriptures, the determining factors in thinking about nature, as about every other subject, are the all-controlling rights and power of God. "The earth is the Lord's and the fullness thereof" (Ps 24:1); this can be carried so far even as to have practical consequences for human social organization, as in the principles underlying the law of Jubilee, that no human being can ever own land outright but must be regarded as a tenant installed by God (Lv 25:1-34).

(b) Under this overall sovereignty of God, humankind does have a position of control over nature, which is approved by God and which is meant to be exercised in a spirit of respect and responsibility. Skills and technology of all kinds may be admirable, but the tyrannical or greedy use of human power over nature is a failure deriving from human sin, not from God's intention in creation.

(c) Humanity's proper control over nature is made possible because the realization that God is One and Supreme, and therefore transcendent, effectively desupernaturalizes the world, ridding it of superhuman personal power, whether divine or demonic, and placing humans in a position to use their powers rationally in dealing with nature.

(d) Nevertheless, nature is not to be evaluated simply in terms of human needs and interests; to think that it is, is simply a mark of folly. God created the greater part of the world for its own sake—a point that comes home even more strongly to us, with our knowledge of the infinite universe—and wisdom consists fundamentally in recognizing this and the limitations it imposes upon us. Technology may explore and exploit nature, but it will never discover the way to wisdom (Jb 28). The truly wise person never imagines that he or she knows fully what God was about in creation.

(e) Since God, however, has a moral and rational character, humans must in the end submit to things as they are, as a genuine revelation, so far as they can grasp it, of ultimate goodness and wisdom. Hence the careful and comprehensive observation of nature will yield indications for human behavior, which were part of God's intention in creating in the first place and which therefore have the status of moral imperatives for humans. We must ultimately be guided by respect for the intricate character and needs of the natural order.

(f) If we are so guided, then we may hope even to improve the condition of nature, which does not as yet embody God's character as human beings have come to know this through their communion with him. Nature is not perfect; there is a work of salvation to be done in it, as well as in humanity, as part of God's eschatological purpose, and this salvation is part of human responsibility for nature.

In contrast with the Hebrew Scriptures, the New Testament has relatively little to say about nature. The reasons for this are some fortuitous, some sociological, but some are inherent in the nature of the primitive Christian community and its world view. The fortuitous reasons arise purely from the scale and character of the New Testament material. To start with, the volume of the New Testament is only thirty percent of that of the Old. The bulk of its contents falls within a period of forty years, and the outside limits of its dating bracket only a century, compared with the nine centuries between the earliest and latest passages of the Hebrew Scriptures. The New Testament is the work of a relatively small community with highly selective interests, whereas the Old is the product of a whole nation's wider issues and situations. Hence it is no surprise to find in the Hebrew Scriptures far greater diversity of literature than in the Christian Scriptures. There is nothing in the New Testament, for example, to parallel the large collections of "observations on life and the world-order," which we call the wisdom literature of the Hebrew Scriptures, or its extensive range of liturgical poetry, or the detailed corpus of its laws on what we would regard as secular matters. The very types of material, therefore, in which an attitude to nature might be most likely to be reflected are precisely those missing from the New Testament.

Sociologically, it is hard to escape the impression that most of the New Testament writers are urbanized, compared with the predominantly agricultural orientation of the mind of the Hebrew Scriptures. The gospel material, especially in the teaching of Jesus, with its use of images from nature and husbandry, is nearest to rural society and to the world of the Hebrew Scriptures; James is thought by some scholars to be addressed to the Palestinian church. But otherwise there is little sign in the writers of any attention to nature; their audiences, where known, are almost exclusively urban. While it is true that this would not have been as strong a distinction in the Roman world as it is in our own megalopolitan culture, nevertheless it is probably fair to say that nature was not one of the things in the center of the mental focus of the early Christians; this is partly related to their sociological classification.

There were, however, other reasons, inherent in the earliest church and its gospel that conspired to minimize concern with the question of human attitudes to nature. The first was the approach of primitive Christianity to scripture. For Christians of the first century, the Hebrew Scriptures were the Bible, the only inspired word of God. It might be thought that this would have awakened some interest at least in all the various subjects with which the Hebrew Scriptures deals, but one overriding factor prevented this. The first Christians were interested in the Hebrew Scriptures primarily as a vast source book of predictions, some clear, some enigmatic, of the coming of Christ, his nature, life, death, resurrection, redeeming work, and heavenly glory, and of the mission and destiny of the church. The literal sense of any passage was, in most cases, of much less importance than its prophetic meaning, which had to be disentangled by allegorical or typological exegesis. Nor were they interested on the whole in the total range of an argument or the total message of a book. These are characteristically modern ways of using scripture. For them, every verse, sentence, or phrase could be taken, out of context if need be, and its reference to Christ extracted by what seems to us at times over-ingenious exposition, but which, given the thought-forms of the day, simply sprang naturally from their exuberant and untiring obsession with the gospel. Given this situation, it can be seen that many of those elements in Judaism that we have been considering were effectively blanked off from early Christian consciousness.

Second, there is the fact that the Christian message was initially a gospel of personal salvation. It impinged on ordinary life only at the points of religious belief and personal morality. The criticism of much present-day Christian preaching as being too much concerned with these two things instead of having something to say on corporate or global issues must, if it is to be both honest and helpful, face the fact that in the foundation (and still authoritative) documents of the church precisely these were the overwhelming dominant concerns. Christianity was from the start a religion of individual faith and morals, its corporate consciousness related not to membership of humankind but to membership of the elect community drawn out from the human race by its response to the gospel. The question whether anything which is specifically Christian, yet of wider import, can develop from this basic character is, of course, a general concern of the church today. But it was not ever thus. The members of the church at Corinth received much instruction from St. Paul, but none of it was directed at the matters we are considering. Indeed, when St. Paul does happen to mention a relevant text from the Hebrew Scriptures—"You shall not muz-

zle an ox when it treads out the grain" (Deut 25:4) — he does so simply to
apply it by a kind of allegorical interpretation to the economic support of
those who preach the gospel. No doubt St. Paul was not anti-oxen, but he
is quite clear that God would not waste valuable inspired wordage on such
a subject: "Is it for oxen that God is concerned? Does he not speak entirely
for our sake?" (1 Cor 9:9–10).

The third and perhaps most important of all reasons is, of course, that
the earliest Christians felt themselves to be those "upon whom the end of
the ages has come" (1 Cor 10:11). The "form of this world" was passing
away, the new age was about to dawn; and it was a serious question what
would happen to the bodies of those who had not yet died when the last
day came, and so could hardly be resurrected (1 Cor 15:51). Since, therefore, the created order did not have long to run, there was no incentive to
develop a constructive long-term attitude to nature as it was. It is to their
successors of the second generation that we have to look for most of the
modest amount the New Testament church has to say on this issue.

Turning now to this positive side, we note first that the underlying tonality, so to speak, of the New Testament is the same as that of the Old;
namely, the created order is God's work and as such is good. In the gospels
God's providential care extends to the most insignificant of animals, and
the beauty of flowers springing up in the fields of Galilee is greater than
that of Solomon in all his glory (Mt 5:6 = Lk 12:24; Mt 10:29 = Lk 14:6;
Mt 6:28f.). There is no food that is unclean; impurity is a moral quality (Lk
7:19). In his parables Jesus assumes care and concern for animals, even if
only in illustration of his main point (Lk 13:15; 15:4; Mt 12:11 = Lk 14:5).
In St. Paul the wonders of the creation are sufficient in themselves to lead
the open and rational mind to God (Rom 1:20). He accepts, despite his
rigorous Jewish upbringing, the insight of Jesus that nothing is in itself
unclean (Rom 14:14; cf. Acts 10:9-16, 28; 11:5-10); in discussing the question of meat offered to idols, while respecting the tender consciences of
the more scrupulous brethren, he makes it clear that for himself, with his
robust Jewish monotheism reinforced by the revelation of God in Christ (1
Cor 8:4-6), there can be no problem, for "the earth is the Lord's and
everything in it" (1 Cor 10:26-28). This fundamentally affirmative and confident attitude to the creation is reinforced by the doctrine of *creatio ex
nihilo* (Heb 11:3), which, as we noted, was not available to the writers of
the Hebrew Scriptures, emerging as it does in the intertestamental period.
In the Acts of the Apostles we find the classic position again clearly stated:
"The living God made heaven and earth and sea and everything in them.
In past ages he allowed all nations to go their own way; and yet he has not
left you without some clue to his nature, in the kindness he shows; he sends
you rain from heaven and crops in their seasons, and gives you food and
good cheer in plenty" (14:15-17). In the same work there are signs of a
very positive theology of the natural order developing with the assimilation
of the Middle Platonist thought of Hellenistic Judaism: God the Unknow-

able, who created the world and everything in it, is not far from each one of us, for in him we live and move, in him we exist, indeed, "We are his offspring" (17:23-24, 27-28).

Nevertheless, even though the basic tonality, to pursue our metaphor, is that of the major key, it is shadowed from time to time by more somber material in the minor. This is a reflection of the pessimism and anxiety afflicting the Mediterranean world around the turn of the era. In Judaism it found expression in that apocalyptic despair that in certain circles regarded the whole of the present created order as beyond redemption and looked for a cataclysmic irruption of God to establish a new order from which evil would be banished. The wide dissemination in the Near and Middle East at this time of dualistic faiths, the staple of that religious phenomenon loosely labeled Gnosticism, was another manifestation of the same malaise; while in Hellenism many suffered from a "sense of helplessness in the hands of fate" which made them "wonder whether it is possible to be at home in the world at all." Because the world had become "a hostile, alien place," they turned to astral cults. "The lower world was not centered in itself, but was under the control of the stars. . . . Hence, in the last resort all activity here is trivial and meaningless, and if it seems to be independent, that is mere illusion" (Bultmann, chap. 2).

These contemporary trends are reflected in the New Testament, partly in vigorous reaction against such beliefs, not by denying the reality to which they referred, but by claiming that in the gospel men were delivered from helpless subjection to that reality. Thus, in such passages as Galatians 4:3, Colossians 2:8,15, and Ephesians 6:12, Christians are exhorted to enter into the freedom Christ has won for them, and to fight against the domination of the hypercosmic powers. Again, in Romans 8:9-22, Paul seems to echo the Stoic views of the aging of the world, as well as the Jewish apocalyptic conception of its subjugation by evil powers responsible for human sin and the disruption of nature. But he puts all this in a new theological perspective. The passage presents notorious difficulties of translation, but certain convictions of Paul stand out. If God was ultimately responsible for the universe's state of frustration, nevertheless this was always imposed within a context of hope: "The universe is itself to be freed from the shackles of mortality, and enter upon the liberty and splendor of the children of God." In other words, the kind of transfigured, eternal existence promised to humanity in the resurrection of Jesus is to have its counterpart in the transformation of the cosmos. The groans of the universe, then, are not the expression of hopeless anguish; they correspond to the cries of a mother in childbirth, they are the pangs of bringing forth a new order. It is true that the general diagnosis of the cosmic situation is not very different from that made by many other sects and schools of thought at the time. The Pauline tradition does not say, "This is rubbish! All this talk of deep-seated corruption and bondage to Fate throughout the created order is nonsense." On the contrary it is taken very seriously; all that Christianity claims is that it has a better answer to the crisis. But that answer is not a program for redeeming the world of nature as well as the human soul, so that they can then live in harmony to create the kingdom of God on earth as it is, but a spiritual liberation of those men and women who believe in Jesus as the prerequisite of a total remaking of the cosmos by God's Spirit and in God's own time. The book of Revelation, with its vision of a new heaven and a new earth (21:1), is the logical culmination of this approach.

As time went on a more optimistic note became discernible, chiefly in opposition to the false asceticism characteristic of the dualistic sects. Thus 1 Timothy 4:3-4 commends the right use of God's gifts in the order of creation. And there was one theological concept in particular in the later New Testament writings that offered a theoretical foundation for a more affirmative attitude to nature. This was the idea of the cosmic Christ. In various forms the conception was developed that the pre-existent divine Christ was himself the divine agent in creation, and that the existence of all things was upheld by him. We find this in such diverse writings as Hebrews (1-3) and Colossians (1:16f.), but the best-known instance is the prologue to the gospel of John (1:1-4). The implications of this idea for a theology of nature are not, of course, worked out in the New Testament itself, but, obscure as the thought-forms undoubtedly are to us, there does shine through them a conviction that the whole universe, could we but see it, is in its essential nature in harmony not merely with some unknown divine power but specifically with God as revealed in Jesus, and that therefore there must be some *modus vivendi* between humans and nature which, even if not yet attained, is in keeping with all that is best in both.

In seeking for any kind of theology of humanity and nature, the Christian cannot but be grateful that his or her Bible does not consist merely of the New Testament. Even the final point, that of the cosmic Christ, would be virtually unusable were it not built on the world-affirming monotheism of the Hebrew Scriptures. But in conclusion can we see in the Bible as a whole insights that are not present in either Testament by itself? What cannot be ignored is the unresolved tension between the theological view that puts all the weight on God's wisdom in creation and the excellence of the cosmos thus created, on the one hand, and the theology which thinks eschatologically and looks to God primarily to redeem the cosmic order, on the other. The cosmic Christ concept can be used with either emphasis. Teilhard de Chardin employed a version of it eschatologically: in Christ is revealed *"le Dieu d'en-avant,"* the *telos* appropriate to an evolving creation, which in humanity has at last attained the self-determining freedom of reflective beings. What the Old and New Testaments together seem to say is that on their understanding of God the character of the primordial and the eschatological must be the same; there must always have been in God from the beginning that which is needed for him to be Savior in the end. Creation and redemption are two expressions of the same Ultimate Being, its power and wisdom and love, even though the "mystery" of this Being was for long ages hidden and has been definitively revealed only in Christ and in the developing understanding of existence of which he is the source. The diptych of the creation story in Genesis 1 and the Isaianic vision of a new and perfected cosmos finds a counterpart in the New Testament terminology applied to Christ: he is "the first and the last" (Rv 1:17); he exists "before everything"; in him "everything was created," and "all things are held together in him" (Col 1:16f.). But at the same time, "the whole universe has been created for him," and "through him God chose to reconcile the whole universe to himself" (Col 1:16, 20). He "is its origin," but also destined "to be in all things alone supreme" (Col 1:18); he is the one who "himself receives the entire fullness of God" (Eph 1:23), but who also descended to our world and ascended again "so that he might fill the universe" (Eph 4:10). Underlying this kind of language is without doubt a view of *redemptio* as *redintegratio*, the recovery of an original perfection that has been lost; this is the synthesis that seeks to reconcile the incompatibles of the priestly theology, for which Eden is something lost, and the prophetic, for which it is something that has never been found. Our own greater knowledge of the history of the universe puts us firmly on the side of the prophetic. But theologically we may still find the instinct of the New Testament synthesis significant, that in God himself there is a fullness and perfection that is unchanging and outside space and time, and that it is this which makes God the proper *telos* for a creation in which the mystery of that fullness is unpacked only through the ages of the evolutionary process, which passes through a series of increasingly critical stages and is now precariously poised in a dependence on the rational response of free creatures. Insofar as the crucial factor for the future of nature on this planet at the moment is humankind, the New Testament claim that the reconciliation of the universe is made possible through Christ has distinctive meaning. In Jesus, as portrayed in the Gospels, we see certain basic attitudes, which may seem overly simple but are in fact adequate foundations for an approach to nature. The first is a conviction that the natural order need not be written off as in bondage to evil — the apocalyptic view — but contains both clues to the nature of God (Mt 5:45) and conditions within which we can learn to be authentic children of our Father in heaven. The second is his equal conviction that we never shall so learn without a repentance, which among other things learns to trust the existence with which we have been endowed as the gift of one to whom we can say, Abba. These basic attitudes do not assume that nothing can be done to improve nature — no countryman would ever be so silly anyway — but they do presuppose a readiness to learn from nature and to be content with the limitations that even at maximum development it still cannot but impose upon us. The tendency of human beings here as in so many other fields is to say not, "What can be done?" but, "What do I want?" and to seek to extort that from nature, whether it is feasible or not. Our responsibility toward nature cannot be fulfilled simply by developing our positive and creative skills; it also involves denying ourselves and taking up the cross daily. All we can do will not be enough of itself to turn earth into paradise, but that after all is something for which we have to wait upon him who is both Alpha and Omega. The new heaven and earth are not of a kind to be evolved on our drawing boards; all we can hope for here are images and foreshadowings of them.

WORKS CITED

Bultmann, Rudolf. *Primitive Christianity: In Its Contemporary Setting*. Trans. Reginald Fuller. Philadelphia: Fortress Press, 1980.
Griffiths, Bede. *Return to the Centre*. Springfield, IL: Templegate, 1976.

2

Covenant and Creation

Wesley Granberg-Michaelson

Relating covenant to justice and peace is a task already initially embraced both theologically and in the practice of the churches today. The same, however, cannot be said about the integrity of creation. For the most part, our churches have been inattentive to the growing threats facing the life of the creation. And our theological and biblical understandings often have minimized and ignored the significance of God's creation when expressing the meaning of Christian faith.

Our challenge, then, is to relate the insights of the Christian tradition to the crisis that today threatens the essential integrity of the creation. In so doing we can discover neglected yet empowering dimensions of God's covenant. Moreover, we can call upon the members of our church communities to respond through covenanting for the very survival and renewal of the gift given in God's creation.

GOD'S COVENANT EMBRACES THE CREATION

This is the biblical truth that forms the foundation for upholding the integrity of creation and provides the basis for the church's response to the perils threatening the life of the world.

God's action as Creator did not consist simply of God making the world.

For Wesley Granberg-Michaelson, director of the sub-unit on Church and Society of the World Council of Churches, God's covenant as depicted in the Bible consists of promises not only to humans but to all of creation as well. In thematizing the concept of covenant and showing its relevance to the crises now faced by life on earth, Granberg-Michaelson uncovers an oft-neglected resource within the Christian tradition. The perspectives and material in this essay originally were developed by the author as part of a consultation by the World Alliance of Reformed Churches exploring the meaning of covenant for justice, peace, and integrity of creation, and as preparation for their World Assembly.

Rather, as Creator, Redeemer, and Sustainer, God chose the creation. Through grace alone, God identified the world as the beloved creation. "For God so loved the world . . ."

Within most Christian thought and particularly in Reformed theology, covenant has been understood as God's promises to humanity. Biblical scholars have revealed the nature of covenant agreements in the world of the Hebrew Scriptures. This background has led to insights concerning the various ways in which covenant was understood by the people of Israel. In some cases covenant promises between God and a people were seen as conditional, and dependent upon appropriate responses. Another tradition came to stress the abiding and unconditional character of God's covenant. Yet, most all such reflection has assumed that the scope of covenant is only God and humanity.

That limited perspective has contributed to the church's inattention to the crisis facing the world's environment. The assumption that God's promises extend simply to humanity has left little room for regarding the creation as central to the message of Christian faith. This has allowed an anthropocentric bias to dominate our interpretation of the biblical message. Further, attitudes that sanction the ruthless domination of nature have been theologically tolerated and even strengthened from the view that God's promises and covenant have no practical relevance for the earth.

Our fresh and hopeful discovery, however, is that the biblical message resounds with declarations of the creation as God's loved possession and gift. The promises of God, and the work of redemption in Jesus Christ, encompass the whole created order. Moreover, the creation is a partner in covenant with God. In fact, the covenant tradition biblically is linked to the creation from the earliest prehistory to the future promises of a new creation.

Christian faith today faces the critical task of renewing its theological tradition through recovering the central place of creation in the biblical message. The community of believers is confronted with the clear calling to participate in the heart of the struggle throughout the world to uphold the integrity of creation. The realities that jeopardize life on this planet make clear that our response is imperative if our hope in God's promises is genuine.

A FUNDAMENTAL BREAKDOWN AT THE HEART OF THE ECOLOGICAL CRISIS

At the heart of the global ecological crisis lies a fundamental breakdown in the modern world view of Western culture. Since the Enlightenment and the scientific revolution, Western culture came to assume that humanity had both the right and duty to dominate nature. Objective, scientific knowledge became an absolute value. And the purpose of such knowledge was to exercise power over the creation. The view of life became secularized;

we came to understand the world apart from any reference to God. The creation became "nature"—raw materials that existed only to be given value through exploitation.

The pragmatic benefits of these developments for civilization are remarkable in many ways. Humanity has been afforded protection against many ancient threats to life. However, this mindset now is presenting humanity with more curses than blessings. Technology has become a social drug. We are addicted to technological solutions to any problem. Power seems the same as truth. Thus we split the atom because we could do it. Instead of solving problems, that action gave humanity the godlike power of life and death over created order.

Modern humanity has become too confident in its own power and has trusted far too deeply in its dominance over the creation. It has constructed a world view that places human power and glory at the center of the universe. We have become like gods, masters over creation's destiny, and ready to demand any sacrifice for our enjoyment—even the destruction of the environment upon which all life depends.

This same mindset also results in the domination of women by men. A hierarchy of values justifies not only the exploitation of nature but identifies female characteristics with nature; both are regarded as weaker, and become subject to male mastery and oppression. The same mistaken biblical interpretation that justifies the rule of men over women also blesses man's unbridled exploitation of creation. Moreover, this stance of mastery over nature has justified the oppression by white people of others who, like women, have been treated as "lower" and associated with nature as objects for exploitation.

Therefore, if the Christian tradition is to play some part in upholding the integrity of the creation in our own time, we must recognize the depth of our challenge. Rather than simply acknowledging immediate environmental problems that need remedy, our task is confronting the basic modern mindset that spawns and rationalizes environmental ruin. This requires nothing short of the power of the gospel.

The message of new life in Jesus Christ overturns the values and cultural assumptions that lie at the foundation of modern ecological ruin. We are called to conversion; such conversion frees us from the ways of thought and life that are hastening the earth's destruction and calls us through the Spirit to live in ways that protect and nourish the gift of God's creation. The power of the gospel beckons us to confront the economic, cultural, and technological assumptions that are destroying life on earth and offer a vision for upholding the creation.

EARLY REFORMED THEOLOGIANS AND THE UNIVERSAL SCOPE OF THE COVENANT

Bullinger maintained that God's covenant did not originate with Abraham but was renewed. Covenant began with Adam and Noah. Zwingli also argued that the covenant was one whole, reaching to the entire human race, and then to the people of Israel through Abraham. Karl Barth underscored the broad scope of the covenant as understood by such early Reformers, and pointing ultimately to the intended destiny of all humanity.

In Calvin, the kingdom of God is portrayed as the special end and goal of the creation. Thus, creation and redemption become united. In this truth, we can understand how humanity's destiny is fully linked with the destiny of creation itself.

The promises of the covenant, then, find their foundation in God's steadfast relationships to the creation. Indeed, the first explicit biblical reference to God's covenant comes in the story of Noah, and establishes the creation, not only humanity, as a partner in the covenant with God. When the creation, with all of its life, is reestablished as Noah and all the animals come forth from the ark, God's covenant is announced. And it is a covenant with "every living creature," a covenant God describes as "between me and the earth" (Gn 9:13). To underscore the promise, the integrity of the earth's cycles, "seedtime and harvest, cold and heat, summer and winter, day and night" is also assured (Gn 8:22); as the Lord promises, "I will never again curse the ground" (Gn 8:21). Five times in the ninth chapter the scope of this covenant is repeated, extending to "all living things on earth of every kind." And the rainbow is described by the words of God as the sign "of the covenant between myself and the earth."

In other expressions of God's covenant promises in the Hebrew Scriptures, the place of creation remains prominent. The Abrahamic covenant (described in Genesis 15 and 17), for example, involves the land, given as God's gift to his descendants. Indeed, in the later giving of the law, the Sabbatical and Jubilee laws rest on the proper treatment of the land, to allow the just sharing of its fruits. The Mosaic covenant at Sinai, often regarded more as a covenant conditional on the actions of the people of Israel, also encompasses God's relationship to all the creation. In Exodus 19, before the ten commandments are given, the Lord reminds Moses that "all the earth is mine" (v.5). In the account of the same events in Deuteronomy 10, when Moses sets forth God's requirements to "fear the Lord your God, to walk in all his ways, to love him, to serve the Lord your God with all your heart and with all your soul, and to keep the commandments" (vv.12-13) he then immediately declares, "Behold, to the Lord your God belong heaven and the heaven of heavens, the earth with all that is in it" (v.14).

Following the Noahic and Abrahamic covenants, the tradition of the unconditional covenant also found expression in the promises to the throne of David. Seen initially as God's guarantee to rule through the Jerusalem kings in the line of David, this covenant finds affirmation in God's reign over all creation. The justice and righteousness at the foundation of David's throne rest upon God's intention to bring shalom, and right relationships, in all the creation. The "Royal Psalms" refer continuously to God's power to rule and accomplish divine intentions in all the world. Rightly understood, kings were to serve as the servants upholding and preserving such dominion in the creation, because it all belongs to God.

This underscores the links between covenant and shalom. Covenant implies a rightly ordered relationship, whether between people, with God, or with the creation. In the biblical view these relationships become inseparable. Shalom is the vision of the harmony, fulfillment, and fellowship among God, humanity, and the creation; its result is justice, peace, and the integrity of creation. In the understanding of covenant we discover God's pledge of faithfulness, intention, and grace to bring about shalom in all that is created.

Establishing such right relationships, and a legitimate order, is initiated through God's identification with the weak, poor, and oppressed. This theme resounds through the pattern of biblical covenants, revealing a movement of solidarity with what is broken, outcast, and rejected. And this pattern extends to the creation. For in the midst of its brokenness and suffering, resulting from "nature" being exploited, we discover that God's solidarity extends to the creation itself, longing for its liberation and wholeness.

Covenant, then, portrays God's predisposition toward humanity and all creation. Simply because of the grace of God, all that God has created becomes loved, chosen, and destined for glory.

God's intention for the creation, underscored by covenant, provides the basis of hope for creation's destiny. For the people of Israel, such hope became refined and purified through the experience of exile and desolation, which shattered their self-aggrandizing dreams. In this time the vision of the prophets returned again to covenant and creation.

In the later part of Isaiah the prophet sets forth the vision of God's work of renewal and salvation. And that vision finds roots in the faithfulness of God's covenant promises. God's work as creator and ruler over all the earth is sounded with fresh power to the people. And the redemptive work of God results in a cosmic renewal and transformation. God's righteousness upholds and brings new life to the whole of creation.

Thus, biblical faith comes to place its hope for the fulfillment, healing, and renewal of creation in the covenant promises, which look to God's redemptive activity. We hear the power and expanse of this hope in Hosea's words:

And I will make for you a covenant on that day with the beasts of the field, the birds of the air, and the creeping things of the ground; and I will abolish the bow, the sword, and war from the land; and I will make you lie down in safety. And I will betroth you to me for ever; I will betroth you to me in righteousness and in justice, in steadfast love, and in mercy. I will betroth you to me in faithfulness; and you shall know the Lord.

And in that day, says the Lord, I will answer the heavens and they shall answer the earth; and the earth shall answer the grain, the wine, and the oil, and they shall answer Jezreel; and I will sow him for myself in the land. And I will have pity on Not pitied, and I will say to Not my people, "you are my people"; and he shall say, "Thou art my God" (Hos 2:18-23).

GOD'S COVENANT PROMISES FIND THEIR FULL EXPRESSION IN JESUS CHRIST

The depth of God's grace—the faithful, long-suffering, sacrificial love of God—is fully embodied in God's Son. And in the saving and redeeming work of Christ all creation finds its promise of fulfillment and glory.

Christ announced and inaugurated the kingdom of God. This kingdom consists of the full reign of God in the world, a reign that restores right relationship among God, humanity, and the creation. Shalom finds its expression. A new order, divinely initiated, breaks into history. And in this all, the initial promises of covenant with creation and humanity become manifest in the life of the kingdom of God.

Thus, the New Testament builds on this foundation, which integrates creation into the work of God's redemption. God's role as creator and sustainer is ascribed to Jesus Christ in understanding the incarnation. John says of Christ, "All things were made through him, and without him was not anything made that was made" (1:3). Colossians repeats this description with this worshipful declaration: "In him all things were created, in heaven and on earth . . . all things were created through him and for him. He is before all things, and in him all things hold together" (1:16-17).

When the work of God's redemption in Jesus Christ is discussed by New Testament writers, the reconciliation achieved through the life, death, and resurrection of Christ extends to the creation. The Colossians passage, for example, continues by declaring, "For in him all the fullness of God was pleased to dwell, and through him to reconcile to himself all things" (1:19-20). This is the same "all things" that were created through Christ. Several other New Testament passages underscore how Christ's defeat of all the rebellious powers results in the restoration of God's purpose and intended order in all the creation.

God's saving activity once expressed legalistically through the commandments and laws from Sinai now is embodied through the one commandment of love demonstrated in the life of Jesus. And the foundational scope of the covenant, embracing the whole of creation, is taken up in Christ, the source and reconciler of all things, who initiates the new creation. This is celebrated in the eucharist, the feast which acknowledges our belonging to this new covenant relationship as the body of Christ and opens all life to the promise of new creation.

RESPONSE TO GOD'S COVENANT ACTIONS

The initiative of God's covenant actions always asks for response. Faced with the crisis confronting the life of creation itself, the church today is compelled to offer to the world a decisive commitment for preserving the integrity of creation as a witness to the promise of God's love. In covenant, the solidarity of God with the created world is declared as an everlasting promise. What is chosen as God's own must now be embraced in solidarity by God's people.

The church's response to creation is rooted, above all, in gratitude. Even in the midst of the calamitous destruction inflicted on the created order by human sin, we still can receive God's creation as the gift of grace. This grace sustains all life, momentarily, through air, water, land, and energy. It opens humanity to the possibility of fellowship with God and to the potential of justice and peace in relationship to others. From God's covenant with creation we discover and receive all life as gift. And our response is one of joyous gratitude and praise to God's glory.

Such gratitude compels resistance. As the church, our response to God's covenant with creation must certainly place us in stalwart resistance to all that breaks the integrity of creation, all that treats the earth as an object for our possession rather than God's gift, and all that subjugates the creation to destruction and ruin rather than saving the creation through fellowship with it. Such resistance brings the power of the gospel to convert the most fundamental attitudes and values in modern culture, which has assumed that the creation can be severed from its belonging to the Creator, and which has placed its highest goal as the industrial and technological exploitation of the earth rather than its preservation.

In Romans we read that all creation longs for liberation from the bondage imposed on it by human sin. And in this longing the creation looks to "the full manifestation of the children of God" (Rom 8:19). For the creation and the children of God are to share together in the kingdom of glory. This is the divine intention of God's covenant action through history.

The church is called to participate in the liberation of creation through entering into fellowship with it in response to God's grace. And here, the struggles for the integrity of creation and for justice and peace all become indivisible parts of one whole.

The creation hungers for its transformation and freedom promised by God. In its suffering, the creation is waiting for the church—waiting for the people of God to embrace, protect, and renew the world as God's well-loved gift. Creation exists to give God glory and honor. Its possession by God is the ground of its final destiny and sustains the church's response in covenant for a renewed creation.

THREATS TO SURVIVAL

By the end of this century the greatest threats to the survival of life on earth may well arise from the destruction of the God-given environment. What can guide the church in its response to this momentous crisis? How can the church witness to God's covenant promises intended for the creation?

First, the church must identify concrete issues threatening the integrity of creation, which must be addressed, and cannot be ignored, for the sake of enabling the ongoing gift of life. The following are examples, interrelated to one another.

The Greenhouse Effect

A dramatic rise in the temperature of the earth over the next few decades, which scientists now say could occur, would result in global catastrophe second only to nuclear war. The church must join with other groups to urge governments of industrialized countries to reduce the burning of fossil fuels by at least fifty percent in the next twenty-five years. Alternative, renewable energy resources throughout the world must be encouraged as essential to global stability. Sustainable agriculture less dependent on chemical fertilizers—another cause of the greenhouse effect—must be aggressively promoted. In short, the churches' mission to the world must now include the saving of the world's climate and atmosphere.

Deforestation

The devastation of tropical forests throughout the world poses critical threats to peoples within the third and fourth worlds, increasing erosion of irreplaceable soil, creating greater water shortages, and contributing to drought and desertification. Further, deforestation is the chief cause of species extinction, as well as adding to the greenhouse effect. Curbing such deforestation, and planting trees, can be a vital form of the church's witness for preserving creation's integrity.

Acid Rain

The contamination of atmosphere, particularly from the burning of fossil fuels, has already destroyed forests and lakes, as well as human lungs, in many regions of the northern hemisphere. Crossing political and ideological barriers as it is carried in the atmosphere, acid rain is spreading through many parts of the globe. The church can encourage international cooperation as well as changes in energy policies, which are required for preserving air that gives life rather than death.

Population Expansion

The issue of global population cannot be considered in isolation from questions of lifestyle and consumption of resources, cultural realities, and prospects for economic justice. But neither can the population issue be ignored by the church. Even with reductions in the maldistribution of global resources, the unprecedented expansion of population over the next few decades will stretch the carrying capacity of the earth to its breaking point. Population growth must become an ethical and theological issue addressed by our churches.

Unlimited Economic Growth

Industrialized societies continue to believe that they can grow economically without any limits. The so-called developing societies often aspire to these same goals. Yet, scientific analysis, as well as practical common sense, make clear that the limits to the earth's resources impose constraints on the level of economic development. The church must encourage the search in modern societies for new understandings of economic life that are rooted in ecological realities. Biblical wisdom underscores the inescapable harmony between human economic welfare and the integrity of the created order. Our world today stands in critical need of such a prophetic and saving message.

Yet, before our churches consider the nature of our witness within society concerning the integrity of creation, we must examine the shape of our own lives as believing communities. The initial steps we must take in response to God's covenant with the creation are those that would bring our own corporate lives more faithfully under the Lordship of Christ's reconciling presence, upholding all the creation.

Some concrete measures can be suggested. Our churches own large amounts of land, for church buildings, camps, and schools as well as for investment purposes. How well do we demonstrate the gift of God's creation on lands that are in our control? What form of witness do we make through the ways in which we tend, nurture, and cherish those portions of land entrusted to us?

Similarly, our buildings, including their architectural design and their use of energy, are expressions of our witness. Certainly there are vast differences of geography and wealth among the member churches in the ecumenical family. Yet we all share the responsibility of relating our material structures to our spiritual beliefs. In a time when the actual survival of many people will depend on radical shifts in the world's patterns of energy consumption, churches can be salt and leaven within their societies through the ways we conserve and use energy resources.

Beyond any doubt preserving the integrity of creation will require dramatic changes in the lifestyles particularly of those living in the North and the West. And the changes in personal patterns of consumption by Christians need the support of the gathered church community. Responding to God's covenant with creation will deepen our understanding of being called into the covenant community, living in love, interdependence, and sharing with our sisters and brothers in Christ's body.

For any of these responses to take root in the lives of our member churches, a strong emphasis must be given to the biblical and theological teaching we offer at all levels concerning God's creation and humanity's relationship to the environment. Though these themes resound in the Bible, we have ignored and neglected them. Heresies have often taken their place. We deny the goodness of the material world and suppose that spiritual realities can be separated from worldly existence. We assume that biological life suffers under God's curse rather than God's blessing, and we fail to see how ongoing decay and death in the natural world bring forth new life. We don't believe that God's redemptive action in Jesus Christ reaches out to the whole creation or that new life in Christ can restore a healing relationship to the earth. In all these ways and more our churches stand in need of God's word and truth.

God's covenant with the creation offers the world the true hope for the preservation of its life and invites the response of God's people. Preserving the integrity of creation must become for our churches in the years ahead a central part of our witness and life in our societies.

3

New Testament Foundations for Understanding the Creation

Paulos Mar Gregorios

Recently I was present at a special function at our presidential palace. Zail Singh, the president of India, bestowed a privately endowed honor on one of our most creative friends of nature: Sunderlal Bahuguna. Bahuguna is well known and written about, both in India and abroad. He initiated the Chipko movement, which has been an important factor in awakening Indians to the environmental question, particularly the importance of conserving the forest trees in the Himalayan region.

The mindless and tragic decimation of the Himalayan forests was the result of the government's thoughtless felling of trees in that region. It resulted in heavy soil erosion, desertification, and climate change. After trying many ways of stopping the government, Bahuguna finally launched the "Embrace [*chipko*] the Trees" movement. He trained the village people to go and embrace a tree as the government workers came to cut it down. The people understood Bahuguna's goal and took on the concerns of the

Christians interested in ecological theologies have much to gain from an encounter with other religions. Sometimes this encounter, as exemplified in McDaniel's essay later in this work, will result in an appropriation of insights of other perspectives. Yet sometimes it will result instead in a sympathetic yet critical rejection of non-Christian perspectives through which Christian views are themselves elucidated. Paulos Gregorios' essay illustrates the latter approach in its relevance to the development of a Christian theology of nature. Emerging out of an encounter with Hinduism, we find in this Indian Orthodox writer's essay a biblical and Christian understanding of the created order. By framing three ecological principles for the environmental movement, he shows the resourcefulness of an Orthodox point of view for ecological concerns. This essay first appeared in *Tending the Garden, Essays on the Gospel and the Earth* (ed. Wesley Granberg-Michaelson, Grand Rapids, MI: William B. Eerdmans, 1987, pp. 83–92) and is used with permission. Translations of scripture are by Gregorios himself.

movement with enthusiasm. The highest government officials had to make major decisions to reduce the cutting of trees, decisions that would have been politically impossible without the Chipko movement.

Bahuguna is a simple Gandhian. At this function in his honor he said publicly that he was ill at ease on the green lawns of the presidential palace; he wanted to be back among the forest trees and the mountain people. He accepted the award bestowed on him very reluctantly, but expressed happiness that in the process the movement was being recognized.

In his acceptance speech Bahuguna presented three principles for the environmental movement which have stayed in my mind:

1. Nature is to be worshiped, not exploited.
2. One who takes less from nature and society should receive greater respect than one who takes more.
3. There is a world inside a person that is richer and more worthy of cultivation than the outside world.

Bahuguna is a Hindu; I am a Christian. As such I must reflect on these principles further rather than accept them at face value. And it is in this context that I seek, trusting in the grace of God and in the power of the Holy Spirit, to examine three passages from the New Testament in order to frame my own principles for the environmental movement. In what follows I will offer my own translation of each of these passages and then discuss the three basic ecological principles I extrapolate from them.

I

For I regard the troubles that befall us in this present time as trivial when compared with

the magnificent goodness of God that is to be manifested in us. For the created order awaits, with eager longing, with neck outstretched, the full manifestation of the children of God. The futility or emptiness to which the created order is now subject is not something intrinsic to it. The Creator made the creation contingent, in his ordering, upon hope; for the creation itself has something to look forward to — namely, to be freed from its present enslavement to disintegration. The creation itself is to share in the freedom, in the glorious and undying goodness, of the children of God. For we know how the whole creation up till now has been groaning together in agony, in a common pain. And not just the nonhuman created order — even we ourselves, as Christians, who have received the advance gift of the Holy Spirit, are now groaning within ourselves, for we are also waiting — waiting for the transformation of our bodies and for the full experiencing of our adoption as God's children. For it is by that waiting with hope that we are being saved today. We do not hope for something which we already see. Once one sees something, there is no point in continuing to hope to see it. What we hope for is what we have not yet seen; we await its manifestation with patient endurance (Rom 8:18-25).

First Principle: Human redemption can be understood only as an integral part of the redemption of the whole creation.

For a long time now we have been conditioned to understand the redemption in Christ primarily—and too often exclusively—in terms of personal salvation. A basic requirement for a healthy Christian approach to the human environment seems to be a shift of gears in this regard.

What is a "person" whose salvation Christ effects? A person exists only in relation—in relation to other human persons (his or her father and mother, to begin with) and to nonhuman realities (light, air, water, food, and so on). It is not possible for a person to come to be or to grow without relation to other persons and things. The earth and the sun as well as other people are essential parts of our existence. Without them we cannot exist. Both the Pauline and the Johannine witnesses in the New Testament strongly affirm this redemption of the whole creation—cosmic redemption, if you like, of the participation of all creation in the liberation of humanity from the bondage of sin and death. This strongly contradicts the Gnostic-Hellenic-Hindu notion that is most characteristically expressed by Plotinus, the so-called founder of Neoplatonism in the third century:

No, if body is the cause of Evil, then there is no escape; the cause of Evil is Matter (Enneads 1:8:8).

Thus, it is quite correct to say at once that Matter is without Quality (in itself) and that it is evil; it is evil not in the sense of having Quality, but precisely, in not having it (Enneads 1:8:10).

In this tradition the body is the source of bondage and evil. Unfortunately this tradition is also very strong among Christians, who—like Hellenists, Hindus, and Neoplatonists—believe that the soul alone is to be saved and that the body and other material objects, whether living or nonliving, do not participate in or benefit from the redemption in Christ. This Gnostic influence in Christianity is what has pervaded our understanding of the Old and the New Testaments. Why do we magnify the prophetic and underplay the priestly? We prefer the prophetic because it fits better with our Gnostic temperament, which despises the material and the corporate, the sacrificial and the ritual, and prefers to focus on the individual soul and the prophetic word. I will come back to this point later, but here we only need affirm what St. Paul and St. John so strongly affirm, contrary to the Gnostic-Hellenic-Hindu tradition, and in the true spirit of the Hebrew

Scriptures: that the whole creation—not just a few human souls—has been redeemed and reconciled in Christ.

Human beings have existed and do exist only as integral parts of a system that includes sources of sustenance—meat, grains, and vegetables—as well as sun and earth, light and water, air and fire. To make a false distinction between nature and history, to limit the presence and action of God to history, to deny God's action in nature—these cannot be regarded as Christian.

Nature, in the way in which we use it, is not a biblical notion. *Nature* (*physis* in Greek) in the sense of nonhuman self-existent reality does not occur in the Old or the New Testament; it is a concept alien to the biblical world. Insofar as the word *nature* refers to something as it exists by itself, it is contrary to the Johannine affirmation that not a thing came into being without Christ the Logos. If the Hebrew Scriptures use the word *nature*, it is only in the Book of Maccabees, and there it puts the word in the mouth of a Greek (Antiochus) rather than of a Hebrew.

In fact, there is no Hebrew word for nature. Hebrew uses "creating" (*bara*) as a verb, but it seldom uses *beriah*, a feminine noun, to refer to the whole creation. It does not make an entity out of creation, though it recognizes the act that produces and sustains the creation. The Hebrew Scriptures may make all the trees of the wood rejoice (Ps 96:12) and ask the trees and animals to praise the Lord (Ps 148), but they do not speak about nature or the creation as an entity representing the whole created order. The New Testament also does not speak of nature as the ensemble of created entities. If it uses the word *nature* (in expressions like *physis, physikos, kata physin*), it is to distinguish between natural and unnatural or natural and artificial (see Rom 1:26, 27; 2:27; 11:21, 24), or to speak about what is spontaneous or connatural. It can speak of our being partakers of the divine nature (in 2 Pt 1:4, *theias koinonoi physeos* literally means "sharers in the nature of the Godhead"), but not of any nature existing independently of God.

Neither is the noun *history* a common biblical notion. Certainly the Bible does not know a God who acts in "history" but does not act in "nature"; it does not distinguish nature from history, as we do. A *historia* is a carefully researched narrative of a series of events, not a realm of exclusively human or divine action unrelated to nature. The noun *historia* does not occur in the Hebrew or Greek Scriptures. The verb *historeo* occurs once (in Gal 1:18), but it is used to mean "visit."

We have seriously distorted the biblical perspective on redemption by introducing alien categories like nature and history into it, and by understanding redemption only in terms of souls and persons. In reacting against the exclusive emphasis on personal salvation, liberalism and neo-orthodoxy fell into the trap of false categories, claiming that God acts in history but not in nature, and that history rather than nature is the realm of God's revelation. These emphases can be traced to a Gnostic bias that detests nature and sacrament as material, but can see history and word as somehow nonmaterial and (therefore?) spiritual.

A new understanding of the redemption in Jesus Christ will then have to take into account at least the following: (a) personal and corporate salvation; (b) spiritual reality and material reality in the creation and in the incarnation; (c) the created order as the object and field of the redeeming order; and (d) the human person as integrally related to the whole cosmos. When we keep these relationships in mind, we will have a picture of our own faith that will facilitate a more respectful approach not to nature but to the created order as a whole. The continuity between the order of creation and the order of redemption, rather than their distinction and difference, should be the focus of our interest. Humanity is redeemed *with* the created order, not *from* it.

II

He, Christ, the Beloved Son, is the manifest presence (icon) of the unmanifest God. He

is the Elder Brother of all things created, for it was by him and in him that all things were created, whether here on earth in the sensible world or in the world beyond the horizon of your senses which we call heaven, even institutions like royal thrones, seats of lords and rulers—all forms of authority. All things were created through him, by him, in him. But he himself is before all things; in him they consist and subsist; he is the head of the body, the Church. He is the New Beginning, the First-born from the dead; thus he becomes in all respects pre-eminent. For it was (God's) good pleasure that in Christ all fullness should dwell; it is through him and in him that all things are to be reconciled and reharmonized. For he has removed the contradiction and made peace by his own blood. So all things in the visible earth and in the invisible heaven should dwell together in him. That includes you, who were once alienated, enemies in your own minds to God's purposes, immersed in evil actions; but now you are bodily reconciled in his fleshly body which has tasted death. Christ intends to present you—holy, spotless, and blameless—in God's presence, if you remain firm in the faith, rooted and grounded in him, unswerving from the hope of the good news you have heard, the good news declared not only to men and women on earth, but to all created beings under heaven. It is this gospel that I, Paul, have also been called to serve (Col 1:15-23).

Second Principle: Christ himself should be seen in his three
principal relationships: (1) to members incorporated into his
body; (2) to the human race; and (3) to the other-than-human
orders of created existence in a many-planed universe. Each
of these is related to the other.

A Christology based on this principle will not conceive of a Christ as somehow other than the created order. Today much of Christology sees Christ as being separate from the world, from culture, and so forth; we try to affirm the lordship of Christ *over* world and culture by conceiving even the incarnate Christ as somehow totally distinct from the created order. We then think of him as Lord of the world, Lord of the church, and so on. In the more individualistic versions of Christology-soteriology, some make him *sole mediato* between the person and God. This perception involves three realities: God, Christ, and the individual. God is there, the individual is here, and Christ stands in between. And the world and the church are fourth and fifth realities.

This kind of disjunctive thinking has to give way to an integral and participative way of understanding Christ. Jesus Christ is not an abstract or "purely spiritual" entity. He is incarnate. He took a material body, becoming part of the created order while remaining unchanged as one of the three persons in the Trinity who is Creator. He is one of us. He is fully consubstantial with us.

As Christians we are united with him in an especially intimate way. By baptism and by faith he has incorporated us as members of his body. By participation in his body and blood, we grow to be integral parts of him. Once he had a human body like ours. In fact, he still does—though it has already been transformed and resurrected and is therefore no longer subject to the ordinary laws of our physics, which govern only mortal bodies and material objects. But he has chosen to have a larger body, partly in heaven (that is, beyond the horizon of our senses) and partly on earth. We belong to that body as a whole, but particularly to the earthly part of it. Christ is always with us, the members of his body, particularly as he continues to fulfill his ministry as high priest of creation and as prophet and servant to the world.

Christ incarnate is a human being, consubstantial with all other human beings. He did not become simply an individual human person or a Christian. He became *humankind*—male and female. He assumed the whole of human nature, and now there is no humanity other than the one which Christ took on—our humanity, in which all human beings participate, whether or not they believe in Christ, whether or not they recognize the nature of their humanity. This aspect of the Redeemer's relationship to the whole of humanity, independent of human faith, is seldom fully recognized by Christians and its implications worked out. No humans are alien to Christ, whether they be Hindu, Muslim, Communist, or Buddhist. They share in Christ's humanity in ways that we have to spell out elsewhere. They are not members of the body of Christ, but they are not unrelated to Christ.

Christ the Incarnate One assumed flesh—organic, human flesh; he was nurtured by air and water, vegetables and meat, like the rest of us. He took matter into himself, so matter is not alien to him now. His body is a *material* body—transformed, of course, but transformed *matter*. Thus he shares his being with the whole created order: animals and birds, snakes and worms, flowers and seeds. All parts of creation are now reconciled to Christ. And the created order is to be set free and to share in the glorious freedom of the children of God. Sun and moon, planets and stars, pulsars and black holes—as well as the planet earth—are to participate in that final consumption of the redemption.

The risen Christ is thus active, by the Spirit, in all three realms: in the church, in the whole of humanity, and in the cosmos. Each of these relationships is fundamentally different, but all are real and meaningful to Christ, the Incarnate One.

Our theology's weakness has been its failure to recognize the wider scope of the redemption beyond the "individualized soul" or the person. Liberalism still spiritualizes the incarnate Christ by confining his actions to so-called history, as if that were a realm in which nature and the material elements of creation were not present. We must move beyond personal salvation to declare and teach the three basic dimensions of the redemption.

III

At the source-spring of all, the Logos is and was. The Logos is God vis-à-vis, and the

> Logos is God. It is this Logos that in the beginning was face to face with God. It is through the Logos that all existing things have come to exist. Without him not a single thing could have come into being. In him was also life. Life is light in human beings. The light shines in the midst of the darkness, and the darkness has not comprehended or overcome the light (John 1:1-5).

Third Principle: Christ and the Holy Spirit are related to the whole created order in three ways: by creating it, by redeeming it, and by finally fulfilling it in the last great consummation.

There is no need to elaborate these points. The act of creation is a corporate act of the three persons of the Trinity. God's relation to plants and trees, to air and water did not begin with the redemption in the incarnate Christ. Not a single thing exists that did not come into being without

Christ and the Holy Spirit, including the primeval water over which the Spirit was hovering at the time of creation (Gn 1:2). Neither art nor literature, neither mountain nor river, neither flower nor field came into existence without Christ and the Holy Spirit. They exist now because they are sustained by God. The creative energy of God is the true being of all that is; matter is that spirit or energy in physical form. Therefore, we should regard our human environment as the energy of God in a form that is accessible to our senses.

We have already discussed the relationship of the human environment, of the whole cosmos, to the redemption. It is a redeemed cosmos that we meet in our environment, and as such it is worthy of respect.

It is the final *apokatastasis*, the fulfillment at the end, that still needs to be stressed. The consummation, which Paul calls *anakephalaiosis*, means adding up everything (Eph 1:10) — that is, the consummation of the whole created order in Christ. Take the three numbers 5, 7, and 14. When one adds them up, one gets 26. At first it may not be obvious that the three smaller numbers are contained in the larger number, but they are there; they are not lost. Analogous to this is the process in the final *apokatastasis*, about which Peter preached in Solomon's Portico in Jerusalem. There he talked about "Christ Jesus, whom the unseen realm must keep until the times of the final restitution of all things, about which God spoke through the mouths of his holy ones the prophets from ages ago" (Acts 3:21; my translation).

The Christian understanding of the status of the world, of all life and of inorganic matter, is determined by these three factors:

Q. How did they come to be, and how are they sustained?

A. By creation.

Q. How does the incarnation of Jesus Christ affect them?

A. They share in the destined freedom of the children of God.

Q. What is their final destiny?

A. To be incorporated, through transformation, in the new order that fully emerges only at the end, in the final recapitulation.

The whole created order comes from God the Holy Trinity, is redeemed by the incarnate Christ, and will be brought to fulfillment after transformation by the same Christ and by the Holy Spirit, the perfecter of all.

REFUTING BAHUGUNA

Now that we have explored these three basic Christian principles, we are in a position to look again at Sunderlal Bahuguna's three principles. As for his first principle, Christians cannot say that nature is to be *worshiped* and not exploited. Christians would say that the created order (not nature) is to be *respected* as the order that has given birth to us, sustains us, and will still be the framework for our existence when the whole process of creation-redemption has been consummated. We respect the created order both because it comes from God and is sustained by him, and because it is the matrix of our origin, growth, and fulfillment as human beings. But we do not worship the creation; worship is reserved for the Creator. We have to *tend* the creation, use it for our own sustenance and flourishing, but we also have to respect it in itself as a manifestation of God's creative energy and cooperate with God in bringing out the full splendor of the created order as reflecting the glory of the Creator. Bahuguna's second principle—that one who takes less from nature is to be more honored than one who takes more—is also dubious from a Christian perspective. Simplicity of life is a high value, but enforced poverty is not. And the poor are to be respected not because they take less from nature but because they are friends of God and the victims of injustice. Christians can choose from two lifestyles: the simple life à la John the Baptist, who lived on locusts and wild honey in the desert, and the fuller life of our Lord, who prayed all night and worked all day, but who ate and drank with others. Neither of these lifestyles would, however, justify the mindless affluence of our consumer society. To impose austerity on a society may be unwise, but it is even more unwise to impose affluence on a nation through hidden persuasion and to make some people more affluent than others. In taking what is given by nature, we should be careful to give back to nature what it needs to maintain its own integrity and to supply the needs of the future.

Bahuguna's third principle—that the individual's inner life is more worthy of development than the outside world—is also wrongheaded. Christians need not despise or reject the outer world in order to develop the inner world. And we should not think of the inner world as an individual realm. Rather, we should think of it as the unseen, the heavenly, that which lies beyond our senses. It is a different perception, one that Paul talks about when he says, "If then you have co-risen with Christ, seek the higher things, where Christ now is enthroned at the right hand of God. Meditate on and will the heavenly realities, not the earthly ones" (Col 3:1-2; my translation). We should not speak of the inner world but of the final fulfillment that is already present in the realm beyond our senses, and that now moves our world as its norm and goal. Even when we are thinking about the environment or socio-economic and political life—*ta ano phroneite*, we should focus our minds and wills on the higher realities (not the inner), which must be manifested in the earthly realities—now partially, but in the end, fully.

4

A Sacramental Approach
to Environmental Issues

John Habgood

Orthodox theology makes much of the relationship between the microcosm and the macrocosm. In the words of Kallistos Ware:

> The human person is not only microcosm, the universe in miniature, but also microtheos, God in miniature. Each of us is not simply *imago mundi*, image of the world, but also *image Dei*, image of God. Each is a created reflection of the uncreated Deity, a finite expression of God's infinite self-expression. That is why Gregory of Nazianus states ... that man is "a second cosmos, a great universe within a little one" (Peacocke, 203).

Such a claim may sound absurdly anthropocentric. Who are we, mere specks in a vast universe, the accidental products of a process that far exceeds us and, even in earthly terms, only one among myriads of life forms, who are we to dignify ourselves with such a central role in the ordering of things? Yet the inescapable truth remains that all our knowledge of the cosmos is *our* knowledge, filtered through the medium of our own minds

---

For many Christians, participation in the sacraments is a more immediate and more fundamental way of discovering the presence of God than is the reading of abstract theological treatises. Through them, as John Habgood explains, "material reality is shown to be capable of bearing the image of the divine." In this essay Habgood carries this suggestion much further, showing how a sacramental approach to nature can give us a deep-seated respect for the earth and other living beings, and how it can, at the same time, guide us in developing technologies that help—rather than frustrate—the fulfillment of divine purpose. For those for whom sacramentalism is at the very heart of Christian faith, this essay offers an indispensable resource for seeing the relation between worship and environmentally responsible action.

My thesis exactly

46

and expressed in terms ultimately derived from our own thoughts and experience. The alternative may be even more arrogant. The quest for completely objective knowledge and the supposition that we can somehow give an account of the universe from some independent nonhuman standpoint fly in the face of the facts. Our perspective is, and always remains, human.

To say this is not to deny that we can achieve in some fields of knowledge a high degree of objectivity. Nor is it to deny that the totality of things is much greater and more mysterious than our minds can grasp. There is a proper sense in which knowledge, like prayer, ends in silence. But insofar as our knowledge admits its human limitations, the claim that microcosm and macrocosm are related, and may reflect one another, is not absurd.

The theological basis of the claim rests, as Kallistos Ware makes clear, on the belief that humanity is created in the image of God. If this is true of humanity then it must in some sense extend to the whole cosmos because Christ, the perfect image of God, is also in St. Paul's thought the agent and fulfillment of creation.

These are high and abstract thoughts, which may seem very distant from the main concerns of this book. I state them without argument as a prologue to some thoughts about sacramental theology, because sacramental theology itself may seem an absurdly narrow route along which to tackle practical questions about the environment. But if small things can reflect large ones, it may not be such a bad route after all. An eleventh-century Chinese administrator is said to have complained about Buddhists: "When they try to understand what is lofty without studying what is lowly, how can they have a proper understanding of what is lofty?"

I have no wish to make exclusive claims for sacramental theology. For some Christians the sacraments form only a small part of their religious experience. For others, among whom I include myself, they lie at the heart of worship. They hold together in a unique manner the inner relationship with God and the outer relationship with material reality, reaching out to embrace a universe whose meaning is finally disclosed in Jesus Christ. In the sacraments microcosm and macrocosm meet.

Sacramental theology centers on the perception that items of material reality—water, bread, and wine—can be given a new meaning and status by being brought within the saving action of God in Christ. This is both a revelation and a transformation. The true potential of bread, for instance, is revealed by its transformation into a means of communication with God. This is beautifully summed up in the ancient offertory prayer:

> Blessed be God through whom we have this bread to offer, which earth has given and human hands have made. It will become for us the bread of heaven.

The prayer is a subtle balance between recognizing God's gift, acknowledging our human role in developing and using it rightly, and accepting its potential as a conveyer of God's own reality. Bread, at once the most basic and ancient of foods, is also the human product that perhaps more than anything else, made possible the civilized world. This fundamental support of life, says the prayer, will reveal a new level of meaning, made possible and actual by God's own involvement in material reality through Christ.

Behind the prayer lies a theology of the incarnation and, more immediately, the discourse on the bread of life in the sixth chapter of St. John's Gospel. Whether the author of the Gospel meant this to be his substitute for an account of the Last Supper need not concern us here. The point is that it is impossible to read it now without seeing the bread as the body of Jesus given for the life of the world in a eucharistic context. But it is significant that it is not confined to a eucharistic context. The bread given by Jesus is not just contrasted with ordinary bread, profoundly important though that is, but with the manna eaten for forty years by the Israelites in the wilderness. In other words even miraculous food, food that had saved a nation from starvation, food that lay at root of its self-understanding as a people saved by God, even this was not to be compared with the bread now promised. The "bread from heaven" is no incidental feature of life with Jesus. Its meaning spreads out to embrace the totality of relationship with him. "I am the living bread which came down from heaven. If a man eats of this bread, he will live for ever" (Jn 6: 51). And it points beyond Jesus himself. "I am" in the sentence "I am the bread of life" picks up and echoes the most profound and mysterious title of God, "I am that I am" (Ex 3: 14).

Some of those who have no doubts about the value of the sacraments in their proper liturgical context find themselves uneasy when sacramental theology appears to "take off" in an apparently illegitimate fashion and to claim sacramental significance in everything. The process of widening sacramental horizons has already begun in John 6, which is why I have used it as the basis for my exposition. It fits well with a theology of worship and of the church which interprets them as expressing on a small scale and in an explicit way truths, often hidden, about what God is doing in the whole human drama. To think like this is not to ecclesiasticize everything. In fact, precisely the reverse. Church and sacraments are the making visible of what is already there but might otherwise remain unrecognized.

The essential point is that material reality is shown to be capable of bearing the image of the divine. It rests on the staggering claim that this is what happened in Jesus and what constitutes the truth in the doctrines of the incarnation and of salvation. Thus what happens to water, bread, and wine when they are used as vehicles of God's grace is no isolated miracle. All matter shares this potential, and specific sacramental actions, which themselves belong within a specific historical, theological, and liturgical context, are the God-given means by which this truth is safeguarded and made known.

They are not the exclusive means, however. Thomas Traherne in *Cen-*

turies of Meditations, saw the same truth as part of a childlike vision of the world before the distortions and separations of adult consciousness take over:

> You never enjoy the world aright, till the sea itself floweth in your veins, till you are clothed with the heavens, and crowned with the stars: and perceive yourself to be the sole heir of the whole world, and more than so, because men are in it who are everyone sole heirs as well as you. Till you can sing and rejoice and delight in God, as misers do in gold, and kings in scepters, you never enjoy the world (Traherne, 29).

At a much lower level of awareness there can be a sense of the goodness, or meaningfulness, or value of the world, which forms part of many people's basic religious awareness, even if it is only glimpsed in fleeting moments. What such experiences tend to lack, though, is the complex interplay between what God has given and what human beings must do, and the illumination that comes from setting individual experience within a developed and subtle religious tradition.

I contend, therefore, that the sacraments themselves remain one of our best clues as to how we should treat the world aright, and in what follows I sketch out in a preliminary fashion how this might help the environmental debate.

THE RECOGNITION OF POTENTIAL

What might it mean to live in practice as if anything or everything might become a vehicle of divine grace?

Perhaps it is easier to start by imagining the opposite, a universe in which anything or everything is ripe for exploitation. The essence of such a regime is that human needs and desires are sovereign, and the stuff of the world can be bent to human purposes with no respect paid to what it is in itself or what it might become within the purposes of God. In the sacramental vision the world is seen as created by God, owned by God, and ultimately finding its fulfillment in God.

Paradoxically the practical consequences of these two visions may not always be very different. Rubbish, for instance, may be seen as a resource by the sacramentalist who is concerned not to dismiss anything as mere waste, as well as by the commercially minded entrepreneur who sees that there is money to be made from it. Deep motivation may be one thing, but seeing a problem as an opportunity is not confined to those who share a particular philosophy of life.

Equally, there may be very different motives for wishing to preserve, say, a forest or an animal species. Long-term prudential considerations can provide reasons for holding back even within a general philosophy of exploitation. An attempt to recognize and respect divine potential might take various forms. It might include, for instance, respect for the evolutionary process as the means whereby in practice most of the potential within the living matter of the universe has so far been released. To let a forest be, or to protect a species, is to acknowledge that they still have within them a greater potential for life, growth, and development, and that their being may therefore form part of the larger purposes of God in using evolution as a means of creation.

Alternatively there might be a more direct respect due to them for what they can reveal of God in being themselves. This is a difficult idea to carry through into practical programs. To let everything be, to respect its right to be itself, and to allow it to develop in its own way, would, if carried to extremes, make human life impossible and negate our own creativeness. Forests also have the potential to become fuel or furniture or agricultural land, and some of the greatest human achievements have resulted from seeing a potential in things that was decidedly not a consequence of letting them be.

Human beings have interfered decisively and irreversibly in many kinds of animal breeding, often bringing out latent potentials that have been hugely to our benefit. We now stand on the threshold of wielding far greater genetic powers, with incalculable consequences for the future. This need not be mere exploitation, though with such powers available the dividing line between drawing out potential and arrogantly trying to play God may be a narrow one.

The key religious insight would seem to be that, whether things are let be or whether they are developed by human ingenuity for human purposes, they belong to God and not to ourselves. There is a respect due to them, an awareness of human limitations, a fine balance to be struck between penitence for what we have done to God's world in the past and hopeful creativeness for the future.

Sacramentally such an attitude would seem appropriate toward inanimate things, at least toward things of a certain complexity, as well as toward living creatures. A flowing stream, a clear sea teeming with life, a mountain landscape, surely deserve respect and care despite the large subjective element that enters into our appreciation of them. They can be treated in specific ways that still further reveal their potential. The great eighteenth-century creator of English landscapes, Capability Brown, earned his nickname for his skill, not in imposing his will on a recalcitrant nature, but in drawing out its aesthetic capabilities. A sculptor carving a particular stone or lump of wood may describe this work in similar ways; the finished object is somehow seen as being already there in the natural formation of the raw material, waiting only to be revealed. An engineer may see a valley as waiting to be dammed, a chasm as waiting to be bridged, an ugly and unhealthy swamp as potentially a place of beauty and usefulness. Such actions can in their own way become secular sacraments, an enhancement, a liberation of what is already there, a transformation that does not violate a thing's essential nature.   *NOT VIOLATE? I'm not sure*

I fully admit that such a way of speaking creates acute difficulties for those who are more used to seeing the universe as a torrent of change. "Essential natures" do not have much place in evolution. Clearly, by itself the recognition of potential is not enough. But sacramentalism is also about God's work complementing and giving substance to ours in a world still in process of creation.

THE NEED FOR COOPERATION

The offertory prayer speaks of bread "which earth had given and human hands have made." Cooperation with natural processes, working with the grain of nature rather than against it, is now part of the conventional wisdom among conservationalists. Can the sacramental context add anything significant to this already familiar idea?   *apt phrase*

The eucharist is a complex act of giving and receiving in which the worshipers as well as God are both givers and receivers. At its highest it is a mutual exchange of love. But all this is set within the context of what God has already done. Despite the mutuality, therefore, the key word is response. In the exchange of love "we love because he first loved us" (I Jn 4: 19). Sacramental action is thus essentially a matter of cooperation rather than co-creation. As human beings we share a role with God in drawing out the divine potential of the world, but only because God has already himself taken the decisive steps.   *cf. native Americans*

The theme of cooperation receives further emphasis in the communion, which forms the climax of the whole. There can be no true giving and receiving with God unless others form a part of it. As those who are themselves loved by God, worshipers caught up in this action are commanded and enabled to love their fellow human beings. And this communion with others spreads still further to embrace "angels and archangels and all the company of heaven." The microcosm of love and mutuality in response to the love of God experienced by those engaged in sacramental worship ultimately has to include the macrocosm.

But how far should this mutuality spread? Should it for instance include battery hens? There is an evolutionary case for including battery hens in some kind of relationship with human beings as very distant cousins, and this common membership of the community of life constitutes some kind of moral claim, albeit not a very strong one. If the sense of community goes further than this, if it is possible to hold that at a very rudimentary level there can and should be a cooperative relationship between human beings and hens, the moral claim is strengthened. If, to put the point more strongly, God gives hens a being of their own and values them prior to their usefulness as a cheap source of food, then the hen's point of view as a partner in this larger communion begins to assume some importance.

Admittedly it is not easy to know what a hen's point of view is, but in the case of battery hens there would seem to be a fairly simple test. In a battery the human element in the relationship with hens so dominates the conditions of life that the possibility of co-operation virtually disappears altogether. The hen is reduced as far as possible to machine-like operation.

Animal husbandry at its best has always contained an element of cooperation.

Even when the relationship ends in death it can be marked by respect for the life taken. The rituals surrounding animal sacrifice in cultures where sacrifice was the almost inevitable preliminary to eating meat witness to the seriousness of taking life, unpleasant though some of the rituals were. Here again the theme of communion with the life sacrificed can perhaps help modern Westernized consciousness develop a different feel for the products of industrialized scientific agriculture. Organic farming, for instance, may not fulfill the quasi-scientific claims for it, but may have moral and spiritual benefits for societies that see the need to develop a more sensitive relationship with the natural world.

The limits of cooperation become all too evident, however, when there is a mosquito in the bedroom. Letting things be themselves, discerning their point of view, looking for the divine potentiality in what is lowly, cannot become a recipe for the passive acceptance of whatever befalls us. Our human place in God's purposes is to cooperate with him in the process of creative change. Sacramental thinking points to a world which has to be redeemed before it can truly reveal the face of God. There is an inescapable element of struggle, discrimination, suffering, and tragedy in the process, and any theological approach to ecological issues that belittles or ignores these is hopelessly unrealistic. Hence, my third and final heading.

TRANSFORMATION BY REDEMPTION

The sacraments are sacraments of Christ's death and resurrection. Suffering and the transformation of suffering belong to their very essence. This is plain from the New Testament account of their origins.

Sacramental theology has no excuse, therefore, for underrating the extent to which the divine potential of the world is denied, frustrated, distorted, defaced, and ignored. Nor need it shrink from accepting that the very means of creation through evolution entails conflict and suffering. Sacramental awareness is not at all the same as sentimentality. The perceptions of divine glory in a world capable of bearing God's image have to be matched by the belief that God bears the weight and suffering of his own creation on the cross.

All this is basic Christianity. To interpret the cross in the light of the sacraments can help to strengthen the bridge between the redemption of human sin and suffering and the redemption of the rest of creation. St. Paul's language about creation "groaning and travailing" (Rom 8:22) and "waiting for the redemption of the sons of God" (Rom 8:23) is another way of expressing the same link.

To put it in sacramental terms has an advantage in that it can suggest a means by which the link is actually operative. The sacraments entail human cooperation with divine initiative, a cooperation which is essentially priestly. This is so whether we think in terms of the priesthood of all believers or the representative priesthood of individuals within the body of the church. The point is that there is a human role whereby, under the grace of God and in the midst of an ambivalent and partially evil world, ordinary things can be offered, consecrated, broken, and transformed as a means of anticipating heaven on earth. The priestly role of all human beings toward the world of nature entails a similar offering through prayer and through the recognition that all belongs to God already, a similar transformation by the release of new potential and by the discovery that even in the world of nature there can be glimpses of heaven on earth.

Implicit in this priestly role is the dual character of human life as belonging to the world of nature yet transcending it. The priest is a mediator, and our common human priesthood as cooperators with God in his creation entails coming to terms both with our createdness and with our God-relatedness. There are other ways of expressing this within Christian theology. The description of human beings as both "beasts and angels" is perhaps the most famous. But the link between sacramental theology and priesthood makes the idea of mediation particularly apposite.

As ourselves part of the process that has to be offered and transformed there is no room for arrogance or for the exploitative mentality which assumes that the created world is "ours." But as those who also stand on the godward side of the process, and who dare to describe ourselves as "made in the image of God," we also have a responsibility not simply to accept the world as it is but see and pursue its possibilities for revealing more fully the glory of God. All our environmental thinking has to take place between these two poles. And the value of a sacramental approach to it lies in the richness and diversity of images, rooted in common Christian experience, such a theology can provide.

WORKS CITED

Peacocke, A., and G. Gillett. *Persons and Personality.* Oxford: Blackwell, 1987.
Traherne, Thomas. *Centuries of Meditations.* I. New York: Harper and Row, 1960.

PART 2

New Ethical Horizons

"*And who is my neighbor?*" *(Lk 10:29) So the lawyer asked Jesus, and so Christians rightly ask themselves. Many in Christian communities now recognize that the boundaries of Christian ethical concern have been drawn too narrowly. A study of Christian history shows that all too often Christians have had too narrow an understanding of "neighbor." We have deemed fellow Christians — or those of our own race, class, and gender — as the only legitimate subjects of moral concern. We have forgotten that all people — regardless of their religion and regardless of their race, class, and gender — are subjects of God's love and bearers of the divine image.*

The consensus among many of the theologians in this section, however, is that the extension of Christian care to all people is still too restrictive. Many of the crises we face today, as members of the species Homo sapiens, arise because we have failed to extend moral consideration to those creatures beyond our species, or where we have extended such consideration, we have done so inadequately. Many members of the human family, particularly the poor, now face destruction precisely because we have been so destructive of the earth. Moreover, other living beings deserve respect in their own right, even if our well-being is not dependent upon them. Our horizons have been severely limited by our speciesism. In this section three authors — Charles Birch, Tom Regan, and Lois Daly — attempt to overcome this limitation.

5

Christian Obligation
for the Liberation of Nature

Charles Birch

Ethics is the infinitely extended responsibility toward all life (Schweitzer, 241).

We need a cosmology that attributes intrinsic value to life, mind, and the cosmos as a whole if we are to have an appropriate environmental ethic flowing out of it (Haught, 146).

I establish my covenant with you ... also with every living creature ... the birds, the cattle and every beast of the earth (Gn 9:10).

Christians see themselves as having an obligation to work for the liberation of the oppressed. Yet there is one group that has caused little concern among Christians, who seem to have left the task of this particular liberation to secular movements. Nonhuman animals are an oppressed group. We treat them as if they were things to be used as we please rather than as

---

Like Albert Schweitzer, and like Daly and Regan in this book, Charles Birch would have ethics extended to all life. Speaking as a Christian and as a biologist, Birch argues that the Christian obligation to work for the liberation of the oppressed includes an obligation to work for the liberation of the nonhuman oppressed. Birch argues that a life-centered ethic—while seeking to maximize the well-being of all life—must recognize that the interests of different organisms often conflict, and that humans often must decide between competing interests. In order to help make such decisions Birch suggests that Christians distinguish between "degrees of intrinsic value" based on different organisms' capacities for sentience. From Birch's perspective contemporary Christians seeking to develop ecologically sensitive theologies must simultaneously recognize the intrinsic value of all life and, at the same time, offer practical, workable guidelines for valuing some lives over others.

beings with lives of their own. We oppress animals in factory farming when we deny them such elementary freedoms as space in which to walk or stretch their limbs, in cruel animal experimentation, and in the destruction of habitats. This latter is the main cause of the present-day extinction of whole populations. Some forms of so-called development are so oppressive that species themselves are becoming extinct at an alarming rate. In the process there is much suffering and misery. A conservative estimate of the current rate of extinction is one thousand species a year. By the 1990s the figure could easily rise to ten thousand species a year (one species an hour). These and other instances of the oppression of animals have been documented in great detail in numerous books and treatises, especially in the last decade (see Singer, 1985). Yet the churches remain largely unmoved by this particular holocaust. Within Western society in general the predominant moral injunctions are concerned to promote the welfare of human beings, treating the welfare of anything else as a matter of moral indifference. Yet it can be argued that animal liberation will require greater altruism on our part than any other liberation movement, since the animals themselves are incapable of demanding it for themselves or of protesting against their exploitation by votes, demonstrations, or bombs. Gustafson argues for the extension of the meaning of justice from "the right relations between persons to the right relations between human activity and the rest of the world" (Gustafson, 1983, 503).

Why, then, this serious neglect by the churches? There is the fear that concern for the plight of animals would detract from the concern for the plight of oppressed humans. One billion people live in poverty. Some forty thousand die each day from hunger and related causes. Countless others live under political oppression that removes most human freedoms from their lives. We don't seem to be doing much of a job in redressing the human plight, why add to that another gigantic problem for our concern? The question indicates not only the narrow horizon of our concern but our misunderstanding of that plight as well. Is our one and only objective to be healthy and free people, and if so do we really believe we can achieve that without concern for the rest of the living world? This is not a case of either/or but both/and. There is another objective with a wider horizon: healthy (whole) people in a healthy (whole) environment with healthy relations to that environment, an environment that necessarily includes other living creatures. By contrast, the modern world has a lot of unhealthy people unable to fulfill their lives in an unhealthy environment in which little concern is given to the other living creatures that share the planet with us. In the long run we look after ourselves by looking after the environment and its inhabitants because they look after us.

There is this empirical reason for being concerned about nonhuman lives. It is very often the main argument of conservationists. It is not sufficient.

A second reason why our concern for oppression does not include nonhuman animals is that we give them no more than this instrumental value. If we do decide to look after them it is only because they look after us. In other words, we treat them as means and not ends in themselves. We see them as objects and not as subjects. This is to deny them any intrinsic value to themselves and for that matter to God. This is a secular view of nonhuman animals. For example, in arguing for experimentation on animals Michael A. Fox gratuitously assumes that animals lack intrinsic value on the unsupported proposition that only beings capable of assigning value can have intrinsic value (see Fox).

ANIMALS AS ENDS AS WELL AS MEANS

Intrinsic value resides in the experiencing of value. Only feeling confers intrinsic value. We recognize intrinsic value in humans because they are experiencing entities. They are not simply objects but subjects. They are not simply means but ends in themselves. My experiences are the most real thing about me.

They are of value to me. Why the tremendous urge to live, even in the face of enormous suffering? We want to live. The fundamental urge to live is what life is. This urge to live is also a feature of the lives of nonhuman animals. Perhaps it is the most central feature of life. A theocentric ethic affirms that each life—human and nonhuman—has value not only to the one who experiences that life but also to God. Intrinsic value means value in itself for the creature who experiences value and to God who experiences all value.

No one can have my experiences. Nevertheless I attribute experience to the other. There is just as much reason to recognize experience and feelings of joy and suffering in chimpanzees and dogs and cats—and why not also frogs and snakes—as there is to recognize experience in other human beings besides myself. Hence the revelation of the question Voltaire posed to the vivisector:

> You discover in it all the same organs of feeling that are in yourself. Answer me, machinist, has nature arranged all the means of feeling in this animal so that it may not feel? (Voltaire, quoted in Regan and Singer, 68).

Most people are willing to grant that their pets experience joy and suffering. Responsible owners of pets do their best to enhance the quality of life of their pets. But why draw the line with those animals we know best? Bird lovers include birds as sensate creatures. Wherever we find a nervous system we may suppose there is something akin to what we call feeling. The intensity of feeling and therefore the degree of richness of experience of life may well be related to the complexity of the nervous system. Any ranking based on this would put humans higher and jellyfish lower in a hierarchy. There is neurophysical evidence to support pan-experientialism. For example, the anti-anxiety agents benzodiazepines have a similar effect on nonhuman animals as on humans. Furthermore, sensory receptors for these chemicals have been found in all vertebrates except cartilaginous fishes such as sharks. This would suggest that a wide range of vertebrates may experience some sort of suffering akin to anxiety in humans. A wide variety of vertebrates also are known to have "reward circuits" in their brains.

These are pathways of nerves involved in feelings of pleasure given by a reward. But why limit experience to those creatures that have a nervous system? Why draw the line there? There are good reasons (given below) for saying that no line can be drawn between feeling entities and non-feeling entities as we go down the hierarchy of natural entities. The importance of all this is that the recognition of intrinsic value in creatures besides ourselves makes an ethical claim upon us to recognize our obligation toward them. In this sense we can speak of animals having rights that we should recognize and work to uphold (see Birch and Cobb, 1981, 153-62).

THE NEED FOR A METAPHYSICAL FOUNDATION FOR A BIOCENTRIC ETHIC

Whether or not we regard animals as subjects with feelings akin to our own depends also upon our general vision of the world. Therefore how we treat them will depend upon our metaphysical, theological, and philosophical views about life. A strong case has been made for a biocentered ethic based on process theology and process philosophy (Armstrong-Buck). A materialistic view of life is unlikely to sustain a deeply ethical concern for all life. An anthropomorphic view of life often fails to sustain any deep concern for nonhuman life. Christians, in particular, have a clear-cut responsibility to develop, promote, and act upon a nonanthropomorphic or biocentric ethical concern. I believe we might also call this a theocentric ethic, because I believe that God is concerned about all life and not only human life. If human life in its intrinsic value is of value to God, it follows that wherever there is intrinsic value there is value to God. Process theology recognizes this in two senses. On the one hand, God is the source of all value, and second, God is the recipient of all experienced value. God not only gives to the world, God also receives from the world as God feels the joys and sufferings of the creation. The world in this sense is appropriately called God's body (Hartshorne, 185; McFague, 69; Jantzen). Hence McFague argues that when we put the world at risk with our unbridled exploitation of nature, God, the God who is incarnate within the creation, is at risk in human hands. The Christian obligation becomes a caring for God's body—the world!

The intrinsic value of a life is a function of richness of experience of that life. The appropriate attitude toward life is respect. "Behold the lilies of the field" is not merely saying "look at those lilies." The word *behold* implies a respect, a kind of tenderness, which suggests that living things have a life akin to ours and an intrinsic value to themselves and to God. To behold means to stand among things with a kind of reverence for life that does not walk through the world of non-self with arrogance and unconcern. To behold implies a relationship of the creature beheld, to others, and to God. It is to respect that relationship. When we break that relationship of integrity we do evil.

The sixth Assembly of the World Council of Churches in Vancouver in 1985 called for a program on justice, peace, and the integrity of creation. The phrase *integrity of creation* was not then spelled out. The phrase needs to be given precise meaning. Integrity of creation should refer to the recognition of the integrity of the intrinsic value of every living creature and the maintenance of the integrity of the relations of each creature to its environment. In other words, it calls us to respect the life of kangaroos and elephants and the relations they have with their environments so as to enhance their lives.

A great deal of human activity today is destructive of the life and relations of nonhuman creation. Restoration is the task before us. The appropriate word for restoration of a broken relationship is salvation. Salvation is an ecological word because it is about restoring a right relationship that has been corrupted. After I had addressed the fifth Assembly of the WCC in Nairobi in 1975 on these and related matters, the conference newspaper had as its headline the next day, "Salvation for Elephants." That was appropriate. I find a similar evaluation in the Zen teaching that says "we save all beings by including them." In an address on this subject Joseph Sittler quoted St. Thomas: *"Gratia non tollet naturam, sed perficit"* — "Grace does not destroy nature but perfects it." A theology that addresses humanity only and leaves the rest of the cosmos unaddressed is an incomplete theology. Yet for biblical and early Christianity, salvation is basically a cosmic matter: the world is saved (McFague). Basil the Great composed a prayer for animals: "And for these also, O Lord, the humble beasts, who bear with us the heat and burden of the day, we beg thee to extend thy great kindness of heart, for thou hast promised to save both man and beast, and great is thy loving kindness, O Master." In quoting this prayer John Passmore comments, "Note that Basil thinks of God as having promised to save both man and beast" (Passmore, 198).

In the history of the Christian churches there has been no unanimous attitude to animals and how we should treat them. Views have been as various as Basil who pleaded for the beasts and Augustine, who said that since beasts lacked reason and therefore have no rights, we need not concern ourselves with their suffering (Passmore; Santmire). Lynn White, in raising the question of whether compassion should be extended to nature, says that scripture warrants any of three human attitudes to nature. The overwhelming and dominant one in Western Christian thinking is the assumption of our absolute rule over the rest of nature. It assumes that all things were created for our use and for no other purpose. A second attitude is that man is a trustee responsible to God for the care of our fellow creatures. Adam is placed as a gardener in Eden "to dress it and to keep it." Third is the attitude adopted by St. Francis that man is a fellow companion of other creatures all of whom rejoice in the beneficence of God (White, 105).

In the Western world today Christian churches have not been in the forefront of movements to promote concern for nonhumans. The dominant tendency has been to see nature as none other than the stage on which the drama of human life is performed. Nonhuman creatures are merely props, having no value other than their value to us; intrinsic value resides in humans alone. This view has often been taken as biblical. It is not. In the Genesis account of nature God finds goodness in things before and quite apart from the creation of Adam. Jesus expressed the divine concern for the sparrows, even the grasses of the field. If man is worth many sparrows then a sparrow's worth is not zero.

Theologians as well as the churches in our time have been slow to appreciate this. Notable exceptions have been process theologians and philosophers such as John Cobb, Charles Hartshorne, David Griffin, and Jay McDaniel. Joseph Sittler's "Called to Unity," his address to the third Assembly of the World Council of Churches in New Delhi in 1961, was notable for putting Christian unity in the larger setting of the value of nature. But it was largely ignored. Jürgen Moltmann promotes a view similar to that of process theology when he says

> According to the anthropocentric world view, heaven and earth were made for the sake of human beings, and the human being is the crown of creation; and this is certainly what is claimed by both its supporters and its critics as "biblical tradition." But it is unbiblical. . . . So if Christian theology wants to find the wisdom in dealing with creation which accords with belief in creation, it must free that belief from the modern anthropocentric view of the world (Moltmann, 31).

Likewise James Gustafson affirms that the universe does not exist for the sake of human beings and God does not order it solely for us. He too widens the ethical context from the human individual to human communities and then to all sentient life. "Humankind is not the exclusive or ultimate center of value in creation" he writes.

> Our capacities enable us to participate in the cultivation and sustenance of many values that are proper to ourselves, and we rightly value things in relation to our proper interests. But our interdependence qualifies our tendencies to anthropocentrism. We can be sure that if many aspects of the natural world could speak and claim rights

they would say that the activities of many are frequently detrimental to them and their world (Gustafson, 1984, 284).

I have argued that in our culture there has been a dominant presumption that all things exist for the sake of man, and that this has been backed by Christian theology as well as other beliefs. On the basis of this presumption all that is "below" man can be put to the service of man; it can be used for human ends regardless of the consequences for other aspects of life in the world. What is good for human beings has determined the evaluation of all other things. This has provided a general rank ordering of values. ... Ethics from a theocentric perspective raises a serious question about this traditional presumption (Gustafson 1984, 307).

An exception to the general neglect by the churches of a justice that includes concern for the whole creation is the eco-justice movement in the United States. It grew out of concern by staff of the American Baptist Convention that ecological concerns not be emphasized at the expense of justice nor justice at the expense of ecology. Eco-justice is defined as the well-being of all humankind on a thriving earth respectful of the integrity of natural systems and of worth of nonhuman creatures (Hessel). Perhaps what this movement needs most is a strong affirmation about a theology of nature that gives a solid foundation to its program of action.

TOWARD A CHRISTIAN BIOCENTRIC ETHIC

A Christian biocentric ethic takes the neighbor to be all that participates in life. The needs of neighbor stretch beyond human needs, as does the reach of love. It poses a central question to traditional Western ethics: What values should we seek to maximize in ethical behavior? "Our task," says John Cobb "is to decide which general statement, from among several alternatives, is correct" (Cobb, 312). He proposes the following possibilities:
1. So act as to maximize value for yourself in the present.
2. So act as to maximize value for yourself in the rest of your life.
3. So act as to maximize value for all humanity for the indefinite future.
4. So act as to maximize value in general.

The first is hardly to be viewed as an ethical principle at all. It says eat, drink, and be merry, for tomorrow we die. The second principle is a maxim of selfish prudence. The third is the utilitarian principle of the greatest good for the greatest number of people. But why limit action to human value? This could be a valid ethical principle only if subhuman entities had no intrinsic value. A central argument of this essay is that intrinsic value is not limited to human beings. Man is not the only pebble on the cosmic beach. Therefore only the fourth principle is sufficiently encompassing to be acceptable.

The recognition that the nonhuman animal is an end in itself and not merely a means to human ends explodes the assumption of traditional ethics. What is needed is a biocentric ethic that recognizes in every animal as well as humans, both ends and means. Conservation movements rest on insecure foundations as long as they do not go beyond instrumental ethics for their justification. In a world in which humans are fast annihilating other species a conservation ethic requires that humans reduce their demands on the environment in favor of other species.

Four sorts of instrumental ethics are invoked by conservationists (for a discussion of these sorts of arguments, see Godfrey-Smith, 311). There is the "silo argument," for maintaining the existence of all those organisms useful to us; the "laboratory" argument for maintaining those organisms needed for experimental studies; the "gymnasium" argument of nature for leisure; and the "cathedral" argument of nature for aesthetic pleasure. All these may well be valid arguments. However, when conservationists try to oppose polluters and developers solely with pragmatic arguments about the value to human welfare of, for example, gene pools in rain forests, they have been maneuvered into fighting on the same ground as their opponents. Their pragmatic arguments for the long-term value of species will be weighted against pragmatic arguments for the immediate needs of some human beings. If a judge rules that the arguments of the developers are more compelling and that a flood control dam will provide more tangible benefits to humanity than will endangered species, to whom will the conservationists appeal? To some extent the argument for preservation of whales has reached this point. Most of the products derived from whales can now be produced from other sources just as well and in any case the most economic use of whales, so some have argued, would be to harvest the lot now and thus circumvent the necessity year after year. What then will save the whales? We are left with an appeal to the intrinsic value of whales to themselves and to God.

The central principle of a biocentric ethic is that we deal with living organisms appropriately when we rightly balance their intrinsic value and their instrumental worth. When the state of Rwanda decided that land on which elephants lived was too valuable for elephants and was needed for the cultivation of food for humans, they did not kill the elephants as pests. They airlifted them by helicopter to a reserve in a neighboring state. Their action suggests that, despite their recognition of elephants as pests, they also recognized that elephants had intrinsic value and had a right to live. So far so good. But then comes the rub. How is one to balance intrinsic value and instrumental value? Up to now ethics has not faced up to this issue. We have no rules to go by. Albert Schweitzer's "reverence for life" and other "egalitarian" ethics, which rate all forms of life of equal value, are not practical guides. Such an ethic could hardly applaud the successful campaign of the World Health Organization to eradicate the smallpox virus or the present campaign to eradicate malaria-carrying mosquitoes. A human being is worth more than one mosquito. I would be prepared to lengthen the odds to an infinite number of Anopheline mosquitoes. But how to take into account the need for land for humans and also for elephants when there may not be enough for both? Is the elephant to account for zero in that equation?

In 1981 John Cobb and I suggested a criterion for assessing the relative intrinsic value of different creatures, namely their richness of experience (Birch and Cobb). The difficulty, of course, is that we have no experience of even another person's richness of experience let alone that of an elephant or a kangaroo. It is reasonable to suppose that the inner experience of an animal bears some relation to the complexity of its nervous system. It would then follow that chimpanzees and whales have more intrinsic value than worms and mosquitoes. In other words, it is reasonable to posit a hierarchy of intrinsic value. In a sense we already operate by some such assessment intuitively when we are more concerned about the death of a monkey in space flights than about the death of fruit flies in such experiments. We need to be more conscious of what should be involved in such assessments. We have not yet begun to rethink the basic theories of the economic world so that they incorporate our intuitions.

If we adopt the principle of seeking to maximize all value (not just human value) for all time (not just our lifetime) we are extending the utilitarian principle as it is usually stated. It is true that Bentham and Mill, for example, believed that animals are subjects and that it is inconsistent to exclude them from ethical consideration. But they did not deal with the questions this raises for the utilitarian system. On the other hand, Peter Singer (see Singer, 1976 and 1985) has consistently argued for a utilitarian ethic that includes all animal life. He does not base his ethic on relative richness of experience of different creatures but on capacity to suffer. The ethical task for Singer is to reduce unnecessary suffering in the world. He carries this to the extent of strongly advocating vegetarianism for all on the grounds that eating animals is one of the greater causes of animal suffering in the world today. Laudable as is Singer's objective, it is not enough. Even if animals in factory-farms were anesthetized, and thus could not suffer, there would still be reason to protest at depriving them of their natural fulfillments. The responsible owner of a cat or a dog is not only unhappy when the pet suffers pain but works to enhance its general enjoyment of life.

Richness of experience is more than reduced suffering. It has a positive component as well. We should seek to be neighbor to nonhumans in a way analogous to the way we seek to be neighbor to our human fellow creatures: to succor those who fall by the wayside and to try to remove the causes of suffering and to provide a room in the inn.

To suit the convenience of owners of pets who cannot take pets on holidays with them and who prefer a new pet on return, a company, Disposapup Ltd., rears and supplies puppies, takes them back and kills them at holiday time, and supplies replacements on demand (Attfield, 172). This is to be condemned as immoral, even if pets are disposed of without suffering. It is immoral to deliberately deprive the puppies of lives of possible pleasure and fulfillment of their canine possibilities. To live and to live abundantly need not be just a human aspiration for humans. It can be a human aspiration for our nonhuman neighbors as well.

I have confined this essay to animals. But what about the rest of creation? An evolutionary perspective leads to the concept of a continuity between all levels of life in evolutionary history. This and other evidence leads process theology to argue for a continuity in nature of all natural entities from the electron type to humans. All natural entities are seen as subjects with some degree of self-determination or freedom and with some degree of sentience or feeling, though the meaning of these words is very different at the level of the human as compared to that of a DNA molecule or an electron. Intrinsic value is thus extended to all natural entities. Since intrinsic value of electrons and atoms must be slight, from all practical points of view and therefore for ethical purposes, it can be ignored. The same is true of "aggregates" of natural entities such as rocks. The intrinsic value of a rock is only the sum of the intrinsic value of the molecules, atoms, electrons, and so on that compose it. Entities of these types may reasonably be treated as means.

A living cell is more than an aggregate. Unlike a stone it has an inherent unity and its own internal relations with its environment. The value of the created universe to God must have become intrinsically greater as evolution proceeded from electrons to atoms to molecules to cells. A world of cells is more valuable than a world without cells. Nevertheless, it is a rare circumstance when the perspective of cells as such would loom large in ethical considerations. Their primary value is instrumental. Some people would make an exception of one cell, the fertilized human ovum. In official Roman Catholic doctrine it is ascribed the intrinsic value of a human being. From the perspective of process theology the fertilized ovum does not have the experience, nor can it have, of a mature human being. It has the potentiality of eventually becoming a creature that may have that experience, but as such its intrinsic value must be very much less than that of a mature human being. Between eighteen and thirty days of fetal development a nervous system can be recognized with the closure of the neural tube forming the spinal cord and the brain. With the further development of the nervous system later in development one may posit the emergence of unified fetal experience. The fertilized ovum can be recognized as having some intrinsic value but less than that of the newly born infant. To apply to the killing of a fetus the same language used for the killing of a human person is an obstacle to reasonable reflection on this contentious subject. It is more reasonable and in line with our biological understanding of development to suppose that the capacity for experience, and therefore intrinsic value, increases with the developing person from the fertilized ovum onward. It follows that intrinsic value will be greatest when experience is rich and fulfilled. With some people whose faculties disappear with advanced age, intrinsic value may be supposed to have reached its peak early in life. This digression about the cell is relevant because of the confusion and contrary views of the intrinsic value of the fertilized human ovum.

Plants come into a category different from that of animals. They do not possess a nervous system, and the unity of the plant is of a nature different than that of the animal. Yet they are not mere aggregates of cells. They are complex societies of many different sorts of cells. Nevertheless the intrinsic value of the plant is probably no more than that of the cells that compose it. Plants are appropriately treated primarily as means and, of course, critically important ones for life on earth.

SOME ETHICAL GUIDELINES FOR PRACTICAL PROBLEMS IN THE TREATMENT OF ANIMALS

The guiding principle proposed is that we are morally obliged to reduce suffering and to enhance the quality of life of animals that share the earth with us. The greater obligation is entailed toward those creatures that have more significant experience. This entails detailed consideration of many of the practices that go largely unquestioned, particularly in Western society.

Experimentation

Today over 100 thousand vertebrates are used in research laboratories all over the world. Some eighty-five percent of these are rats and mice. Frogs, pigeons, hamsters, dogs, cats, pigs, and primates constitute almost all the rest. About five percent are used for teaching purposes, another five percent for diagnosis of disease, twenty percent for production of biological substances ("biologicals") and for toxicity testing, thirty percent in development of drugs and their testing, and forty percent for other research activities such as the present work in genetic engineering to increase the size of sheep and pigs. A Dutch survey indicates that fifty percent of all animal experimentation involve a risk of appreciable discomfort to the animals (Tannenbaum and Rowan). Tannenbaum and Rowan recognize six different ethical stances toward experimentation with animals ranging from total acceptance (for example, Adrian) to total rejection (for example, Linzey) with a variety of positions in between. More has been published supporting total rejection than on all the other views. The issues are complex. However, a minimal requirement must be that animal experimentation should not be undertaken without counting the cost to the animals involved. The cost is usually some form of suffering. Or it also may be, as with chimpanzees (now classified as an endangered species), the possible annihilation of the species altogether. In all cases experimentation should not be done unless absolute necessity can be demonstrated and all alternative possibilities have been excluded after serious consideration.

The existence of ethical review committees in many countries today means that some sorts of experimentation done in the past will no longer be permitted. One example is the experimentation of Harry J. Harlow and his colleagues (from 1961 onward) on Rhesus monkeys. This experimentation involved severe maternal and sibling deprivation described by Michael A. Fox as "nightmarish and regrettable experiments" (Fox, 103) and by Mary Midgley as completely unnecessary for the purposes for which they were done (Midgley 1981). The churches should align themselves with watchdog organizations that monitor the treatment of animals in laboratories in their own community. (Some of these organizations may adopt extreme methods—which is all the more reason why churches should be involved to help make these activities responsible and fair.)

Food

There is a variety of ethical stances on the eating of animals ranging from no objection to total rejection (e.g. Regan 1983). A minimal stance again surely holds that treatment of animals as renewable resources having value only to human interests is immoral. Farm animals should be treated with the respect they are due. It is wrong to maintain animals used as food in a manner that causes them discomfort and denies them the opportunity to live in conditions that are reasonably natural. This consideration renders the battery cage system for hens as immoral. Switzerland and Sweden have passed legislation to phase out this system. The standard method of rearing calves in the United States for the production of luxury veal is extremely cruel. These procedures have already been declared illegal in the state of Victoria in Australia and in Great Britain.

The advocacy of increasing meat consumption in the rich world should be questioned on a number of grounds. First, such consumption multiplies the cruelty of crowded yards, crowded transports, and abattoirs. Second, there are sound health reasons to increase the component of vegetables in the human diet in the rich world. Third, meat production is, in many instances, a wasteful way of producing food. As world population increases more and more people will, of necessity, have less meat and more vegetables in their diet. We should anticipate this change, which is already part of life in poor countries. There are good arguments for vegetarianism. The most important one is that it reduces one major cause of animal suffering.

All animals in the creation story in Genesis are vegetarian. They live on grass, and the humans live on nuts and fruit. It is only when humans in the account become evil that they become enemies of other animals and take them for food. In the book of Isaiah the day is foreseen when paradise is regained, and everyone not only goes back to a nonmeat diet, but the friendliest relations subsist between all species. The wolf shall dwell with the lamb, the leopard shall lie down with the kid, and a little child shall lead them! In the book of Job God puts questions to Job that show up human egotism and indicate that nonhuman creation has value other than that determined by human use. Who has made it rain on the land where no man is to cause the tender grass to spring forth? Who has provided food for the wild ass and the wild ox that can't be domesticated or put to work? The author of Psalm 104 even says that God made Leviathan as a pet, so that God could play with it. In these references God made things for their own sake and for God's sake.

Genetic Engineering

The successful transplantation of the gene for growth hormone into the fertilized ovum of mice has produced "super mice." This is a model for possible "improvement" of livestock by genetic engineering. The first steps in this have already been accomplished with the transplanting of additional genes for growth hormone into sheep in Australia to produce larger animals and therefore more wool. In the first generation the metabolism of these sheep has been greatly disturbed. It remains to be seen what the offspring of these genetically altered sheep will be like. One might imagine chicken farmers wanting to produce a chicken with four drum sticks instead of a mere two. What sort of alteration of the animal is ethical? By standard procedures of artificial selection we have produced farm animals that are vastly different from their wild progenitors. Are the consequences of genetic engineering on animals different in principle?

Zoos, Circuses, Gladiatorial Shows, and Hunting

We are obliged to question the morality of confining animals for display and entertainment unless the conditions are virtually natural for the animals concerned. The day of wire cages and cement pits should have long passed but hasn't. What might have been claimed as an educational role of zoos in the past has been superseded by superb wildlife films such as those produced by Sir David Attenborough for the BBC. Zoos have a role for saving threatened species but perhaps little else. There is no role for performing animals in circuses in a biocentric ethic. The same goes for shows of fighting cocks and bullfights, which are legal entertainment in some countries. The emotions to which these so-called sports pander and the morality they condone are akin to those that led people to find entertainment in watching Christians being thrown to lions. Mary Midgley cogently remarks that bull-baiting has not been replaced by bulldozer-baiting because active personal conflict is essential to such "sport" (Midgley 1983, 16). This seems to be regarded as an essential component of hunting also. Greyhound dogs seem to be satisfied with chasing mechanical rabbits in greyhound racing, but some owners do what they can to slip in the benighted live rabbit if they can get away with it. Open seasons for shooting ducks and other wildfowl involve much suffering, some of it in lingering death. The suffering is even more horrific when the hunt is for wild mammals such as kangaroos. Again we may well ask of the churches what they are doing about combating these cruel conventions in their own community?

Animals in the Wild

In some respects this is the most difficult of all the problems we face in our treatment of animals. In every continent now the habitats of wild animals are being encroached upon by agriculture. Wild animals are being displaced by domestic cattle, and their habitats changed mostly to the disadvantage of the wildlife, which sometimes is driven to extinction. There are exceptions. The two most abundant species of kangaroos in eastern Australia have become more common as a result of sheep farming in their habitats. This seems to be because of the increased supplies of water farming brings with it. But the farmer, often without supporting evidence, more often than not regards kangaroos on his property as pests and seeks to destroy them. Because of the abundance of kangaroos on and near farms, farmers are given quotas to kill. This raises great opposition from conservationists. An alternative to killing the kangaroos is turning the farms over to them, since much of the country is marginal for sheep anyway. Sheep don't thrive there nearly as well as kangaroos. Moreover, kangaroos don't reduce the habitat to a dust bowl in dry years, as do sheep. But what then happens to the farmer? In some cases the farm could be taken over by the state for national kangaroo parks. Or the kangaroos could be harvested for food and leather instead of sheep. But in this latter case we have the prospect of beloved native mammals being slaughtered like the domesticated mammals they replaced. If we were to put the greatest value on the reduction of suffering then the kangaroo park might be the best solution. But if we put more value on the products from the land, then some form of farming will be chosen, as it has been chosen in the past. In any case a major problem—certainly in Australia and it seems to be the case elsewhere—is the conservative attitude of farmers who are not interested in changing age-long habits for newfangled ideas about rights of animals. So education becomes increasingly important. In this the churches have a part to play.

CONCLUSION

The task of working out a biocentric ethic for our time has yet to be done. Initially we need to discover in our tradition and from an understanding of modern biology some fundamental principles on which to build such an ethic. That includes an appreciation of the continuity between humanity and the rest of nature while at the same time emphasizing the distinctiveness of the human. The development of such an ethic means that values we place high on the human agenda, such as justice, must be extended to include the rest of nature. It involves a recognition of the intrinsic value of creatures besides ourselves and their value not simply to us but to themselves and to God. Taking our biocentric ethic seriously in practice will mean a dramatic change in our behavior toward nature. The ethical task before us is to liberate all life from the constraints of oppression, human insensitivity, and dominion in whatever form they take.

The great achievement of the Enlightenment, says Mary Midgley, was to build a theory of the rights of man that made possible enormous advances towards social justice (Midgley 1983, 51).

A great achievement of our time could be to extend the concepts of rights and justice to all living creatures not only in theory but in the practice of a nonanthropocentric, biocentric ethic.

The Prayer of the Donkey

O God who made me
to trudge along the road
always,
to carry heavy loads
always,
and to be beaten
always!
Give me great courage and gentleness.
One day let somebody understand me—
that I may no longer want to weep
because I can never say what I mean
and they make fun of me.
Let me find a juicy thistle—
and make them give me time to pick it.
And, Lord, one day, let me find again
my little brother of the Christmas crib.
—Carmen Bernos de Gasztold

WORKS CITED

Adrian, Lord. *Experiments With Animals*. Science in Society Project. London: Association for Science Education, 1986.

Armstrong-Buck, Susan. "Whitehead's Metaphysical System as a Foundation for Environmental Ethics." *Environmental Ethics* 8 (1986):241-59.

Attfield, Robin. *The Ethics of Environmental Concern*. Oxford: Blackwell, 1983.

Bernos de Gasztold, Carmen. *Prayers From the Ark*. London: Macmillan, 1963.

Birch, Charles, and John B. Cobb. *The Liberation of Life: From the Cell to the Community*. New York: Cambridge University Press, 1981.

Cobb, John B. "Ecology, Ethics and Theology." *Toward a Steady State Economy*.

Ed. H. E. Daly. San Francisco: W. H. Freeman, 1973, pp. 307-20.

Fox, Michael A. *The Case for Animal Experimentation: An Evolutionary and Ethical Perspective.* Berkeley: University of California Press, 1986.

Godfrey-Smith, W. "The Value of Wilderness." *Environmental Ethics* 1 (1979): 309-19.

Gustafson, James N. "Ethical Issues in the Human Future." *How Humans Adapt: A Biocultural Odyssey.* Ed. Donald J. Orther. Washington, D.C.: Smithsonian Press, 1983, pp. 491-515.

―――. *Ethics From a Theocentric Perspective. Ethics and Theology.* Vol. 2. University of Chicago Press, 1984.

Hartshorne, Charles. *Man's Vision of God.* Chicago: Willet Clark and Co., 1941.

Haught, John F. "The Emergent Environment and the Problem of Cosmic Purpose." *Environmental Ethics* 8 (1986):139-50.

Hessel, Dieter T., ed. *For Creation's Sake: Preaching, Ecology, and Justice.* Philadelphia: Geneva Press, 1985.

Jantzen, Grace. *God's World, God's Body.* Philadelphia: Westminster Press, 1984.

Linzey, Andrew. *Animal Rights: A Christian Assessment of Man's Treatment of Animals.* London: SCM Press, 1976.

McFague, Sallie. *Models of God: Theology for an Ecological, Nuclear Age.* Philadelphia: Fortress Press, 1987.

Midgley, Mary. "Why Knowledge Matters." *Animals in Research.* Ed. David Sperlinger. New York: Wiley, 1981, pp. 319-36.

―――. *Animals and Why They Matter: A Journey Around the Species Barrier.* Harmondsworth, Middlesex, England: Penguin, 1983.

Moltmann, Jürgen. *God in Creation: An Ecological Doctrine of Creation.* The Gifford Lectures 1984-85. London: SCM Press, 1985.

Passmore, John. "The Treatment of Animals." *Journal of the History of Ideas,* 36 (1975):195-218.

Regan, Tom. *The Case for Animal Rights.* Berkeley: University of California Press, 1983.

Regan, Tom, and Peter Singer (eds.). *Animal Rights and Human Obligations.* New Jersey: Prentice Hall, 1976.

Santmire, H. Paul. *The Travail of Nature: The Ambiguous Ecological Promise of Christian Theology.* Philadelphia: Fortress Press, 1985.

Schweitzer, Albert. *Civilization and Ethics.* London: Adam and Charles Black, 1949.

Singer, Peter. *Animal Liberation: A New Ethic for Our Treatment of Animals.* London: Jonathon Cape, 1976.

―――. "Ten Years of Animal Liberation." *The New York Review of Books* 31: nos. 21 and 22 (1985):46-52.

Tannenbaum, Jerrold, and Andrew N. Rowan. "Rethinking the Morality of Animal Research." *Hastings Center Report* 15, no. 5 (1985):32-45.

White, Lynn. "The Future of Compassion." *Ecumenical Review* 30 (1978):100-09.

6

Christianity and Animal Rights: The Challenge and Promise

Tom Regan

In its simplest terms the animal-rights position I uphold maintains that such diverse practices as the use of animals in science, sport, and recreational hunting, the trapping of fur-bearing animals for vanity products, and commercial animal agriculture are categorically wrong—wrong because these practices systematically violate the rights of the animals involved. Morally, these practices ought to be abolished. That is the goal of the *social* struggle for animal rights. The goal of our *individual* struggle is to divest ourselves of our moral and economic ties to these injustices, for example, by not wearing the dead skins of animals and by not eating their decaying corpses.

Not a few people regard the animal-rights position as extreme, calling, as it does, for the abolition of certain well-entrenched social practices rather than for their "humane" reform. And many seem to imagine that once the label "extreme" is applied, the need for further refutation evaporates. After all, how can such an "extreme" moral position be correct?

I addressed this question in a recent speech, reminding my audience of a few "extreme" moral positions upon which we are all agreed:

The murder of the innocent is *always* wrong.

Rape is *always* wrong.

Tom Regan is among the foremost ethicists of our time who argue for the rights of nonhuman animals. Christians who are concerned with the liberation of the oppressed must listen to the voices of such ethicists; they must begin to hear the demand that we see the wrongfulness in the mistreatment of nonhuman animals—a demand Regan takes to be absolute. In such a demand, so Regan insists, many Christians are faced with an individual—and a parallel social—choice: to live out of hypocrisy or to act for the transformation of oppressive and evil habits and institutions.

Child molestation is *always* wrong.

Racial and sexual discrimination are *always* wrong.

I went on to note that when an injustice is absolute, as is true of each of the examples just adduced, then one must oppose it absolutely. It is not a reformed, "more humane" rape that an enlightened ethic calls for; it is the abolition of all rape that is required; it is this *extreme* position we must uphold. And analogous remarks apply in the case of the other human evils I have mentioned.

Once this much is acknowledged it is evident—or at least it should be—that those who oppose or resist the animal rights question will have to do better than merely attach the label "extreme" to it. Sometimes "extreme" positions about what is wrong are right.

Of course there are two obvious differences between the animal rights position and the other examples of extreme views I have given. The latter views are very generally accepted, whereas the former position is not. And unlike these very generally accepted views, which concern wrongful acts done to human beings, the animal-rights position concerns the wrongfulness of treating animals (nonhuman animals, that is) in certain ways. Those who oppose or resist the animal rights position might seize upon these two differences in an effort to justify themselves in accepting extreme positions regarding rape and child abuse, for example, while rejecting the "extremism" of animal rights.

But neither of these differences will bear the weight of justification. That a view, whether moral or otherwise, is very generally accepted is not a sufficient reason for accepting it as true. Time was when the shape of the earth was generally believed to be flat, and time was when the presence of physical and mental handicaps were very generally thought to make the people who bore them morally inferior. That very many people believed these falsehoods obviously did not make them true. We don't discover or confirm what's true by taking a vote.

The reverse of the preceding also can be demonstrated. That a view, moral or otherwise, is not generally accepted is not a sufficient reason for judging it to be false. When those lonely few first conjectured that the earth is round and that women are the moral equals of men, they conjectured truly, notwithstanding how grandly they were outnumbered. The solitary person who, in Thoreau's enduring image, marches to a different drummer, may be the only person to apprehend the truth.

The second difference noted above is more problematic. That difference cites the fact that child abuse and rape, for example, involve evils done to human beings, while the animal-rights position claims that certain evils are done to nonhuman animals. Now there is no question that this does constitute a difference. The question is, Is this a *morally* relevant difference—a difference, that is, that would justify us in accepting the extreme opposition we judge to be appropriate in the case of child abuse and rape, for example, but which most people resist or abjure in the case of, say, vivisection? For a variety of reasons I do not think that this difference is a morally relevant one.

Viewed scientifically, this second difference succeeds only in citing a biological difference: the victims of rape and child abuse belong to one species (the species Homo sapiens) whereas the victims of vivisection and trapping belong to another species (the species *canis lupus*, for example). But biological differences *inside* the species Homo sapiens do not justify radically different treatment among those individual humans who differ biologically (for example, in terms of sex, or skin color, or chromosome count). Why, then, should biological differences *outside* our species count morally? If having one eye or deformed limbs does not disqualify a human being from moral consideration equal to that given to those humans who are more fortunate, how can it be rational to disqualify a rat or a wolf from equal moral consideration because, unlike us, they have paws and a tail?

Some of those who resist or oppose the animal-rights position might have recourse to "intuition" at this point. They might claim that one either *sees* that the principal biological difference at issue (namely, species membership) is a morally relevant one, or one does *not* see this. No *reason* can be given as to why belonging to the species Homo sapiens gives one a superior moral status, just as no *reason* can be given as to why belonging to the species *canis lupus* gives wolves an inferior moral status (if wolves have a moral status at all). This difference in moral status can only be grasped immediately, without making an inference, by an exercise of intuitive reason. This moral difference is self-evident — or so it will be claimed by those who claim to intuit it.

However attractive this appeal to intuition may seem to some, it woefully fails to bear the weight of justification. The plain fact is, people have claimed to intuit differences in the comparative moral standing of individuals and groups *inside* the human species, and these alleged intuitions, we all would agree, are painful symptoms of unquestioned and unjustifiable prejudice. Over the course of history, for example, many men have "intuited" the moral superiority of men when compared with that of women, and many white-skinned humans have "intuited" the moral superiority of white-skinned humans when compared with humans having different skin colors. If this is a matter of intuition, then no reason can be given for this superiority. No *inference* is or can be required, no evidence adduced. One either sees it, or one doesn't. It's just that those who do see it (or so they will insist) apprehend the truth, while those whose deficient intuitive faculties prevent them from seeing it fail to do so.

I cannot believe that any thoughtful person will be taken in by this ruse. Appeals to intuition in these contexts are symptomatic of unquestioned and unjustifiable moral prejudices. What prompts or encourages men to "see" their moral superiority over women are the sexual prejudices men bring with them, not what is to be found in the existence of sexual differences themselves. And the same is true, *mutatis mutandis*, of "seeing" moral superiority in racial or other biological differences among humans. In short, appeals to intuition, when made *inside* the species Homo sapiens, and when they purport to discover the moral superiority latent within existing biological differences—such appeals can gain no admission to the court of fair judgment.

That much established, the weakness of appeals to intuition in the case at hand should be apparent. Since intuition is not to be trusted when questions of the comparative moral standing of biologically different individuals *inside* the species Homo sapiens are at issue, it cannot be rational to assume or insist that such appeals can or should be trusted when questions of the comparative moral standing of individuals *outside* this species are at issue. Moreover, since appeals to intuition in the former case turn out to be symptomatic of unquestioned and unjustifiable moral prejudices, rather than being revelatory of some important moral truth, it is not unreasonable to suspect that the same diagnosis applies to appeals to intuition in the latter case. If true, then those who "intuit" the moral superiority of all members of the species Homo sapiens over all members of every other species also emerge as the unwitting victims or the willful perpetrators of an unquestioned and unjustifiable moral prejudice.

Speciesism is the name commonly given to this prejudice. This idea has been characterized in a variety of ways. For present purposes let us begin with the following twofold characterization of what I shall call *categorical speciesism*.

> *Categorical speciesism* is the belief that (1) the inherent value of an individual can be judged solely on the basis of the biological species to which that individual belongs, and that (2) all the members of the species Homo sapiens have equal inherent value, while all the members of every other species lack this kind of value, simply because all and only humans are members of the species Homo sapiens.

In speaking of inherent value, both here and throughout what follows, I mean something that coincides with Kant's famous idea of "end-in-itself." Individuals who have inherent value, in other words, have value in their own right, apart from their possible utility for others; as such, these individuals are never to be treated in ways that reduce their value to their possible usefulness for others. They are always to be treated as "ends-in-themselves," not as "means merely." Categorical speciesism, then, holds that all and only humans have this kind of value precisely because all and only humans belong to the species Homo sapiens.

I have already indicated why I believe that appeals to intuition cannot succeed in establishing the truth of categorical speciesism as so characterized. But that a given view has not been proven to be true is not tantamount to showing that those who believe it are prejudiced. No one has yet proven that the "Big Bang" theory is true. But it hardly follows from this that those who accept this theory must be in the grip of some prejudice. By analogy, therefore, it is apparent that those who believe in categorical speciesism (speciesists, so-called) are not shown to be morally prejudiced simply because their appeals to intuition turn out to be rationally inadmissible. How, then, might the prejudicial character of speciesism be established?

Part of that answer is to be found when we pause to consider the nature of the animals we humans hunt, trap, eat, and use for scientific purposes. Any person of common sense will agree that these animals bring the mystery of consciousness to the world. These animals, that is, not only are *in* the world, they are aware *of it* — and also of their inner world. They see, hear, touch, and feel; but they also desire, believe, remember, and anticipate. If anyone questions my assessment of the common-sense view about these animals, then I would invite them to speak with people who share their lives with dogs or cats or horses, or others who know the ways of wolves or coyotes, or still others who have had contact with any bird one might wish to name. Common sense clearly is on the side of viewing these animals as unified psychological beings, individuals who have a biography (a psychological life-story), not merely a biology.

Of course, if common sense happened to be at odds with our best science over this issue, it would be difficult to be altogether sanguine in siding with common sense. But common sense is *not* in conflict with our best science here. Indeed, our best science offers a scientific corroboration of the common-sense view.

That corroboration is to be found in a set of diverse but related considerations. One is evolutionary theory, which implies that (1) the more complex has evolved from the less complex; (2) members of the species Homo sapiens are the most complex life form of which we are aware; (3) members of our species bring a psychological presence to the world; (4) the psychological capabilities we find in humans have evolved over time; and (5) these capacities would not have evolved at all and would not have been passed on from one generation to the next if they (these capacities) failed to have adaptive value — that is, if they failed to offer advantages to our species in its ongoing struggle to survive in an ever-changing environment.

Given these five points, it is entirely consistent with the main thrust of evolutionary theory, and is indeed required by it, to maintain that the members of *some species of nonhuman animals* are like us in having the capacity to see and hear and feel, for example, as well as to believe and desire, to remember and anticipate. Certainly this is what Darwin thinks, as is evident when he writes of the animals we humans eat and trap, to use just two instances, that they differ psychologically (or mentally) from us in degree, not in kind.

A second related consideration involves comparative anatomy and physiology. Everything we know about nature must incline us to believe that a complex structure has a complex reason for being. It would therefore be an extraordinary lapse of form if we humans had evolved into complicated psychological creatures, with an underlying anatomical and physiological complexity, while other species of animals had evolved to have a more or less complex anatomy and physiology, very much like our own in many respects, and yet lacked — *totally* lacked — any and every psychological capacity. If nature could respond to this bizarre suggestion, the verdict we would hear would be, "Nonsense!"

Thus it is, then, that both common sense and our best science speak with one voice regarding the psychological nature we share with the non-human animals I have mentioned — those, for example, many people stew, roast, fry, broil, and grill for the sake of their gustatory desires and delights. When the dead and putrefying bodies of these animals are eaten, our psychological kin are consumed.

Recall the occasion for this review of relevant scientific considerations. Categorical speciesism, which I characterized earlier, is not shown to be a moral prejudice merely because those who accept it are unable to prove its truth. This much has been conceded and, indeed, insisted upon. What more, then, would have to be established before the charge of moral prejudice could be made to stick? Part of that answer is to be found in the recent discussion of what common sense and our best science contribute to our understanding of the nonhuman animals we have been discussing. Both agree that these animals are fundamentally like ordinary human beings — like you and me. For, like us, these animals have a unified psychological presence in the world, a life-story that is uniquely their own, a separate biography. In the simplest terms they are *somebody, not something.* Precisely because this similarity is so well-established, grounded in the opinions, as Aristotle would express this, of both "the many and the wise," any substantive moral position at odds with it seems dubious to say the least.

And categorical speciesism, as I have characterized it, is at odds with the joint verdict of common sense and our best science. For once the appeal to intuition is denied (and denied for good reasons), the onus of justification must be borne by the speciesist to cite some unique feature of being human that would ground the attribution of inherent value exclusively to human beings, a task that we now see is all but certain to end in failure, given the biographical status humans share with those nonhuman animals to whom I have been referring. Rationally considered, we must judge similar cases similarly. This is what the principle of formal justice requires, what respect for logical consistency demands. Thus, since we share a biographical presence in the world with these animals, it seems arbitrary and prejudicial in the extreme to insist that all humans have a kind of value that every other animal lacks.

In response to this line of argument people who wish to retain the spirit of speciesism might be prompted to alter its letter. This position I shall call modified speciesism. According to this form of speciesism those nonhuman animals who, like us, have a biographical presence in the world have some inherent value, but the degree of inherent value they have always is less than that possessed by human beings. And if we ask why this is thought to be so, the answer modified speciesism offers is the same as categorical speciesism: The degree of value differs because humans belong to a particular species to which no other animal belongs—the species Homo sapiens.

I think it should be obvious that modified speciesism is open to many of the same kinds of damaging criticisms as categorical speciesism. What, we may ask, is supposed to be the basis of the alleged superior value of human beings? Will it be said that one simply intuits this? Then all the same difficulties this appeal faced in the case of categorical speciesism will resurface and ultimately swamp modified speciesism. To avoid this, will it be suggested that the degree of inherent value an individual possesses depends on the relative complexity of that individual's psychological repertoire—the greater the complexity, the greater the value? Then modified speciesism simply will not be able to justify the ascription of superior inherent value to all human beings when compared with every nonhuman animal. And the reason it will not be able to do this is simple: Some nonhuman animals bring to their biography a degree of psychological complexity that far exceeds what is brought by some human beings. One need only compare, say, the psychological repertoire of a healthy two-year-old chimp, or dog, or hog, or robin to that of a profoundly handicapped human of any age, to recognize the incontrovertible truth of what I have just said. Not all human beings have richer, more complex biographies than every nonhuman animal.

How are speciesists to get around this fact? For get around it they must, because fact it is. There is a familiar theological answer to this question; at least it is familiar to those who know something of the Jewish and Christian religious traditions, as these traditions sometimes have been interpreted. That answer states that human beings—all of us—are inherently more valuable than any other existing individual because we are spiritually different and, indeed, unique. This uniqueness stems from our having been created in the image of God, a status we share with no other creature. If, then, it is true that all humans uniquely image God, then we are able to cite a real (spiritual) difference between every member of our species and the countless numbers of the millions of other species of creaturely life. And if, moreover, this difference is a morally relevant one, then speciesists might seem to be in a position to defend their speciesism (and this is true whether they are categorical or moderate speciesists) in the face of the demands of formal justice. After all, that principle requires that we judge similar cases similarly, whereas any two individuals—the one human, the other a member of some other species—will not be relevantly similar, given the hypothesis of the unique spiritual worth of all human beings.

Now I am not ill-disposed to the idea of there being something about humans that gives us a unique spiritual worth, nor am I ill-disposed to the idea that the ground of this worth is to be found or explicated in the idea that humans uniquely image God. Not surprisingly, therefore, the interpretation of these ideas I favor, while it concedes this possible difference between humans and the rest of creation, does not yield anything like the results favored by speciesism, whether categorical or moderate.

The position I favor is one that interprets our divine imaging in terms of our moral responsibility. By this I mean that we are expressly chosen by God to be God's viceregents in the day-to-day affairs of the world; we are chosen by God, that is, to be as loving in our day-to-day dealings with the created order as God was in creating that order in the first place. In this sense, therefore, there *is* a morally relevant difference between human beings and every other creaturely expression of God. For it is only members of the human species who are given the awesome freedom and responsibility to be God's representatives within creation. And it is, therefore, only we humans who can be held morally blameworthy when we fail to do this, and morally praiseworthy when we succeed.

Within the general context of this interpretation of our unique imaging of God, then, we find a morally relevant difference between God's creative expression in the human and God's creative expression in every other aspect of creation. But—as should be evident—this difference *by itself* offers neither aid nor comfort to speciesism, of whatever variety. For to agree that only humans image God, in the sense that only humans have the moral responsibility to be loving toward God's creation, in no way entails *either* that all and only humans have inherent value (so-called categorical speciesism) *or* that all and only humans have a superior inherent value. Granted, our uniqueness lies in our moral responsibility to God and to God's creation, including of course all members of the human family. But this fact, assuming it to be a fact, only answers the question, Which among God's creatures are capable of acting rightly or wrongly (or, as philosophers might say, "are moral agents")? What this fact, assuming it to be one, does not answer are the questions: To which creatures *can we act* rightly or wrongly? and What *kind of value* do other creatures have?

As very much a nonexpert in the area of biblical exegesis, I am somewhat reluctant to make confident declamations about how the Bible answers these questions. But like the proverbial fool who rushes in, I shall make bold and hazard the opinion that there is no one, unambiguous, unwavering biblical answer to either question. Many passages lend support to viewing all of nonhuman creation as having no or little value apart from human needs and interests, a reading that tends naturally to support the view that human moral agents act wrongfully with regard to the nonhuman world only if our treatment of it harms some legitimate human need or interest. This is the traditional Christian anthropocentrism. By contrast, other passages support views that are more or less nonanthropocentric. I do not profess to know how to prove that the anthropocentric reading is false or unfounded, or that a lesser or a greater nonanthropocentric reading is true or well-grounded. Indeed, as I already have indicated, I do not myself believe that the Bible offers just one answer to the questions before us.

The upshot, then, to my mind at least, is that we are left with the awesome responsibility of choosing between alternative biblical representations of the value of nonhuman creation, none of which is clearly or incontrovertibly the correct one. And this fact, I believe, should chasten us in our conviction that we have privileged access to the whole Truth, and nothing but the Truth. With minds so feeble, spirits so weak, and a biblical message so open to honest differences of interpretation among people of real faith and good will, all who take spiritual sustenance from the pages of the Bible ought to realize both the value of, and the need to practice, the virtue of tolerance.

Having said this, I may now speak to my own reading of the biblical message and indicate why that message, as I understand it, not only fails to offer aid and comfort to speciesism, it actually can and should serve as a healthy spiritual antidote to this virulent moral prejudice.

I take the opening account of creation in Genesis seriously, but not, I hasten to add, literally (for example, a day, I assume, is not to be understood as twenty-four hours). I take it seriously because I believe that this is the point from which our spiritual understanding of God's plans in and hopes for creation must begin and against which our well-considered judgments about the value of creation finally must be tested. It is therefore predictable that I should find significance in the fact that God is said to find each part of creation "good" before humans came upon the scene and that humans were created by God (or came upon the scene) on the same day as the nonhuman animals to which I have been referring—those whose limbs are severed, whose organs are brutally removed, and whose brains are ground up for purposes of scientific research, for example. I read in this representation of the order of creation a prescient recognition of the close, vital kinship humans share with these other animals, a kinship I earlier endeavored to explicate in terms of our shared *biological* presence and one, quite apart from anything the Bible teaches, supported both by common sense and our best science. If I may be pardoned even the appearance of hubris, I may say, in the language of St. Thomas, that this fact of our common biographical presence is both a "truth of reason" and a "truth of faith."

But I find in the opening saga of creation an even deeper, more profound message regarding God's plans in and hopes for creation. For I find in that account the unmistakable message that God did not create nonhuman animals for the use of humans—not in science, not for the purpose of vanity products, not for our entertainment, not for sport or recreation, not even for our bodily sustenance. On the contrary, the nonhuman animals currently exploited by these human practices were created to be just what they are— *independently good* expressions of the divine love which, in ways that are likely always to remain to some degree mysterious to us, was expressed in God's creative activity.

The issue of bodily sustenance, of food, is perhaps the most noteworthy of the practices I have mentioned since, while humans from "the beginning" were in need of bodily sustenance and had a ready supply of edible non-human animal food sources available, there were no rodeos or circuses, no leg-hold traps or dynamite harpoons in the original creation. Had it been a part of God's hopes in and plans for creation that humans use nonhuman animals as food, therefore, it would have been open to God to let this be known. And yet what we find in the opening saga of creation is just the opposite. The food we are given by God is not the flesh of animals, it is "all plants that bear seed everywhere on the earth, and every tree bearing fruit which yields seed: they shall be yours for food" (Gn 1:29, NEB).

Now I do not believe the message regarding what was to serve as food for humans in the most perfect state of creation could be any clearer. Genesis clearly presents a picture of veganism; that is, not only is the flesh of animals excluded from the menu God provides for us, even animal products—milk and cheese, for example—are excluded. And so I believe that, if, as I am strongly inclined to do, we look to the biblical account of "the beginning" as an absolutely essential source of spiritual insight into God's hopes for and plans in creation, then—like it or not—we are obliged to find there a menu of divinely approved bodily sustenance that differs quite markedly from the steaks and chops, roasts and stews most people, in the Western world at least, are accustomed to devouring.

To a less than optimal or scholarly degree I am aware of some of the chapters and verses of the subsequent biblical record: the fall, the expulsion from the garden, the flood, and so on. There is no debate about *the details* of the subsequent account I could win if paired against an even modestly astute and retentive young person preparing for first communion. I wear my lack of biblical (and theological) sophistication on my sleeve—although even I cannot forbear noting, in passing, that the covenant into which God enters with humanity after the flood is significant for its inclusion of non-human animals. The meaning of this covenant aside, I believe that the essential moral and spiritual truth any open-minded, literate reader of the first chapter of Genesis *must* find is the one I already have mentioned; namely, that the purpose of nonhuman animals in God's creation, given the original hopes and plans of God-in-creation, was not that humans roast, fry, stew, broil, bake, and barbecue their rotting corpses (what people today call meat).

In this reading of God's creative activity, therefore, I find a spiritual lesson that is unmistakably at odds with both the letter and the spirit of speciesism. That lesson, as I understand it, does not represent the non-human animals to whom I have been referring as having no or less inherent value than humans. On the contrary, by unmistakably excluding these animals from the menu of food freely available to us, as granted by God's beneficence, I infer that we are called upon by God to recognize the independent value of these animals. They are not put here to be utilized by us. At least this was not God's original hope. If anything we are put here to protect them, especially against those humans who would reduce these animals to objects for human use. As you might imagine, the message we find in Genesis 1 is celestial music to the ears of one who, like myself, is not embarrassed or silenced by the "extremism" of the animal rights position.

I am aware that some theologians take a different view than I do of Genesis's opening saga of creation. Eden never was, they opine; the perfection of creation is something we are to work to bring about, not something that once existed only to be lost. I do not know how to prove which vision of Eden, if either, is the true one. What I do believe is that, when viewed in the present context, this question is entirely moot. For what *is* clear—clear beyond any doubt, as I read the scriptures—is that human beings simply do not eat nonhuman animals in that fullness of God's creation the image of Eden represents. And this is true whether Eden once was (but was shattered), or is yet to be (if, by the grace of God, we will but create it).

Every prejudice dies hard. Speciesism is no exception. That it is a prejudice and that, by acting on it, we humans have been, and continue to be, responsible for an incalculable amount of evil, an amount of truly monumental proportions, is, I believe, as true as it is regrettable. In my philosophical writings over the past fifteen years I have endeavored to show how this tragic truth can be argued for on wholly secular grounds. On this occasion I have looked elsewhere for support—have in fact looked to the original saga of creation we find in Genesis—in the hope that we might there find a religious or theological account that resonates with the secular case for animal rights. Neither case—secular or religious—has, or can have, the conclusiveness of a proof in, say, geometry. I say "can have" because I am reminded of Aristotle's observation, that it is the mark of an educated person not to demand proof that is inappropriate for a given subject matter. And whatever else we might think of moral thought, I believe we at least can agree that it is in important ways unlike geometry.

It remains true, nonetheless, that my attempt to explain and defend an egalitarian view of the inherent value of human and other animals must face a number of important challenges. For reasons of length, if for no other, I cannot on this occasion characterize or respond to all these challenges, not even all the most fundamental ones. The best I can do, before concluding, is describe and defuse two of them.

The first begins by observing that, within the traditions of Judaism and Christianity, *every form of life*, not simply humans and other animals, is to be viewed as expressive of God's love. Thus, to attempt to "elevate" the value of nonhuman animals, as I might be accused of having done, could be viewed as having the unacceptable consequence of negating or reducing the value of everything else.

I think this objection misses the mark. There is nothing in the animal-rights philosophy (nothing, that is, in the kind of egalitarianism I have endeavored to defend) that either denies or diminishes the value of fruits, nuts, grains, and other forms of vegetative life, or that refuses to accept the possibility that these and the rest of creation are so many ways in which God's loving presence is manifested. Nor is there anything in this philosophy that disparages the wise counsel to treat *all* of creation gently and appreciatively. It is an arrogant, unbridled anthropocentrism, often aided and abetted in our history by an arrogant, unbridled Christian theology, *not* the philosophy of animal rights, that has brought the earth to the brink of ecological disaster.

Still, this philosophy does find in humans and other animals, because of our shared biographical status in creation, a kind of value—inherent value—that other creatures fail to possess, either at all or at least to the degree in which humans and other animals possess it. Is it possible to defend this view? I believe it is, both on the grounds of a purely secular moral philosophy and by appealing to biblical authority. The secular defense I have attempted to offer elsewhere and will not repeat here. As for the Christian defense, I shall merely reaffirm the vital importance (in my view) of Genesis 1, as well as (to my mind) the more than symbolic significance of the covenant, and note that in both we find biblical sanction for viewing the value of animals to be superior to that of vegetables. After all, we do not find carrots and almonds included in the covenant, and we find God expressly giving these and other forms of vegetative life to us, as our food, in Genesis's first creative saga. In a word, then, vegetative life was meant to be used by us, thus giving it utility value for us, which does not mean or entail that we may use these life forms thoughtlessly or even irreverently.

So much for the first challenge. The second one emanates from quite a different source and mounts a quite different objection. It begins by noting the large disparities that exist in the quality of life available to those who are affluent (the "haves") and those who are poor (the "have nots"), especially those who live in the so-called third world. This objection states: It is all fine and good to preach the gospel of animal rights to those people who have the financial and other means to practice it, if they choose to do so, but please do spare us your self-righteous denunciation of the struggling and often starving masses of people in the rest of the world, who really have no choice but to eat animals, wear their skins, and use them in other ways. To condemn these people is to value animal life above human life. And this is misanthropy at its worst.

Now, this particular variation on the familiar theme of misanthropy (at least this is familiar to advocates of animal rights) has a point, up to a point. It would be self-righteous to condemn the people in question for acting as they do, especially if we are acting worse than they are, as well we may be. But, of course, nothing in what I have argued supports such a condemnation, and this for the simple reason that I have nowhere argued that people who eat animals, or who hunt and trap them, or who cut their heads off or burst their intestines in pursuit of "scientific knowledge," either are or must be *evil people*. The position I have set forth concerns the *moral wrongness of what people do, not the vileness of their character*. In my view, it is entirely possible that good people sometimes do what is wrong, and evil people sometimes do what is right.

Indeed, not only is that possible, it frequently happens, and among those circumstances in which it does, some concern the actions performed by people in the third world. At least this is the conclusion we reach if we take the philosophy of animal rights seriously. To make my meaning clearer, consider the following example. Suppose we chance upon a tribe of hunter-gatherers who annually, on a date sacred to their tradition, sacrifice the most beautiful female child to the gods in hope that the tribe will prosper in the coming year. In my view this act of human sacrifice is morally wrong and ought to be stopped (which does *not* mean that we should invade with tanks and flame-throwers to stop it!). From this moral assessment of what these human beings do, however, it does not follow that we should judge them to be evil, vicious people. It could be that they act from only the best intentions and with nothing but the best motives. Nevertheless, what they do, in my judgment, is morally wrong.

What is true of the imaginary case of this tribe is no less true of real-life cases where people in the third world raise and kill animals for food, cruelly subject other animals to forced labor, and so on. Anytime anyone reduces the inherent value of a nonhuman animal to that animal's utility value for human beings, what is done, in my view, is morally wrong. But it does not follow from this that we should make a negative moral judgment about the character of the human moral agents involved, especially if, as is true in the third world, there are mitigating circumstances. For it often happens that people who do what is morally wrong should be *excused* from moral blame and censure. A person who shoots a family member, for example, in the mistaken belief that there is a burglar in the house, does what is wrong and yet may well not be morally blameworthy. Similarly, people in the third world who act in ways that are prohibited by respect for the rights of animals do what is wrong. But because of the harsh, uncompromising exigencies of their life, where they are daily faced with the demand to make truly heroic sacrifices, where indeed it often is a matter of their life or their death that hangs in the balance, the people of the third world in my view should be excused from our harsh, uncompromising judgments of moral blame. The circumstances of their life, one might say, are as mitigating as any circumstances can be.

In light of the preceding remarks, I hope it is clear why it would be a bad reading of the philosophy of animal rights to charge its proponents with a hearty appetite, if not for animal flesh then at least for self-righteousness. When we understand the difference between morally assessing a person's act and that person's character, and when we take cognizance of the appropriateness of reducing or erasing moral blame in the face of mitigating circumstances, then the proponents of animal rights should be seen to be no more censorious or self-righteous than the proponents of any other philosophy.

Finally, then, in closing, I wish to make a few observations closer to home, as it were. Most of us who were in attendance at the Annecy conference traveled hundreds or thousands of miles at the cost of irreplaceable fossil fuels, the production and combustion of which, when added to the total from other sources, contribute to the pollution of air and water, and the deforestation of the earth's woodlands. We were housed in a lovely setting, slept in comfortable beds, were the beneficiaries of indoor plumbing and hot showers—all this while the great majority of our fellow humans scraped by, catch-as-catch-can, from one day to the next. And we journeyed there, and were gathered together there, leisurely to discuss issues relating to the integrity of creation. Truly we are among the lucky ones—the sons and daughters of a capricious dispensation of privilege—to enjoy such benefits.

Just as surely, in my view, we daily run the risk of succumbing to a detached hypocrisy. For the questions we must face concern not only the idea of the integrity of creation, they also ask how we—you and I—should live if we are to express our allegiance to this idea in our day-to-day life. That ancient question has no simple answer. There is much good that we would do, that we do not. And there is much evil that we would not do, that we find ourselves doing. The challenge to lead a good, respectful, loving life just in our dealings within the human family is onerous and demanding. How much more onerous and demanding must it be, therefore, if we widen the circle of the moral community to include the whole of creation?

How might we begin to meet this enlarged challenge? Doubtless there are many possible places to begin, some of which will be more accessible to some than to others. For my part, however, I cannot help believing that an appropriate place to begin is with the food on our plates. For here we are faced with a direct personal choice, over which we exercise absolute sovereign authority. Such power is not always within our grasp. How little influence we really have, you and I, on the practices of the World Bank, the agrarian land-reform movement, the call to reduce armed conflicts, the cessation of famine and the evil of abject poverty! These large-scale evils stand beyond the reach of our small wills.

But not the food on our plates. Here we are at liberty to exercise absolute control. And here, then, we ought to be asking ourselves, Which of those choices I can make, are most in accord with the idea of the integrity of creation?

When we consider the biographical and, I dare say, the spiritual kinship we share with those billions of animals raised and slaughtered for food; when, further, we inform ourselves of the truly wretched conditions in which most of these animals are raised, not to mention the deplorable methods by which they are transported and the gruesome, blood-soaked reality of the slaughterhouse; and when, finally, we take honest stock of our privileged position in the world, a position that will not afford us the excuse from moral blame shared by the desperately poor who, as we say, really have no choice—when we consider all these factors, then the case for abstaining from animal flesh has the overwhelming weight of both impartial reason and a spiritually-infused compassion on its side.

True, to make this change will involve some sacrifices—in taste perhaps, in convenience certainly. And yet the whole fabric of Christian *agape* is woven from the threads of sacrificial acts. To abstain, on principle, from eating animals, therefore, although it is not the end-all, can be the begin-all of our conscientious effort to journey back (or forward) to Eden, can be one way (among others) to reestablish or create that relationship to the earth that, if Genesis 1 is to be trusted, was part of God's original hopes for and plans in creation. It is the integrity of this creation we seek to understand and aspire to honor. In the choice of our food, I believe, we see, not in a glass darkly, but face to face, a small but not unimportant part of both the challenge and the promise of Christianity and animal rights.

7

Ecofeminism, Reverence for Life, and Feminist Theological Ethics

Lois K. Daly

Feminist theological ethics claims to be informed by an analysis of the interlocking dualisms of patriarchal Western culture. These include the dualisms of male/female, mind/body, and human/nature. In fact, as feminists argue, none of these dualisms will be overcome or transformed until the connections between and among them are named and understood. This means that we cannot rest with examining the consequences of subjugating body to mind or female to male. We must also look at the ways in which the distinction between what is human and what is nonhuman authorizes the widespread destruction of individual animals, their habitats, and the earth itself. And, in doing theological ethics, we must also explore what this means for understanding the relationship between human beings and the divine. In other words, feminist theological ethics must ask about the implications of a transformed human/nonhuman relationship for understanding the human/divine relationship.

Feminist theologies are among the most promising of contemporary theological options. As these theologies often make clear, the ways of thinking that have led to a destruction of the earth and an exploitation of animals are often the very ways of thinking that have led to an exploitation of women. To overcome male-centeredness is also to overcome human-centeredness.

Speaking as a feminist, Lois K. Daly reviews the argument that male-centeredness and human-centeredness have gone hand-in-hand and then proposes a new ecofeminist alternative to both, drawing on the perspective of Albert Schweitzer. She suggests that Schweitzer's theme of reverence for life provides a helpful antidote to the dualisms that have dominated patriarchal culture in the West and that have contributed to the subjugation of nature and women to men. Inherent in Daly's appropriation of Schweitzer is the advocacy of an ethical absolute: that we affirm and treat compassionately and nonviolently *all* life. Such an imperative takes life-centered ethical and theological thinking to its utmost possibilities.

This essay will describe the connections between feminist concern about the status of women and the status of nonhuman nature, point to a theological ethic that reconsiders the relationship between human beings and other living beings, and explore the theological and ethical implications of those two steps. Reverence for life, as articulated by Albert Schweitzer, will serve as a primary resource in this project. Though decidedly not feminist in any self-conscious way, Schweitzer's position does provide resources for reconceptualizing the relationship between human beings and the nonhuman, or "natural," world and for examining the theological implications of such a reconceptualization. This theological task, the task of conceptualizing the relationship between human beings and God in light of a different way of thinking about human life in relation to the nonhuman world, is critical for feminist theological ethics.

ECOFEMINISM

Ecofeminists, or ecological feminists, are those feminists who analyze the interconnections between the status of women and the status of nonhuman nature. At the heart of this analysis are four central claims: (1) the oppression of women and the oppression of nature are interconnected; (2) these connections must be uncovered in order to understand both the oppression of women and the oppression of nature; (3) feminist analysis must include ecological insights; and (4) a feminist perspective must be a part of any proposed ecological solutions (Warren, 4). A closer look at each of these claims will illuminate the concerns of ecofeminism.

The Oppression of Women and the Oppression of Nature Are Interconnected.

One way to talk about the connections between women and nature is to describe the parallel ways they have been treated in Western patriarchal society. First, the traditional role of both women and nature has been instrumental (Plumwood, 120). Women's role has been to serve the needs and desires of men. Traditionally, women were not considered to have a life except in relation to a man, whether father, brother, husband, or son. Likewise, nonhuman nature has provided the resources to meet human needs for food, shelter, and recreation. Nature had no purpose except to provide for human wants. In both cases the instrumental role led to instrumental value. Women were valued to the extent that they fulfilled their role. Nature was valued in relation to human interests either in the present or the future. Women and nature had little or no meaning independent of men.

A second parallel in the treatment of women and nature lies in the way the dominant thought has attempted "to impose sharp separation on a natural continuum" in order to maximize difference (Plumwood, 120). In other words, men are identified as strong and rational while women are seen as weak and emotional. In this division of traits those men who are sensitive and those women who are intellectually or athletically inclined are marginalized. They are overlooked in the typical (stereotypical) description of men as opposed to women. The same holds true for distinctions between what is human and what is not. The human being is conscious, the nonhuman plant or animal is not; the human is able to plan for the future, to understand a present predicament, the nonhuman simply reacts to a situation out of instinct. These distinctions are drawn sharply in order to protect the privilege and place of those thought to be more important.

These parallels are instructive but they do not explain why they developed. Two theologians were among the feminists who first articulated the link between women and nature in patriarchal culture. They were Rosemary Ruether, in *New Woman, New Earth* (1975), and Elizabeth Dodson Gray, in *Green Paradise Lost* (1979). Both of them focused on the dualisms that characterize patriarchy, in particular the dualisms of mind/body and nature/culture. In her work Ruether traces the historical development of these dualisms in Western culture. She points to the way in which Greek thought, namely dualistic thought, was imported into ancient Hebraic culture. The triumph of this dualism came in the development of a transcendent or hierarchical dualism in which men

master nature, not by basing themselves on it and exalting it as an independent divine power, but by subordinating it and linking their essential selves with a transcendent principle beyond nature which is pictured as intellectual and male. This image of transcendent, male spiritual deity is a projection of the ego or consciousness of ruling-class males, who envision a reality, beyond the physical processes that gave them birth, as the true source of their being. Men locate their true origins and natures in this transcendent sphere, which thereby also gives them power over the lower sphere of "female" nature (Ruether 1975, 13-14).

In this way, transcendent dualism incorporates and reinforces the dualisms of mind/body and nature/culture as well as male/female. In addition these distinctions are read into other social relations, including class and race. As a result, ruling-class males lump together those whom Ruether calls the "body people": women, slaves, and barbarians (Ruether 1975, 14; see also Plumwood, 121-22).

While agreeing with the reasons for the development of transcendent dualism, Dodson Gray's response to it differs from Ruether's. Ruether's tack is to reject transcendental dualism outright; Dodson Gray appears to embrace the dualism but to reevaluate the pairs. In other words, she maintains the distinction but insists that being more closely tied to nature does not detract from women's worth. Instead, for Dodson Gray, it enhances it.

As others have pointed out, Dodson Gray "come[s] dangerously close to implicitly accepting the polarities which are part of the dualism, and to trying to fix up the result by a reversal of the valuation which would have men joining women in immanence and identifying the authentic self as the body" (Plumwood, 125).

A similar division of opinion can also be traced in other feminist writings. It is the difference between the nature feminists and the social feminists (Griscom 1981, 5). The nature feminists are those who celebrate women's biological difference and claim some measure of superiority as a result of it. The social feminists are those who recognize the interstructuring of race, class, and sex, but who tend to avoid discussing nature exploitation precisely because it invites attention to biological difference. Both kinds of feminists have positive points to express, but another sort of feminism, one that transcends these, is needed in order to understand the connections between the oppression of women and the oppression of nature.

These Connections Must Be Uncovered in Order To Understand Both the Oppression of Women and the Oppression of Nature.

Feminist analysis of the transcendent dualism identified by Ruether shows that there are three basic assumptions that govern the way the dualism's elements are treated (see Ruether 1975, 1983). These assumptions lie behind the parallels between the oppression of women and nature described above. First, the elements in the dualism are perceived as higher and lower relative to each other. The higher is deemed more worthy or valuable than the lower. Second, the lower element is understood to serve the higher. In fact, the value of the lower is derived in instrumental fashion. Third, the two elements are described as polar opposites. That is, "the traits taken to be virtuous and defining for one side are those which maximize distance from the other side" (Plumwood, 132). In other words, men are "not women" and women are "not men." The same holds true in traditional conceptions of human and nonhuman nature. These three assumptions lead to a logic of domination that repeatedly identifies differences and controls them in such a way as to protect the "higher" element in the dualism. In this way, from the point of view of the "higher," difference automatically implies inferiority.

In patriarchal culture these three assumptions are at work in a "nest of assumptions" that also includes (1) the identification of women with the physical and nature, (2) the identification of men with the intellectual, and (3) the dualistic assumption of the inferiority of the physical and the superiority of the mental (Plumwood, 133). Once this nest of assumptions is unpacked the differences between the social feminists and nature feminists and the deficiency of each become more clear. On the one hand, the social feminists simply reject the identification of women with nature and the physical and insist that women have the same talents and characteristics as men. These feminists focus on the interaction of sexism, racism, and classism (Griscom, 6). On the other hand, the nature feminists embrace the identification of women with nature but deny that nature or the physical is inferior. But neither of these responses represents a sufficient challenge to the dualistic assumptions themselves since both leave part unquestioned. Social feminists do not ask about the assumed inferiority of nature, and nature feminists do not ask about the assumed identification of women with nature. In this way, both "remain within the framework in which the problem has arisen, and . . . leave its central structures intact" (Plumwood, 133).

A thoroughgoing ecofeminism must challenge each of the dualisms of patriarchal culture (see King, 12-16). The issue is not whether women are closer to nature, since that question arises only in the context of the nature/culture dualism in the first place. Rather, the task is to overcome the nature/culture dualism itself. The task can be accomplished first by admitting that "gender identity is neither fully natural nor fully cultural," and that neither is inherently oppressive or liberating (King, 13). Second, ecofeminists need to learn what both the social feminists and nature feminists already know. From social feminists we learn that "while it is possible to discuss women and nature without reference to class and race, such discussion risks remaining white and elite" (Griscom, 6). And nature feminists remind us that there is no human/nonhuman dichotomy and that our bodies are worth celebrating (Griscom, 8).

Feminist Analysis Must Include Ecological Insights.

One result of the way the oppression of women and the oppression of nature are linked in these dualisms is that feminist thought and practice must incorporate ecological insights. To do otherwise would not sufficiently challenge the structures of patriarchal domination. The most direct way to illustrate this is to discuss the repercussions of the feminist assertion of women's full humanity in light of the interlocking dualisms described above. The fact that male/female, human/nature, and mind/body dualism are all closely linked together means that feminism cannot rest with proclaiming women's full humanity. To do this without also raising the question of the human/nature relationship would be simply to buy into the male-defined human being. In other words, if women and men are now to be reconceptualized non-dualistically, the choices available are either to buy into the male definition of the human (as the social feminists tend to do) or to engage in a reconceptualization of humanity as well. But, as soon as we begin to redefine humanity, the question of the human/nature dualism arises (Plumwood, 134-35). This is also the case when we ask about the status of race or class. Thus, any thorough challenge to the male/female dichotomy must also take on the other dualisms that structure Western patriarchy.

At this point it becomes clear that ecofeminism is not just another branch of feminism. Rather, ecofeminists are taking the feminist critique of dualism another step. What ecofeminism aims for transcends the differences between social and nature feminists. What is needed is an integrative and transformative feminism that moves beyond the current debate among these competing feminisms. Such a feminism would: (1) unmask the interconnections between all systems of oppression; (2) acknowledge the diversity of women's experiences and the experiences of other oppressed groups; (3) reject the logic of domination and the patriarchal conceptual framework in order to prevent concerns for ecology from degenerating into white middle-class anxiety; (4) rethink what it is to be human, that is, to see ourselves as "both co-members of ecological community and yet different from other members of it"; (5) recast traditional ethics to underscore the importance of values such as care, reciprocity, and diversity; and (6) challenge the patriarchal bias in technology research and analysis and the use of science for the destruction of the earth (Warren, 18-20).

A Feminist Perspective Must Be Part of Any Proposed Ecological Solutions.

Just as feminism must challenge all of patriarchy's dualisms, including the human/nature dichotomy, ecological solutions and environmental ethics must include a feminist perspective:

> Otherwise, the ecological movement will fail to make the conceptual connections between the oppression of women and the oppression of nature (and to link these to other systems of oppression), and will risk utilizing strategies and implementing solutions which contribute to the continued subordination of women [and others] (Warren, 8).

In particular, two issues in the ecological movement and environmental ethics need to be addressed in the context of ecofeminism: the status of hierarchy and dualism, and the place of feeling.

As already indicated, ecofeminism works at overcoming dualism and hierarchy. Much of current environmental ethics, however, attempts to establish hierarchies of value for ranking different parts of nature (Kheel, 137). It does this by debating whether particular "rights" ought to be extended to certain classes of animals (Singer). This is another way of assigning rights to some and excluding them from others and of judging the value of one part as more or less than that of another. These judgments, then, operate within the same framework of dualistic assumptions. As a result, this debate merely moves the dualism, as it were; it does not abandon it. Human/nonhuman may no longer be the operative dualism; instead, sentient/nonsentient or some other replaces it.

Another way in which environmental ethics has perpetuated traditional dualist thought lies in its dependence on reason and its exclusion of feeling or emotion in dealing with nature. The dualism of reason/emotion is another dualism under attack by feminists. In this case environmental ethics has sought to determine by reason alone what beings have value and in what ranking and what rules ought to govern human interactions with nature (Kheel, 141). This procedure is flawed according to ecofeminists since "the attempt to formulate universal, rational rules of conduct ignores the constantly changing nature of reality. It also neglects the emotional-instinctive or spontaneous component in each particular situation, for in the end, emotion cannot be contained by boundaries and rules" (Kheel, 141).

Ethics must find a way to include feeling, but including feeling does not mean excluding reason. Again, the task is to overcome the exclusive dualism.

Ecofeminism, then, involves a thoroughgoing analysis of the dualisms that structure patriarchal culture. In particular ecofeminists analyze the link between the oppression of women and of nature by focusing on the hierarchies established by mind/body, nature/culture, male/female, and human/nonhuman dualisms. The goal is to reconceptualize these relationships in nonhierarchical, nonpatriarchal ways. In this way, ecofeminists envision a new way of seeing the world and strive toward a new way of living in the world as co-members of the ecological community.

What ecofeminism lacks, however, is an analysis of what Ruether and Dodson Gray agreed was hierarchical or transcendent dualism, the dualism that they think undergirds the others. Ecofeminists, largely philosophers and social scientists, have not attended to the specifically theological dimensions of patriarchy. Meanwhile, feminist theologians and ethicists have focused primarily on the interrelationship of sexism, racism, and classism without sufficiently articulating or naming the interconnections between these forms of oppression and the oppression of nature. Yet the analysis of these critically important social justice questions would be strengthened when it is understood that the same dualistic assumptions are operative in each of these forms of oppression.

Furthermore, feminist theology needs to explore the relationship between human beings and God in light of those dualistic assumptions and the impact of the new way of seeing human beings that results from linking the oppression of nature with other forms of oppression. When reconceptualizing the male/female dualism entails reconceptualizing the human/nature relation because male/female is embedded in human/nature, as ecofeminists argue, then the human/divine relationship also needs reworking, since male/female is also embedded in human/divine. In other words, if feminist theology is serious in attempting to transform patriarchal dualisms, it must go further than reworking the dualistic imagery used to refer to God; it must discover how the images themselves support a dualistic relationship between human beings and God with the same assumptions as the traditional male/female and human/nonhuman dualisms.

Two contemporary theologians, Isabel Carter Heyward (1982) and Sallie McFague (1987), have begun this task. They contrast their respective conceptions of God with the traditional idea of a God "set apart from human experience . . . by the nature of 'His' impassivity" (Heyward, 7), or the idea of a "monarchical" God (McFague, 63-69). In other words, both challenge the dualistic assumptions that typically characterize the relationship between human beings and God. They argue that human beings are not simply subordinate to God but are co-workers with God, and consequently, that human beings are not simply instrumentally related to God and that God and human beings are not polar opposites. For Heyward, God is the "power in relation" (Heyward, 2), while for McFague, God is more appropriately conceived using the models of mother, lover, and friend within the context of the image of the world as God's body (McFague, xi).

What I am suggesting is a position that goes further than these authors even while it shares certain characteristics with them. The main difference lies in the extent to which Heyward and McFague have really reworked their conception of the relationship between human beings and the nonhuman world. In Heyward's case it is clear that she wants to include the creation in the relationships effected by God as the power in relation; however, this desire appears to be qualified. For example, Heyward writes:

In relation to God, as in any relation, God is affected by humanity and creation, just as we are affected by God. With us, by us, through us, God lives, God becomes, God changes, God speaks, God acts, God suffers and God dies in the world. . . . The constancy of God is the activity of God in the world wherever, whenever, and for whatever reason, humanity acts to create, liberate, and bless humanity (Heyward, 9).

Creation, including the nonhuman elements, may be included in what affects God, but what happens to it in the talk about God's activity in the world? Is it only God's activity when the activity benefits humanity? Even more absent is any discussion of the kind of behavior toward the nonhuman world required of human beings in order to "incarnate God."

McFague goes further than Heyward when she discusses the necessity of adopting an "evolutionary, ecological perspective" due to our interconnections and interdependence with aspects of the world (McFague, 7-8) and when she includes in her descriptions of the models of mother, lover, and friend an explanation of the ethic which follows from the model. These are, respectively, the ethics of justice, healing, and companionship (pp. 116-24, 146-56, 174-80). What is missing in these ethics is a frank discussion of the hard decisions that confront us as soon as we begin to see "ourselves as gardeners, caretakers, mothers and fathers, stewards, trustees, lovers, priests, co-creators, and friends" of the world (p. 13). In other words, how far does McFague's transformation of the dualistic relationship between human beings and the nonhuman world go?

Finally, neither Heyward nor McFague does what ecofeminists claim must be done, namely, to articulate the links between forms of oppression, especially the oppression of women and of nature. Heyward's and McFague's concentration on the transformation of the human/divine relationship away from dualist assumptions is extremely helpful, but it needs to be joined with concrete descriptions of and efforts to transform the other dualisms that structure Western patriarchy. In other words, Heyward and McFague appear to reconceptualize the divine/human dualism without sufficiently exploring the consequences for other powerful dualisms, including but not limited to male/female and human/nonhuman.

REVERENCE FOR LIFE

Albert Schweitzer's notion of reverence for life provides some clues for feminist theological and ethical efforts to reexamine the relationship between human beings and the nonhuman world and between human beings and God despite the fact that he offers no analysis of oppression. Instead, what Schweitzer does is begin with a description of human beings that links us both with nonhuman nature and with God in a way that does not appear to presuppose those dualistic assumptions of subordination, instrumentality, and polarity. For this reason, his position is highly instructive.

Schweitzer begins with a description of the self as "life which wills to live, in the midst of life which wills to live." This, he says, is the "the most immediate and comprehensive fact of consciousness" (Schweitzer 1949/1981, 309). As will-to-live, the self is volitional, free, driven to perfect itself, and living in relation to others who will to live. More important, however, is the fact that Schweitzer refuses to describe the self simply as "life," for "life continues to be a mystery too great to understand" (Schweitzer 1936/1962, 182-183). He knows only that life is good since the self continues to will to live.

Ethics, for Schweitzer, emerges with thinking about the experience of the will-to-live. There are two kinds of knowing for Schweitzer: intuitive and scientific. The intuitive is an inward reflection on the contents of the will-to-live. By living out these ideas, the self finds meaning and purpose in its actions (Schweitzer 1949/1981, 282). Scientific knowing, the second kind of knowing, is knowledge of the world. Science describes "the phenomena in which life in its innumerable forms appears and passes"; it may sometimes "discover life where we did not previously expect it." Hence, scientific knowledge "compels our attention to the mystery of the will-to-live which we see stirring everywhere" (Schweitzer 1949/1981, 308). Together, the two kinds of knowing allow the self to describe what science finds by using an analogy with itself as will-to-live. In this way the self knows and, for Schweitzer, feels that "the will-to-live is everywhere present, even as in me" (Schweitzer 1936/1962, 185). The self, therefore, becomes aware of its inward relation to the wills-to-live present in the world.

Schweitzer gives one important qualification to both kinds of knowing: neither one can explain what life is. "We cannot understand what happens in the universe. . . . It creates while it destroys and destroys while it creates, and therefore it remains to us a riddle" (Schweitzer 1934, 1520). As a result human beings have no grounds for placing themselves at the center of a moral universe or at the apex of moral order in the universe. "We are entirely ignorant of what significance we have for the earth. How much less then may we presume to try to attribute to the infinite universe a meaning which has us for its object, or which can be explained in terms of our existence!" (Schweitzer 1949/1981, 273).

Because no purposiveness or prioritizing of phenomena is evident in the events of the world, no hierarchy of meaning and value can be constructed from the evidence of intuitive or scientific thought. As Schweitzer points out, "we like to imagine that Man is nature's goal; but facts do not support that belief" (Schweitzer 1936/1962, 181).

The inability to find meaning in the world and the recognition of the interrelationship of all wills-to-live lead to what Schweitzer calls an ethical mysticism. This mysticism is a mysticism of the will. The volition found in the will-to-live becomes an activist ethic. As Schweitzer explains:

> Ethics alone can put me in true relationship with the universe by my serving it, cooperating with it; not by trying to understand it. . . . Only by serving every kind of life do I enter the service of that Creative Will whence all life emanates. I do not understand it; but I do know (and it is sufficient to live by) that by serving life, I serve the Creative Will. This is the mystical significance of ethics (Schweitzer 1936/1962, 189).

Union with the Creative Will, or infinite will-to-live, Schweitzer's philosophical name for God, is achieved through active service and devotion to all that lives. Hence as an ethical mysticism, Schweitzer's is directed toward those particular manifestations of the infinite will-to-live that come within the reach of the individual.

Schweitzer's mysticism, then, provides him a way to combine the drive for self-perfection, which is contained in the will-to-live, and devotion to others. Self-perfection in the context of this mysticism becomes a drive to attain union with that which the human will-to-live manifests, namely, the infinite will-to-live (Schweitzer 1949/1981, 301-2). In human beings, as Schweitzer points out, "the craving for perfection is given in such a way that we aim at raising to their highest material and spiritual value both ourselves and every existing thing which is open to our influence" (Schweitzer 1949/1981, 282). That is, I make a reality of my own dedication to the infinite only by devoting myself to its manifestations. "Whenever my life devotes itself in any way to life, my finite will-to-live experiences union with the infinite will in which all life is one" (Schweitzer 1949/1981, 313). Self-perfection, or self-fulfillment, is therefore, reciprocally related to devotion to others.

In addition, Schweitzer's mysticism provides another way into his refusal to place human beings at the center of the moral universe. The self as will-to-live is not the source of its own value. Instead, the will-to-live given in the self has value as a result of its relationship to the infinite. The source or origin of value is the universal will-to-live or infinite being. As Schweitzer points out, through the will-to-live

> my existence joins in pursuing the aims of the mysterious universal will of which I am a manifestation. . . . With consciousness and with volition I devote myself to Being. I become of service to the ideas which it thinks out in me; I become imaginative force like that which works mysteriously in nature, and thus I give my existence a meaning from within outwards (Schweitzer 1949/1981, 305).

Meaning comes not simply from my own estimation but also from the fact that my will-to-live is a manifestation of the universal will-to-live. At the same time, all other wills-to-live are also manifestations of that same universal. Hence their value and my value have the same source. The fact that the self cannot discern the meaning of any of these lives from the world as it is experienced means that it cannot determine that any one manifestation of the will-to-live is more important or more valuable than any other manifestation. The mystical and mysterious relatedness of every will-to-live in the universal will-to-live prohibits assigning gradations of value to individual manifestations of the will-to-live, whether in humans or viruses. The will-to-live establishes value but not distinctions in it. There-fore, Schweitzer insists, all attempts to bring ethics and epistemology together must be renounced (Schweitzer 1949/1981, 289).

The ethic that follows from thinking about the will-to-live is the ethic of reverence for life. The self lives in the midst of other wills-to-live. Hence Schweitzer says, "If I am a thinking being, I must regard other life than my own with equal reverence" (Schweitzer 1936/1962, 185). Actions in accord with my will-to-live, such as upbuilding, deepening, and enhancing the optimism, value, and affirmation given in the will-to-live, are required in relation to other manifestations of the will-to-live (Kraus, 47). "Ethics consist . . . in my experiencing the compulsion to show to all will-to-live the same reverence as I do to my own" (Schweitzer 1949/1981, 309). In the language of Schweitzer's mysticism, "reverence for life means to be in the grasp of the infinite, inexplicable, forward-urging Will in which all Being is grounded" (Schweitzer 1949/1981, 283).

According to Schweitzer, the ethic of reverence for life cannot foster, condone, or excuse injuring or killing of any sort. Three reasons support this judgment. First, reverence for life is what Schweitzer calls an absolute ethic. That is, its claim is absolute because it arises from the inner necessity of the will-to-live to be true to itself. Second, reverence for life is a universal ethic. The inner compulsion to show reverence to life extends to all that can in any way be considered as life.

> The absolute ethics of the will-to-live must reverence every form of life, seeking so far as possible to refrain from destroying any life, regardless of its particular type. It says of no instance of life, "this has no value." It cannot make any such exceptions, for it is built upon reverence for life as such (Schweitzer 1960, 187-88).

Neither species nor sentience presents a barrier that qualifies this universality.

The third reason why the ethic of reverence for life does not justify killing or injury is its refusal to allow human beings to locate themselves at the center of a moral universe, its inability to base any ranking of value on information about the world that comes from external sources. There is no moral hierarchy that says that decisions to destroy infectious bacteria in human beings or other animals are the right decisions. There is no sure way to judge any being, human or not, as less worthy and therefore insignificant enough to allow it to be killed.

> The ethics of reverence for life makes no distinction between higher and lower, more precious and less precious lives. It has good reasons for this omission. For what are we doing, when we establish hard and fast gradations in value between living organisms, but judging them in relation to ourselves, by whether they seem to stand closer to us or farther from us. This is a wholly subjective standard. How can we know what importance other living organisms have in themselves and in terms of the universe? (Schweitzer 1965, 47).

Universality, absoluteness, and the absence of any clear objective moral order "out there" prevent Schweitzer's reverence for life from condoning any form of killing or harming of life. His ethic will not compromise; it points to limitless responsibility.

These reasons clearly do not mean that choices to kill are not made. Schweitzer knows that human beings as well as other forms of life depend for life on killing and that, in many situations, decisions to save one means death to another (Schweitzer 1965, 22-23). This is all part of what he calls the "dilemma" of the will-to-live (Schweitzer 1949/1953, 181).

According to Schweitzer we must recognize that "the universe provides us with the dreary spectacle of manifestations of the will to live continually opposed to each other. One life preserves itself by fighting and destroying other lives" (Schweitzer 1965, 24-25). Conflict in the world prevents Schweitzer from being able to find a basis for ethics in the patterns and purposes seen in the world. Hence, he turns inward to the will-to-live. It is precisely Schweitzer's realistic description of the world in terms of conflict that drives him to the ethic of reverence for life. The only sure meaning and purpose for activity comes, for Schweitzer, in the certainty of the volition of the will-to-live found and experienced in the self.

Because of its absolute and universal character, then, the ethic of reverence for life cannot provide any specific guidelines for making life-and-death decisions even though it knows these decisions must be made. The fact that reason and the will-to-live can find no objective moral ordering means that there are no objective moral standards by which to judge. Reverence for life

> knows that the mystery of life is always too profound for us, and that its value is beyond our capacity to estimate. We happen to believe that man's life is more important than any other form of which we know. But we cannot prove any such comparison of value from what we know of the world's development. True, in practice we are forced to choose. At times we have to decide *arbitrarily* which forms of life, and even which particular individuals, we shall save, and which we shall destroy (Schweitzer 1936/1962, 188).

The decision, for Schweitzer, is always subjective, arbitrary:

> In ethical conflicts man can arrive only at subjective decisions. No one can decide for him at what point, on each occasion, lies the extreme limit of possibility for his persistence in the preservation and furtherance of life. He alone has to judge this issue, by letting himself be guided by a feeling of the highest possible responsibility towards other life (Schweitzer 1949/1981, 317-318).

No one else knows the limits of one's ability to aid and protect another. The ethic of reverence of life means limitless personal responsibility. In decisions to harm or destroy one "bears the responsibility for the life which is sacrificed" (Schweitzer 1949/1953, 181).

Schweitzer's restriction of ethics to activity that does no harm reveals the extent to which reverence for life is not an unbreakable rule or law.

> In the conflict between the maintenance of my own existence and the destruction of, or injury to, that of another, I can never unite the ethical and the necessary to form a relative ethical; I must choose between ethical and necessary, and, if I choose the latter, must take it upon myself to incur guilt by an act of injury to life (Schweitzer 1949/1981, 324).

The necessity of killing or harming does not challenge the authority or validity of reverence for life. As absolute and universal, reverence for life continues its demands even in the face of overwhelming odds, namely, the fact that the will-to-live is divided against itself. It may be, for example, that it is better to kill a suffering animal than to watch it slowly die (see Schweitzer 1960, 83-84). The tension between the ethical and necessary is maintained by facing the reality of conflict. "We are living in truth, when we experience these conflicts more profoundly. The good conscience is an invention of the devil" (Schweitzer 1949/1981, 318).

A pressing issue facing individuals who must kill is the intensity of guilt incurred in actions that kill or harm and the possibilities there are to alleviate that guilt. For Schweitzer the principal way to do this is to increase service to others: "Some atonement for that guilt can be found by the man who pledges himself to neglect no opportunity to succor creatures in distress. . . . When we help an insect out of a difficulty, we are only trying to compensate for man's ever-renewed sins against other creatures" (Schweitzer 1965, 23, 49).

His answer, then, is renewed determination to reverence all forms of life. Again, the reality of destruction does not compromise the demand. Part of the reason for this is the mystical nature of reverence for life. "The more we act in accordance with the principle of reverence for life, the more we are gripped by the desire to preserve and benefit life" (Schweitzer 1965, 31). "Reverence for life means to be in the grasp of the infinite, inexplicable, forward-urging Will in which all Being is grounded" (Schweitzer 1949/1981, 283).

According to Schweitzer, the ethic of reverence for life has a profoundly religious character (1949/1953, 182). This is most clearly seen in his mysticism. Reverence for life is a way of relating to the "multiform manifestations of the will-to-live," which comprise the world. Only through action in devotion to others do I come in contact with the infinite will-to-live, God. Religion is not, for Schweitzer, a matter of accepting creeds or knowing the history of dogma. Instead, it is the ethic of reverence for life (Schweitzer 1934, 1521).

In a letter to Oskar Kraus, one of Schweitzer's early critics, Schweitzer explains his use of language with respect to philosophy and religion.

Hitherto it has been my principle never to express in my philosophy more than I have experienced as a result of absolutely logical reflection. That is why I never speak in philosophy of "God" but only of the "universal will-to-live." But if I speak the traditional language of religion, I use the word "God" in its historical definiteness and indefiniteness, just as I speak in ethics of "Love" in place of "Reverence for Life" (Kraus 1944, 42).

Schweitzer's philosophy is at the same time his theology. The universal will-to-live manifest in the world and in my will-to-live is Schweitzer's way of speaking philosophically about God. And reverence for life is the ethic of love, the ethic of Jesus. In fact for Schweitzer, "Christianity, as the most profound religion, is to me at the same time the most profound philosophy" (Schweitzer 1939, 90).

Schweitzer defines Christianity as an "ethical theism" (Schweitzer 1939, 80-81). But Christianity's theism, Schweitzer argues, is ambiguous: "It presupposes a God who is an ethical Personality, and who is, therefore, so to speak, outside the world . . . [and] it must hold fast the belief that God is the sum total of the forces working in the world — that all that is, is in God" (Schweitzer 1939, 81).

This ambiguity is not resolved in Christian faith. As Schweitzer puts it: "In the world He is impersonal Force, within me He reveals Himself as Personality. . . . They are one; but how they are one, I do not understand" (Schweitzer 1939, 83). Theism and pantheism remain unreconciled. This ambiguity in the conception of God is not something that concerns Schweitzer. Attention to intellectual conceptions of God is, for Schweitzer, an abstraction. Concern about the particular relation of theism to pantheism leads one away from active devotion to the individual manifestations of the will-to-live in the world. Christianity, according to Schweitzer, is more a way of acting in the world than a way of knowing, and this way of acting is not dependent on a full or complete understanding of how the world works or of God's intrinsic nature. Piety, according to Schweitzer, "depends not on man being able to subscribe to a historically traditional conception of God, but on his being seized by the spirit and walking in it" (cited in Langfeldt, 52-53). Ultimately, "theism does not stand in opposition to pantheism, but rises out of it as the ethically definite of the indefinite" (cited in Langfeldt, 51).

For Schweitzer, Christians are called to surrender themselves to the ethical will of God. This surrender corresponds exactly with how Schweitzer develops the contents of the will-to-live: Service to other forms of life is also service to God. Christianity, therefore, appeals not only to the historical revelation but also to "that inward one which corresponds with, and continually confirms the historical revelation" (Schweitzer 1939, 83). Experience of the will-to-live corresponds with and confirms, then, the teachings of the historical Jesus. For Schweitzer, this means the teachings of the kingdom, especially as they are found in the Sermon on the Mount. These are Jesus' teachings concerning love. In response to them the will-to-live as devotion to others becomes the will-to-love. Devotion to others construed as will-to-love is at the heart of Christianity, according to Schweitzer, in the same way that devotion to others is a necessary part of self-perfection in a philosophical construal. For both philosophy and theology, it is service to others as individuals that brings about union with the ultimate.

Christianity, according to Schweitzer, provides no more account of the world, its meaning and purpose, than reason. The inward revelation of God as universal will-to-love and the self as one of its manifestations does not reveal anything which makes life less mysterious or tells of the final destiny of human beings.

When Christianity becomes conscious of its innermost nature, it realizes that it is godliness rising out of inward constraint. The highest knowledge is to know that we are surrounded by mystery. Neither knowledge nor hope for the future can be the pivot of our life or determine its direction. It is intended to be solely determined by our allowing ourselves to be gripped by the ethical God, who reveals Himself in us, and by our yielding our will to His (Schweitzer 1939, 78).

Moreover, Christianity

assigns man a place in this world and commands him to live in it and to work in it in the spirit of the ethical God. Further, Christianity gives him the assurance that thereby God's purpose for the world and for man is being fulfilled; it cannot, however, explain how. For what significance have the ethical character and the ethical activity of the religious individual in the infinite happenings of the universe? What do they accomplish? We must admit that the only answer we have to this question is, that thereby the will of God is fulfilled (Schweitzer 1939, 73-74).

Christian teachings do not give human beings a privileged place in relation to other manifestations of the will-to-live. What Christianity does is confirm what we already experience through our own will-to-live in its relations to others.

TOWARD AN ECOFEMINIST THEOLOGICAL ETHIC

Although I want to argue that Schweitzer's position provides clues for feminist theological ethics, it is important to point out two places where his thought is seriously lacking. First, Schweitzer has little sense of the sociality of the self. Instead, his will-to-live is the radical individual, who, despite being related to other wills-to-live in an ethical mysticism, does not really live socially or communally. The human will-to-live works, according to Schweitzer, to better the situation of other wills-to-live as individuals. Furthermore, he focuses his attention so exclusively on the individual and the individual's actions that the ways in which lives are shaped and affected by social structures are ignored. Significantly, justice is not a high priority for Schweitzer (Schweitzer 1939, 18-19). For feminists, particularly those who are schooled in the social feminist analysis of the structures of oppression, this is a serious failure. Schweitzer writes as if most suffering takes place as a result of individuals acting on other individuals. Feminist analysis insists, in contrast, that social structures and cultural expectations affect not only the conditions under which people live but also severely restrict the choices they perceive themselves to have.

The second problem is a consequence of the first: Schweitzer does no social analysis. For Schweitzer, human beings are ahistorical individuals, who learn to reverence life through self-reflection. There is no attention to social structures which limit or enhance those individuals. As a result, Schweitzer does not address institutionalized oppression in any way. For example, his position is a good example of the way in which *man*, as male, is taken as normative for both male and female without any hint that male experience is not normative for females. He makes no effort to rethink the meaning of the human (or *man*, as he would say) that experiences itself as will-to-live and that is one manifestation among others of the infinite will-to-live. In other words, although Schweitzer reworks the human/nonhuman dichotomy by using the will-to-live terminology, he fails to take seriously the destructiveness of the male/female dualism embedded in the traditional conceptions of human/nonhuman relationships. And, despite his home in Africa and his attention to individual patients, there is no analysis of two other destructive dualisms embedded in a traditional description of human beings: racism and classism.

Nevertheless, Schweitzer's position clearly involves a reevaluation of the relationship between human beings and nonhuman forms of life along the lines suggested by ecofeminists. That is, despite the absence of any analysis of oppression, Schweitzer does attack the dualistic structure of Western patriarchy. The relationship between human beings and nonhuman forms of life is not characterized by subordination, instrumentality, or polarity. Schweitzer has no basis for judging that nonhuman lives simply serve human interests or that they have no value apart from their service to human lives. He refuses to construct a moral hierarchy with human beings at the top. And, his use of "will-to-live" as the description of all that lives means that the polarity assumption has also been discarded. Human and nonhuman cannot be polar opposites since both are manifestations of the same will-to-live.

Furthermore, Schweitzer's use of will-to-live to describe not only all living beings but also the divine suggests a transformation in the divine/human relationship away from the transcendent dualism feminist theologians criticize. Human beings and God are not conceived as polar opposites or as over against each other. God is not, according to Schweitzer, an external "other," external to the world or to human beings. As Schweitzer explains, "I carry out the will of the universal will-to-live which reveals itself in me. I live my life in God, in the mysterious divine personality which I do not know as such in the world, but only experience as mysterious Will within myself" (Schweitzer 1949/1981, 79). This idea of living life in God sounds very much like Isabel Carter Heyward's notion that human beings "incarnate God" as they work to bring about justice in the world (Heyward, 159).

It may be argued, however, that Schweitzer retains at least one dualism even while he transforms others. In particular, Schweitzer is open to challenge concerning his apparently exclusive attention to all that lives. Using "will-to-live" as the primary category suggests that nonliving, nonhuman nature, such as rocks, air, and water, is excluded from the ethic of reverence for life. Feminists, in contrast, are increasingly calling for ways to include the so-called nonliving as morally significant (see Warren and Kheel). For the most part Schweitzer's will-to-live refers to plant and animal life, although, in at least one place, he does include the crystal as a form of will-to-live (Schweitzer 1949/1981, 282). In addition, he uses the language of "Being" in several places as well (Schweitzer 1949/1981, 304-6). These suggest some attention to nonliving nature. A more fruitful way to look at this issue is to recall Schweitzer's openness to science and scientific knowledge. As science through its investigations increasingly blurs the distinction between living and nonliving, will-to-live will become a less accurate way to describe what Schweitzer is trying to express.

One way for Schweitzer to include the nonliving as relevant is to emphasize the relatedness of wills-to-live, or the fact that "I am life which wills to live, *in the midst of* life which wills to live" (emphasis added). This relatedness, or interrelatedness in the context of Schweitzer's mysticism, in addition to his insistence that we do not know what life is (which means that we have no grounds for limiting it) moves Schweitzer in the direction of including the nonliving in moral discussions. Further, the possibility of seeing rocks and water as morally relevant tests Schweitzer's insistence that the reason something has value is not its analogical proximity to human life but its relationship to the divine as somehow a manifestation of the universal will-to-live.

The weight of evidence concerning the retention of hierarchical dualism in Schweitzer's thought suggests that he is more interested in transforming such dualisms. In addition to his use of "will-to-live" in the context of the human/nonhuman dualism, there are at least two other patriarchal dualisms that Schweitzer refuses to maintain. First, like feminists, Schweitzer does not divorce reason from intuition or affectivity. The two kinds of knowing for Schweitzer work in concert with each other to describe the self's relations with others in the world and to allow the self to feel those relations. Moreover, one of the most important elements in Schweitzer's ethic is compassion, and reverence itself is not a rational category. In these ways Schweitzer's ethic embraces the feelings and affectivity of the agent. In like manner feminists insist that the whole person be involved in judging and acting (Harrison, 3-21). As Marti Kheel points out, "We cannot even begin to talk about the issue of ethics unless we admit that we care (or feel something)" (Kheel, 144).

Second, Schweitzer's position works to transform the dualism of mind and body. Schweitzer's description of human beings as participants in the dilemma of the will-to-live, or its self-division, is done in such a way that he does not disparage the body. In other words, if Schweitzer was a firm supporter of a mind/body dualism, the fact that the body lives at the expense of other wills-to-live provides an occasion to deny bodily needs in favor of the "superior" mind. Schweitzer does not do this. Instead, it is the self as a whole as will-to-live that lives at the expense of others. And it is the self as a whole that must work to overcome the dilemma. Clearly feminist ethicists also attack the mind/body dualism.

In addition to overcoming these dualisms, Schweitzer's articulation of the ethic of reverence for life shares certain key features with feminist theological ethics. First, he depends on experience for his description of the interrelatedness and interdependence of all of life. For Schweitzer, the experience of the individual will-to-live in the midst of other wills-to-live presupposes a network of relation and interrelation. In Schweitzer's ethical mysticism, each being is a manifestation of the universal will-to-live and as such is related to every other being. More important, this experience of the self as will-to-live provides the only basis for understanding the self and others, including God. Feminists likewise depend on women's experience of themselves in relationship to others for their description of the world. For both, then, experience is crucial.

Second, both Schweitzer and feminists refuse to systematize ethics. Neither proposes absolute principles, which must be obeyed no matter what the situation or consequences; nor do they propose a telos or utilitarian goal. In both cases there is attention to the situation and an attempt to respond to the situation as it presents itself. For Schweitzer, ethics cannot be systematized because reverence for life, including love and compassion, must attend to the situation in which it finds itself. For example, in one situation compassion may mean saving a bird at the expense of the worms and bugs it will eat. In another circumstance, however, it may mean allowing the bird to remain where it has fallen in order to protect some other life, whether the worms and bugs, an injured cow, or the starving child I am trying to assist. In either case reverence for life cannot be removed or abstracted from the situation. Schweitzer's vision of ethics, then, sounds very much like the ethics of care that many feminists describe (see Warren and Gilligan).

Third, both feminist theological ethics and Schweitzer's ethic are activist ethics. Feminists are not simply interested in theory; rather we are interested in transforming oppressive social structures and living in nonpatriarchal ways. That entails concrete activity. Similarly, Schweitzer's reverence for life is far more than a way to reflect on the relationship between self and world. Reverence for life seeks to aid those in need and to transform the conditions of the will-to-live in the world. It does not accept present circumstances, especially the dilemma of the will-to-live as eternally or supernaturally given. The world as populated by manifold manifestations of the universal will-to-live is not static.

Fourth, Schweitzer's ethic is life-affirming. This includes not only his optimism about the possibilities for constructive action but also his attention to this world. Schweitzer's ethic does not support any form of nihilistic rejection of this world or any sort of religious otherworldliness. Individuals, for Schweitzer, come into contact with the divine not by withdrawing from others but by actively serving them in this world. This ethical mysticism lies at the heart of Schweitzer's position. It supports the sort of world-affirming and life-affirming ethic insisted upon by feminists such as Beverly Harrison, Isabel Carter Heyward, and Sallie McFague.

To conclude: Ecofeminist concerns and Schweitzer's reverence for life provide both challenges and resources for feminist theological ethics. Ecofeminists help us to see the connections between forms of oppression maintained by patriarchy at the level of dualistic assumptions. At the same time they challenge us not to lose sight of those connections when we move to the specifically theological dualism of human/divine. Schweitzer's ethic of reverence for life provides an example of an ethic that takes very seriously a non-dualistic description of the relationships between human beings and the world and between human beings and God. He challenges us to add to this the analysis of the dualistic structures that characterize human social relationships.

In short, what feminist theological ethics must recognize is that three fundamental relationships must be addressed simultaneously. These three relationships—between human beings and the nonhuman world, between human beings and God, and among human beings—are all defined dualistically by Western patriarchy. What we must see is that the way in which human beings are described in one of these relationships affects all the others. What we must remember is that no one or two of these relationships will be transformed without the transformation of all three.

WORKS CITED

Gilligan, Carol. *In a Different Voice*. Cambridge, MA: Harvard University Press, 1982.

Gray, Elizabeth Dodson. *Green Paradise Lost*. Wellesley, MA: Roundtable Press, 1979.

Griscom, Joan L. "On Healing the Nature/History Split in Feminist Thought." *Heresies: A Feminist Journal of Art and Politics* 4, no. 1 (1981): 4-9.

Harrison, Beverly. *Making the Connections*. Ed. Carol S. Robb. Boston: Beacon Press, 1985.

Heyward, Isabel Carter. *The Redemption of God: A Theology of Mutual Relation*. Washington, D.C.: University Press of America, 1982.

Kheel, Marti. "The Liberation of Nature: A Circular Affair," *Environmental Ethics* 7 (Summer 1985):135-49.

King, Ynestra. "Feminism and the Revolt of Nature." *Heresies: A Feminist Journal of Art and Politics* 4, no. 1 (1981): 12-16.

Kraus, Oskar. *Albert Schweitzer: His Work and His Philosophy*. Trans. I. G. McCalman. London: Adam and Charles Black, 1944.

Langfeldt, Gabriel. *Albert Schweitzer: A Study of His Philosophy of Life*. Trans. Maurice Michael. London: George Allen and Unwin, 1960.

McFague, Sallie. *Models of God: Theology for an Ecological, Nuclear Age*. Philadelphia: Fortress Press, 1987.

Plumwood, Val. "Ecofeminism: An Overview and Discussion of Positions and Arguments," *Australasian Journal of Philosophy* 64, Suppl. (June 1986):120-138.

Ruether, Rosemary Radford. *New Woman, New Earth*. New York: Seabury Press, 1975.

————. *Sexism and God-Talk: Toward a Feminist Theology*. Boston: Beacon Press, 1983.

Schweitzer, Albert. "Religion and Modern Civilization." *The Christian Century* 51 (28 November 1934):1519-21.

————. "The Ethics of Reverence for Life," *Christendom* 1 (Winter 1936): 225-39. Reprinted in Henry Clark, *The Ethical Mysticism of Albert Schweitzer: A Study of the Sources and Significance of Schweitzer's "Philosophy of Civilization"*. Boston: Beacon Press, 1962, pp. 180-94.

————. *Christianity and the Religions of the World*. Trans. Johanna Powers. New York: Henry Holt, 1939.

————. *Out of My Life and Thought: An Autobiography*. Trans. C.T. Campion. New York: Holt, Rinehart and Winston, 1949. Reprint ed. New York: New American Library, 1953.

————. *The Philosophy of Civilization*. Trans. C. T. Campion. New York: Macmillan, 1949. Reprint ed. Tallahassee, FL: University Presses of Florida, 1981.

————. *Indian Thought and Its Development*. Trans. Mrs. Charles I. B. Russell. Boston: Beacon Press, 1960.

————. *The Teaching of Reverence for Life*. Trans. Richard and Clara Winston. New York: Holt, Rinehart and Winston, 1965.

Singer, Peter. *Animal Liberation: A New Ethics for Our Treatment of Animals*. New York: Avon Books, 1975.

Warren, Karen. "Feminism and Ecology: Making Connections," *Environmental Ethics* 9 (Spring 1987):3-20.

PART 3

Voices from Africa, Asia, and Latin America

The majority of today's Christians live in Africa, Asia, Latin America, and Oceania. Clearly their voices represent the very leading edge of Christian consciousness and Christian history. As liberation theologies have made so clear, many of these people have experienced, and still experience, forms of economic and political subjugation that are unknown to the affluent minorities of the world, and that are the result, at least in part, of Western colonial influence. The emerging theologies of Africa, Asia, Latin America, and Oceania understandably emphasize freedom from Western cultural influence. Their call is for distinctively African, distinctively Asian, distinctively Latin American, and distinctively Oceanic forms of Christian self-understanding.

Their call is also for justice and peace. Here justice means freedom from poverty and freedom for self-determination; and peace means freedom from violence and freedom for harmonious relations with other people. Increasingly, however, these theologies emphasize that justice and peace are not enough, at least if these social ideals are limited in their application to interhuman relations. What is needed, they suggest, is a more holistic perspective, which sees human life as in community with all life and liberation itself as a liberation of life. If the words justice and peace suggested this broader, more life-sensitive perspective, they would be sufficient. But since they so often carry only Western, humanistic connotations, they are insufficient. To peace and justice, it seems, a third phrase is needed: one that underscores the need for harmonious relations with the land and with fellow creatures.

The World Council of Churches—itself so deeply shaped by African, Asian, Latin American, and Oceanic points of view—offers that third phrase. It is the integrity of creation. Taken as a whole, so the World Council suggests, peace, justice, and the integrity of creation name the appropriate ideal of contemporary Christian commitment. According to the World Council, respect for the integrity of creation is important, not only because people depend on the earth and other creatures for our survival, but because the earth and fellow creatures have value in their own right as aspects of divine care.

The essays in this section illustrate how important such respect has become for African, Asian, and Latin American theologies. They capture one of the central themes of this book, that life as a whole, and not human life alone, is in need of liberation from oppression. The three essays in this section illustrate this new, ecological consciousness in theologies from Africa, Asia, and Latin America. First, there is an essay by Ingemar Hedström, who, having lived in Costa Rica for fifteen years, identifies deeply with Latin American liberation theologies. Hedström is a pioneer in articulating the new ecological direction that such theologies can and should take. After Hedström's essay, there is an essay by Jong-Sun Noh, a Minjung theologian from Korea who cries out against unecological theologies by which his own country has been plagued. Finally we have an essay by one of the most prominent African theologians of our time — Harvey Sindima — who shows how a traditional African emphasis on life, understood as the very power of the divine, can be an antidote for his continent, and for other parts of the world as well, to unecological thinking.

8

Latin America and the Need for a Life-Liberating Theology

Ingemar Hedström

All the great civilizations of the world began with the felling of the first tree . . . the majority of them disappeared with the felling of the last (Combe and Gewald).

During the 1970s, when I visited the capital of El Salvador on several occasions, I was able to observe the thousands of swallows that would fill the power lines every evening across from the National Theater in Morazan Plaza. Like endless strings of white pearls they covered the entire electrical layout of the plaza, as well as the small ledges on the theater building. The same phenomenon was observed for many years in the city of Escuintla, located to the southwest of Guatemala's capital city.

This custom of gathering together to sleep and rest at night (*roosting* in English) is practiced by a few animals, including white herons, mammals,

In the latter decades of the twentieth century, the phrase *liberation theology* often has been used synonymously with *Latin American liberation theology*. This reflects the immense influence that Latin American theologians have had on the global Christian community. Can Latin American theologies, too, be part of the emerging consensus that life in its totality, and not human life alone, deserves liberation? Indeed they can, at least from the point of view of Ingemar Hedström. Hedström, living in Latin America for many years and deeply influenced by liberation perspectives, has published several works at the interface of liberation theology and ecology. His proposal is that Latin American liberation perspectives can and must be committed to the integrity of creation if they are to meet the needs of the human poor. Hedström's essay, abridged by the editors of this book and translated by Kathlyn Smith, combines sections from two of his books: *We Are Part of a Great Balance: The Ecological Crisis in Central America* (3d ed., published in San Jose, Costa Rica, by Editorial DEI, 1988) and *Will the Swallows Return? The Reintegration of Creation from a Latin American Perspective* (Editorial DEI, 1988).

and some species of butterflies. It is believed that, given the high number of captures by predators, the chances of individual survival are greater.

My native companions informed me that these swallows of San Salvador had been practicing the custom of roosting together in Morazan Plaza for many, many years. Some citizens had written beautiful poems in homage to the swallows, while others argued that they soiled the streets and tried to get rid of them—with gunshots, buckets of water, or fireworks. In spite of this, the swallows continued arriving every evening to cover the cables and spend a peaceful night in the plaza.

Ten years later, upon returning to San Salvador, I could not see a single swallow in Morazan Plaza. What had happened to them? Why did they not appear as usual in the evenings? I asked several of my friends in the capital, but no one could give me a definite reason. Among other things, they told me that owls had come to the plaza in search of prey, and that the swallows had fled in a panic. This reason, like the others they had offered, did not seem to me a very satisfactory explanation.

I have been thinking about the apparent disappearance of the swallows in San Salvador as well as in Escuintla. For me, they have become a very concrete symbol of what is happening in Latin America; I am referring to the environmental deterioration of the continent and in particular of El Salvador. When the swallows could find nothing to eat in the vicinity of the capital, what choice did they have but to move on or die? We wonder: Will the swallows return, or are they, are we ourselves, headed toward premature death and irreversible destruction?

The disappearance of swallows in El Salvador is by no means an isolated incident. It is part of a much larger pattern of abuse and exploitation, of the earth and of people, which has occurred in South and Central America, and which is itself part of an age-old historical pattern of ecological destruction. It is worth our while to review this age-old pattern and then to look at its exemplification in South and Central America.

THE PATTERN OF DESTRUCTION

The Landscape of Greece: A Decayed Skeleton

Let us recall that centuries ago in ancient Greece more than half the country was covered by green forests. Today it is estimated that only one-twentieth of this country is wooded; apparently, scarcely two percent of the old layer of humus (fertile organic remains of dead plants and animals) has been conserved in Greece (Edberg, 150).

The famous Greek philosopher Plato (438-347 B.C.E.) founded the Greek Academy. Following extensive travels throughout his country he lamented the fact that the delicate, fertile part of the Greek soil had been washed away through rains and the lack of vegetation in the country (Edberg, 149-50). Of the landscape nothing remained but a decayed skeleton. The temple ruins on the hills of Attica to the north of Athens, the capital, today are silent, along with the natural world that surrounds them. A great many species, among them many birds, have now abandoned this dry, semi-sterile environment in order to survive.

The Roman Empire

Centuries later on the Italic peninsula this same drama was being repeated. During the Roman Empire the flatlands were already suffering from excessive cultivation. The Roman peasants were obliged to go higher and higher into the Apennine Mountains for arable land. The fertile soil lost its humus layer, which was washed by the rains into the rivers and then deposited forever in the Mediterranean Sea. Once there, it fouled the water and killed the aquatic fauna.

So the Roman Empire was soon forced to seek new lands on the other side of the Mediterranean Sea — in Northern Africa, in what is now Algeria and Tunisia. The Romans thus acquired in their African colonies provisions and olives enough to continue living "on bread, wine, and pleasure" in the city of Rome.

The Romans also exploited the lands on the island of Sicily in the same way as in Northern Africa. Let us remember the legendary city of Carthage, which lies close to the capital (Tunis) — how it had to be literally "destroyed to please the Romans." Carthage had to feed not only itself and the neighboring villages — whose populations are calculated to have been about three times the present population — but the Roman population as well, including a very large migration of people who were then looking for new opportunities in Rome.

Northern Africa

With the exploitation of natural resources that was practiced throughout this epoch, the natural environments of Italy, Sicily, and Northern Africa had to pay a very high price to be able to satisfy the excesses of the Empire. Furthermore, what the Romans did not manage to destroy during this period was finished off by domestic animals, mainly goats or kids. These animals not only eat the green parts of the plants, but consume the roots of the vegetation as well. The region in which Hannibal of Carthage captured elephants for his army — the mountains of Northern Africa where today these beautiful animals are no longer found — became a semi-desert, along with southern Italy and Sicily. Today history informs us that the vegetation of this landscape died with the Roman Empire itself.

The Clearing of European Forests

At this point I should add that not only the environment of the great Southern European empires was sadly damaged. In the tenth century, when the original European forests began to be converted to farmland and pasturage, ninety percent of the entire continent was covered by trees; today only twenty percent of these trees remains (Myers 1979, 121).

Often the despoliation occurred with amazing rapidity. In the eighteenth century, when the Swedish naturalist Carolus Linnaeus (1707-78) returned in his later years to an island of the Gothenburg (Sweden) archipelago, he was surprised at the absence of trees, which had been there when he was a young man. The cliffs facing the sea were practically bare because the trees had become raw material for the construction of ships and of wooden barrels for preserving the famous Nordic herring.

Disappearance of North American Virgin Forests

About the tenth century, when the ancient Scandinavians, the Vikings, were frequenting North America, the humid portion of the east, as far as the mid-east of what is now the United States of North America, was covered by a dense forest of 1.6 million square kilometers. Today less than five percent of this forest is still virgin (see Myers 1979, 121).

Spain

If we move forward in the course of European history, we find that at the time when Spanish kings were trying to build their own empire, trees were cut down in Spain, also, to produce lumber for shipbuilding, and great expanses of forest were converted to pastureland. But all of the wealth that Spain had managed to amass during the sixteenth century was lost in the Spanish trade crisis of the following century. Spain's environment was greatly affected, and today on the Iberian Peninsula we find a severely eroded landscape, virtually dead rivers, and bare mountains.

The Naked Coasts of the Mediterranean

I have been able personally to observe several of these areas and their present appearance as resulting from overexploitation in Southern Europe: felling of trees and excessive pasturing in Greece, Turkey, Italy, and southern Spain, as well as in North Africa—Morocco, Algeria, and Tunisia. All of these large areas are now dry and eroded because of the poor land management mentioned above.

A New Land to Exploit: America

Long ago the Spanish and the Portuguese settled in Central and South America. It may be supposed that Central America at the time of the conquistadors' arrival presented an area covered almost completely by forests. On his fourth voyage, when Christopher Columbus reached the coast of what is now Costa Rica, the admiral found an enormous wealth of forest in the area:

Before Spanish colonization, the natives cultivated the soil using rudimentary, subsistence-level methods; therefore, the exploited geographic areas were very limited. The forests predominated; plant cover was maintained on cultivated ground, thereby renewing its organic material and nutrients, or natural fertility; the climate contributed efficiently to agricultural yield, and the rivers and underground springs were plentiful and of excellent quality; the fauna was abundant (Espinoza, 168).

In South America, in what is now Peru, the subjects of the Incan Empire had developed terrace cultivation, by which they obtained better harvests and also avoided soil erosion.

In Mexico the high plateau populations used water-rationing methods for centuries in their farming, which made possible the flourishing of an area that today is totally dry and eroded due to lack of measures to prevent a permanent water shortage in the region.

The Fall of the Mayas

Another illustrative case, though not an altogether clear one, is the collapse of Mayan civilization about one thousand years ago. Of the proposed theories regarding its fall, the role of agricultural productivity in the lowlands has been discussed in the majority of the studies done on the subject (see Fonseca Zamora). It is believed that the Mayas upset the balance between humans and nature, although the fall of their civilization probably corresponded to "a network of interaction in which any difficulty could have had repercussions on the whole" (Fonseca Zamora, 505).

The Mayas attained a high degree of efficiency in mathematics, writing, and astronomy, but probably not in the rational management of soil and forest. Roughly by the year 250 B.C.E., the clearing of forests and the over-cultivation of Mayan agricultural lands had caused a great deal of soil erosion (see Deevey, et al.). One proof of their mistaken farming methods may lie in a discovery made on Mexico's Yucatan Peninsula, where after a meter's excavation into the light-brown fertile soil, a stratus of black was unexpectedly found: this probably means that this civilization practiced burning off vegetation in order to expand their arable lands (see the studies in *Dagens Nyheter*).[1] Repeated burnings promote destruction of soil productivity in any part of the world.

The Aboriginal Population of Central America

Certain parts of Central America were densely populated during the pre-Columbian period, reaching their peak density by 1520, when the Europeans arrived. The most important nuclei of aboriginal population were in Guatemala, El Salvador, and certain parts of Honduras (Fournier, 50), while Nicaragua, Costa Rica, and Panama were a sparsely populated region.[2] The aboriginal population then decreased eighty to ninety percent over the following twenty-five to fifty years (Corrales Rodriguez, 114-15).

Imported Agricultural Systems

The Spaniards who came to Central America saw as backward and primitive the native system of soil cultivation, which was *migratory* or *itinerant* agriculture, involving prolonged rotation (Hall, 122-23). They therefore replaced the indigenous tradition with agricultural systems imported, literally, from Spain and with models of land use which were well-suited to the Mediterranean regions but completely alien to the tropics.[3] When the Spaniards settled in Costa Rica, all lands, including those of the aborigines, became the property of the Spanish Crown. True to Spanish tradition, the pastures and cleared fields, which had no place in the aboriginal ecosystem, were initially designated as public lands, but in practice many of them were gradually absorbed as private property (Hall, 123). Espinoza summarizes the situation well:

> The Spaniards invaded the region by pillaging nature; they appropriated vast tracts of land, monopolizing the best soil, introduced livestock, and enslaved the natives for clearing forests, creating pastureland, and tending livestock, thus establishing land-cattle fiefs. With oxen they implemented animal traction, or cultivation of the soil with ploughs, thus intensifying erosive agricultural practices and the soil compaction caused by livestock's trampling of the ground (Espinoza, 168).

Today, the depletion of minerals, forests, and other natural resources in Central America is considerable, just as is soil depletion in the areas of greatest development. Changes in the possession and overdevelopment of land have affected the people in the past and continue to do so today. The Spaniards and their descendants, in less than four centuries, changed great stretches of countryside into an unbalanced, half-naked environment. We continue this destruction in the present through practices at the heart of our economies. By way of illustration, consider the pattern of destruction in light of its relation to the meat-eating habits of North Americans.

THE "HAMBURGERIZATION" OF THE FORESTS OF CENTRAL AMERICA

Forest management, agriculture, and extensive cattle-ranching are the principal activities upon which Central America's economy rests.[4] Of these, cattle-ranching has developed the most during recent decades. For this reason the majority of Central American countries could be called "hamburger republics," though the cattlemen of the region do not themselves perceive it in this way. They see their activity as fair and profitable enterprise. Cattle-ranching still represents a fairly secure flow of income into Central America.

Now, what the cattlemen refuse to acknowledge is that meat production in Central America is intimately linked to destruction of the forests. This is due primarily to the fact that cattle-ranching in this region is a process of colonization based upon extensive exploitation of large amounts of land, including forests. Consider the following statistics concerning individual countries in Central America.

Costa Rica

In Costa Rica, between 1960 and 1980, pasturage and cattle increased by about seventy-five percent, while the rain forests decreased by about forty percent during this same period, being converted to pasturelands (Myers 1981, 6). The *hatos* (cattle pastures) account for one-half of the landed property in Costa Rica and one-third of the country's total area.

In 1972 Tosi had already summed up very precisely the consequences of irrational utilization of Costa Rica's virgin lands, to the detriment of the natural balance. His account is worth extensive quoting.

When it left the Central Valley, agricultural colonization became cattle-based and extensive, occupying great areas of land in order to sustain a dispersed population. The invaded regions were, in general, warmer . . . much rainier, and characterized by a topography that was often rugged and uneven. . . . The land was ill-suited for continual cultivation. New fields cultivated on top of the debris of a recently cleared forest . . . did not last more than two or three years. Given these limitations, colonization was characterized by a frontier that advanced rapidly upon virgin forests with tree-cutting . . . , burning, and temporary cultivation, and by a large area in its wake where abandoned farmland, instead of being allowed to turn into natural secondary forests thus renewing its fertility and guarding against erosion, was converted into cattle ranches. Whenever there was a dry season of sufficient length for the annual burnings, the brushlands were made into natural pasturelands. Since cattle require a wide expanse of this barren land in order to be profitable, the colonists indiscriminately cleared forests in every kind of climate, topography, and soil. Even watersheds important to the lowland water supply were completely shorn of their protective forests.

We know the process well. It is not just persisting, but is getting worse at present, spreading over the slopes and upper river basins of the country's mountain ranges. . . . It has gained new momentum, impelled not by the poor colonist searching for land with which to support his family, but rather by the commercial cattleman seeking short-term profits in the new and expanding international beef market.

Popularly regarded as progress, this colonizing process has reached a point where it does not lead to authentic development in the country, but leads instead to its impoverishment and to the eventual biological and economic death of the land. In most cases, primary forests are cleared along rivers and streams. This destruction of elements vital to the ecology and renewal of the land—elimination of entire communities, their flora and fauna, their roots and seeds, their organic soils. . . . When there are no vestigial forests close by, natural repopulation of secondary forests and wildlife becomes impossible. . . . Worse yet, much of this land is unsuitable for use as pastureland and, when used for such purposes, is gradually ruined for any future use, including forestation (Tosi).

Nicaragua

Beginning in the sixties, cattle-ranching in Nicaragua was enormously revitalized (see Slutsky, 100). Meat exports came to constitute the country's third largest export product, surpassed only by cotton and coffee.

Cattle-ranching in Nicaragua has been conducted traditionally in the form of land-leasing and sharecropping, which the great landowners have given to the *campesino* (Slutsky, 100). The sharecropper would clear and farm the land and leave it planted with grass before moving on in search of more land; the *campesino*'s function from the sixties on, then, basically has been that of "increasing the value of land that will later be occupied by the big cattlemen" (Slutsky, 100).

Panama

Or consider Panama. In 1950 Panama had about 570,000 head of cattle and approximately 550,000 hectares of pasturage; by 1970 the number of cattle had risen to 1.2 million head and the pasturage to 1.1 million hectares (Heckadon Moreno 1984b, 18).

Regarding Panama, S. Heckadon Moreno says:

The tropical-forest zones are being incorporated into the national economy, at a high ecological and social cost, due to the rapid expansion of extensive cattle-ranching. . . . This colonization is characterized by rapid destruction of the tropical forest, substituted first by cultivation of cleared lands and later by pastures which are burned annually. When the forests disappear and the soil loses its fertility, social organization is altered. Class structure changes, and traditional, mutual-assistance institutions are weakened. . . . These transformations contribute to the cycle which continually displaces the *campesinos* from old to new frontiers of colonization (Heckadon Moreno[a], 133).

Food for Export and Not for Central Americans

The increase in meat production in Central America did not come about in order to satisfy internal consumption . . . but rather for the purpose of exportation.[5]

Why the exportation of meat, and not rice and beans or other popular foods so badly needed by the hungry populace? Why cattle-raising, so extensive in its use of the most limited resource in all of Central America, the soil, and so unintensive in its use of labor while thousands are looking for work? Just as in the other operational categories of the World Bank, its interest in promoting cattle-ranching in Central America does not seem to correspond to a desire to confront the conditions and structures produced by man and by poverty. Instead, an answer must be sought as we examine the role of Central American cattle-ranching in the world meat market, and especially capitalism's interest in its development (Keene, 202).

In some countries of Central America, as is the case in Costa Rica, Guatemala, and Honduras, one can see that meat production went from being insufficient in satisfying internal consumption needs to a position of importance among export products, following coffee, sugar, and bananas.

For example, studies conducted by the Nutrition Institute of Central America established that for the average conditions of Costa Rica an average of ninety grams of meat should be eaten daily. According to findings of the country's National Production Council, in 1983 the daily consumption per person was twenty-three grams.[6] Per capita consumption of meat for Costa Ricans declined after that, in spite of the fact that consumption was already at an unacceptable level for supporting basic protein nutrition. According to some sources, such as Myers, even though meat production in Costa Rica tripled during the period 1960-70 internal consumption fell to a point where each person ate "less meat than a domestic cat receives annually in the United States" (Myers 1981, 6).

The increase in meat production is designated almost entirely for export; more than thirty percent is sent to the United States (see Parsons). The meat produced in Central America is usually frozen and flown to Miami, where it enters the processed-foods production chain (see Andersson).

It could be contended that the eating habits of North Americans and their country's politics are determinants in the promotion of cattle-ranching in Central America. According to Andersson, some United States government programs stimulate ranching activity in Central America. The U.S. State Department's Agency for International Development, for example, has carried out various assistance programs for profitability in that industry.

The "Hamburgerization" of Central America

On the other hand, after 1955, when the first "hamburgers to go" restaurant opened in Chicago, there was a veritable revolution in the eating habits of North Americans (Hubler, 1). In 1960 there were already more than 200 McDonald's restaurants in the United States alone, with a consumption of meat that was truly immense. The problem at that time was how to obtain so many tons of meat at a low price. The best alternative turned out to be the meat produced in Central America, on the basis of the extensive grazing and natural pastures of the region. Inexpensive meat would mean inexpensive hamburgers. So, beginning in 1960 a "bonanza era" of cattle-ranching came to be. Few people had any idea of the high cost that would be paid in the Central American forests.

In summary, we would point out that from 1960 to 1980 beef production in Central America increased 160 percent; of the 400,000 square kilometers of rain forest that existed in 1960 in Central America less than one-half remained by 1980 (Myers 1981). We find ourselves faced, then, with a "hamburgerization" of Central America.

THE NEED FOR A LIFE-LIBERATING THEOLOGY

In light of this ravaging of people and land in Central America, we realize that the preferential option for the poor, characteristic of Latin American liberation theologies, must be articulated as a preferential *option for life*. To exercise this option is to defend and promote the fundamental right to life of *all* creatures on earth. The right to life in all its fullness involves partaking of the material base of creation, that is, of the material goods that permit life. All people, and not the powerful alone, must be availed of such goods; all people, not the powerful alone, must do so in a way that preserves rather than despoils the earth and other forms of life. In order to exercise this right in a just and sustainable way, we must rediscover our primal roots in the earth, and creatures of the earth.

This rediscovery will not be easy. Many modern people are detaching themselves, consciously or unconsciously, from their primal roots, from the *origins* of their existence: the earth and its natural resources, self-renewing sources of food, raw materials, energy, and so on. They are doing so because they are obsessed with profit and an eagerness to dominate nature. Indeed, this obsession has become an ideology.

The basic characteristic of this ideology seems to be unlimited growth, constant expansion. In the case of capitalism we have a pattern of consumption and waste that attacks humanity itself. This ideology is the basis for a mode of production, especially in the affluent countries, whose thirst for profit and for irrational expansion has not only promoted the pauperization of the majority of the planet's human population but has also led to the plundering and pollution of nature. Thus has life been endangered not only for the poor, but for all sectors of the human population and for many of the creatures with which we share the earth.

It would seem that we have only two options. On the one hand, there is the traditional, persistent, and negative interpretation of *anthropocentrism*. According to it, human beings are in the front rank, trying to control the natural environment for his own benefit.

On the other hand, we have a new and more attractive valuation of nature. We might call it *ecocentrism* (see Sale). According to this interpretation human beings are but one among many species, and not much more. We have no right to continue our present behavior, as if we were the only species on earth and, moreover, as if the present generation were the last. Rather we must recognize ourselves as of the same order as other animals, in no way more valuable.

I believe we ought not limit ourselves to either of these concepts. Rather, we must somehow discover and combine the positive elements contained in each. That is, we must establish a new concept based on a *balance* between these two ideas, thereby achieving an interpretation of the harmonious relationship that is aspired to between human being and the rest of nature.

What we need is a greater understanding of the *environmental limits* which most certainly exist regarding human intervention into nature. The acceptance of these environmental limits may not guarantee us an equitable distribution of society's wealth, but — and this is the crucial point — the idea of *balance and environmental limits* offers the prospect of a more just society. This is because respect for these limits is essential to any social body that aspires to a qualitatively better life for all. Traditional industrial society, as we know, has not really presented us with this possibility.

In other words, we must develop a new ethic and, to be frank, a new logic with relation to nature, based on the conviction that, as Father Gustavo Gutiérrez of Peru says, "life and not death has the last word." We rightly insist that God opposes death because God is the Creator and the giver of life.

Thus, as Christians in Latin America we choose life over death by combating the deterioration of the natural environment and the pollution of soil, air, water, and other elements. Always keeping in mind the environmental limits, we put ourselves on the side of life rather than death, among other reasons, so that all of us will have the chance to satisfy the basic necessities: work, food, home, health, education. Such must be our new, life-liberating ethic.

By way of conclusion, then, let us recall the plight of the swallows mentioned in the introduction, noting that if we are not careful, their plight may become our own.

The swallows that once occupied the power lines in the Morazan Plaza of El Salvador's capital are migratory birds. They, along with 150 other species of birds (which is equivalent to two-thirds of the birds in North America's forests), move each year from North America toward Central America and the Caribbean, going as far as South America, in order to spend the North American cold season in warmer latitudes.[7]

Central America lies on the route of many species of migratory birds. The isthmus is shaped more or less like a funnel, which channels the birds that migrate along diverse paths and come together in the narrow isthmus. Every time that the swallows and other birds fly south, they find their habitat more and more deteriorated. As a result, one to four percent of migratory birds disappear each year (Myers 1986). In other words, the individuals of each species of migratory bird are slowly diminishing in number. It is calculated that within some fifteen years, more than half of the migratory birds will have disappeared. If this is happening with wild animals, we may easily guess who is to follow.

NOTES

1. *Dagens Nyheter*, Stockholm, 30 April 1979. "Skogsvard död för Maya" ("Poor Forest Management Causes the Ruin of the Mayas"). These studies were carried out on the Yucatan Peninsula in the 1970s by the agronomist Gerald Olson, Cornell University, United States.

2. When the conquistadors arrived there were, in Costa Rica at least, no more than 27,000 natives, according to Bishop Thiel. Seventy years later, given the abuse to which they were subjected, they had decreased to about 17,000, which dwindled to 9,000 by 1801. In other words, in three hundred years the aboriginal population in Costa Rica was reduced by almost two-thirds. Today only one percent of the country's total population is aboriginal, the lowest percentage in Central America (see Cevo Guzman, et al., 224).

3. Pre-Columbian aboriginal communities required access to a large area of forest, and they would reduce the land's yield after one or two harvests; they would abandon the farmed lands so that the forest would grow back and would clear another strip for cultivation. In this way the forest protected the soil, the plants, and the wild animals which, together with fish and shellfish, provided the aborigines with valuable sources of energy and nutrients (Hall, 122-124).

4. In the mid-seventies El Salvador had sixty-five percent, Costa Rica fifty- four percent, Honduras and Nicaragua thirty-five percent, and Guatemala thirty-two percent of their land area in agricultural use (see Soria 1976).

5. For a more in-depth study on the World Bank's cattle politics in Central America, see Keene.

6. See *Libertad*, Costa Rica. "Desnutrición y consumo de carne en Costa Rica," 23-29 November 1984.

7. In the opinion of Bill Marleau, forest ranger with the Adirondack Reserve, New York State, United States, the abuse of pesticides is the main cause of the

recent disappearance of swallows and other animals from this famous reserve. He relates: "I remember how it used to be, when millions of swallows perched on the power lines here. Every year around the 26th of August, they would assemble in large flocks and then migrate south. Last year, however, for the first time in twenty years, we didn't have even one to build its nest. For four years now, not a single pair has been able to feed its young due to lack of insects in the area. . . . The two kinds of swallows common here had always raised two broods per year. Last year, when as usual I was counting the number of swallows assembled to migrate south, I could only see about fifteen; no more. As I said earlier, there used to be thousands. The same thing is being seen with other species of birds, and with mammals and insects, within our reserve" (Landin, 146-47).

WORKS CITED

Andersson, W.T. "A más ganado, menos carne para el pueblo." *Noticias Aliades*, no. 2 (24 January 1985): 3-4.

Cevo Guzman, et al. *Costa Rica: nuestra comunidad nacional, estudios sociales sétimo año*. San Jose, Costa Rica: Universidad Estatal a Distancia, 1984.

Combe, J., and N.J. Gewald eds., *Guía de campo de los ensayos forestales del CATIE en Turrialba, Costa Rica*. Costa Rica: Centro Agronómico Tropical de Investigaciones y Enseñanza, 1979.

Corrales Rodríguez, D. *Impacto ecológico sobre los recursos naturales renovables de Centro América*. Managua, Nicaragua: Instituto Nicaragüense de Recursos Naturales y del Ambiente, 1983.

Deevey, E. S., et al. "Mayan Urbanism: Impact on Tropical Karst Environment." *Science* (19 October 1979).

Edberg, R. *Spillran av ett moln (The Remains of a Cloud)*. Stockholm, Sweden: Litteratur-främjendet, 1966.

Espinoza, E. "Recursos naturales de aprovechamiento agropecuario." *Actas* of the Segundo Seminario Nacional de Recursos Naturales y del Ambiente. Managua, Nicaragua: Instituto Nicaragüense de Recursos Naturales y del Ambiente, 1981.

Fonseca Zamora, O.M. 1979. "El colapso maya." In *Anuario de Estudios Centroamericanos*. Costa Rica: Editorial Universidad de Costa Rica, 1979, pp. 489-505.

Fournier, O. *Ecología y desarrollo en Costa Rica*. San José, Costa Rica: Editorial Universidad Estatal a Distancia, 1981.

Hall, C. *Costa Rica: Una interpretación geográfica con perspectiva histórica*. San José, Costa Rica: Editorial Costa Rica, 1984.

Heckadon Moreno, S. (a) "Dinámica social de la 'cultura del potrero' de Panamá el caso de Tonosí." *Colonización y destrucción de bosques en Panamá*. Ed. S. Heckadon Moreno and A. McKay. Panama: Asociación Panameña de Anthropolgía, 1984.

———. (b) "La colonización campesina de bosques tropicales en Panamá." *Colonización y destrucción de bosques en Panamá*. Ed. S. Heckadon Moreno, and A. McKay. Panama: Asociación Panameña de Anthropología, 1984.

Hubler, D. "El rey de la hamburguesa en Estados Unidos." *La Prensa Libre*, Costa Rica (6 March 1985).

Keene, B. "Incursiones del Banco Mundial en Centroámerica." *El Banco Mundial: un caso de "progresismo conservador."* Ed. H. Assman. San José, Costa Rica:

Departmento Ecuménico de Investigaciones (DEI), 1981.

Landin, B. *Om träd kunde grata (If Trees Could Cry)*. Stockholm: Prisma, 1986.

Myers, Norman. *The Sinking Ark*. Oxford: Pergamon Press, 1979.

————. "The Hamburger Connection: How Central America's Forests Become North America's Hamburgers." *Ambio* 10, no. 1 (1981): 3-8.

————. "Economics and Ecology in the International Arena: The Phenomenon of Linked Linkages." *Ambio* (Sweden) 15 (1986):296-300.

Parsons, J. J. "Forest to Pasture: Development or Destruction? *Revista de Biología Tropical* 24, suppl. 1 (1976): 121-38.

Sale, K. "The Forest for the Trees: Can Today's Environmentalists Tell the Difference?" *Mother Jones* 11, no. 8 (1986):25-33, 58.

Slutsky, D. "El avance de la frontera agrícola con especial referencia a la cost Atlántica de Nicaragua." *Actas del segundo Seminario Nacional de Recursos Naturales y del Ambiente*. Managua, Nicaragua: Instituto Nicaragüense de Recursos Naturales y del Ambiente, 1981.

Soria, V. J. "Los sistemas de agricultura en el Istmo Centroamericano." *Revista de Biología Tropical* 24, suppl. 1 (1976): 57-68.

Tosi, J. A. *Los recursos forestales de Costa Rica*. San José, Costa Rica: I Congreso Nacional sobre la Conservación de los Recursos Naturales Renvoables, 1972.

9

The Effects on Korea of Un-Ecological Theology

Jong-Sun Noh

There were two pretty fish
that lived in a small pond
by the path deep in the mountain.
On a certain clear summer day,
the two pretty fish fought each other.
One fish floated on the water,
her flesh decayed.
The water was polluted at the same time.
Now, in that little pond by the path
deep in the mountain.
No life can survive.
   —from Minkee Kim's "Two Fishes"

TWO FISHES: THE DIVISION OF NORTH AND SOUTH KOREA

This poem is a song that the young, conscientized university students love to sing in Korea. When they sing the song, the small pond refers to

In the following essay the Korean theologian Jong-Sun Noh provides a telling analysis of injustice and suffering—human and nonhuman—in Korea. Writing from the perspective of *Minjung* theology—a school of liberation theology specifically centered on the oppressed peoples of Korea—Noh reports inductively on the sorts of oppression that often arise from, or are validated by, what the *Minjung* theologians call division theologies. These are theologies that reflect and endorse first world and imperialistic or colonialistic interests. In Korea we see the result of ways of thinking that have failed to be ecological and liberating. Noh's inductive and socio-historical method lays bare the result of unecological thinking. His concerns, and the concerns of many like him, have played a large part in motivating the thinkers represented in this book, who are working toward a more inclusive vision.

the Korean peninsula, and the two fish refer to the divided north and south. As most of us know, North and South Korea have been divided for over forty-three years. Often, they have fought each other like two fish. Tragically, it is possible that, in the future, the pond as a whole—the peninsula itself—will be polluted by conflict in such a way that no life will be possible.

To many young Christians who sing this song, the song has two distinctively theological meanings. First, it means that the Korean peninsula was once beautiful, that it was created by God for God's glory. The sun, the stars, the heavens, the earth, and that particular part of earth called Korea were designed to praise the Lord. Second, it means that this peninsula may someday become a place that cannot support life. It may become a place in which the integrity of creation of which the World Council of Churches speaks and toward which Christians rightly exercise respect, may become a mere wasteland of disintegration.

What are we to make of this song? What can the song mean for us? Should it mean that the death of the Korean peninsula—its people and its nonhuman life as well—is imminent? Should it mean that the biosphere in Korea will be so totally devastated that the waters, the fish, and the human beings there will die? Perhaps it can have an even broader meaning. Perhaps the little pond of death in the song can refer to the planet earth as a whole and to the global biosphere. Perhaps the song is instructive to both Koreans and to the people of the world in pointing toward the destructiveness of a certain kind of unecological theology—what we in Korea call division theology—that legitimates an oppression of people, of other animals, and of the earth itself. In what follows I will explain what I mean by division thinking, showing its influence on Korea, the land I know best.

KOREA

In the pond by the name of Korea, the people of the north and the people of the south have fought and killed each other for over forty-four years. This conflict has been in fact a proxy war to benefit imperialist superpowers. Both North and South Korea have been the scapegoats for this neo-colonial proxy war, what amounts to a war of imperialist beasts, the dragons of the book of Revelation. Under the structure of this war, females and males of the human species have been and are currently dying, oppressed and exploited, even while they are unaware of the cause of their suffering or the cause of the division of Korea. Korean Christians have advocated and supported faiths, ideologies, and economics that legitimate division and are themselves divisive.

These division theologies (Bundan Shinhak) divide, violate, and destroy the integrity of God's creation. Korean Christians must confess our responsibility here, for we have sometimes accepted such theologies as our own. At the same time, however, the politico-economic elites within the military-industrial complexes of the super, imperialistic, and hegemonic powers must confess their sin of destroying the pond, the Korean peninsula, of destroying a beautiful and integral part of God's creation for their own political and economic ends. Let us review some of this history.

Although the Korean peninsula was once a unified community of nature and people, it has consistently been divided by outside forces. The sin of division and separation, breaking the one into two, was first plotted by Toyotomi Hideyosi, the Japanese general, and Weehahhoe, the Chinese general, in 1593, almost four hundred years ago. They proposed the division of Korea as a means of balancing power between the Japanese and Chinese hegemonies. They failed to respect that *community* which was the Korean people itself, along with the land they loved and the flora and fauna who dwelt among them. Division thinking begins by failing to respect existing communities of this sort.

The effects of such division thinking were exacerbated in the nineteenth century. In 1894 John W. Kimberly, the Minister of Foreign Affairs for Great Britain, the colonial power and chief oppressor of colonized people in the world at that time, again proposed the division of the Korean peninsula in order to make peace between Japan and China. This plan, designed from so-called first-world perspectives, essentially made Koreans scapegoats. It is noteworthy that President Truman and General MacArthur did not divide Japan, the war criminal, in 1945; instead, they divided Korea, the victim of world war and of colonial powers. In dividing Korea these men committed the sin of dividing and destroying a part of the integral order of creation itself. An integral order is deeply ecological in the sense that it involves a people in communion with their land. It is a community in the sense noted above: an ecological community of people living in meaningful degrees of harmony with one another and with the earth.

A few in the West recognized the need to respect such community. Averill Harriman, then the United States ambassador to Moscow, protested against MacArthur's plan to divide Korea because he knew that Korea had a history as one community with one race, and that no one should divide her. But the structures of MacArthur's consciousness—which was built over a long period of his life with guns and swords—were full of ruling ideologies, which wrongfully justified using the oppressed people as scapegoats for what he supposed to be justice, peace, and order. Though a so-called Christian working for justice, peace, and order in the created world, MacArthur did so from a consciousness informed by the hegemonic ideologies of the first world, ideologies that sought to divide existing communities. Thus Germany was divided after World War II. In Asia, by similar logic of division, Japan ought to have been similarly divided. But instead Korea was divided. This incident is not an accidental one.

The cause of this injustice can be traced back to 1905 when a secret agreement was made between President Taft (United States) and Prime Minister Katsura (Japan).[1] The secret agreement was made because Japan wanted Korea as a colony and the United States wanted the Philippines;

each agreed to support the other in these respective aims. The Philippines and Korea were the "food" for a coalition of Japanese and American imperialists. From 1910 to 1945 the leaders of the oppressed Korean people who tried to assert the self-reliance and independence of a united Korea were put into prisons, deported, exploited, tortured, politically assassinated, and martyred. The stories of their lives were not permitted to be put into print and were totally suppressed.

The people and their leaders who resisted the division of Korea could not enjoy the life spans given to them by God. Some, like Kim Koo, were killed by guns or stabbed to death by the hands of Cain, by the hands of men who rebelled against the will of God. Some, like Reverend Chun Dukee, were tortured to death. The length of their lives was shortened arbitrarily by the forces of the imperialist superpowers.

The sin of rebelling against God through the violation of the integrity of creation, through the destruction of the beauty and harmony of the Korean peninsula, was ultimately committed by military-industrial elites in collaboration with these superpowers, with Western European and North American colonial powers, and with Japan in Asia. This is a continuing sin based on action that followed the division thinking of the Taft-Katsura mentality.

DIVISION THEOLOGY, IMPERIALISM, AND THE VIOLATION OF LIFE

A kind of quasi-theology arose from the Taft-Katsura model. This quasi-theology is exemplified in the lives of men like the medical missionary Dr. William B. Scranton. Scranton was born in New Haven, Connecticut, graduated from Yale University, and received his M.D. degree from Columbia University in New York City. He was in certain respects a dedicated, loyal, and faithful servant of God, and he spent his life in Korea treating countless numbers of patients. He was one of the founders of the Sangdong Methodist Church, one of the first churches in Seoul City, and was at one time a district superintendent of the Methodist Church in Korea. In 1905 Imperial Japan forced Korea with guns and swords to sign a protectorate treaty and arrested all the diplomatic rights of Korea. This was the first stage of the colonialization of Korea by Japan. The Young Adult Association in the Sangdong Methodist Church began an active but nonviolent protest against Japanese Imperial colonialization. In response, Dr. Scranton, with the power of the district superintendent of the Methodist Church, disbanded the Young Adult Association of the church.

Dr. Scranton also took action against the pastor of the church, warning him not to make any political protests against the Japanese colonialization of Korea. This pastor, Chun Dukee, was very active in organizing the Shin Min Hwoe (New People's Meeting), which had been working for the self-reliance, independence, and self-development of Korea, working in opposition to threats of colonialization by Japan. Numerous national leaders met with Chun Dukee, using the church as a secret gathering place. Among these were Yi Dongwhee, who later organized the Korean Communist Party, the first Communist Party in Asia; Kin Koo, who was respected as one of the genuine leaders of the Korean people for an undivided Korean peninsula and who was later assassinated by ultra-right-wing terrorists; and Yi Choon, the patriot who killed himself for the peace and independence of Korea.

Scranton's warning to Chun Dukee and his disbanding of the Young Adult Association indirectly and directly contributed to the processes of enslavement and destruction of life. Scranton's faith was informed by the Taft-Katsura model; it was centered in the interests of the imperialists. This first-world orientation led him unwittingly to support the destruction of humans and other living beings in Korea. In the language of the World Council of Churches, his actions against the people and the natural communities in the Korean peninsula were actions against the integrity of creation.

The Japanese colonial government, that resulted from the colonization, suppressed Christianity. It prohibited Korean ministers from reading the story of Exodus, the story of another enslaved people which rose up against another imperialist force; and from reading the book of Revelation, the story of passive resistance against the Roman Empire. Indeed, Korean Christians were not allowed to sing "Onward Christian Soldiers" because the Japanese government thought this hymn—and the biblical stories mentioned—would conscientize the people to fight against Japanese colonialism. These were the strategies of Japan to suppress the anti-Japanese independence movements among Korean Christians and to distort their faith.

What was the situation of human ecology in Korea under the Japanese colonial government? Young men in the Korean peninsula went to the proxy war and died there for the Japanese version of world peace and justice in Asia. Young women were forcefully "volunteered" to the Women's Volunteer Corps and then misused as military prostitutes. Each woman was responsible for fifty to one hundred Japanese soldiers per day. They were systematically raped and subsequently died. There is no single memorial statue for the 200 thousand Korean women who died for the cause of the so-called justice and peace of the world.[2] It is fair and essential to remember that many Christians supported these historical sins of imperialism, these and other cruelties by which imperialistic colonialism systematically destroyed the created order of nature, men, and women in the Korean peninsula.

Unlike the Israel of prophecy in Ezekiel, chapter 37, a Korea liberated from the Japanese in 1945 was still not a unified land. As noted above, the American general MacArthur divided Korea at this time. He and the United States divided Korea into two without any consent or even prior notice to any single Korean. This action was a clear violation of the rights of the Korean people. It further destroyed the life of the people and forcefully divided the members of countless families. Indeed, my own grandmother has been in North Korea since 1945, and my family has not heard anything of her for forty-three years. Division theologies fail to attend to those communities which are families, and which are among the most beautiful creations of God.

The United States decision to divide Korea clearly destroyed the integrity of many families. The south was placed under the Interim Military Government of the United States. Those who advocated unification were arrested, imprisoned, killed, eliminated from society, and labelled procommunist and leftist. Most of the Christians in the south, informed and guided by division faith, division ideology, and division theology, supported the "south-only election," which assured permanent division of the north from the south.

Division theologies—by which families are separated, cultural traditions undermined, and natural communities destroyed—characterized even some of the most astute of Western theologians. For example, John C. Bennett, one of the greatest Christian political ethicists and former professor at Union Theological Seminary, supported the United States foreign policy as a sort of manifestation of the justice, peace, and will of God.[3] In actual fact, his support was the affirmation of the separation of families, husbands and wives, and the division of a whole people in the Korean peninsula. His theology was, as far as it concerned the Koreans, an imperialistic division theology. Later, in his book *Radical Imperative: From Social Ethics to Theology*, Bennett confessed his mistakes, and came to see that his view of American foreign policy in the 1940s and 1950s, a view that took American policies as manifestations and realizations of the kingdom of God, was gravely in error.

Reinhold Niebuhr also made mistakes in understanding Korea. In 1950 he interpreted the Korean War as a war against Russian communist world expansionism. His perspective had been centered on the U.S. and Russia and did not do justice to the Koreans, the scapegoats in this proxy war between the superpowers (see Noh, 1983). In his *Intellectual Autobiography* Niebuhr, like Bennett, confessed his misinterpretation and his lack of fair attention to the destiny of Koreans and Vietnamese, scapegoats under the situations of proxy war (Niebuhr). Division ideologies, division faiths, and division theologies of the Koreans were products in many ways of the theologians of the superpowers. Such ideologies would eventually lead to the destruction of both human ecology and the biosphere in the Korean peninsula.

THE HUMAN AND NONHUMAN CONSEQUENCES

What have been the practical consequences of these persistent efforts to divide Korea? Let us look. They include the sexual exploitation of women and the murder of protesters on Cheju Island; the development of a dependency upon nuclear powers; and an increasing dependence on polluting industry.

Cheju Island: Sexual Exploitation and Death

There is a beautiful island called Cheju in the southernmost part of the Korean peninsula. There are many oranges produced on this island, and it is one of the most popular honeymoon sites. It is also a popular place for international tourists in general and Japanese men in particular. This island is known as an island with an abundance of three things: wind, rocks, and women!

How romantic to see that there are many women in the southernmost island of Korea! However, not many people realize that there is a reason there are many women in that southernmost island with lots of oranges, tourists, and newlyweds. In fact, no one seems to ask the serious human ecological question of why there are so many women proportionally to men. Historical data on this matter has been legally banned from being published in any form for the last forty years. On 1 March, 1947, at a memorial rally on the island for the independence movement of 1919, two people were killed by government forces. Incidents on 3 April, 1948, led to the killing of eighty thousand islanders—out of a total of 300 thousand who were labelled communist guerillas or pro-communists. Nearly one-third of the population on the island was killed. Almost all the males were eliminated. It will be the research task of engaged theological and biocentric ethics to know how many noncombatant civilians were killed in that massacre. According to the secret documents of the Far East Command, United States, later released to the public, the slogans of the Cheju Islanders were for the establishment of a self-reliant, unified Korean government and denied the division of the Korean peninsula, denying the south-only elections which eventually divided Korea permanently (see Merrill).

In 1988, on this island where almost all males were killed, there are many Geisha houses for *non-Korean men only*, each of which can entertain three hundred to five hundred Japanese men, men who do not need visas to come to the island for sex tourism. Is this a manifestation of the beautiful order of God's creation? The descendants of the women of the Japanese Women's Volunteer Corps who were forced into military prostitution have, in the 1980s, dedicated themselves to the sex tourism of Japanese men. In a twisted way, their work has been praised as patriotic and nation-building because it brings foreign money into the country. In a sermon, the pastor of one of the largest Pentecostal churches on the island called the action of the Geishas patriotic and then declared that these women should give more to the church from their income. Researchers at the International Christian Seminar on Women and Sex Tourism held on 20 April, 1988, at the Y.M.C.A. on Cheju Island reported that the Geishas, chatting to one another, said, "We need to have more Japanese tourists, so that we can give more to the church." Is this destruction of the human ecology representative of the integrity of God's perfectly harmonized order of creation? This destruction involves the oppressed women of the most severely oppressed people in Korea. Such a violation of human ecology must be analyzed with regard to the domination of Korea by foreign powers and the divide-and-conquer strategies that continue to dehumanize the victimized people of the third world. So, too, must the current problems of nuclear weapons dependency. So, too, must the destruction of the ecological biosphere.

Nuclear Dependency

Currently the Korean peninsula is not self-reliant but is rather absolutely dependent on the nuclear war strategies of the superpowers in general and those of the United States in particular. It has been reported by many sources that there are more than enough nuclear bombs in South Korea to destroy the peninsula biologically forever. Reports indicate that there are from 120 to twelve hundred United States nuclear bombs in South Korea, and that there are approximately forty thousand United States ground troops stationed there. Russian nuclear weapons are targeted at South Korean military installations. American ground troops and civilians have efficient evacuation plans ready in case of emergency nuclear war. But there have been no reports on evacuation plans for the forty million Koreans in the south (it is not fair to comment on the case of North Korea without clear evidence).

Recently the Philippines has legislated a law declaring that those who bring nuclear weapons into the territory of the Philippines will be imprisoned for a sentence of at least six years and up to a maximum of thirty, and that all airplanes or ships carrying nuclear bombs will be arrested.[4] There have been indications that the United States has explored plans to relocate the United States military from the Philippines to Taiwan. Such a relocation was strongly opposed by Taiwanese women delegates to the recent International Christian Seminar on Women and Sex Tourism, who insisted that it could result in making Taiwan a place of sex tourism for American soldiers. In the face of potential opposition, the United States has also examined the possible relocation of forces in the Philippines to Korea. Is it the case that the divided Korean peninsula will be the United States spare depot for nuclear bombs? Without prior notice to the NATO nations, United States troops are not allowed to use nuclear weapons in Europe. But in the case of the Korean peninsula, United States troops do have the power to start using nuclear weapons without any consent from the people, including the Korean commanders.

As was the case when Korea was divided in 1945, a decision-making structure that totally and intentionally ignores the opinions of any single

Korean—including the current Korean Commander-in-Chief of the military forces in Korea—is applied now to nuclear-war strategies in Korea. From the time of the Korean War in 1950, an American was until just recently the commander-in-chief of all military forces, including the Korean forces, in South Korea. The decision-making structure still is not only an obstruction of internal justice, but it is a violation of international justice and of the sovereignty of Korea.

Korean life is threatened and the basic biological rights of Koreans are critically violated by the nuclear strategies of the United States. Neither can Russian responsibilities be ignored, since their nuclear weapons are ready to strike any part of the Korean peninsula. In the unfortunate case of nuclear war, Pyungyang City might be bombed by the nuclear warheads. What does this say of the survival of people in Seoul City? If Wonsan City is bombed, could the people of Kangnung City, Sokcho City, or Woolsan City in the south expect to survive? And what of nonhuman life in both the north and the south? What of the biosphere of the peninsula itself? What of even the fish in the Imjeen River or in the seas west and east of Korea? Americans in Korea have efficient evacuation plans, but the Koreans and the other living beings on the peninsula do not have such an escape. The entire peninsula and all its inhabitants are threatened with absolute devastation.

Japan declared an anti-nuclear policy by her constitution. Legally Japan is nuclear-weapon free. The Philippines also does not want to house nuclear weapons. Then why should Korea become the victim of the nuclear weapons of Russia and the United States?

But there are other problems.

Pollutant-Dependent Industry

Not long ago tens of thousands of people mourned the death of a fifteen-year-old boy who died of toxic poisoning as the result of working only six months in a mercury-producing factory. This is but a single example of how a once united land has become the scene of continued exploitation, and the example must be understood set against a recent background of general violence, division, and exploitation of Korean people and Korean land.

In April 1970, following a 1969 Nixon-Sato communique, the Mitsuya plan was proposed and subsequently implemented. The plan's main points were as follows:

1. A unitary Japan-Republic of Korea (ROK) economic cooperation zone should be created to operate in the 1970s so that the two countries can develop a sort of Asian EEC (common market).

2. Japan will relocate to the South Korean industrial zone its steel, aluminum, oil refining, petrochemical, shipbuilding, electronics, plastics, and other industries that cannot be maintained in Japan because of pollution.

3. In view of the shortage of labor in Japan, Japan will also shift its labor-intensive industries to the ROK.

4. The ROK government will strictly prohibit labor disputes at factories for these Japanese-ROK joint ventures.

5. Flexible domestic measures will be taken within the ROK to facilitate this mode of operation (see Noh 1983).

This plan, one which again commits crimes of the Taft-Katsura type and of division theologies, is clearly exploitative. As with the problem of nuclear weapons, it clearly conjoins exploitation of and threats against the well-being of human beings with the exploitation of and threats against all of nature. This plan has been realized in what is now a pollution-dependent Korea through the cooperation of Japan and the United States. Ultra-right-wing theologies in Korea have interpreted the transfer of pollution-dependent industry to the ROK as a blessing, as a manifestation of God's miraculous assistance toward economic growth. But this transfer of technology and industry from—and the resulting reality of a dependency on—the United States and Japan threatens the entire biosphere, the entire Korean peninsula. The mass destruction of human life—as in the Bhopal incident in India or the Chernobyl nuclear incident in Russia—could happen at any moment in Korea. The annihilation of human and nonhuman life is increasingly possible.

The economic policies of this plan have resulted in the systematic destruction of the sphere of food production in Korea, which now imports fifty to sixty percent of its total needs, mostly from the United States. Korea is now a country dependent for its food on the United States, although Korea had been self-reliant in terms of food production for thousands of years.

Up until the 1960s, eighty percent of the total population was located in the farming countryside. Now only twenty-seven percent lives in the agricultural sectors of the land. As is happening in so many parts of the world where Western models of development have prevailed, rural communities have been destroyed. Because of increasing food imports, there is no way for farmers to survive without giving up food production and that ecological sphere in which they once worked. Food is a weapon in neo-colonialistic capitalism. The food-dependent state cannot be politically self-reliant. In the Korea of today, Korean bachelor men who remain to live as farmers in the countryside are unable to find brides. Their livelihood is threatened from all sides. Because of imports of beef from the United States, farmers have had to kill their own cows—and often themselves—because of debts they have incurred in the current economic situation. Farmers have consistently lost their lands to become mere tenants. These peasants—so connected as they have been to the earth—have been the heart of the Korean nation. In 1894, Korea experienced the literal fall of a nation when peasants were killed in the Peasants' Revolutionary War (see Noh 1987 and Noh 1988).

TOWARD A THEOLOGY OF SILVER FISH IN THE IMJEEN RIVER

To overcome the current critical situation, a theology of Jubilee must be declared in the land. Korean theologies have directly or indirectly supported the division of Korea, the violation of the integrity of creation, and the division-based psychoses and insecurities that have resulted from this violation and from the manipulation, intervention, and invasion of foreign superpowers. Korean theologies have been division theologies. They have led Korea toward an almost absolute submission to domination by the superpowers, a dehumanizing and degrading submission that has resulted in depressive frustration and neurotic inferiority complexes. As a consequence of this submission, Korean leaders and police have vented their frustrations by torturing their people, violating human rights, and raping subversive women students (as in the case of Deacon Moon Kiidong). These reactions are the symptoms of the collective division psychosis suffered by almost all the Korean people, a psychosis that has developed for over forty-four years. The only medication for such a sickness is the autonomy, self-reliance, and self-determination of the nation in an ecologically responsible way. A process for strengthening the people's power and reunifying a land that has been systematically victimized by the superpowers calls for a theology of reunification and self-reliance. The Korean situation calls for a theology like the one embodied in the following story of fishes in a divided land, a theology of silver fish.

In January 1987 Park Chongchul, a Seoul National University student, was arrested by the police, who simply wanted to question him about another friend's whereabouts. After overnight torture with water, and as a result of this torture, Park died. The police cremated his body hurriedly and tried to eliminate the evidence by throwing the ashes into the streams of the Imjeen River, which runs between the divided north and south of Korea. The life of one student, who shouted out for the autonomy, self-reliance, and reunification of a divided land and for the democratization of military dictatorships, was chemically reduced to a few grams of calcium, nitrogen, and so on. After the cremation, these chemical elements—the ashes—were thrown into the river. I dreamed that they became the numerous silver-colored fishes in the river. My hope is that these silver fish will live forever, or at least for as long and as far as the Imjeen River flows. They will swim in the demilitarized zone that divides Korea into two.

What we need is a theology of silver fish, a theology that moves beyond division thinking toward respect for the integrity of creation. A theology of silver fish will guide us into that beautiful unity of people in relation to one another and in relation to the earth, but it must do so by overcoming the division ideologies of foolish theologians and the division faiths of misguided Christians. If a theology of silver fishes emerges, one that respects the integrity of the Korean people and their beautiful peninsula, division theologies based on the division psychosis will be transformed into theologies that respect living communities of people and land. Then the memory of Park Chongchul, and the many others like him who have suffered so much, can be redeemed. Then the silver fish of the Imjeen river can themselves enjoy the unpolluting peace of the living Christ.

NOTES

1. Ki-baik Lee writes, "Roosevelt felt, moreover, that it was necessary to acquiesce in Japanese domination of Korea as a quid pro quo for Japan's recognition of U.S. hegemony over the Philippines. This deal between the U.S. and Japan is revealed in the secret Taft-Katsura Agreement of July 1905. England, too, in renegotiating the terms of the Anglo-Japanese Alliance in August 1905, acknowledged Japan's right to take appropriate measures for the 'guidance, control, and protection' of Korea" (Lee, 309).

2. A monument related to this problem has been built recently in Chiban Prefacture, Japan. See Chung-Ok Yoon (a professor at Ewha University) 1988.

3. John C. Bennett writes: "I recognize in myself a too bland acceptance of national trends in the 1940's and 1950's. The fact that there was considerable harmony between my ethical convictions and the policies of the United States Government during the Second World War and during the early years of the cold war contributed to this" (Bennett, 9-10).

4. *Chosun Daily News*, 27 May 1988.

WORKS CITED

Bennet, John C. *The Radical Imperative: From Theology to Social Ethics*. Philadelphia: Westminster Press, 1975.

Lee, Ki-baik. *A New History of Korea*. Trans. Edward W. Wagner. Seoul: Ilchokak, 1984.

Merrill, John. "Chejudo Rebellion." In *The Island That Never Sleeps*. Ed. Youngmin Noh. Seoul: Onnuree, 1988.

Neibuhr, Reinhold. "Intellectual Autobiography" in *Reinhold Niebuhr: His Religious, Social, and Political Thought*. Ed. C. W. Kegley and R. W. Bretall. New York: Macmillan, 1967.

Noh, Jong Son. *First World Theology and Third World Critique*. New York: Sung Printing Co, 1983.

————. *Religion and Just Revolution*. Seoul: Voice Publishing, 1987.

————. *Toward a Theology of Reunification: Third World Christian Ethic*. Seoul: Hanwoolsa, 1988.

Yoon, Chung-Ok. "Report at the International Christian Conference on Women and Sex Tourism," Chejudo Y.M.C.A, 20 April 1988.

10

Community of Life: Ecological Theology in African Perspective

Harvey Sindima

How we think about the world affects the way we live in it. In particular, our understanding of nature—our cosmology—affects the way we understand ourselves, the way we relate to other people, and, of course, the way we relate to the earth and other forms of life. For some time the people of Africa have been influenced by a cosmology inherited from the West: the mechanistic perspective that views all things as lifeless commodities to be understood scientifically and to be used for human ends. Yet these people have an alternative way of looking at the world, an alternative cosmology, which can better serve their needs for cultural development and social justice in an ecologically responsible context. This alternative way might be called a life-centered way, since it stresses the bondedness, the interconnectedness, of all living beings. In what follows I will (1) examine

That Christian theology throughout its history has been transformed by sources outside of Christianity is a well-known fact. That it *should* be open to transformation through the insights of the various traditions, that it *should* be open to the possibilities of creative transformation by contact with the wisdom and vision of other sources, is highly controversial. Many of the authors in this book, however, are committed to such openness as an essential part of their own Christianity. Moreover, most would argue that we must repent of some aspects of the Christian experience that have been exploitive or destructive to peoples and to nature. In this essay African theologian Harvey Sindima proposes a traditional African view of life and community, which opposes the mechanistic world view that has so dominated Christianity in the West since the Enlightenment. It is the mechanistic world view, imported to Africa, which has been largely responsible for many eco-crises faced by Africa and which has led us in many ways to the global crises we face today.

the sort of cosmology imposed on African thinking by the West and (2) explore the traditional African view of creation and life as a healthy alternative to this vision. The chapter is divided into two sections corresponding to these aims.

THE PROBLEM

The Mechanistic World View

The problems that are arising from a misuse of science and technology — our loss of ecological balance, for example — demand that we look seriously at different ways of thinking and living in the world. The present ways of understanding the world and the models of living informed by these views are leading humanity to self-destruction. The African concept of the *bondedness of life*, to which I will return in the second part of this chapter, is a viable alternative that could provide a foundation for a doctrine of creation and for the transformation of society. If a vision of the bondedness of all life informed and regulated the structures and actions of government and church, it would transform the way socio-political, economic, and ecological decisions were made. The ministries of the church — preaching, pastoral care, and the church's general involvement in the life of the people and nature — would be transformed.

What prevents the traditional vision of the bondedness of all things from influencing government policies and church ministries in Africa? The answer to this all-important question obliges us to analyze the last two centuries or so of Africa's socio-political biography. During that period the West intensified its contacts with Africa because of the growing demand for African resources and labor overseas. The early titles of the African novelist Chinua Achebe, *Things Fall Apart* and *No Longer at Ease*, capture what happened in the two centuries following this intensified contact. Achebe's novels show the African attempt to fight against European domination of thought and values.

The West introduced a system of thought and a manner of living new to Africa. This system of thought manifested itself in various ways, particularly in a cultural imperialism, which was taught in schools and preached in the churches. Any system of domination uses three modes of control: coercion and reward; dependence; and thought control (Baker). The last mode is the most subtle of all forms and is a technique that seeks to uproot a people and impose on that people a value system different from their own, doing so until the people become obsessed with the values so imposed. The higher one's education, the greater his or her disorientation. This disorientation process begins with corrupting thought and language, for people interpret and understand their experience or reality, that is, their cosmology, through these media. Consequently, people's emotions and relationships become conditioned by a new "reality." If a people's thought system is corrupted, their value system is destroyed; the "world" or cosmology that informs their way of life has been ruined. This corruption continues as long as the people do not come to a realization of who they are. Without such self-consciousness a people cannot reject the disorienting language, that is, the process of alienation becomes total. This is what Western cultural imperialism sought to do to Africans.

With the imposition of Western cultural views, the African hermeneutical process — the process by which African people appropriated their own heritage — became so impaired that the Africans ceased to understand their world through their own cultural system or through the symbolic interpretation given by their cosmology. Today this impairment prevents the traditional concept of the bondedness of life from being an organized logic informing African life and practice.

In this chapter I use the word *mechanistic* to refer to that view of the world and its attendant manner of living that informed the thinking and behavior of the Westerners who brought this impairment. The mechanistic view takes the world to be like a machine with many parts, each working according to the laws of nature. To understand the world, one has only to know these laws. Society, as well, is conceived as a megamachine[1] in which nature and people are objectified. The model of living in this megamachine is accordingly mechanical. People are seen as atomistic individuals whose interactions and interrelationships are valued according to function and utility alone. Feelings and emotional needs are not important. Hence, concern and care do not enter everyday living. Moral conduct in a mechanistic society is often guided by self-interest, and often there is no agreement on what is "moral." Mechanistic society undermines the ties that bind persons and their communities to one another and to the cosmos.

The mechanistic perspective which has now shaped Africa itself has a history, originating in the seventeenth and eighteenth centuries with work in philosophy and science by thinkers such as Descartes, Bacon, Newton, and others. In this era, nature was reduced to mathematics or transformed into quantitative physical phenomena which could be grasped by rationality. Nature was purely *other* and merely material to be subjugated and manipulated. It had only instrumental value, determined by the extent to which people could use it. With this vision of nature in place, the stage was set for the rise of materialistic philosophy and its attendant manner of life. This way of life has captivated much of Western civilization ever since, and has been exported to all places this civilization has gone in its quest of material resources and to fulfill its expansionist philosophy.

Part of the mechanistic perspective involves adherence to the myth of progress. For Descartes, Bacon, and Newton, science implied unlimited growth. Technology became the application of the rules of nature established by science to specific needs for human ends. Through science and technology, human mastery over nature seemed complete and progress assured.

The notion of progress has been very compelling in Western civilization. Many believed progress was the way in which misery would be eliminated in the world. However, as the centuries have shown, the alliance of progress, science, and technology has not eliminated misery. On the contrary, destitution has emerged and the future of all creation hangs in the balance. Progress through (industrial) technology creates exploitation of resources and people and has often damaged the ecological balance and threatened the livelihood of those who depend upon that balance. This alliance of progress, science, and technology has led to social, ecological, and spiritual bankruptcy.

Exploitation

Let us consider some examples of this exploitation. First, the ivory trade. The demand for ivory abroad is the reason for the large decrease of elephants in Africa. But elephants play a very important role in the ecological balance. They contribute significantly to the welfare of other animals. Elephants are the only animals with an extra sense to locate water in the ground. With their tusks elephants make a hole in the ground to get at water as deep as three feet below the surface. Elephants drink about sixty-five gallons of water at a given time. They also like mud because they play and bathe in it. Furthermore, mud serves as moisturizer for their unusually dry skin. Because of this great need for water, elephants make a hole in the ground large enough for their massive bodies. In the process they make a pool from which other animals find water they need. This explains why many animals are found in areas where elephants are in large numbers. Kill elephants for their tusks to satisfy aesthetic beauty abroad, and many animals will die of thirst at home. The ecological balance to which elephants have contributed is destroyed.

Ecological balance is also destroyed when people want to take more from nature at one time than nature's internal mechanism allows for the balance of the system. Science has the ability to promote life when rightly applied, but its potential to destroy ecological systems is great. Informed by marine biologists, an effort was made in the 1960s to increase tonnage of fish caught in Lake Victoria, Africa's largest lake. To increase tonnage, marine biologists recommended introduction of Nile perch, some of which grow to be six feet long. The perch took to the lake with a vengeance and have destroyed scores of all fish. Once again, the ecological balance was changed. It does not take much thinking to know that the introduction of the perch into Victoria had a negative result for the people who depend on the lake for their livelihood and protein. The desired increased tonnage is still in the future!

Attempts for high productivity may be appropriate, but the price and who will pay the price must always be taken into account. Usually it is those already struggling to make ends meet who pay the price for national gambles. Science, or at least its technological application, has much to answer for in Africa in this respect. In the name of high productivity Africans were encouraged to use fertilizers. Most of these fertilizers were not tested for the particular soils in which they were being used. This resulted in the use of the wrong types of fertilizers. Consequently, soils were burnt with the wrong salts applied to them and made unable to produce as much as had been hoped.

Malawi

Malawi, my own country, provides a more specific example of some of the problems identified above. In Malawi the staple diet for a large population of the country is made from corn flour. In an attempt to increase production of corn, agriculture experts recommended introduction of a hybrid corn, *Malawi Hybrid*, commonly known as MH 12, 15, or 32. The numbers stand for specific hybrid categories. This corn grows two to three long cobs with big ears on one stock, and it grows faster than the traditional corn. Its big ears, however, are softer and therefore absorb water much more quickly than the traditional corn. Because of its softness and quick absorption of water, MH 15 and the others get rotten very fast. Insects quickly infest the ear. To preserve it for some time, even for a few months, insecticides have to be used. For reasons best known to agricultural "experts" in the country or because of economic considerations, the insecticide commonly used by farmers or stocked by local farmers' clubs is dichlorodiphenyl-trichloroethane (DDT). How safe is DDT for human consumption? Furthermore, this breed of corn is unsuitable for the tropics because of the high rainfall these areas get. The corn begins to rot even before it is harvested. For Malawi, the problem is compounded by the fact that rain water permeating through the walls of traditional granaries gets to the corn. The walls of traditional granaries are made of bamboo or twigs and their roofs are thatched grass. A roof on top of the granary prevents the corn from direct exposure to rain but does very little to keep it from getting rotten. Thus a family that worked very hard for months may find it has less food to carry it through to the next harvest because all its corn is rotten. Worse still, the family will have no money, yet it has to pay back a loan from the local farmers' club from which it got the MH 15 seed. All this, for high productivity!

The result of these and other examples has been suffering on the part of people and other creatures. Until people learn to be responsible in their relations with nature, until people realize that they are a part of nature and that nature is part of them, unnecessary suffering will abound. People need to learn to take care of nature.[2]

THE RESPONSIBILITY OF EXPERTS AND OF WESTERN CHRISTIANITY

The examples I have given above indicate what happens when moral responsibility is replaced by greed, and when the mechanistic perspective prevails. Over the past two centuries the mechanistic concept of the world and its attendant manner of living, a manner of living inundated with greed, has destroyed the African system of thought and values; it has ruined our vision of and interaction with nature. Our ability to interpret the world as we understood it and live accordingly has been weakened; not only has our sense of basic values been affected but our very vision of life has been undermined. Our very identity has experienced a crisis.

Illustrative of this identity crisis has been an overreliance on mechanistically inclined "experts" at the expense of trusting in the intelligence of traditionally minded African people. For example, in the last few decades the crisis has been compounded by the recommendations that Africa has received from the "development experts." Indeed, the very concept of development has its roots in the notion of progress and is essentially a materialist philosophy bent on unlimited growth of exploitation and accumulation. The African bureaucrats and political elite who operate within the Western vision of the world continue the philosophy of accumulation under the heading of development. This explains why politicians and the bureaucratic elite are unable to draw on our concept of the bondedness of life as they decide on national policies.

Even Christianity cannot be excused. Christianity, though a Middle-Eastern phenomenon, came to Africa in the last century as part and parcel of Western culture and civilization. That being the case, Christianity only compounded the problem of the crisis of values for Africans. Through preaching and education churches changed traditional value systems. As traditional values crumbled, the hermeneutic ability of our people became deeply affected. This is to say, Christianity weakened or impaired our ability to interpret and reconstruct systems of values and norms that give meaning to our lives. All the more important that Africans, particularly African Christians, rediscover traditional African values and rethink Christianity in a non-Western, African way. As we will see, this envisioning process may have relevance to people in other parts of the world as well.

THE AFRICAN CONCEPT OF CREATION

The African understanding of the world is life-centered. For the African, life is the primary category for self-understanding and provides the basic framework for any interpretation of the world, persons, nature, or divinity. For Malawians, life originates in the divine *Moyo*. Part of the very process of life involves a tendency toward self-transcendence, which itself aims toward *umunthu*, or the fullness of life. In the human sphere the process of life achieves fullness when humans are richly connected to other people, to other creatures, and to the earth itself. Humans realize their own fullness by realizing the bondedness of life.

To reclaim this notion of life, of life as characterized by a deep and thorough bondedness, is to find a correction to the mechanistic view which has been imposed upon African thinking, and which has led to the exploitation and suffering of humans and other creatures alike. In what follows, I briefly explore (1) *Moyo* as the foundation of life, (2) *umunthu* as the aim of life, and (3) notions of justice and community which are entailed by life itself.

Moyo as the Foundation of Life

In a Public Broadcasting Service documentary series titled *The African* (1986), Ali Mazrui, one of the leading African political scientists, finds an example of the African vision of interrelatedness and bondedness with nature in the way Africans think of the forest. Mazrui pointed out that the forest provides the African with all basic needs—food, materials for building a home, medicine, and rain; it also provides a sanctuary for religious practices as well and a home for the fugitive; in addition, it serves as a cemetery and the abode of ancestral spirits. In short, the forest is everything for the African.

In so many ways nature in general plays an important role in human life and in the process of human growth. It provides all that is necessary for a person to live and develop. This means that nature and persons are one, woven by creation into one texture or fabric of life, a fabric or web characterized by an interdependence between all creatures. This living fabric of nature—including people and other creatures—is sacred. Its sanctity does not mean that nature should be worshipped, but does mean that it ought to be treated with respect. John Mbiti comments on this vision of nature as follows:

It emerges clearly that for African peoples, this is a religious universe. Nature in the broadest sense of the word is not an empty impersonal object or phenomenon; it is filled with religious significance. . . . This is one of the most fundamental heritages of the African peoples. It is unfortunate that foreign writers, through great ignorance, have failed to understand this deep religious insight of our peoples; and have often ridiculed it or naively presented it as "nature worship" or animalism. . . . The physical and spiritual are but two dimensions of one and the same universe. These dimensions dove-tail into each other to the extent that at times and in places one is apparently more real than, but not exclusive of, the other. To African peoples this religious universe is not an academic proposition: it is an empirical experience, which reaches its height in acts of worship (Mbiti, 73-74).

For the Malawians the universe is full of sacred life, full of life that transcends itself through fecundity, that in its abundant creativity continues to cross frontiers and break forth into new dimensions, always recreating itself and presenting people with ever new possibilities.

Moyo is the Malawian word for such life. *Moyo*, written with a lower case *m*, is both physical and spiritual. In part, *moyo* is life as it is manifested in biological existence. As such it is shared by, and bonds together, all living things. But *moyo* is also spiritual and sacred: even *moyo* as it is manifested in biological existence is rooted in the Mystery. Divine life, signified by the capitalized *Moyo*, is the source and foundation of all *moyo*. All life—that of people, plants and animals, and the earth—originates from and therefore shares an intimate relationship of bondedness with divine life; all life *is* divine life. Mulago speaks of this vision of life as follows:

> It is a whole of life, individual inasmuch as it is received by each being which exists, communal or collective in as much as each being draws from a common source of life . . . It is life as it has been derived from the source of "power," as it turns towards power, is seized by it and seizes it (Mulago, 138).

Holding that human life is inseparably bound to nature, and that both human life and that of other creatures are one with the divine, the Malawians find it alien to objectify nature as the other or to see nature as having only instrumental value. The African notion of the bondedness of all beings in sacred *moyo*, in one texture of life, fosters a sense of care for all of creation. It entails a manner of living guided and enriched by respect, by a stance that allows the rhythms of life to flow.

Nature has rhythms and patterns through which *moyo* flows. It is our responsibility to keep ourselves from interrupting the flow of *moyo*; it is imperative that we avoid changing or reversing these rhythms and patterns. The future of a people depends upon how that people relates to nature and exercises its human responsibility.

Umunthu: *The Aim of Life*

For the African, human life is a fiber in the fabric of the totality of life. The phrase "being-in-plenitude" best describes the African notion of persons because it emphasizes the unity or connectedness of persons to one another and to nature. We cannot understand persons, indeed we cannot have personal identity, without reference to other persons. Nor can we understand ourselves without reference to nature. People understand themselves and gain identity only in a total framework of life. They are defined as they engage in work, ritual practice, and symbolic activities. But they must also understand themselves as belonging to nature, as living the life of nature. It is through their relationships with nature that people discover their identities and approach the possibility of living life fully. As nature opens itself up to people, it presents possibilities for experiencing the fullness of life, possibilities for discovering how inseparably bonded people are to each other and to all of creation.

Furthermore, when traditional Africans think of creation they think of the relation between human life and nature; a world without people is unthinkable to them, for it is an incomplete world. *Moyo* continually breaks frontiers and reaches superabundance. It continuously transcends itself as it aims at greater and greater fullness of life. Human life completes the picture of this process of creation. Through their rich relationships with life, with nature, and with one another, individuals give themselves new meaning and achieve *umunthu*, fullness of life. Similarly, creation achieves new meaning through these persons. In many ways, *moyo* transcends itself as the possibilities for the realization of *umunthu* are created.

Community and Justice

In the African view of the world, the word community refers to more than a mere association of atomic individuals.[3] The term itself suggests bondedness; it refers to the act of sharing and living in communion and communication with each other and with nature. Living in communication allows the stories or life experiences of others to become one's own. The sharing of life's experiences affirms people and prepares them for understanding each other. To understand is to be open to the life experience of others and to be influenced by the world of others. In community, we share and commune with selves who are other than ourselves and yet united to us by both *moyo* and *Moyo*. In being open to the other, we are given possibilities for transformation and for reaching *umunthu*.

Persons are not individual entities or strangers to one another. They are nature itself seeking fullness in the actuality of present life. Since people belong to the fabric of life, their life—like nature—must be respected. This call for respect is also a charge to the community to create possibilities for persons to realize full personhood. In a community of life where all are bonded together, everyone is responsible for everyone else:

> What falls on one, falls on all. In such a relationship, the issue is the re-establishment of community, the re-establishment of the circulation of life, so that life can go on transcending itself, go on bursting the barriers, or the intervals, the nothingness, go on being superabundant (Boulaga, 81).

A community of life emphasizes being-together for the purpose of allowing life to flow and for the purpose of creating possibilities for achieving *umun-*

thu. The notion of being-together is intended to emphasize that life is the actuality of living in the present together with people, other creatures, and the earth. Justice in such a community must be based on a sense of the bondedness and oneness of life:

We must repair every breach of harmony, every wound and lesion. We must demand reparation for ourselves because we are not merely ourselves, and for others because they are also ourselves, the what-and-who of our pre-existence and survival, the what or who of some manner of our "presupposing" ourselves (Boulaga, 81).

Justice is how we live in the web of life in reciprocity with people, other creatures, and the earth, recognizing that they are part of us and we are part of them.

CONCLUSION

As we see, *moyo, umunthu,* community, justice, nature, and the power of life are inseparable. Together they represent the bondedness of life. This notion of the bondedness of life has informed some African Christian thinking where that thinking has attempted to transcend the mechanistic views imposed on Africa by the West, where that thinking has drawn upon the rich heritage of Africa itself. But such life-centeredness could also serve as a vital basis for all Christian thinking and action, as a guide and an empowering vision for the Christian movement to alleviate the suffering and exploitation of living creatures worldwide.

And there is urgent need to consider a model for the transformation of society, a model which will take bondedness and the relationship between people and other creatures seriously.[4] Social structures and policies must find a basis in life itself, and in the notion of justice as it is entailed by the life we creatures share with each other and the divine. Community must be based in a consciousness that all creatures are part of all others, that humans share a common destiny with nature. Community, and the vision that puts forth that community, must be dedicated to the fullness of life for people, for other animals, for plants, for the Earth, indeed for all expressions of the divine *Moyo.*

NOTES

1. This is a term Lewis Mumford has designated in describing the differences in visions and ways of life of Western and other societies.

2. There are a few examples where projects exhibiting care for nature have been embarked upon in Malawi. The restoration of the country, which begins every year in December with the tree planting day, December 21, is a good sign of care for nature. The project is done by all Malawians. The Ministry of Forestry through its

nurseries throughout the country sells the seedlings at a cheap price, about three cents a seedling, cheap enough for most people to afford. Game parks are another sign of hope, especially when attention is given to animals that may soon be endangered species, such as the twenty-four hundred elephants now under special protection in the Game Parks. In an attempt to preserve nature, Malawi in 1982 became the first country in the world to create an underwater national park designed to protect fish. According to ichthyologists, Lake Malawi has nearly a thousand species of fish, many of which exist nowhere else in the world. But what will happen to this park if Malawi follows the U.N. proposal to introduce fresh water sardines into Lake Malawi? According to U.N. marine biologists, these sardines could produce as much as ten thousand tons of protein. At what price will that be in terms of the ecological balance of the lake? What will be the future of the sixteen thousand Malawians whose livelihood depends on the lake?

3. The differences between African and Western concepts of community are well-argued by Menkiti (Menkiti, 179).

4. I have described the question of transformation in another work, *Community of Life: Foundations for Religious and Political Transformation*.

WORKS CITED

Achebe, Chinua. *Things Fall Apart*. London: Heinemann, 1962.

———. *No Longer at Ease*. London: Heinemann, 1963.

Baker, Donald. *Politics of Race: Comparative Studies*. Westmead and Lexington, MA: D.C. Heath, 1975.

Boulaga, F. Fboussi. *Christianity Without Fetishes: An African Critique and Recapture of Christianity*. Trans. Robert R. Barr. Maryknoll, NY: Orbis Books, 1984.

Mazrui, Ali. *The Africans*. A Public Broadcasting Service television series, 1986.

Mbiti, John S. *African Religions and Philosophy*. New York: Doubleday, 1970.

Menkiti, Ifeanyi A. "Person and Community in African Traditional Thought." *African Philosophy*. Ed. Richard A. Wright. Lanham, MD: University Press of America, 1984.

Mulago, Vincent. "Vital Participation: The Cohesive Principle of the Bantu Community." *Biblical Revelation and African Beliefs*. Ed. Kwesi Dickson and Paul Elingworth. Maryknoll, NY: Orbis Books, 1971.

Mumford, Lewis. *The Myth of the Machine, Part Two: The Pentagon of Power*. A Harvest Book. New York: Harcourt Brace Jovanovich, 1970.

Sindima, Harvey. *Community of Life: Foundations for Religious and Political Transformation*. Cambridge: Cambridge University Press. Forthcoming.

PART 4

New Sensibilities

Christianity is an evolving tradition. It grows, in part, when its members explore new ways of thinking in light of the most urgent needs of the time. It also grows through criticisms and challenges from outside its tradition, including challenges from other religions and from the earth itself. Indeed, Christianity is an ongoing process of creative transformation, sometimes from within and sometimes from without.

All of the authors in this section believe that new, radically ecological thinking is needed in our time. Indeed, they believe that more than new thinking is needed; rather, new feeling is needed, new spirituality. They challenge Christians toward new, ecologically responsive modes of thought, feeling, and action. In our view, the emergence of ecologically sensitive traditions in Christianity will involve new thinking of the sort proposed in these essays, as well as thinking that draws from the Bible and tradition, as proposed in the first section. In the coming decades some forms of ecological theology will be traditional; others will be post-traditional; and still others will be both.

11

The Spirituality of the Earth

Thomas Berry

The subject with which we are concerned is the spirituality of the earth. By this I do not mean a spirituality that is directed toward an appreciation of the earth. I speak of the earth as subject, not as object. I am concerned with the maternal principle out of which we were born and whence we derive all that we are and all that we have. In our totality we are born of the earth. We are earthlings. The earth is our origin, our nourishment, our support, our guide. Our spirituality itself is earth-derived. If there is no spirituality in the earth, then there is no spirituality in ourselves. The human and the earth are totally implicated each in the other.

Not to recognize the spirituality of the earth is to indicate a radical lack of spiritual perception in ourselves. We see this lack of spiritual insight in the earlier attitude of Euro-Americans in their inability to perceive the spiritual qualities of the indigenous American peoples and their mysticism of the land. The attack on these spiritual qualities by Christians constitutes one of the most barbaric moments in Christian history. This barbarism turned upon the tribal peoples was loosed also upon the American earth with a destructive impact beyond calculation.

The fragility of the earth has not yet impressed itself upon us. The crassness of our relation to the earth cannot but indicate a radical absence of spirituality in ourselves, not the lack of a spiritual dimension of the earth.

For Thomas Berry and for those who follow him, the earth, in a very real sense, is our *mother*. We are born from this mother, from Gaia; we are extensions of the earth and the cosmos of which it is a part. This means that our conceptualizing and our spirituality also extend from the spiritual dimension of the cosmos and the earth. As Berry makes clear, Christians have often failed to acknowledge the spirituality and numinous presence of the earth. But we are also experiencing a turn in our awareness, developing new consciousness in dialogue with the sciences, with other faiths, with ourselves as men and women, and with the earth itself.

The opaqueness is in our understanding of the earth, not in the earth's structure which expresses an abiding numinous presence. The earth process has been generally ignored by the religious-spiritual currents of the West. Our alienation goes so deep that it is beyond our conscious mode of awareness. While there are tributes to the earth in the scriptures and in Christian liturgy, there is a tendency to see the earth as a seductive reality, which brought about alienation from God in the agricultural peoples of the Near East. Earth worship was the ultimate idolatry, the cause of the Fall, and thereby the cause of sacrificial redemption by divine personality. Thus, too, the Christian sense of being crucified to the world and living only for the savior. This personal savior orientation has led to an interpersonal devotionalism that quite easily dispenses with earth except as a convenient support for life.

We can produce Christian spiritualities that function in a certain isolated context without regard for the larger society. But such redemptive spiritualities are not liable to be effective in our present world. They speak a rhetoric that is not available for our world, or, if it is available, widens rather than lessens the tragic inner division between the world of affairs and the world of divine communion. They do not offer a way of interpreting the inner life of the society itself in a rhetoric available to the society. They do not establish an understanding of that authentic experience in contemporary life oriented toward communion with creation processes. Indeed, they do not recognize that the context of any authentic spirituality lies in the creation myth that governs the total life orientation.

Creation in traditional Christian teaching is generally presented as part of the discussion concerning "God in himself and in relation to his creation." But creation in this metaphysical, biblical, medieval, theological context is not terribly helpful in understanding the creation process as set forth in the scientific manuals or the textbooks of the earth sciences as they are studied by children in elementary or high school, or later in college.

These classroom studies initiate the child into a world that has more continuity with later adult life in its functional aspect than does the catechetical story of creation taken from biblical sources. This schoolroom presentation of the world in which the child lives and finds a place in the world is all-important for the future spirituality of the child. The school fulfills in our times the role of the ancient initiation rituals, which introduced our children to the society and to their human and sacred role in this society. The tragedy is that the sacred or spiritual aspect of this process is now absent. It is doubtful if separate catechetical instructions with their heavy emphasis on redemptive processes can ever supply what is missing.

It may be that the later alienation of young adults from the redemptive tradition is, in some degree, due to this inability to communicate to the child a spirituality grounded more deeply in creation dynamics in accord with the modern way of experiencing the galactic emergence of the universe, the shaping of the earth, the appearance of life and of human consciousness, and the historical sequence in human development.

In this sequence the child might learn that the earth has its intrinsic spiritual quality from the beginning, for this aspect of the creation story is what has been missing. This is what needs to be established if we are to have a functional spirituality. Just how to give the child an integral world — that is the issue. It is also the spiritual issue of the modern religious personality. Among our most immediate tasks is to establish this new sense of the earth and of the human as a function of the earth.

We need to understand that the earth acts in all that acts upon the earth. The earth is acting in us whenever we act. In and through the earth spiritual energy is present. This spiritual energy emerges in the total complex of earth functions. Each form of life is integrated with every other life form. Even beyond the earth, by force of gravitation, every particle of the physical world attracts and is attracted to every other particle. This attraction holds the differentiated universe together and enables it to be a universe of individual realities. The universe is not a vast smudge of matter, some jelly-like substance extended indefinitely in space. Nor is the universe a collection of unrelated particles. The universe is, rather, a vast multiplicity of individual realities with both qualitative and quantitative differences all in spiritual-physical communion with each other. The individuals of similar form are bound together in their unity of form. The species are related to one another by derivation: the later, more complex life forms are derived from earlier, more simple life forms.

The first shaping of the universe was into those great galactic systems of fiery energy that constitute the starry heavens. In these celestial furnaces the elements are shaped. Eventually, after some ten billion years, the solar system and the earth and its living forms constituted a unique planet in the entire complex of the universe. Here on earth life, both plant and animal life, was born in the primordial seas some three billion years ago. Plants came out upon the land some six hundred million years ago, after the planet earth had shaped itself through a great series of transformations forming the continents, the mountains, the valleys, the rivers and streams. The atmosphere was long in developing. The animals came ashore a brief interval later. As these life forms established themselves over some hundreds of millions of years, the luxuriant foliage formed layer after layer of organic matter, which was then buried in the crust of the earth to become fossil formations with enormous amounts of stored energy. One hundred million years ago flowers appeared and the full beauty of earth began to manifest itself. Some sixty million years ago the birds were in the air. Mammals walked through the forest. Some of the mammals — the whales, porpoises, and dolphins — went back into the sea.

Finally, some two million years ago, the ascending forms of life culminated in the awakening human consciousness. Wandering food gatherers and hunters until some eight thousand years ago, we then settled into village life. This life led us through the neolithic period to the classical civilization which has flourished so brilliantly for the past five thousand years.

Then, some four hundred years ago, a new stage of scientific development took place which in the eighteenth and nineteenth centuries, brought about human technological dominance of the earth out of which we had emerged. This stage can be interpreted as the earth awakening to consciousness of itself in its human mode of being. The story of this awakening consciousness is the most dramatic aspect of the earth story.

The spiritual attitude that then caused or permitted humans to attack the earth with such savagery has never been adequately explained. That it was done by a Christian-derived society, and even with the belief that this was the truly human and Christian task, makes explanation especially harsh for our society.

Possibly it was the millennial drive toward a total transformation of the earth condition that led us, resentful that the perfect world was not yet achieved by divine means, to set about the violent subjugation of the earth by our own powers in the hope that in this way the higher life would be attained, our afflictions healed.

While this is the positive goal sought it must be added that the negative, even fearful, attitude toward the earth resulting from the general hardships of life led to the radical disturbance of the entire process. The increasing intensity shown in exploiting the earth was also the result of the ever-rising and unsatiated expectation of Western peoples. Even further, the natural tensions with the earth were increased by the Darwinian principle of natural selection, indicating that the primary attitude of each individual and each species is for its own survival at the expense of the others. Out of this strife, supposedly, the glorious achievements of earth take place. Darwin had only minimal awareness of the cooperation and mutual dependence of each form of life on the other forms of life. This is amazing since he himself discovered the great web of life. Still, he had no real appreciation of the principle of intercommunion.

Much more needs to be said on the conditions that permitted such a mutually destructive situation to arise between ourselves and the earth, but we must pass on to give some indication of the new attitude that needs to be adopted toward the earth. This involves a new spiritual and even mystical communion with the earth, a true aesthetic of the earth, a sensitivity to earth needs, a valid economy of the earth. We need a way of designating the earth-human world in its continuity and identity rather than in its discontinuity and difference. In spirituality, especially, we need to recognize the numinous qualities of the earth. We might begin with some awareness of what it is to be human, of the role of consciousness on the earth, and of the place of the human species in the universe.

While the scholastic definition of the human as a rational animal gives us some idea of ourselves among the biological species, it gives us a rather inadequate sense of the role we play in the total earth process. The Chinese have a better definition of the human as the *hsin* of heaven and earth. This word *hsin* is written as a pictograph of the human heart. It should be translated by a single word or phrase with both a feeling and an understanding aspect. It could be thus translated by saying that the human is the "understanding heart of heaven and earth." Even more briefly, the phrase has been translated by Julia Ch'ing in the statement that the human is "the heart of the universe." It could, finally, be translated by saying that we are "the consciousness of the world," or "the psyche of the universe." Here we have a remarkable feeling for the absolute dimensions of the human, the total integration of reality in the human, the total integration of the human within the reality of things.

We need a spirituality that emerges out of a reality deeper than ourselves, even deeper than life, a spirituality that is as deep as the earth process itself, a spirituality born out of the solar system and even out of the heavens beyond the solar system. There in the stars is where the primordial elements take shape in both their physical and psychic aspects. Out of these elements the solar system and the earth took shape, and out of the earth, ourselves.

There is a certain triviality in any spiritual discipline that does not experience itself as supported by the spiritual as well as the physical dynamics of the entire cosmic-earth process. A spirituality is a mode of being in which not only the divine and the human commune with each other, but we discover ourselves in the universe and the universe discovers itself in us. The Sioux Indian Crazy Horse called upon these depths of his being when he invoked the cosmic forces to support himself in battle. He painted the lightning upon his cheek, placed a rock behind his ear, an eagle feather in his hair, and the head of a hawk upon his head. Assumption of the cosmic insignia is also evident in the Sun Dance Ceremony. In this dance the symbols of the sun and moon and stars are cut out of rawhide and worn by the dancers. The world of living moving things is indicated by the form of the buffalo cut from rawhide, and by eagle feathers. The plant world is represented by the cottonwood tree set up in the center of the ceremonial circle. The supreme spirit itself is represented by the circular form of the dance area.

So the spiritual personality should feel constantly in communion with those numinous cosmic forces out of which we were born. Furthermore, the cosmic-earth order needs to be supplemented by the entire historical order of human development such as was depicted on the shield of Achilles by Homer and on the shield of Aeneas by Virgil. Virgil spends several long pages enumerating the past and future historical events wrought on the shield of Aeneas by Vulcan at the command of Venus, the heavenly mother of Aeneas. All these cosmic and historical forces are presently available to us in a new mode of appreciation. The historical and the cosmic can be seen as a single process. This vision of earth-human development provides the sustaining dynamic of the contemporary world.

That there is an organizing force within the earth process with both physical and psychic dimensions needs to be acknowledged in language and in imagery. It needs to be named and spoken of in its integral form. It has a unified functioning similar to the more particular organisms with which we are acquainted. When we speak of earth we are speaking of a numinous maternal principle in and through which the total complex of earth phenomena takes its shape.

In antiquity this mode of being of the earth was indicated by personification. "Earth" itself designates a deity in Hesiod and in the Homeric hymns. This personification is expressed as Cybele in the Eastern Mediterranean and as Demeter in the Greek world. Biblical revelation represents a basic antagonism between the transcendent deity, Jahweh, and the fertility religions of the surrounding societies. There is a basic effort here to keep the asymmetry in the relationship between the divine and the created. In the doctrine of the Madonna in later Christian history there are many passages indicating that Mary was to be thought of as the Earth in which the True Vine is planted and which had been made fruitful by the Holy Spirit. Probably it belongs to the dialectics of history that direct human association with unique historical individuals, the savior and his mother, had to develop before any adequate feeling for the mystique of the earth could take place. Perhaps, too, full development of redemption processes was needed before this new mode of human-earth communion could find expression in our times.

However this may be, a shift in attention is now taking place. Several things are happening. The most notable single event is that modern science is giving us a new and more comprehensive account of our own birth out of the earth. This story of the birth of the human was never known so well as now. After the discovery of the geological stages of earth transformation and the discovery of the sequence of life in ancient fossil remains by Louis le Clerc, James Hutton, and Charles Lyell, came the discovery of the emergence of all forms of life from primordial life forms by Charles Darwin, presented in his *Origin of Species* in 1859. While Darwin saw the human appearing only out of the physical earth, Teilhard de Chardin saw the human emerging out of both the physical and the psychic dimensions of the earth. Thus the whole burden of modern earth studies is to narrate the story of the birth of the human from our Mother the Earth.

Once this story is told, it immediately becomes obvious how significant the title Mother Earth is, how intimate a relationship exists, how absolute our gratitude must be, how delicate our concern. Our long motherless period is coming to a close. Hopefully, too, the long period of our mistreatment of earth is being terminated. If it is not terminated, if we fail to perceive not only our earth origin but also our continuing dependence on our earth-mother, then our failure will be due in no small measure to the ephemeral spiritualities that have governed our own thoughts, attitudes, and actions.

In this mother-child relationship, however, a new and fundamental shift in dependence has now taken place. Until recently the child was taken care of by the mother. Now, however, the mother must be extensively cared for by the child. The child has grown to adult status. The mother-child relationship needs to undergo a renewal similar to that in the ordinary process of maturing. In this process both child and mother experience a period of alienation. Then follows a reconciliation period when mother and child relate to each other with a new type of intimacy, a new depth of appreciation, and a new mode of interdependence. Such is the historical period in which we are now living. Development of this new mode of earth-human communion can only take place within a profound spiritual context. Thus the need for a spirituality that will encompass this process. As a second observation concerning our newly awakening sense of the Earth, we could say that a new phase in the history of the madonna figure of Western civilization has begun. Association of the Virgin Mother with the Earth may now be a condition of Mary returning to her traditional role in Western civilization. Her presence may also be a condition for overcoming our estrangement from the earth. In the Western world the earth known only in itself as universal mother is not sufficient. It must be identified with an historical person in and through whom earth functions in its ultimate reaches. Phrases referring to Mary as the Earth are found throughout Western religious literature. Whether this is anything more than a simple rhetorical device needs a thorough inquiry at the present time. But whether or not this relationship is given in any extensive manner in prior Christian literature, it is a subject of utmost importance for our entire civilizational venture. Few, if any, other civilizations were so deeply grounded in a feminine mystique as the medieval period of Western Christendom. A vital contact with this earlier phase of Western civilization is hardly possible without some deep appreciation of its feminine component. Thus we cannot fail to unite in some manner these two realities: Earth and Mary. In Western Christian tradition earth needs embodiment in an historical person, and such an historical person needs an earth identity to fulfill adequately her role as divine mother.

A third observation is that emergence of the new age of human culture will necessarily be an age dominated by the symbol *woman*. This, too, depends on the identification of woman with the earth and its creativity. Woman and Earth are inseparable. The fate of one is the fate of the other. This association is given in such a variety of cultural developments throughout the world in differing historical periods that it is hardly possible to disassociate the two. Earth consciousness, woman consciousness; these two go together. Both play a stupendous role in the spirituality of humans as well as in the structure of civilizations. Our alienation from the earth, from ourselves, and from a truly creative man-woman relationship in an overly masculine mode of being, demands a reciprocal historical period in which not only a balance will be achieved but even, perhaps, a period of feminine emphasis.

A fourth observation I would make is to note our new capacity for subjectivity, for subjective communion with the manifold presences that constitute the universe. In this we are recovering the more primitive genius of humankind. For in our earlier years we experienced both the intimacy and the distance of our relation with the earth and with the entire natural world. Above all we lived in a spirit world, a world that could be addressed in a reciprocal mood of affectionate concern. This is what gave rise to sympathetic magic as well as to the great rituals, the majestic poetry, and the awesome architecture of past ages. Nothing on earth was a mere "thing." Every being had its own divine, numinous subjectivity, its self, its center, its unique identity. Every being was a presence to every other being. Among the more massive civilizations, China gave clearest expression to this intimacy of beings with each other in its splendid concept of *Jen*, a word that requires translation according to context by a long list of terms in English, terms such as love, goodness, human-heartedness, and affection. All beings are held together in *Jen*, as in St. Paul all things are held together in Christ. But perhaps an even better analogy is to say that while for Newton, the universal law of gravitation whereby each particle of matter attracts and is attracted to every other particle of matter in the universe indicates a mere physical force of attraction, the universal law of attraction for the Chinese is a form of feeling identity.

For this reason there is, in China, the universal law of compassion. This law is especially observable in humankind, for every human has a heart that cannot bear to witness the suffering of others. When the objection was made to Wang Yang-ming in the fifteenth century that this compassion is evident only in human relations, Master Wang replied by noting that even the frightened cry of the bird, the crushing of a plant, the shattering of a tile, or the senseless breaking of a stone immediately and spontaneously causes pain in the human heart. This would not be, he tells us, unless there exists a bond of intimacy and even identity between ourselves and these other beings.

Recovery of this capacity for subjective communion with the earth is a consequence and a cause of a newly emerging spirituality. Subjective communion with the earth, identification with the cosmic-earth-human process, provides the context in which we now make our spiritual journey. This journey is no longer the journey of Dante through the heavenly spheres. It is no longer simply the journey of the Christian community through history to the heavenly Jerusalem. It is the journey of primordial matter through its marvelous sequence of transformations—in the stars, in the earth, in living beings, in human consciousness—toward an ever more complete spiritual-physical intercommunion of the parts with each other, with the whole, and with that numinous presence that has been manifested throughout this entire cosmic-earth-human process.

12

Religious and Cosmic Homelessness: Some Environmental Implications

John F. Haught

In recent philosophical and theological literature concerning the world's current environmental crisis the root cause is often identified as our relentless anthropocentrism. An exaggerated impression of human significance concentrates valuation so intensely on our species that intrinsic importance is drained away from the rest of nature. No doubt the self-centeredness of our species is a factor in the neglect of the rest of nature. But if we are to come to the roots of the problem, we have to go deeper into the mythic, theological, and scientific ways of thinking upon which our anthropocentrism is erected. Our anthropocentrism is intimately related to, perhaps based upon, a pervasive sense of *cosmic homelessness*, which we must recognize first if we are to understand the role of anthropocentrism. For anthropocentrism is a secondary reaction to the fear engendered by our species' apprehension of its sense of being "lost in the cosmos." It is an understandable and forgivable groping for significance that follows a prior

If we are to meet the environmental needs of our time, it is important that we accept our surroundings—the earth and the universe itself—as a hospitable habitat, a home. Yet much of the theology and science that we inherit as Christians leads us to a different way of experiencing our surroundings, to a sense of cosmic homelessness. Indeed, some sense of homelessness is at the heart of what many of us know as religion. Must this latter sense of homelessness be entirely rejected? John Haught argues not. While criticizing the nature-denying tendencies of religious homelessness, Haught finds value in that aspect of homelessness that elicits in us a sense of adventure. Like Thomas Berry, he affirms that we are very deeply connected to the cosmos even *in* our self-transcendence; our sense of adventure is itself part of the adventure of the universe itself. In his own way Haught underscores what many Christian theologians of nature wish to affirm: Nature itself is not a fixed, static whole, but rather an unfinished process of which our own lives, and our own hopes and dreams, are expressions.

disenfranchisement of the specifically human from a value-bestowing cosmic matrix. Thus it is of little ethical value for us to attack frontally our anthropocentric tendencies. Instead I suggest that we examine and address the feeling of cosmic exile, to which anthropocentrism is an inappropriate and indeed disastrous "solution."

Even apart from its contributing to the rise of anthropocentrism, however, the feeling of not being at home in nature is environmentally consequential. The contemporary environmental crisis is closely connected to inherited ways of thinking that have fostered a feeling in us that we are not really at home in the universe. As long as we fail to experience how intimately we belong to the earth and the universe as our appropriate habitat, we will probably not care deeply for our natural environment.

Both theology and science have promoted cosmically homeless habits of thought in the past. Today there are signs in both of these disciplines that some of us are tiring of cosmographies that have left us exiles in the universe. But these new developments have not yet become dominant. They continue to meet resistance among the orthodox of both camps. They appear at times to be pseudo-scientific to the mainstream scientists, and the corresponding developments in religion are accused of succumbing to naturalism. In some instances such critiques are justifiable, but at other times they are out of place.

Only those ways of thinking that allow us to look on earth and universe as "home" can be environmentally wholesome. But this formula already raises questions for the religious. For is not one of the major themes of the religions that we *should* feel out of joint and even out of place in our immediate environment? Ever since the so-called axial period (from about the middle centuries of the first millennium B.C.E.) some of the major traditions have had strong other-worldly leanings and have promoted spiritual disciplines that have made us feel alien to the physical universe. At times these traditions have asked us to withdraw from the world since "we have here no lasting home." Homelessness has been idealized rather than suppressed. The Buddha leaves his wife and family. In our own traditions the call of Abraham to move into an unknown but promising future has been a central paradigm of self-transcendence. "The Son of Man has nowhere to lay his head." "We are only pilgrims on earth." Unless we feel somewhat out of place in terms of our immediate world we will hardly experience the religious stimulus to self-transcendence. For, according to the religions, it is only in a continually "going beyond" present actuality that humans achieve authenticity.

The biblical movement into history allegedly exiles us from "nature," and we are told that it is regressive piety to seek refuge from the "terrors of history" by returning to the regularities of nature. Even our "natural" sacraments are overlaid with historic meaning. We share with Hinduism and Buddhism some need to feel out of place as a condition for moving forward. And this exilic motif can easily be interpreted as a demand to move beyond the ensnarements of the physical cosmos.

What are we to make of such teachings at a time when it is becoming increasingly urgent to make the natural world our beloved habitat lest we perish of our own recklessness toward it? Is it not too easy to interpret the religious requirement of homelessness as a cosmic homelessness? Are they one and the same? If they are, then religion and religious thought will inevitably remain anti-environmental. And to many ethically sensitive people religions will become more and more irrelevant. Hence we need a hermeneutic of religions that distinguishes religious homelessness from cosmic exile. For if they are identified in a simplistic way, then being religious will continue to foster that very posture that provokes anthropocentrism as a defensive reaction.

focus

On the other hand, we cannot abandon the religious idealization of homelessness without violating our traditions. Being religious requires our not fitting too comfortably into present actuality. Religions of course tolerate homelessness only as part of the quest for our true home. It is not that religions are opposed to home, but rather that they resist our settling for something as home that is really not an adequate domicile for our infinite restlessness. Nothing less than inexhaustible mystery can be the appropriate abode for the human spirit. But does not the restlessness resident in religious visions perhaps encourage an escapism with respect to the cosmos? Or can we interpret religious homelessness in such a way as actually to foster a sense of being at home with the natural world? There are developments occurring in both science and theology today that not only allow but actually advocate such a synthesis. In a special way the image of the cosmos as itself a story or an *adventure* into mystery provides the key to such a hermeneutic.

As we explore these issues our itinerary will be as follows: (1) we shall look first at several ways in which reflection on science has contributed to the feeling of cosmic exile and therefore to our environmental carelessness; (2) then we shall examine how theologies from our own Christian tradition that have hovered closely, even though critically, around modern scientific cosmologies have perpetuated the same feeling of cosmic exile; and (3) finally we shall look briefly at how a cosmological understanding of religion centering on the notion of adventure can both reconcile us to the evolving universe and at the same time allow us to embrace the feeling of religious homelessness present in religious teachings.

SCIENCE AND COSMIC EXILE

Scientism

It is clear that our hostility to nature flows partly from a vision of the cosmos in which we humans are only accidentally present and essentially absent. Though the roots of this attitude can be found in ancient mythic and religious forms of thought, in the past three centuries the estrangement of human subjects from the natural world in turn has been built up in our imaginations under the influence of certain types of scientific epistemology and cosmology. Expulsion of the human subject from nature is implied in the scientific method of knowing which puritanically (one is tempted to say Gnostically) segregates the human knower from nature, and in the materialism, mechanism, or "hard naturalism," which follows from a severe logical divorce of physical reality from mental reality. By isolating the knowing subject from the object-world, dualism repudiates in principle the ecological presupposition of the interrelatedness of all entities in the cosmos. For in such an interpretation the knowing subject is no longer a part of the scientifically known universe. Subjectivity is epistemologically absent from the very universe that, according to scientific knowledge, gave rise to it in the first place.

Few will seriously deny that scientific objectivity is a worthy ideal for science. Questions arise only when a method that seemingly exalts impersonality, disinterest, and detachment is made into a cultural ideal governing all human knowledge and life. For the more widely an ideal of pure objectivity is applied across physical, biological, human, and cultural strata, the more likely we are to feel ourselves absent from the world.

The temptation to objectivist thinking is enormous. It seems to have borne much fruit in the advance of knowledge. The level of achievement in modern science seems to have occurred in direct proportion to the banishment of anthropomorphism from our explanatory schemes. Biology, for example, is said to have begun making considerable progress only after it got rid of the ideas of teleology and vitalism. Notions of purpose and life began to recede from biological interest as chemical explanation progressed. And in the human sciences the ideas of person, freedom, and dignity got in the way of a neutrally objective accounting for human reality. The way to move forward in science is apparently to exile life and eventually even personal subjects from the cosmos.

The scientific method of seeking explanation of all things, including the activity of persons, as far as possible in impersonal terms is a fruitful and worthy one. But this method, which deliberately leaves so much out (such as considerations of value, beauty, and purpose), has been taken by scientism as the only legitimate road to the real. This cognitional policy has dismissed, as irrelevant to true knowledge, all those "personal" aspects of knowledge that actually energize the whole project of pursuing scientific truth. It systematically denies, for example, the fiduciary aspects of knowing and relegates the element of discovery in science to the field of psychology. Thus, as Michael Polanyi says, it has led to a "picture of the universe in which we ourselves are absent" (Polyani 1964, 142).

The remote ancestry of this homelessness in scientism lies in the (religious) myth of dualism. Dualism prepares the way for scientism by rendering nature mindless and lifeless. And then through a series of philosophical transformations in our intellectual and spiritual history, it turns mind and life into strangers in the universe. They become "epiphenomenal" intruders into an inherently inanimate, mindless world. In spite of its explicit suspicion of religion, scientism remains tied to the same dualistic myths that have caused Christian and other religious spiritualities to distrust and even despise the natural world. Scientific and religious puritanism have a common ancestry, a fear of the physical in its swampy, wild, and untamed naturality.[1]

Scientism's roots in dualistic myth and in otherworldly religious Gnosticism can be readily traced. Its complicity in the power obsession of an industrial age and the resultant pollution is already widely acknowledged. There is no need here to elaborate further on the negative consequences of scientism for environmental ethics. We might mention, however, two related ideals often cultivated in our universities. The first is that of complete explanation of all natural phenomena, including life and mind, in terms of their particular constituents. And the second is the modern obsession with clarity and the corresponding revulsion toward any mistiness in the cosmos that might lie off limits to the control of scientific knowledge. The disdain for mystery implied in these two intimately connected standards of exploration has dramatically negative implications for how we regard the natural world in a scientific age.[2] Even though initially the quest for clarity and simplicity seems innocent enough, unless carefully contained it can become a weapon of power wielded ruthlessly to hack away the rich undergrowth of vagueness that goes along with any cherishing of mystery.

Thus to the extent that an environmental ethic would have to grow out of at least some appreciation and reverence for the mystery of nature, modern ideals of clear and exhaustive explanation can easily prove deleterious if they overrun their legitimate epistemological margins. One of the essential contributions of a theology of nature to the reshaping of our environmental outlook would be that of providing a new mystagogy, namely, a cosmically centered pedagogy into mystery, fully informed by modern scientific discovery. It would rethink the religiously indispensable idea of mystery from the perspective both of science and of religion. Without what Thomas Berry has called a "mystique of nature" we cannot cultivate the attitude of reverence that would be required to ignite an environmental ethic. Because of their obsession with reduction and clarity current scientistic attitudes hardly encourage such a mystique.[3]

On the other hand, theology remains for the most part out of touch with the discoveries of modern science, and so it fails to direct its mystagogical expertise toward a natural world that corresponds to a plausible cosmology. Christian theology, for example, continues to locate the arena of mystery primarily in the areas of history or existential subjectivity rather than nature. What it requires now is the development of a new mystique of nature that does not reject the subject and history, but which places them in a cosmic setting. Such a reenchantment of nature, one that avoids naivete, has been undertaken to some extent by process theology and by Jürgen Moltmann and creation-centered theology. In North America it has been developed most explicitly by Thomas Berry and the growing number of his students. And now the emerging scientific narrative of the universe as adventure provides a favorable backdrop for a new mystique of nature and a novel synthesis of science and religion.[4]

Scientific Materialism

The sense of exile from the cosmos is also promoted by scientism's scion, scientific materialism. Scientific materialism is the view that "matter" alone is real and that all phenomena in the universe can be adequately understood as special applications of the laws of chemistry and physics. It has its proximate origin in a number of assumptions brought to a head during the seventeenth century. Of particular interest to us here is the distinction of primary qualities such as mass, momentum, shape, and position from the secondary qualities (such as color, taste, sound, smell, and texture). The latter have been viewed in modern philosophy as the creations of a "subject," a subject isolated from the "real" world, that is, from the world of primary qualities. Ontological primacy has been given to the substrate valueless world of primary qualities, while the world of values has been relegated to the ontologically rarefied and highly subjective realm of secondary qualities.

The gulf between the isolated human subject and the "real," material world of primary qualities can be bridged only by the filmiest of webs, known in psychology as *projection*, an imaginative throwing forth of our wishes onto a cosmos intrinsically alien to our desires. Such projection can give us the illusion that we live in a compatible environment, but as long as we give ontological primacy to "primary" qualities we shall suspect, underneath it all, that our illusions are simply covering up the real world momentarily. We eventually realize that projection is hardly powerful enough to make us feel at home in the cosmos, and so we remain exiles from nature.

Among the projections precariously reconnecting us to the natural world as so envisaged are poetry, art, and religion. Symbolic or metaphoric modes of reference project a warm coating of color onto the cosmos, and this makes it a bit more habitable. But it is still not quite home, because we suspect deep down that the world is *fundamentally* alien to our projections. So in spite of religious myth and symbol we are still lost in the cosmos. We remain absent from the very universe we strive so mightily to understand with our sciences. Once we conceive our cultures and religions as projections, and perhaps concede to them a capacity to warm our hearts a bit, they are still not sufficiently substantive to call us back from exile.

This absence of a feeling of vital interrelationship with nature cannot but enfeeble a truly ecological vision. It fosters an attitude of cosmic homelessness that has provoked us to anthropocentrism as one way of salvaging some significance for ourselves in a world that gives no backing to our projects. In turn it has justified our disregard of an environment that seemingly fails to nurture our estranged subjectivity. Thus there is little hope for our recovering a feeling of truly belonging to the cosmos as long as we hold onto the assumptions about physical reality (such as the primacy of primary qualities and cognate assumptions) underlying scientism and materialism.[5] For we will continue to have a gnawing suspicion that the *real* world is so different from our projections that we are still without a home in the universe as it runs on colorlessly and meaninglessly beneath our secondary and tertiary "subjective" projections.

But what is the alternative to this modern view of a valueless noumenal nature existing underneath our impressions and rendering us value-seeking beings quite out of place on such terrain? First, we would have to recognize that the so-called primary qualities are really not so primary after all. Recent physics has challenged the assumptions of classical physics that gave priority to these easily quantifiable aspects of nature. And even apart from developments in physics, philosophers like Whitehead have shown that they are actually mathematical abstractions from a concretely complex and value-laden world, which hardly corresponds in fact to the sharp edges of the primary quantities. However, in a very subtle and persistent way the assumption of the primacy of primary qualities, or some noumenal substrate modeled on them, continues to affect much of our thinking today. And as I shall note a bit later, it still persists in a great deal of contemporary theology. We continue to suspect that the symbols and myths that reconcile us to the earth as our home have the same derivative and unreal status as the secondary qualities of Lockean philosophy. And as long as we doubt our religious symbols' realism they cannot deeply take hold of us or motivate us. Nor, for that matter, can they reconcile us with the cosmos. For we will look upon them as mere projections. Even psychologists like Jung, who was most favorably disposed toward the therapeutic value of the symbolic life, still have doubts about the ontological substantiality of religious myth and symbol. (Jung, for example, spoke often about their "psychological truth," an epistemologically vague expression, but not much about their possible ontological or revelatory integrity.)

As an alternative to the psychological interpretation we might begin to think of our symbols, myths, metaphors, and religions in a cosmological way, that is, not as psychic projections but as the flowering forth of energies and mysteries welling up from the depths of the universe itself. We need to outgrow our long held suspicion that human symbolic creativity is just futile gesturing done only by lonely subjects in an uncaring universe. At times, of course, our symbols may be little more than projections. But they may also be reflections of, or at least gropings toward, reality. Our symbols may be expressions of the universe rather than alien projections thrown back onto it by lost human subjects. Our religious symbols and stories are possibly no less a blooming of the *universe* than is a tropical rain forest. Symbolic activity is the cosmos itself groping toward further discovery through human organisms totally continuous with the evolutionary process.

Still, we cannot envisage our symbolic creativity in this way until we become convinced that we *ourselves* are an expression, a germinating from the depths of the universe, and not aliens imported from some other world. Myths of dualism still prevent us from deeply internalizing this insight. We have a long way to go before we can really *feel* our continuity with the cosmos without at the same time having to abandon the religious idea that human existence is in some sense also homeless wandering.

Scientific Materialism and Our Environmental Crisis

The philosophy of scientific materialism fails to provide a cosmological vision sufficiently grounded in the value orientation needed to promote a life-centered ethic. In spite of the environmental concern of many scientific authors who follow either a hard or soft naturalism, their theoretical (if not practical) acquiescence in the essentially hopeless view of a universe cannot inspire the trust in life needed for lasting ethical aspiration. Instead, if taken seriously as the basis for human life and thought, materialism would strangle any ethical aspiration. As far as an environmental ethic is concerned, the still dominantly materialist orientation of contemporary science is unable to provide the cosmic vision essential for lasting commitment to the preservation of the earth's life systems. We need a religious vision conceptualized in the form of a scientifically enlightened theological idiom.

Many scientists and scientific thinkers who embrace a materialistic naturalism are nevertheless ardent supporters of environmental reform. And the same cosmic pessimists who despair about any meaningful cosmic destiny, or who think the universe will ultimately culminate in a lifeless and mindless "heat death," are themselves often ethically committed to the flourishing of life and consciousness in our terrestrial quarters. Is there perhaps some irony in the fact that on the one hand they allow no ultimate significance to things, yet on the other hand they consider our environment to be worthy of care and reverence?

Perhaps not. To the materialists and cosmic pessimists there is really no contradiction; the inherent purposelessness of the web of life is not at all a good reason for our not caring for it. In fact, as far as cosmic pessimists are concerned the very indifference of the universe at large makes the local domain of life by contrast even more worthy of preservation. Our awareness of life's dubious perch on the slopes of entropy allows us to venerate it all the more intensely. Its precariousness gives life an exceptional value over against the insensate backdrop that makes up the bulk of cosmic reality. The very improbability of life makes it stand out all the more valuably in contrast to its mundane and inanimate cosmic setting.

So materialist scientists and philosophers can readily support environmental causes. They might even be suspicious that a teleological view of the cosmos would take our attention away from life's special status in our own earthly garden. Too much trust in an *ultimate* cosmic purpose might diminish our spontaneous respect for the delicacy of living forms to which evolution has unconsciously and painfully given birth on our insignificant planet. Would not a teleological cosmology allow us to postpone indefinitely any genuine concern for our immediate environment? Might not religions that posit a cosmic purpose allow us to remain indifferent to present environmental conditions? Is it even possible that the solace of some far off or *final* purpose might allow us to tolerate environmental abuse in the present?

This materialist grounding of an environmental ethic on a purely naturalistic and cosmically tragic foundation challenges us to rethink theologically the issue of cosmic purpose in a scientifically compatible and environmentally fruitful way. What religiously teleological vision, if any, might be more favorably disposed than a tragic naturalism toward inspiring an environmental care? Might not cosmic pessimism with its sharp intuition of the perishability of life be quite as capable of fostering a genuine love of our natural environment as would any religious teleology?

At first sight materialism's sensitivity to life's ephemerality might seem to be a sufficient reason for our cherishing the biosphere. But metaphysically speaking it is inadequate. For it can be argued that the mere perishability of something is hardly a rationally satisfactory basis for our valuing it. Followers of Whitehead, for example, would suggest that mere perishability alone is not a value. Perishability is even an argument against a thing's intrinsic importance. Any valued entity must possess some characteristics other than sheer evanescence in order to arouse our value sensitivity. Perishability alone will not suffice. It cannot adequately explain why life may be intrinsically (and not just instrumentally) valuable.[6] The reason we value life is not for its fragility, but for its beauty (see Haught 1986, 139-50). Beauty, not precariousness, is the basis of the intrinsic value of things. We often confuse the two since they are tied up so closely with each other. But they are not identical. In Whitehead's vision beauty is the harmony of contrasting elements. We are aesthetically attracted to those things, whether natural or artificial, that combine a wide variety of complexity, nuance, or shades of difference. Living beings, for example, arouse our aesthetic valuation because they integrate into themselves an almost incalculable number and variety of components. They have an intrinsic value that consists of their beauty.[7] The value of life, then, does not consist in its precariousness, but in the fact that it is an instance of intensely ordered novelty, of harmonized contrast, that is, of beauty. Beauty, of course, is always in danger of degenerating into monotony on the one hand or chaos on the other. It has an inherent instability that sometimes, especially in the biosphere, makes it temporary and precarious. But precariousness is not itself the basis of intrinsic value. The delicacy or frailty of living things is a consequence of their being syntheses of order and novelty or of harmony and complexity. In living beings there is an aesthetic tension between complexity and order that renders them exceedingly fragile. But the fragility is not itself the ground of their value. Their intrinsic value resides in the intensity of their beauty. Our reverence for nature and its ecological patterning can be situated best within this aesthetic vision.

Scientific materialism and less extreme forms of naturalism lack such a vision of nature's intrinsic value. They generally see beauty (and all values) as simply the creation of estranged human subjects, who project their own individual or communal sense of what is beautiful, and therefore valuable, onto the universe. But this universe remains for them inherently valueless and purposeless. So our valuations can only be the flimsy concoctions of cosmically homeless minds alone, and not the reflection of any inherent aspects of nature. Nature itself remains neutral and valueless at the sub-phenomenal level. All value comes only from our own "phenomenal" human estimation. Just as without us primary qualities would be colorless, tasteless, and odorless, so also without us the world would lack any value.

According to this philosophy nothing outside of us humans has intrinsic value, since all value is the product of human creativity. Such an assertion of human specialness may well contribute to a policy demeaning the environmental context over against which our "specialness" shows up by contrast. In the manner of Descartes, Kant, many existentialists, and ancient Gnostics, scientific materialists often presuppose an estrangement of the human mind from the impersonal, objective, natural world. This sense of discontinuity between the isolated scientific subject and the valueless universe is clearly illustrated in these remarks of a respected American philosopher:

> From the standpoint of present evidence, evaluational components such as meaning or purpose are not to be found in the universe as objective aspects of it. . . . Rather, we "impose" such values upon the universe . . . An objective meaning—that is, one which is inherent within the universe or dependent upon external agencies—would, frankly, leave me cold. It would not be mine. . . . I, for one, am glad that the universe has no meaning, for thereby is man all the more glorious. I willingly accept the fact that external meaning is non-existent, . . . for this leaves me free to forge my own meanings (Klemke, 69-72).

Because of its inability to find intrinsic value in the universe, scientific materialism fails as the adequate basis for any serious environmental ethic. Its proponents may personally support environmental causes, but this advocacy is not plausibly based on their cosmology. Rather it arises out of an ineradicable moral and aesthetic sensitivity that inherently contradicts their explicit metaphysics. A philosophy that theoretically resolves the animate world into an inanimate one can hardly provide the foundation for an environmental policy that strives to prevent this reduction from actually taking place (Commoner, 44).

Since such a view is premised upon a dualistic, cosmically homeless vision of things, it remains as environmentally questionable as the other worldly religiosity it criticizes. As the basis for an environmental ethic we would need a cosmology that attributes intrinsic value to life, mind, and the cosmos as a whole. In recent thought Whitehead's cosmology, though not without its own problems, appears to be a more than acceptable philosophical alternative.

THEOLOGY AND COSMIC HOMELESSNESS

However, scientism and materialism are not the only perpetrators of the strain of cosmic pessimism that ultimately undermines our ethical aspirations. Christian theology has also tolerated cosmic pessimism, combining it with an individualistically religious "optimism of withdrawal" from the world.[8] In doing so it has religiously legitimated the cosmic homelessness that underlies our present environmental crisis. Christian theology under the influence of dualism has directed us to look toward a spiritual world independent of the physical universe, and so it has perhaps innocently sabotaged human concern for the earth and life. And it is questionable whether much recent systematic theology has taken serious steps toward a more positive theology of nature. In fact, some current ways of doing theology may actually present obstacles to the construction of such a theology.

In several of its dominant strains Christian theology still clings to the same assumptions of cosmic homelessness that we find in scientism and materialism. In recent decades the most obvious example of this theology of exile is known as existentialist theology, which, especially in its Bultmannian form, continues to influence Western Christian theology, perhaps more than any other single school (see Kegley). Existentialist thought, whether theistic or atheistic, exalts human freedom. But it can find little place for freedom in the context of a deterministically understood natural environment. Thus it goes beyond the realm of nature (typically understood along Newtonian lines) in search of a place to situate human freedom. It has generally swallowed whole the cosmological assumptions of mechanism-materialism, but not being willing to embrace, as far as humans are concerned, the deterministic implications of materialism, it has located the realm of freedom completely apart from nature. There freedom is not subject to the physical laws governing the matter-energy continuum. However, for its apparent independence human freedom has to pay the price of being completely isolated from the cosmos.

Existentialist theology has resigned itself to an inexorable dualism of nature and freedom, thus implicitly endorsing the view that the core of human existence subsists in a domain completely different from the world of nature. We cannot overemphasize the extent to which this vision still reigns over contemporary theology. Perhaps it is partly because of the dominance of this neo-dualism that so few contemporary Christian systematic theologians are sincerely concerned about environmental issues.

The realm in which freedom is at home is called history in contemporary theology. Thus history has been sharply divorced from nature. Any form of natural theology has been held suspect. Correspondingly, the theme of creation has been subordinated to that of the history of (human) salvation. There is now the promise of overcoming this separation of nature and history, for science itself increasingly sees nature itself as a story, while theology is beginning to situate history within the theme of creation.[9] Theologians have for some time questioned the existentialist and historicist exile of subjectivity from nature. Gordon Kaufman, for example, pointed out some years ago that existentialist theology remarkably overlooks the simple fact that every mental or historical event is also an occurrence within nature, not outside of it.[10] And yet the assumptions of dualism and materialism continue to infect our theologies, including some of those that have begun to turn their attention to environmental issues.

If we are to move toward an environmentally wholesome theology of nature we may need to refashion dramatically our ways of understanding religion. I shall propose that we look at it not so much as acts or constructs performed by human beings on the face of a cosmic terrain that is intrinsically indifferent to religion, but primarily as expressions of the universe and the earth. We can have a cosmically adequate theology of nature only if we put the universe first and ourselves later in our theories of religion and in our theological methods. In order to unfold this conception we might draw upon Thomas Berry's simple but explosive statement that *the universe itself is the primary revelation* (Berry, 195).

Unfortunately, Christian theology itself has yet to adopt such an outlook, as does our whole scholarly way of looking at religions. In our universities and seminaries religion, including Christianity, is hardly ever viewed cosmologically instead of from the perspective of the social sciences, which share many of the assumptions of materialism and cosmic homelessness. Social science looks at religious activity and expression as something done *on* the earth by our species, instead of seeing it as something the earth does through us, as a further phase of evolution's groping toward mystery. Psychology and the social sciences are often, without being aware of it, governed by the premise that the human dimension is radically discontinuous with the natural. This is especially evident in the theory that symbolic expression is best understood as human "construction" or "projection." The projection theory of religion and culture feeds parasitically on the assumptions of materialism, such as its dichotomization of primary and secondary qualities, and on the parallel Kantian dichotomy of the noumenal and phenomenal worlds. According to this dualism, culture and religion are little more than the products of human creativity, located ontologically in the same sphere as secondary qualities. They are the "subjective" products of private sensation, subjective caprice or social consensus. By being relegated to this subjective territory they are demoted to the status of being "unreal" in comparison with the truly "real" primary cosmic qualities, which in themselves are odorless, colorless, valueless, and meaningless. This way of setting up the world and its relation to subjects is compelled to consign the whole realm of meaning and importance to that of the subject, for the "objective" world is itself devoid of inner worth.

The human sciences, in spite of some notable exceptions, are still under the spell of this dualistic-materialist way of thinking. They are inclined to make humans appear to be essentially value-creating, meaning-projecting beings, rather than natural emanations of an already value-permeated universe. Since the cosmos itself is intrinsically meaningless, it is up to *homo faber* to fill it with the meaning it lacks.

No one can seriously object to the supposition that creativity is an essential human attribute and responsibility. But this anthropological (and theological) observation has led in modern times to the peculiar position that there is no really significant creativity going on outside of us. Just as Cartesian dualism earlier segregated subjectivity from nature, the corresponding temptation now is to divorce creativity from nature. This dualism amounts to a further devaluation of the cosmos outside of the sphere of human creativity.

Christian theology is today still entranced by the same way of looking at religion that we find in the human sciences. Theology is under the spell of psychology, history, and sociology. It is seldom influenced deeply by cosmology. It too has become obsessed with the theme of human creativity at the expense of cosmic creativity. Theology still participates in a subtle devaluation of the nonhuman cosmos as deficient of that value, namely creativity, that is so highly esteemed in existentialism and humanistic social science. Its pervasive anthropocentrism follows not only from the ancient and modern versions of dualism, but also from the more recent philosophical divorce of creativity from the cosmos and its relocation solely in the human sphere.

Evolutionary thinking has made it possible for us to recover in a dynamic way the ancient intuition of the cosmos as primary creative subject. A theology in touch with this evolutionary vision might recapture the view of the universe or the earth as subject. And then it would locate our own creative subjectivity within the context of a more comprehensive one, that of the universe itself. This shifting of primary subjectivity from ourselves to the earth and the cosmos may run against the grain of our habit of turning nature into a mere object to be manipulated by our subjective control, but it would be both scientifically responsible and environmentally beneficial.

The assumption underlying much contemporary thought is that authentic human existence is achieved only in moments where we become fully conscious of our creativity.[11] The dominant anthropological image is that of *homo faber*.[12] The influence of Marx and existentialism is present here, and these two strands of modern thought are always suspicious of any ideological or religious inclinations to undermine a sense of our human productivity. As I have already suggested, though, worthy as such a suspicion may be at times, it still works sometimes within the horizon of a view of the human as essentially absent from the cosmos. For the world here is seen solely or predominantly as material "out there" to be molded by human creativity. Nature is interpreted as the object of human creating, and human subjectivity is represented as authentic only in the moment of grasping its own creativity over against the resistance and malleability of nature. There is still a subtle dualism operative here that can be overcome only if we recognize nature's inherent creativity even apart from us. Once again we find in cosmological approaches such as Whitehead's and Berry's an acknowledgment of the pervasive creativity of nature, whereas existentialist and psychologically based theologies tend to confine creativity to humans (and God) alone.[13]

Just as Cartesian thought had exorcised nature of any intrinsic mentality, existentialism, the humanistic tradition of sociology, and the theologies based on them, expel from nature its intrinsic creativity. The older dualism drained psyche, mind, and spirit from the physical universe and deposited this complex of mentality in the separated sphere of human subjectivity. Recent thought perpetuates dualism, though of a different sort, by neglecting the inherent creativity in the nonhuman sectors of the cosmos. The *homo faber* image embodied in existentialism, Marxism, and humanistic social sciences saps creativity from the cosmos and squeezes it into a culturally creative human subject or society. Such a vision leaves out the fact that our human creativity indwells a multilayered cosmos of emergent creativity. It is oblivious of the cosmic vision according to which human creativity is first of all a property of the universe and not simply our own subjective self-expression.[14]

RELIGION AND ADVENTURE

For religions, home in the deepest sense ultimately means mystery. Religions require for the sake of religious authenticity that our lives not be embedded too comfortably in any domain short of the inexhaustible mystery that is the ultimate goal and horizon of our existence. Thus fidelity to our religious traditions demands that we embrace the traditional ideal of religious homelessness as the point of departure for self-transcendence. But a commitment to religious homelessness can no longer coincide with an environmentally unhealthy cosmic homelessness, as it has done in the past.

How, though, can we hold together a feeling of fully belonging to the cosmos, while at the same time embracing the insecurity of a genuine religious movement into mystery? And can we do so in such a way that the feeling of being on an endless religious journey actually integrates us more fully with the cosmos instead of inspiring us to take flight from it? This seems to be a key question for spirituality and environmental ethics today.

If we could find an answer to it it would allow us hermeneutically to retrieve the best aspects of our religious traditions. And it would permit this retrieval to occur not in spite of our need to belong to nature but actually for the sake of reconciling us to the cosmos.

The best answer I have been able to find so far to our search for a context harmonizing religious homelessness with a genuine belonging to nature lies in the notion of a cosmic adventure. The idea of the cosmos as an adventure is able to integrate the biblical and other religious ideals of homeless searching with the environmental need to feel totally at home in nature. For nature too, as we now know from science, is and always has been restless. The cosmos itself appears now as the story of an adventurous quest. We can no longer idealize nature as a haven from the adventure of history. For it too is now seen to be fundamentally a story of restless searching. We no longer have to segregate it from history and the realm of freedom. We can now accommodate the cosmos itself to the theme of homeless wandering. If we are to be faithful to nature and our continuity with it, we must accept its inherent "insecurity" as the setting for humanity's spiritual adventure. The cosmos can now be envisioned not only as a point of departure for the spiritual journey but as fellow traveler into mystery. We now realize that we need the companionship of nature not as a paradisal refuge from history (though its beauties are seductive and tempting enough at times). We need its own inherent exploratory restlessness to energize, not to divert, our religious excursions.

Interestingly, we can see now that major developments in the character of scientific knowledge today help to make possible this synthesis of cosmic belonging on the one hand and religious wandering or sojourning on the other. Science, which had formerly presented us with cosmographies of a humanly uninhabitable universe, is now the main stimulus for a new story of the universe hospitable to our twin requirements: It appeals to the religious need for not putting down our roots too deeply as well as to the environmental need to make nature our true domicile.

In what sense? Science has increasingly and almost in spite of itself taken on the lineaments of a *story* of the cosmos. The cosmos has itself increasingly become a narrative, a great adventure. Although there have always been mythic and narrative undercurrents in presentations of scientific theory, the past century has brought forth a scientific vision that, starting from the Darwinian story of life on this planet, has moved back in time to embrace the astrophysical origins of the cosmos fifteen or twenty billion years ago. The most expressive metaphor for what science finds in nature today is no longer *law*, but *story* (Rolston, 119).

The narrative nature of science has enormous implications for issues in science and religion. And it is also of consequence for our problem of integrating traditional spirituality with an environmentally acceptable attitude toward nature. For some time this narrative aspect of cosmology has been a dominant theme in process theology. And it has recently been developed by Holmes Rolston in his book *Science and Religion*, and in a Roman Catholic context by Thomas Berry (see Lonergan and Richards, and Berry, 178-239) and Brian Swimme. Swimme, a Catholic physicist and follower of Thomas Berry, emphasizes how the narrative revolution in science is now capable of placing all our religious and other traditions against the more fundamental backdrop of a cosmic story. We now for the first time in our species' history have a story that can serve as the basis for intercultural and inter-religious encounter.

> The universe, at its most basic level, is not so much matter or energy or information. The universe is story. Bolstering my conviction that story is the quintessential nature of the universe is the story of how story forced its way into the most anti-story domains of modern science, I mean physics and mathematics. For physicists during the modern period, "reality" meant the fundamental interactions in the universe. In a sense, a modern physicist would regard the world's essence as captured by the right group of mathematical equations. The rest of it—the story of the universe in time—was understood as nothing more than an explication of these fundamental laws (Swimme, unpublished paper).

Swimme recalls the famous story of how Einstein himself resisted the narrative implications in his own equations. They indicated that the universe is expanding, in which case it would have had a singular origin and then unfolded sequentially in various phases of a genuine narrative. But "only when Edwin Hubble later showed him the empirical evidence that the universe was expanding did Einstein realize his failure of nerve. He later came to regard his doctoring of the field equations as the fundamental blunder of his scientific career" (Swimme, unpublished paper).

It is common scientific knowledge now that not only life, but the stars, galaxies, planets on the macroscale and the subatomic layers at the micro level are all involved in transformations to which the word story seems more and more applicable. Swimme notes that story

> forced its way still further into physics when in recent decades scientists discovered that *even the fundamental interactions of the universe* were the result of transformations in time. The laws that govern the physical universe today, and that were thought to be immutable and above development of the universe, were themselves the result of the development of the universe. That is, the story—rather than being simply governed by these laws—draws these laws into itself (Swimme, unpublished paper).

But the word story is not quite adequate. We might better characterize the cosmic process as an *adventure* story. Adventure, in the technical meaning given to it by process thought, is the search for ever more intense versions of ordered novelty.[15] The theme of the cosmos as adventure now lies at the center of scientific thought. And the integration of religious traditions with our new story of the cosmos can occur more readily if we see clearly that religion is also essentially adventure, continuous with the cosmos itself.

The cosmos is itself a saga of continual experimentation with novel forms of order, a struggle upward from simplicity toward increasing complexity. This straining for more complexity is not always successful. There are many backward and sideways movements in the story of the universe's struggle upward from the simplicity of its origins. But over the long haul there has clearly been a general trend toward the creation of more elaborate entities. It is this generic ascent of the cosmos toward increasing complexity that we may call adventure. And we may now situate the story of religion within this more encompassing cosmic narrative.

Religion is often understood as the trustful entry into an acknowledged realm of mystery. But this entry into mystery is best characterized as an adventure. The heart of religion is trust. Its orientation is toward mystery. But its distinctive style is adventure. Although much that passes as religion seems undeniably far from adventurous, religion in "essence," if not always in manifestation, is an adventure of the human spirit. But the religious adventure has its roots deep down in the story of an evolving universe out of which it has recently emerged.

When observed within a cosmological vista, religion will appear not just as something *people* do, but as an astonishing and disturbing development in the entire evolution of the *universe*. We are not wont to view religion in this light, but the growing awareness of our species' evolution from the depths of the universe invites us to do so. We are the latest dominant emergent in the earth's evolution, and so all that we humans do and think and say is relevant for our understanding of the cosmos out of which we evolved. The universe is giving expression to itself in giving birth to us. And in our giving birth to religion the universe may well be saying something new and astounding.

Unusual insights into the nature and function of religion can be reached if we learn to look at it from this cosmic perspective. We are gaining a deeper impression today of our intimate ties with nature and its evolution. We can see more clearly now than ever before that the human race is part of an ageless cosmic struggle upward toward more intense versions of organized complexity, and toward a deepening of consciousness. The evolutionary perspective that has taken over in the realm of the sciences also calls for a new understanding of our species' inveterate religious tendencies. We humans have appeared relatively recently in evolution, and our religious habits have evolved along with us. They have apparently been part of us from the very beginning of our journey on this planet. We suspect that we are yet unfinished, and so the same is likely true of our religions.

What this means for the study of religion is that we can no longer legitimately isolate it as a peculiar expression of the human mind or focus on
it as though psychology and the social sciences, or even theology, were the
privileged roads to a contemporary understanding of it. We must also look
at religion *cosmologically*, viewing it as part of the very evolution of the
universe.

A cosmological and evolutionary approach to religion is sorely needed
at this time. For the evolutionary paradigm has come to dominate our ways
of thinking about the world. From astronomy and geology at one end of
the natural continuum to the study of invisible physical events at the other,
science itself has become the *story* of the universe. The accounts of evolution "from the Big Bang to the Big Brain" are essentially narrative in form.
They tell the story of a cosmic adventure. And the story of religion is a
most significant chapter in this cosmic narrative. Thus we may no longer
investigate religion as though it were not also part of the unfolding adventure of cosmic evolution. The story of religion is part of the story of the
universe. The two stories must now be told together.

We need not enter here into disputes as to whether cosmic evolution
has always or generally been progressive. All we need to do is notice that
since the "Big Bang" occurred fifteen or twenty billion years ago some
momentous things have happened, in particular the emergence of life and
mind on our planet (and perhaps elsewhere). Both life and mind have
generally had the tendency to complicate themselves more and more, for
whatever reason. If we think in terms of the epochs of evolution, life and
mind made their evolutionary transition into culture and civilization very
recently, only a flash of time ago. Yet here too the struggle for complexity
continued, and at an alarming rate of speed. The invention of agriculture,
civilization, art, and culture, of nations, politics, education, and science —
all of these developments exemplify the universe's impatience with monotony and urgent need for subtle shading and more intense enjoyment of
beauty, now that it has reached the human phase of its unfolding.

But the cosmic adventure, on our own planet at least, has been extended
in a special way by the religious journey. No human actions or gestures
have reached out more passionately for the unknown or revolted more
compellingly against monotony than has religion. Its surmounting of the
mundane, its reaching beyond ordinariness, its striving for a deeper reality
beneath appearances, and its unquenchable quest for beauty make it appropriate for us to envisage religion as an adventure. The ageless religious
quest for novel forms of order is continuous with, and an extension of, the
universe's own aim toward more intense harmony of contrasts.

For nearly uncountable millennia our universe labored before it was in
a condition of readiness to bring forth life. The heavy chemical elements
required for life (carbon, oxygen, nitrogen, phosphorous, and so forth) took
several billion years of cooking time at the heart of stars before supernovas
eventually dispersed them throughout space. Countless more epochs

elapsed before these elements began to cluster into planetary bodies like our earth. The chemicals that make up our terrestrial home, having finished their previous careers in some now dead star, finally coalesced five billion years ago into our own planet. Then a billion years or so later, after the earth's surface had cooled sufficiently to sustain primitive organisms, life began to appear. And following endless more spans of patient waiting and experimentation, it burst forth into the extravagant arrays of higher organisms such as reptiles, birds, and mammals. Finally, perhaps two million years ago, our immediate prehuman ancestors began to appear in abundance and spread out over the face of the earth. That is not very long ago in terms of evolutionary time, and we can safely surmise that much more of the cosmic journey, perhaps the bulk of it, still lies ahead of us.

We cannot know for sure, but it is highly likely that our ancestors started acting and thinking in something like a religious way at the same time that they became endowed with language and consciousness. Why? Why has our species been so ineradicably religious, so sensitive to a dimension of mystery summoning us to move beyond any absolute contentment with the mere givenness of things? Perhaps it has a lot to do with the inherently adventurous nature of the *cosmos*. The restlessness that launched matter on its pilgrimage toward complexity twenty billion years ago has apparently not yet been quieted. It continues now in our own questioning minds and our spirit of exploration. In the modern development of science we find one of the clearest illustrations of this exploratory restlessness. Science, like religion, is not content to take things at face value. It too seeks a world beyond our customary impressions. But in the story of human religiousness, especially in its post-axial forms, we find perhaps the most stirring manifestation of discontent with mere appearances, and nature's grasping for the seemingly unreachable. Because of our contemporary awareness of the evolutionary, narrative character of the universe, and the growing sense of our species' continuity with this emergent process, we are now in a position to interpret the long search of religion as a prolongation of the cosmic struggle toward more intense beauty. Such a way of looking at religion should prevent us from separating its demand for self-transcendence from the cosmos in which it is rooted.

CONCLUSION

In the story of religion there is so strong a theme of restlessness or homelessness that it is impossible to avoid the suggestion that we are dealing here with adventure in the boldest sense. But what starts out as adventure, as we know from our own experience, can eventually degenerate into a loss of enthusiasm. The effort to sustain any valorous expedition can sag. And the same is true of our species' religious journey. Religions can grow weary of their voyage into mystery and take refuge in the familiar. Religion can lose touch with its primordial zest for the unattainable. It may become transformed into a style of life and thought that does little more than sanction the social or political status quo. Religion can lose its soul, and Whitehead thought that this is what has been happening to religion in the modern age. "Religion," he said, "is tending to degenerate into a decent formula wherewith to embellish a comfortable life" (Whitehead 1967b, 188). Nevertheless, this same philosopher thought he could still see through to religion's authentic core. In its most stalwart manifestations religion provides a "commanding vision" that arouses its devotees to move beyond complacency. Religious worship is "not a rule of safety—it is an adventure of the spirit, a flight after the unattainable. The death of religion comes with the repression of the high hope of adventure" (Whitehead 1967b, 192).

The theme of homelessness, wandering, alienation, and exile is so much a part of our religious traditions that we need to salvage it rather than discard it. The problem before us is how to do so in an environmentally healthy way. For we know how easy it has been for those who have embarked on the religious adventure to interpret nature as though it were a restraint. And the results have been to foster a recklessness about our natural habitat as though it were holding us back from our journey. Our new narrative cosmology, however, allows us to feel the universe itself as the primary subject of adventure. Human and religious wanderings are expressions of the primary revelation of adventure, which is the universe itself. We may care for our natural matrix not in spite of but because of our religious restlessness. The universe itself is an adventure into mystery, and our religions are simply various ways of explicating this inherent character of the universe at the human level of emergence. We do not have to make the natural environment a victim of a theology of homelessness. Theology can hold on to the notion that we may live in homelessness from our universal destiny without feeling lost in the cosmos. Reconciliation with an adventuring universe is the very condition of our releasing our religious instincts to venture forth into mystery. For the destiny of both ourselves and the cosmos is to become lost in mystery.

NOTES

1. Dualism has also been criticized as resulting from a fear of the feminine and the maternal, a point that cannot be developed here.

2. Both Michael Polanyi and Alfred North Whitehead have written important critiques of the modern obsession with abstraction and clarity. See Polanyi 1967 and Whitehead 1968: "The degeneracy of mankind is distinguished from its uprise by the dominance of chill abstractions, divorced from aesthetic content" (Whitehead 1968, 123).

3. See the articles by and about Thomas Berry collected in *Cross Currents* 37, nos. 2 and 3 (1988), pp. 178-239.

4. See Lonergan and Richards. For a popular introduction to this mystique of nature as a cosmic creation story see Brian Swimme 1986.

5. Alfred North Whitehead has identified the underlying assumptions as (1) the assumption of simple location; (2) the assumption of the primacy of primary qualities; and (3) the assumption that clarity and distinctness are more fundamental than vagueness. All three are instances of what he calls the "fallacy of misplaced concreteness," that is, the mistaking of logical abstractions for concrete actuality (Whitehead 1967b, 39-55).

6. I have summarized Whitehead's position in my book on science and religion, *The Cosmic Adventure*. See also Whitehead 1967a, 252-96.

7. It is worth remembering that classical philosophy often considered beauty to be one of the so-called transcendentals, together with being, unity, and goodness. The association of value with beauty is not peculiar to Whiteheadians.

8. The expression "optimism of withdrawal" is that of Teilhard de Chardin, (Teilhard, 45).

9. Jürgen Moltmann's recent book, *God in Creation*, is perhaps the best-known example. But the work of Thomas Berry makes the same point no less forcefully.

10. "It is impossible to speak of history as though it were a realm of freedom and decision entirely separate from nature. Certainly the biblical perspective is not characterized by such nonsense. It is a measure of the desperation of contemporary theology and faith, in the face of the power of the modern scientific world view . . . that this way out was attempted at all" (Kaufman 1972, 122).

11. It is not just existentialist theology that exiles human subjects from the cosmos. I am thinking also of the many recent theologies that have closely followed a psychological and social-scientific paradigm according to which culture is interpreted primarily as a human construct without any reference to the cosmic roots of human creativity. The social sciences are understandably abstract from cosmological questions and schemes. It is not their concern to delve into the cosmic roots of social behavior, although anthropology at times makes this link explicit. But sociology and psychology generally focus narrowly on the specifically human band of the broad spectrum of cosmic layers and do not concern themselves with the universe as such. Like all sciences they deliberately bracket out other layers of cosmic reality. While there can be no objection to this abstracting from the cosmos by the social sciences, we may still question the adequacy of a theology that ties itself too tightly to the social-scientific approach, for it may thereby easily lose sight of the cosmic roots of human existence and behavior. This seems to have happened in recent theological reflection influenced by the sociologist Peter Berger. Berger employed a humanistic social-scientific model in his interpretation of religion, *The Sacred Canopy*. For him authentic religion is the kind that allows us to recognize our creativity and responsibility; inauthentic religion on the other hand masks our creativity from us. Such an approach is a healthy corrective to a theology that leaves us passive, uncreative puppets. But it runs the risk of exaggerating the *homo faber* image of humanity and forgetting the inherent creativity in the entire cosmos.

12. One of the best critiques of the dominance of the *homo faber* image of human existence is still that of Sam Keen.

13. Jürgen Moltmann even cautions against our identifying the divine life with creativity. "If God is 'eternally creative' how can we understand his sabbath rest? . . . If creation is said to be 'identical' with the divine life, how can there be beings who are not *God* and yet *are*?" (Moltmann, 84).

14. I may cite as another instance of a type of theology closely tied to the dualistic paradigm, the recent work of Gordon Kaufman. Even though Kaufman was earlier

critical of existentialist theology's dualism of mind and nature, and in spite of his own recent environmental concerns, his current theological writings exemplify the extent to which the materialist and scientistic paradigm continues to provide the background of theological reflection. In spite of Kaufman's otherwise profound ecological sensitivity, his theology has not completely escaped the philosophical assumptions in terms of which the existentialist theology he criticized has been shaped. Kaufman's theological method begins with the thesis that theology is a human construct. Although he says that religion itself, as distinct from theology, is more than a construction and even has transcendent reference, nevertheless he states that the image of God in religion is a human construct. His theology is patterned on the assumptions in the social sciences that we observed earlier. It is entranced by the image of *homo faber* to such an extent that it makes theology into nothing other than our own human creation, and one gets the impression at times that Kaufman sees religion also as nothing but a human construct. He fully accepts the Kantian view that notions such as God and world have no discernible objective basis in our experience. They are regulatory rather than objectively verifiable ideas. They are noumenal realities covered over by a phenomenal world of our own making (Kaufman 1975). Historians of philosophy can easily demonstrate how this Kantian distinction of an unavailable noumenal world from a vivid, but frothy, phenomenal one, is erected upon the distinction in classical physics between primary and secondary qualities. Kaufman's Kantian method of coming at the subject matter of theology betrays the same old feeling that religion, and hence religious people, do not quite belong to the "real" universe. That religious symbols are seen first as human constructs rather than as the flowering (through us) of deeply cosmic energies is a sign of how stuck theology still is in the framework of homelessness upon which scientism and materialism are based. (For another critique of Kaufman's theology see Gustafson 1981.) It has been pointed out often that a lack of cosmic awareness is present also in much liberation theology. Abstracting from cosmological considerations is quite understandable here since the immediate questions giving rise to this adventurous theology arise out of social and economic inequities. Social injustice sometimes seems far from the preoccupations of a theology of nature. However, as an increasing number of theologians sympathetic to this perspective are now insisting, a socio-economic concern cannot plausibly be separated from a cosmic concern. Thomas Berry has made this point as forcefully as anyone.

In Catholic thought a subjectivist tendency is present in "Transcendental Thomism" and the Kantian turn that still dominate much Catholic theology. The return to cosmology in Catholic theology is taking place to some extent among theological followers of Teilhard who are suspicious of the latter's anthropocentric leanings but find his thought nevertheless a stimulus to environmental concern. Once again Thomas Berry is a good example.

15. For the following discussion of adventure see Alfred North Whitehead 1967a, especially pp. 252-96.

WORKS CITED

Berger, Peter. *The Sacred Canopy*. Garden City, NY: Doubleday Anchor Books, 1969.

Berry, Thomas. "The New Story: Comments on the Origin, Identification and

Transmission of Values." *Cross Currents* 37 (Summer/Fall 1988): 187-99.

Commoner, Barry. "In Defense of Biology." *Man and Nature*. Ed. Ronald Munson. New York: Dell Publishing Co, 1971.

Gustafson, James M. *Ethics from a Theocentric Perspective*. Vol. 1. Chicago: University of Chicago Press, 1981.

Haught, John. *The Cosmic Adventure*. New York: Paulist Press, 1984.

————. "The Emergent Environment and the Problem of Cosmic Purpose." *Environmental Ethics* 8 (1986): 139-50.

Kaufman, Gordon. *God the Problem*. Cambridge: Harvard University Press, 1972.

————. *An Essay on Theological Method*. Missoula, Montana: Scholars Press, 1975.

Keen, Sam. *Apology for Wonder*. New York: Harper & Row, 1969.

Kegley, Charles, ed. *The Theology of Rudolf Bultmann*. New York: Harper & Row, 1966.

Klemke, E.D. "Living Without Appeal." In *The Meaning of Life*. Ed. E.D. Klemke, New York: Oxford University Press, 1981.

Lonergan, Anne, and Caroline Richards, eds. *Thomas Berry and the New Cosmology*. Mystic, CT: Twenty-Third Publications, 1987.

Moltmann, Jürgen. *God in Creation*. Trans. Margaret Kohl. San Francisco: Harper & Row, 1985.

Polanyi, Michael. *Personal Knowledge*. New York: Harper Torchbooks, 1964.

————. *The Tacit Dimension*. New York: Doubleday Anchor Books, 1967.

Rolston, Holmes. *Science and Religion*. New York: Random House, 1987.

Swimme, Brian. *The Universe is a Green Dragon*. Santa Fe: Bear & Co., Inc., 1986.

————. "The Cosmic Creation Story." Unpublished paper.

Teilhard de Chardin, Pierre. *The Future of Man*. Trans. Norman Denny. New York: Harper Colophon Books, 1969.

Whitehead, Alfred North (a). *Adventures of Ideas*. New York: The Free Press, 1967.

———— (b). *Science and the Modern World*. New York: The Free Press, 1967.

————. *Modes of Thought*. New York: The Free Press, 1968.

13

Chance, Purpose, and the Order of Nature

Charles Birch

The central issue in science and religion today is whether nature in its evolution has any purpose or ultimate meaning (Haught, 7).

Neither pure chance nor the pure absence of chance can explain the world (Hartshorne 1984, 69).

According to the traditional scientific picture the universe is a random collection of particles with blind forces acting upon them. Yet the universe

When Bishop William Paley (1743-1805) wrote his *Natural Theology*, he intended his work to be an exaltation of God. Arguing from what he took to be the machine-like nature of the universe, a universe operating like clockwork, Paley felt he could deduce the existence as well as the many divine characteristics of God. His theology—and natural theologies of the time like his—filled out the argument for the existence of God from design with mechanistic understandings of the universe. But such "proofs," such exaltations, came at the great expense of adopting, continuing, and extolling a view of nature we have come to realize as ultimately destructive. The mechanistic, deterministic views of Paley and others like him since the Enlightenment have often led us astray philosophically and theologically. Indeed, as Harvey Sindima's essay in this book attests, mechanistic views have contributed to the threatened destruction of the earth not only in the West but also in Africa. What is needed are alternatives to the mechanistic orientation.

Charles Birch offers one such alternative. In many ways his essay is a response to Paley and those like him. It emerges out of Birch's own dialogue with the best of contemporary science. Birch's aim is to offer a nonmechanistic understanding of nature and to show how such an understanding elicits a new way of thinking about God. For Birch, and for several others in this volume, such as Haught, McFague, McDaniel, and Sindima, the new sensibilities that Christians need in our ecological age include, among other things, more ecological ways of sensing the Divine.

has an elaborate structure and order. How then does a seemingly directionless assembly of entities produce the complex organization that we refer to as the order of nature? What is the origin of this apparent creative activity? This is a deep mystery for science. Sir Karl Popper has described the creativity of nature as the greatest riddle of complexity. Some physicists, such as Leon Legerman, director of the Fermilab in Illinois, have the faith that physics will ultimately reduce this mystery to a single mathematical formula so simple "that you can wear it on your T-shirt"! Others are less sanguine about the capacity of reductionist physics to so explain the order of nature.

OTHER VIEWS ON THE ORIGIN OF THE ORDER OF NATURE

In his satirical song "Friday Morning" Sydney Carter puts a view of the origin of the order of nature thus:

> You can blame it onto Adam,
> You can blame it onto Eve,
> You can blame it on the apple,
> But that I can't believe.
> It was God who made the devil and the woman and the man,
> And there wouldn't be an apple if it wasn't in the plan!

That the order of nature was the product of a predetermined plan or design in much the same way a building is the product of an architect's blueprint executed by the builder was a view widely held prior to Charles Darwin. Nothing is left to chance.

Darwin's theory of the natural selection of chance variations put an emphasis on the role of chance in determining the order of nature in the living world. The evidence from nature, which he accumulated over many decades, no longer supported the religious determinism that saw in the order of nature a predetermined design accounting for every detail from the apple to the man. Indeed the neo-Darwinian view is that these same principles account for the order of nature not only from the apple to the man but from the primeval soup of molecules from which life is supposed to have arisen. The Darwinian alternative allowed no place for a monarchical God in charge of nature and put the spotlight on the role of chance. Opponents of the view that chance has any part to play in the order of nature tried to ridicule it in the famous analogy of the typewriting monkeys, asking if a million monkeys banging at random on a million typewriters could by chance produce one of Shakespeare's plays. A modern criticism in the same vein argues that for higher forms to have evolved by chance is like the chance that a tornado sweeping through a junkyard will assemble a Boeing 747 aircraft from the materials there. Both analogies are glib, meretricious, and false. They completely misinterpret the role Darwinism gave to chance in the evolutionary process. They are false for several reasons. The most obvious of these is that they ignore reproduction and selection.

For many years I have put to students another analogy, which I think gets closer to the Darwinian proposition. Instead of a million monkeys banging at random on a million typewriters, imagine a million, indeed billions of blind painters each sprinkling a few splashes of color on billions of canvases, one before each painter. Of these only the few that show the first feeble suggestion of a meaningful picture are preserved; the rest are destroyed. The selected rudimentary pictures are reproduced a billionfold. And again billions of blind painters add a few random touches of paint to them; again the best are selected and reproduced, and so on millions of times corresponding to the number of generations that have elapsed since life appeared on earth. We might expect that such a process of chance, selection, and reproduction might produce a painting that had some order and meaning to our eyes. This analogy gets closer to what is meant by natural selection of chance variations, though it still does not do justice to the full picture of Darwinian evolution. The analogy has recently been put in much more sophisticated terms by Richard Dawkins in computer models that incorporate random elements, reproduction, and selection, much as in the model of the blind painters (Dawkins). He demonstrates quite convincingly that an ordered outcome can be the product of such operations. What more general conclusions might we draw from this image about the origin of the order of nature?

Dawkins concludes that the order of nature is to be explained solely in terms of such models. Similarly before him the distinguished molecular biologist Jacques Monod claimed that "Chance alone is at the source of every innovation of all creation in the biosphere" (Monod, 110). For Dawkins, Monod, and many of their followers, chance is the one and only principle in nature. They contrast their position with those who seek to find in every detail of nature evidence for deterministic design in which living organisms are compared with contrivances such as a watch, which a watchmaker designs and makes. There is not much room for chance in designing a watch. There is no room at all for chance in designing a space vehicle for the safe transportation of humans. It is thoroughly determined to the last detail by its designers. The deists at the time of Darwin and before said the design of nature was like that. And so do the so-called creationists today. And so do other theists who are bound to the image of God as monarchical and imperialistic. The order of nature for them is the creation of an all-powerful deity who left nothing to chance, nor for that matter, to the entities the deity created. This is the concept of *ex machina*.

But the alternatives we are faced with are not simply a world of chance or a world excluding chance. There is a third possibility, namely, a world of chance and of purpose. One does not exclude the other. In considering this alternative we need to be clear about what we really mean by chance, so as not to be misled by false analogies, and what we mean by purpose, so as not to fall back into the discredited model of design and manufacture. In doing this we need to explore models of God alternative to the imperialistic and monarchical ones many of us have inherited. That implies as well a model of nature that is less mechanistic, less materialistic, and less reductionist than traditional science has tended to bequeath to us.

In pursuing these avenues I have found much inspiration in the thought of process theologians, who have made a conscious effort to interpret Christian faith for our time in terms that appropriate the insights of science. This is not to propose that the only criterion for theology is its fit with the reigning understanding of reality. But as McFague has said, "for theology to do less than fit our present understanding—for it to accept basic assumptions about reality from a very different time—seems blatantly wrongheaded" (McFague, 14).

Besides finding insight from process theology I have found much inspiration in the attempts of McFague to experiment with new models of God to flesh out these new concepts of God's working in nature. Her images of the world as God's body and her models of God as mother, lover, and friend of the world illuminate the more philosophical understanding I derive from process theology.

But first we need to get some clarity into the meaning of chance events in the order of nature that goes beyond analogies of monkeys and painters and computers. I believe that leaves us with the necessity of recognizing that any credible account of the order of nature must accept chance as part of the nature of nature. Then we can proceed to find a meaning of purpose that is relevant to a nature that is not completely determined by some external influence.

There is no role for God in a completely mechanical world any more than there is in the workings of my motorcar. There is no role for God in a world completely dependent upon chance events. Nor is there any role for God in a world that is completely determined from start to finish. I shall argue that we can draw from modern science a vision of nature that accepts the existence of chance and a degree of self-determination and freedom for the entities of the creation. I believe it is possible within this model to find a working out of purpose in the creative process. The world becomes much more a body in which God lives than a machine in which the laws of mechanics reign supreme. A truly incarnational theology is one in which God becomes incarnate in the world as it is created. As self is to the body so God is to the world. Such a theology promotes an ethic of justice and care and a profound acceptance of human responsibility for the fate of the earth.

I am convinced that when we find an understanding of nature that incorporates a role for chance which Darwin emphasized, and a role for purpose, we enlarge the Christian understanding of nature. Bishop John Austin Baker, as dean of Westminster Abbey, put it this way—in a guide to the

Abbey—commenting on the fact that the Abbey is the final resting place of Charles Darwin: "Today most Christians ... are glad that one of the intellectual giants who laid the foundation of our modern understanding of the world should lie here in the house of God in whom he himself did not believe but whom we know so much better as a result of his discoveries."

THE MEANING OF CHANCE IN THE EVOLUTION OF NATURE

The idea that the origin and evolution of plants and animals and all living creatures depends in part upon chance events is largely due to Charles Darwin in the nineteeth century. Darwin didn't always think this way about nature. On the contrary, when he left Cambridge to take part in the epic voyage around the world in the *Beagle* he was a convinced creationist and thus a determinist and a theist. He had read Paley's *Natural Theology* as a student at Cambridge University and was impressed by its arguments for the existence of God from the design of nature. The "doctrine of divine carpentry," as a later vice-chancellor of Cambridge called it, was promulgated by bishops from their pulpits. Students were expected to provide more and more evidence for it. In that respect Darwin became a traitor. His observations on the continents of the southern hemisphere changed his views of the source of the order in nature. The author of *The Origin of Species* had failed to perform what the public expected of its biologists. It was as if the Pope had announced his conversion to Buddhism.

Darwin's conclusions included three critical concepts: (1) Nature was not complete and perfect once and for all time, it was still in process of being made. (2) The process involved a "struggle for existence." (3) The process involved chance. What could have been more devastating for the design thesis than imperfection, struggle, and chance at the heart of the creative process?

The element of chance in Darwin's theory was the genetical variation on which natural selection acted. Instead of the tiger being designed with its stripes for camouflage once and for all time, Darwin invoked the notion that originally tigers had all sorts of patterns on their coats. This was a consequence of chance genetic variation. But only that pattern persisted that gave the animal an advantage in its struggle for existence and that could be inherited. This is the principle of "chance and necessity" Monod considered to be the one and only principle of nature. Darwinism was a shattering blow to the notion that the order of nature was completely determined in all its details by an omnipotent deity outside nature. This does not mean that Darwin showed, as many claimed, that there was no purpose in nature. What he did show was that existing views of design by an external agent were invalid. Darwin's theory did nothing to prove that God did not exist, but it did destroy the only argument by which many people thought the existence of God could be established.

Neo-Darwinism, which is the dominant view of biologists today, is an interpretation of Darwinism in terms of a modern understanding of genetics. The basic source of genetic variation in the living world is chance variation of the DNA molecule. This molecule can come in an infinite variety of forms; which form is a matter of chance. At the beginning of life on earth there may have been just one DNA molecule. The DNA molecule has the peculiar capacity to be able to replicate in the appropriate environment. Had it replicated forever with deterministic perfection, that is, without any chance variations, there would have been no evolution. Evolution was, and is, utterly dependent upon occasional chance in the molecule when it replicates. This is what mutation is in its basic form. It involves a rearrangement of the base-pairs in the steps of the ladder-like DNA molecule. This basic event in evolution is a random or chance change, an accident if you will, during replication. One might well expect that accidental changes in DNA during replication would be deleterious to the organism that harbors the changed DNA. And indeed that is the case. Most mutations are deleterious. Some few are not. By chance they confer some advantage upon the organism that harbors them.

The meaning of chance in this context is quite specific. It is often misunderstood. It does not mean being without a cause. We know many of the causes of mutation, such as radiation. Whether or not a particular mutation will increase the chance of its possessor to survive and reproduce is dependent upon a second chain of events, which is quite independent of the event of mutation itself. This second chain of events has nothing to do with the environment in which the organism finds itself. For example, the DNA of a fly mutates to confer upon its offspring resistance to the insecticide DDT. This chain of events is quite unrelated to whether or not the environment contains DDT. Indeed there is good evidence that such mutant genes were being produced long before DDT was invented. When the environment does not contain DDT the mutation confers no particular advantage upon the organism. It is important to understand that the DDT does not itself cause the mutation. All it does is act as an agent of selection. The important point is that the two causal chains are entirely independent.

We say that mutation is random in relation to the needs of the organism at the time the mutation occurs. That the two chains of events intersect with advantage to the organism is a matter of chance or accident. Darwinism thus introduced an indeterminacy into the concept of the evolutionary process. A determinist might want to argue that there is an omnipotent observer, who sees that the appropriate mutation occurs at the appropriate time so that the two chains of events interact with benefit to the organism. That this is not the case is a scientific fact known from careful experiments. There are no two ways about it. All sorts of mutation occur all the time; most are deleterious. By chance, some few are not.

This schematization of the two pathways tends to exaggerate the separation of chance and purpose. The acceptance of a role of chance in nature does not exclude a role for purpose. Indeed, as I shall argue, it makes a role for purpose possible.

The world of Paley's *Natural Theology* was a completely determined world. The world of Jaques Monod was one of chance and chance alone. There is a third possibility: one of neither pure determinism nor pure chance alone, but chance and purpose together. As Hartshorne has said, "Neither pure chance nor the pure absence of chance can explain the world" (Hartshorne 1984, 69). The recognition of chance and accident in the natural order is critically important for a realistic theology of nature. Without chance there could be no freedom. If the universe and all its happenings were fully determined by some omnipotent power, attributed by some to God, there would be no freedom for the creatures.

To take chance seriously is the first step in moving away from the concept of deterministic design, whether by an omnipotent designer or as some in-built principle of nature. It is also the first step in moving toward a realistic concept of purpose. Monod, who took chance seriously, failed to see its implications for freedom. Chance alone was for him the one and only principle in nature. Darwin never came to this conclusion. Indeed, it seems he was reluctant to admit the reality of chance, despite the role he attributed to it. In this respect he was like Einstein, who said he could not believe that God plays dice. Darwin probably admired the deterministic universe of Newton. Perhaps he saw himself as the Newton of biology. The key to Darwin's thinking on chance and determinism is not to be found in *The Origin of Species* but in Darwin's correspondence, especially with the Harvard botanist Asa Gray in 1860 and 1861. Charles Hartshorne is, so far as I know, the first person to appreciate the significance of this correspondence (Hartshorne 1962, chap. 7; Hartshorne 1984, chap. 3).

The critical passage in Darwin's letter to Asa Gray is the following: "I cannot think that the world . . . is the result of chance; and yet I cannot look at each separate thing as the result of Design. . . . I am, and shall ever remain, in a hopeless muddle" (F. Darwin, 353-54). And "But I know that I am in the same sort of muddle . . . as all the world seems to be in with respect to freewill, yet with everything supposed to have been foreseen or pre-ordained" (p. 378). Darwin repeatedly declared in his letters to Asa Gray as well as to others that chance cannot explain the world as an ordered whole. Again and again Darwin asks: Is it all ordained or is it all a result of chance? Because of his dilemma Darwin gave up theism. At the same time he could see there must be pervasive limitations upon chance since unlimited chance is chaos. Yet he was bewildered. Why?

Hartshorne makes two suggestions: (1) Darwin tended, like many others, to think of science as committed to determinism; he even suggested that what we call chance may not be chance at all; and (2) it was not apparent to Darwin why cosmic purpose should leave anything to chance (Hartshorne 1962, 207). The God of deism was identified with absolute law and non-chance. The dominant theology of his day was of no help to him in this respect. It had no clearly conceived creationist philosophy. God must do everything or nothing. And if God is responsible for everything then why all the evil in the world? Darwin wrote to Asa Gray, "You say that you are in a haze; I am in thick mud; the orthodox would say in fetid, abominable mud; yet I cannot keep out of the question" (F. Darwin, 382).

THE MEANING OF PURPOSE IN EVOLUTION

The "mud" in which Darwin found himself immersed was the opacity that always characterizes a deterministic world view. Darwin argued correctly that the facts of evolution are in conflict with belief in deterministic design by a benevolent designer. But only one of his correspondents suggested to him that God was other than an omnipotent determiner of all the details of nature. The English vicar and novelist Charles Kingsley wrote to Darwin, "I have learnt to see that it is just as noble a conception of Deity, to believe that He created primal forms capable of self-development into all forms needful ... as to believe that He required a fresh act of intervention to supply the lacunas which He himself made" (F. Darwin, 288). And elsewhere Kingsley wrote about Darwin's contribution thus: "Now that they have got rid of an interfering God—a master magician as I call it—they have to choose between the absolute empire of accident and a living, immanent, ever-working God" (quoted in Raven, 177). In his evolutionary epic, *The Water Babies*, which Kingsley wrote for his children just four years after the publication of *The Origin of Species*, he tells of how God makes things make themselves. There is no evidence that Darwin appreciated Kingsley's alternatives to the omnipotent deterministic God of deism.

Darwin needed a Jacques Monod to convince him that chance and accident were essential to the order of nature. He needed also a Charles Hartshorne to persuade him that there was a credible alternative to the deism of Paley and other nineteenth-century divines. But in fact he never did resolve his dilemma of chance and determinism.

Hartshorne hit the nail on the head when he said, "There must be something positive limiting chance and something more than mere matter in matter or Darwinism fails to explain life" (Hartshorne 1962, 210). What is "the something positive" that limits chance and what is the "something more than mere matter in matter"? The answer to these questions depends upon how we conceive of the origin of the order of nature.

Darwinism rules out the concept of an all-determining orderer. In so doing it opens the door to another concept of ordering. There are only two ways of ordering. One is dictatorial. The other is persuasive. Process theology takes its cue from the latter. The "something more than mere matter in matter" is the concept of the entities of nature as not being substance or mere objects. They are subjects, that is to say, they are sentient to the possibilities of their future, within the limitations imposed by their past.

There is no such thing as mere matter. Quantum physics certainly opens the door to a nonsubstantialist concept of matter, where the words freedom and choice are relevant. And so far as those entities we call alive are concerned, the most characteristic feature about them is not the survival of the fittest but their urge to live. Life is anticipation. Whitehead's more complete statement is — *the present is memory tinged with anticipation*. What the entities of creation respond to — "the something positive that limits chance" — are the persuasive possibilities relevant to their future. Order by persuasion is the factor-limiting chance. The possibility of chaos and disorder in a lecture theater full of students is immense. The lecturer who is any good, will by persuasive influence create a high degree of order in a large class. The students are free to make chaos if they wish. Sometimes they do. But under the influence of a persuasive lecturer they choose not to. That is the nature of order in nature. This introduces another meaning to chance: namely, that there is no certainty that at any moment any entity will respond to the lure of creation. Self-determination means that it may or it may not. The degree of that uncertainty is presumably small at the level of the electron but greater with entities such as ourselves.

We can say with Hartshorne, "The only positive explanation of order is the existence of an orderer" (Hartshorne 1984, 71). The orderer is no longer the *deus ex machina* of the deists, which Darwin rightly rejected. Kingsley hinted at the alternative when he said that things tend to make themselves. Creativity exists within the entities of the creation. That is the first step in the argument for order. Many people, indeed many Christians, find this difficult to grasp. For, as Hartshorne says,

> Since teleology has been thought of as unilateral creativity on the part of the deity, unshared in any appreciable degree with the creatures, indications that the world had far reaching potentialities for self-creation were naturally startling. But only because creativity had not been grasped in its proper universality, as the principle of existence itself (Hartshorne 1962, 209).

Today that should be a less startling concept (see Birch and Cobb). Science is leading in that direction as witness, for example, the recognition of "self-organization" as a principle in cosmology (Davies) and in molecular biology (Prigogine and Stengers).

The combination of sentience in natural entities, be they electrons, cells, or human beings, together with the lure beyond themselves for their possible futures is the source of their creativity. Nuts and bolts can't evolve. They are aggregates of natural entities. Aggregates have no intrinsic creativity. That belongs to the natural entities such as atoms and molecules which constitute them. Creativity is not simply rearrangement of bits and pieces of stuff like nuts and bolts in simple or complex arrangements. The relation between the individual natural entity and the ensemble of which it is a part is entirely different in a creative agent as compared with a machine. In a machine the entities that compose it maintain their identity, whether the machine be a washing machine or a computer. Not so in a natural entity such as a living cell. As one moves up levels of organization — electrons, atoms, molecules, cells, and so on — the properties of each larger whole are given, not merely by the units of which it is composed, but by the new relations among these units. It is not that the whole is more than the sum of its parts. The parts themselves are redefined and changed as a result of their new relations to one another in the process of evolution from one level to another. An electron in a lump of lead is not the same as an electron in a cell in a human brain. The mechanical assumption of classical physics that it is the same everywhere is no longer a part of quantum physics. All this means that the properties of matter relevant at, say, the atomic level do not begin to make predictable the properties of matter at the cellular level, let alone at the level of complex organisms.

The parts of a machine, its cogs, levers, transistors, or chips, have external relations only. They can be pushed and pulled in different directions, but their nature remains unchanged. The parts of a natural entity have, in addition to external relations, internal relations to their environment. Their being, indeed their existence, depends upon their internal relations. The idea of an internal relation is a relation that is constitutive of the character and even the existence of something. We are aware of the role of internal relations in the way in which chosen purposes determine what each of us becomes. Our chosen purposes are powerful internal causes in our lives. Goal-directed integration is found wherever there are entities that have some degree of self-determination. Quantum physics recognizes the possibility of similar influences at the level of the electron type of entity. For many quantum physicists these entities are no longer to be called particles. There are no particles because there are no substances in nature. The word *substance* is used in this context in its classical meaning as defined by Descartes: "And when we conceive of substance, we merely conceive an existing thing which requires nothing but itself in order to exist" (quoted in Whitehead 1930, 92). But as Whitehead said "There is no entity, not even God, which requires nothing but itself in order to exist" (Whitehead 1930, 12).

Biology has been slower than physics in moving away from the substantialist prejudice. It recognizes the role of purpose in cultural evolution. At the level of molecular biology the argument becomes complex, but I believe we are beginning to see a meaning for it there (Birch 1988a). Molecular biology, which was the last to come into mechanistic biology may well be the first to opt out. The point I want to make is that science itself is beginning to see the limitations of the substantialist prejudice, the reduction of everything to "mere matter." The new physics and to some extent the new biology recognizes the entities of creation as subjects and not simply objects pushed and pulled like billiard balls (Birch 1988b).

A multitude of creative agents implies the need for the rule of one. Too many cooks spoil the broth! There must be something that sets limits to the confusion and anarchy possible with a multiplicity of creative agents. Individual purposing agents need to be coordinated. The key here is not manipulation of the entities by an external agent but persuasion. The persuasive ordering principle, which coordinates the creativity of a multitude of creative agents, is given the name God in process theology. An orchestra consists of many creative players. Each player interprets the score in his or her own way. But the over-all coordination is provided by the conductor. God is like a composer-conductor who is writing a score a few bars ahead of the orchestra, taking into account their harmonies and disharmonies as he proposes the next movement of the music. God does not determine the outcome. The power of God is the power of persuasion to harmonize the whole. The brilliant television documentary made in 1984 showing Leonard Bernstein conducting rehearsals of his own composition "West Side Story" struck me in this way. The musicians, composer, and conductor became one. Bernstein originated the music. Each player was making an interpretation from what Bernstein had written and from the grimaces on his face. Sometimes the orchestra seemed to exceed the conductor's expectations and he responded with intense delight. It was clear also that every performance was creatively different, both for the orchestra and for the conductor.

Instead of being an all-powerful manipulator of creation, the God of process theology is its persuader, providing each entity with specific goals or purposes and coordinating the activity of all. "What happens," says Hartshorne "is in no case the product of (God's) creative act alone. Countless choices, including the universally influential choices, intersect to make a world, and how concretely they intersect is not chosen by anyone, nor could it be ... Purpose in multiple form, and chance are not mutually exclusive but complementary; neither makes sense alone" (Hartshorne 1967, 58).

This argument carries the principle of cultural evolution all down the line of natural entities from the human and the rest of the living world to entities such as electrons. The idea of cultural evolution, which is most clearly seen in humankind, is that humankind transmits information from one generation to another by teaching and learning so that successive generations learn to purpose their lives in particular ways. For us this has meant learning to control our environment through science and technology and to use them creatively or destructively. Through cultural evolution we take charge of much of our environment and that in turn changes the direction of natural selection of genes. The latter becomes less important as cultural evolution takes over. The main difference between us and the cave people of hundreds of thousands of years ago is cultural and not genetic. We have good evidence that cultural evolution is a feature in the evolution of mammals and birds, and there is evidence that it may apply all down the line (Birch and Cobb). In cultural evolution humans accept the role of purposes that make choice possible. There is no longer any reason to draw a line below which choice no longer operates at all. Of course the nature of the choice and the degree of freedom are very different at the human level compared to that of a frog or an electron.

CHANCE, PURPOSE, AND THE ANTHROPIC PRINCIPLE

The modern discovery is that chance and purpose can live together. Indeed one is not possible without the other. A world without chance is a totally determined world. In such a world there can be no freely chosen purposes; freedom excludes preprogramming. There was a chance that life might not have arisen in the universe. A slightly different sequence of events in the first microseconds of the "Big Bang" would have resulted in a universe of all helium and no hydrogen. Without hydrogen there would subsequently have been no heavy elements such as carbon and iron, which were formed by the fusion of hydrogen nuclei. Heavy elements are essential for life as we know it. One chain of events led to hydrogen and subsequently to heavy elements. Another chain of events led from heavy elements to life. The second chain was dependent upon the first. There were indeed many such chains of causes. For example, if the relative masses of protons and neutrons were different by a small fraction of one percent, making the proton heavier than the neutron, hydrogen atoms would be unstable. Hydrogen, on which the origin of life was dependent, could not then have existed. These and other examples suggest that the universe is finely tuned for our existence. The sequence of necessary events seems to put too great a burden on chance. Hence the formulation of what some physicists have called the anthropic principle asserts there must exist a guiding principle that ensures the fine tuning of the cosmos to enable life to evolve. The early states of the universe are to be explained by the fact that they made subsequent states possible. But it is quite fallacious to infer that because the present is sufficient for inferring the occurrence of a given past history, it explains that history. This is no better than supposing that symptoms of syphilis explain syphilis. Physicists who promote the strong anthropic principle seem to think that this universe has been given exactly those properties that ensure the eventual production of physicists. This is the fallacy of *a posteriori* reasoning or thinking backward. It is the same fallacy embodied in the deistic explanation of nature that Darwin refuted—that God designed nature in all its detail for the benefit of humans. Shades of it are to be found in Hugh Montefiore's advocacy of the anthropic principle in his argument for the existence of God (Montefiore).

If we accept that the universe in all its details is not determined completely by some outside power, and if we accept a role for chance, accident, and some persuasive purpose, there is no need to invoke the strong anthropic principle or its deistic variant. The principle of natural selection at the cosmic level, together with chance and purpose as organizing principles, provide another way of looking at the order of the universe. Our universe may be one of many possible universes that could exist, have existed, or exist now. Ours happens to be the one in which the physical realities are such that life as we know it could evolve. From the foundations of the universe there was the possibility that life could evolve. But it had to wait for the appropriate coincidence of many chains of physical events. Maybe it had to wait trillions of trillions of years. There was no inevitability that the chain of events that led to stable hydrogen and then to heavy elements had to occur. There was always the possibility that they would.

The dinosaurs that had dominated the earth for 100 million years became extinct about 65 million years ago. The early mammals lived in the interstices of the dinosaurs' world. Had the dinosaurs continued, the mammals would probably still be small creatures living in these interstices. A conceivable cause of the extinction of the dinosaurs is the impact of some large extraterrestrial body upon earth. Suppose that without it the dinosaurs might not have died out. We know of only one lineage of primates, a little form called *purgatorius* that lived before this potential asteroid hit. Suppose this lineage had become extinct? Many lineages of mammals did become extinct at that time. The primates would not have evolved again, as we know evolution does not repeat itself detail for detail. In that scenario the impact of a large extraterrestrial body, that greatest of all improbabilities, may have been the *sine qua non* of the development of the primates and hence our existence. And as Gould, who gives us this scenario, points out, hundreds of other historically contingent improbabilities were also essential parts of human evolution (Gould, 103).

THE PRESENCE OF GOD IN THE WORLD

An ecological doctrine of creativity implies a new kind of thinking about God. "The center of this thinking," says Moltmann, "is no longer the distinction between God and the world. The center is the recognition of the presence of God in the world and the presence of the world in God" (Moltmann 1985, 13). And as Whitehead said, "God is not before all creation, but with all creation" (Whitehead 1978, 343). There are three views of the relation of God to creation, only one of which conforms to the ecological doctrine of creativity: (1) God is identified with the cosmos and in all aspects inseparable from it and all that exists. This is pantheism. (2) God is not identified with the cosmos and is in all aspects independent of it. This is called classical theism. (3) God is involved in the cosmos but is not identified with it. God is both within the system and independent of it. This is panentheism.

The position developed by process theology in its ecological model of creation is that of panentheism (neo-classical theism). It has a long tradition that in some of its elements goes back to Hindu scriptures, Lao-tse, and parts of the Judeo-Christian scriptures such as sections in Genesis 1, Psalm

103, Psalm 104:29-30, Proverbs 8:22-31, and various parts of the New Testament. Its modern development in the light of science is largely the work of Alfred North Whitehead and those process philosophers and theologians who have taken their lead from him.

The presence of God in the world is referred to, in Whitehead's terminology, as the primordial nature of God. In the ecological model a constant tension exists between chaos and order since order is neither the outcome of one all-powerful orderer nor of deterministic necessity. At the heart of the universe, even before there were cells or atoms, there must have been the possibility of these entities coming into existence. The general potentiality of the universe is an aspect of God's nature. These possibilities of the universe are realities that constitute a continuous lure to creation. They are in the primordial mind of God. In God's primordial nature God confronts what is actual in the world with what is possible for it. This is that aspect of God which is the same yesterday, today, and forever. God is the ground of order but the order is a changing and developing one as the many become one, else ours is a multiverse and not a universe. The creative activity of God involves the creation of novelty that itself adds to the existing unity. The parts are members of one another. This is both a biblical concept and a principle in quantum physics. God as persuader, lure, and ground of order finds an appropriate expression in McFague's model of God as lover (McFague, 125 ff.). We speak of God as love, she says, but are afraid to speak of God as lover. The gospel of John gives the clue in the phrase "God so loved the world." When the divine love meets the human eros toward God the only appropriate response is with zest, with all one's heart and soul and mind and strength. The response of the creature to the divine eros is passionate and transforming.

Multiple creativity makes some disorder and conflict inevitable. It allows for the possibility of great disorder and evil. In the ecological model evil springs from chance and the freedom that it allows—not from providence (Hartshorne 1979). Providence does not eliminate chance because a world without chance is a world without freedom. For God to completely control the world would be the same as to annihilate it. It follows that it is nonsense to ask why God allowed Vesuvius to pour its molten lava on populated Pompeii or why God allowed the holocaust. People who ask these questions have not been liberated from the concept of God as omnipotent dictator of the universe, who is responsible for everything that happens and who, if he willed, could change the course of events by sheer *fiat*. It is this concept, says Whitehead, that has infused tragedy into the histories of both Christianity and Islam (Whitehead 1978, 342).

The creative working of God's primordial nature includes the concept "in the fullness of time." At each step in the evolutionary process there is a response that is appropriate. There are no shortcuts. A billion years ago there was no possibility then and there of humans becoming a reality on earth. A million years ago human values began to be realized, but there was no possibility of a mature society then and there. A Jesus or a Buddha would have been an anachronism a million years ago. In the fullness of time they appeared out of their own societies, and some were ready to respond to the call. Bertrand Russell said that if he were God he would have skipped the million years of the dinosaurs and gone straight to man. But God is not a magician, though Bertrand Russell seemed to think this was the main quality endowed upon God by theologians.

The doctrine that the divine element in the world is to be conceived as a persuasive agency, not a coercive one, should be looked upon, says Whitehead, as one of the greatest discoveries in the history of religion (Whitehead 1933, 196). It was plainly enunciated by Plato. "Can there be any doubt," asks Whitehead, "that the power of Christianity lies in its revelation in act of that which Plato divined in theory?" (Whitehead 1942, 197).

The power of the Christian gospel is the experience of divine love in human life which transforms life. The God of the universe who touches us as we experience life in its fullness is vaster than our experience of him. When I go down to the Pacific Ocean to swim on its shore I get to know one part of the ocean—its near end. But there is a vast extent of ocean beyond my experience that is nevertheless continuous with that bit of ocean I know. We touch God at the near end, yet that same God extends into the farthest reaches of the universe and there too is persuasive love. This is the full meaning of incarnation. The universe exists by its incarnation of God in itself. It is the sort of universe in which God can be incarnate. God could not be incarnate in a machine! God works in the universe through influence (literally meaning inflowing) as God's universal mode of causation.

To see the universe as a whole in this way with the same God working in the universe at large, in the life of Jesus and in our lives was put in highly symbolic language by Paul in his letter to the Colossians about the Cosmic Christ. The affirmation "In him all things hang together" (Col 1:17) is repeated in the rest of the chapter no fewer than five times. For Paul, God is the God of "all things." Nature as well as human history is the theater of grace. This panorama is caught up also in the prologue to St. John's gospel and becomes particularly pointed in John Robinson's paraphrase which begins

> The clue to the universe as personal was present from the beginning. It was to be found at the level of reality which we call God. It was personal from the beginning. Always it was transcendent to the world, always it was involved in the world, drawing the world to itself, brooding over the face of the earth (Robinson, 98).

In God's primordial nature God draws the world to greater richness of experience as each entity responds to possibilities for itself over eons of evolutionary time. But we ask what value has been achieved if in the long run our earth collapses into the sun and life on earth is no more and indeed if the universe collapses upon itself? That there will come an end to our earth seems inevitable. What then of the purposes of God? What matters matters only if it matters ultimately and it matters ultimately only if it matters everlastingly. And it matters everlastingly only if it matters to the one who is everlasting. We come face to face with the proposition, the faith, and the conviction that God, in addition to being creative out-going love, is also responsive love. This is Whitehead's doctrine of the consequent nature of God or the doctrine of the presence of the world in God.

THE PRESENCE OF THE WORLD IN GOD

In God's consequent nature God responds to the world as the world is created and lives its own life. And that makes a difference to God, for the life of God is enriched by experiencing the new creation. God lives in his world. In Whitehead's image God saves the world in his experience as a sort of memory; God saves all of value that has become concretely real in cosmic evolution and in every moment of the life of the cosmos. The intrinsic value achieved in the experience of each entity will never be nullified. The merest puff of existence has some significance to God. All experience in the cosmos will be retained as imperishable treasure "where neither moth nor rust corrupt and where thieves do not break through and steal" (Mt 6:20). The image—and it is but an image—under which this operative growth of God's nature is best conceived, is that of a tender care that nothing be lost. ... He saves the world as it passes into the immediacy of his life. It is the judgment of a tenderness which loses nothing that can be saved" (Whitehead 1978, 346). God rejoices with the joy of the world and suffers in its travail. This image is part of the Judeo-Christian tradition. The "pathos of God" (as contrasted with the concept of the "impassability" of God), according to the Jewish biblical scholar Abraham Heschel, is the central idea of prophetic theology (Merkle, 494). In McFague's model

> God as lover cannot be aloof like the artist nor identify at a distance like the educator but will be totally, passionately involved in the agency of the evil that befalls the beloved. God's involvement with the world in its struggles with evil will embody passion as both deep feeling and suffering (McFague, 142).

When Jesus said not a sparrow falls to the ground without God knowing, was he portraying God as a counter of dead sparrows? Or did he mean that God was involved in the life of the sparrow such that even its experiences were of value to him? When the writer of Romans 8 speaks of the whole of creation groaning and suffering in travail as in the agony of childbirth, he adds that God is not simply watching from afar as a producer of a play might watch the performance from the wings. God is in the drama feeling every feeling in ways that words cannot express. God is no mere detached spectator of the ocean of feelings that is nature. God is the supreme synthesis of these feelings. Hence Hartshorne says that "all life contributes to the living one who alone can appreciate life's every nuance. He experiences our experiences and that of all creatures. His feelings are feelings of all feelings" (Hartshorne 1979, 60). The chief "novelty of the New Testament," says Hartshorne, "is that divine love . . . is carried to the point of participation in creaturely suffering, symbolized by the Cross taken together with the doctrine of the Incarnation" (Hartshorne 1967, 104).

In this ecological concept of creativity there is an inside story to evolution in addition to the outside story on which science concentrates its attention. Presumably God knows the inside story as direct experience. We cannot have the experience of even another person, let alone that of a tiger or a sparrow or a dinosaur. We can participate in it imaginatively, as indeed we seek to do in the lives of our fellows. The world will then no longer be seen as a factory to provide for our every need, no matter at what cost to the creation. Its eventual worth is not its worth to us, but the contribution it has made to something more enduring than any particular atom or sparrow or any species of plant or animal. The "final beauty" says Hartshorne "is the beauty of holiness" (Hartshorne 1970, 321) — which I take to mean the enrichment of the life of God in God's consequent nature from all the creation.

CONCLUSION

The dominant model of nature derived from science is mechanistic or substantialist. Science investigates nature as if it were machinery. It does not follow that nature is therefore machinery. Science does this by excluding from its consideration all subjective elements of nature, mind, and conscious feeling. The quintessence of this approach is to conclude that nature is the product of chance and necessity. There is no place for purposes as causal agents, or for God other than the God outside the machinery. However, there is a post-modern understanding of science, which seeks a more inclusive view of nature. This finds its deepest expression in quantum physics, which has rejected the substantialist model of nature. It is also highly relevant to biology and is recognized as such particularly by some workers in neurophysiology, development, behavior, and evolution. There is no place for the workings of purposes as causal agencies, or of God as involved in nature, in the substantialist model of nature. However the post-modern model of nature is highly relevant to an understanding of both the role of purposes and the role of God in the creative process. The meeting of science and theology in this context leads to a view of nature that includes the following characteristics: (1) Chance is a component of nature and its evolution; nature is not the product of preprogramming or some deterministic design as might be specified in an architect's blueprint of a building.

(2) Since nature is not one-hundred percent determined, there is room for freedom and a degree of self-determination on the part of the created entities. There is thus a multiplicity of creators. (3) The existence of freedom and self-determination allows for the influence of purposes as causal agencies and therefore of internal relations as well as external relations as influential in nature. (4) Insofar as the entities of creation are themselves creative and to a degree self-determining they are subjects as well as objects. (5) A multitude of creative agents makes some disorder, conflict, and evil inevitable. But a multitude of creative agents also implies the necessity of the rule of one if total chaos is to be avoided. The nature of the rule of one, which coordinates the creativity of a multitude of creative agents, is persuasion, the persuasive love of God in the world. (6) God is present in the world. God as cause is not outside nature as an external coercive agency but is involved in the being of the created entities through persuasive love. The creation has its own degree of freedom in its response to God as lure. (7) The world is present in God. God responds to the creation as it evolves and lives its own life. God experiences the experiences of the created entities in all their joy and their sufferings. The image of incarnation is extended to the whole of creation and it, together with the symbol of the cross, becomes central in the ecological understanding of nature. (8) The ecological model of nature and the involvement of God in nature leads to a view of nature not simply as the stage on which the drama of human life is performed but as itself the drama. Since every creature, not only humans, is a subject with intrinsic value, this leads to an ethic of high responsibility of caring for the world.

WORKS CITED

Birch, Charles (a). "The Post Modern Challenge to Biology." In *The Reenchantment of Science: Post Modern Proposals*. Ed. David Ray Griffin. Albany, NY: State University of New York Press, 1988, pp. 57-78.

—— (b). "Eight Fallacies of the Modern World and Five Axioms for a Postmodern World View." *Perspectives in Biology and Medicine* 32 (1988):12-30.

Birch, Charles and John B. Cobb. *The Liberation of Life: From the Cell to the Community*. New York: Cambridge University Press, 1981.

Darwin, F., ed. *The Life and Letters of Charles Darwin*. London: John Muray, 1888.

Davies, Paul. "The Creative Cosmos." *New Scientist* 17 (1987):41-44.

Dawkins, Richard. *The Blind Watchmaker*. London: Marlow, Longman, 1986.

Gould, Stephen J. Untitled remarks. In *Darwin's Legacy*. Ed. Charles L. Hamdrum. Nobel Conference 18. San Francisco: Harper and Row, 1983.

Hartshorne, Charles. *The Logic of Perfection*. La Salle, IL: Open Court Pub. Co., 1962.

——. *A Natural Theology for Our Time*. La Salle, IL: Open Court Pub. Co., 1967.

——. *Creative Synthesis and the Philosophic Method*. London: SCM Press, 1970.

——. "God and Nature." *Anticipation* 125 (1979): 58-64.

——. *Omnipotence and Other Theological Mistakes*. Albany, NY: State University of New York Press, 1984.

Haught, John F. *The Cosmic Adventure: Science, Religion, and the Quest for Purpose.* New York: Paulist Press, 1984.

McFague, Sallie. *Models of God: Theology for an Ecological, Nuclear Age.* Philadelphia: Fortress Press, 1987.

Merkle, J. C. "Abraham Hershel: The Pathos of God." *Christianity and Crisis* 45 (1985): 493-96.

Moltmann, Jürgen. *God and Creation: An Ecological Doctrine of Creation.* London: SCM Press, 1985.

Monod, Jacques. *Chance and Necessity: An Essay on the Natural Philosophy of Modern Biology.* London: Fontana/Collins, 1974.

Montefiore, Hugh. *The Probability of God.* London: SCM Press, 1985.

Prigogine, L. and I. Stengers. *Order Out of Chaos: Man's New Dialogue With Nature.* New York: Bantam Books, 1984.

Raven, Charles E. *Natural Religion and Christian Theology.* Gifford Lectures. First series: Science and Religion. Cambridge: Cambridge University Press, 1953.

Robinson, John A. T. *Exploration into God.* London: SCM Press, 1967.

Tillich, Paul. *A History of Christian Thought: From Its Judaic and Hellenistic Origins to Existentialism.* New York: Simon and Schuster, 1967.

Whitehead, Alfred North. *Religion in the Making.* Cambridge: Cambridge University Press, 1930.

———. *Science and the Modern World.* Cambridge: Cambridge University Press, 1933.

———. *Adventure of Ideas.* Middlesex, Harmondsworth: Penguin Books, 1942.

———. *Process and Reality: An Essay on Cosmology.* Gifford Lectures. Corrected edition edited by David Ray Griffin and Donald W. Sherbourne. New York: The Free Press, 1978.

14

Imaging a Theology of Nature: The World as God's Body[1]

Sallie McFague

I spent my last sabbatical in England, and I think all will agree that England is a green and pleasant land. I recall an early morning trip to Coventry on the bus: the lovely, gently rolling hills, quaint villages with thatched-roofed cottages—very pastoral, idyllic. There were sheep dotting the hills, but also something else: huge, concrete towers of nuclear plants rising up through the morning mist. It seemed a strange juxtaposition: sheep and nuclear towers—life and potential death. Our cruise missiles also dotted the countryside, though I did not see them. These towers and missiles symbolize a situation unique to our time. We are the first generation of human beings out of all the billions of humans who have ever lived who have the responsibility of nuclear knowledge. In perverse imitation of God, the creator of life, we have become potential uncreators. We have the knowledge and the power to destroy ourselves and much of the rest of life. And we will *always* have this knowledge—regardless of nuclear disarmament. Jonathan Schell in his book *The Fate of the Earth* speaks of the "second death"—the death of life (Schell, 99ff.). The first death is our own individual one and difficult as that is to face, we at least know that birth will follow and others will take our place. But the death of birth is the

---

In this essay, theologian Sallie McFague, author of the influential *Models of God: Theology for an Ecological, Nuclear Age,* engages in what she calls heuristic theology. The aim of such theology is to interpret God, albeit with humility, in an ecologically responsible manner. Such is the need, so McFague claims, of our "ecological, nuclear age." McFague identifies four images that ecologically attuned Christians might find helpful: God as mother, as lover, as friend, and finally, God as embodied by the universe itself. The importance of McFague's thinking is evidenced by the many references to her work in other essays in this anthology. She is one of the leading ecological theologians of our time.

extinction of life and that is too horrendous to contemplate, especially when we know *we would be responsible for it.*

Our nuclear knowledge brings to the surface a fundamental fact about human existence. We are part and parcel of the web of life and exist in interdependence with all other beings, both human and nonhuman. As Pierre Teilhard de Chardin puts it in a moment of insight: "I realized that my own poor trifling existence was one with the immensity of all that is and all that is in process of becoming" (Teilhard 1968a, 25). Or, as the poet Wallace Stevens says, "Nothing is itself taken alone. Things are because of interrelations and interconnections" (Stevens, 163). The evolutionary, ecological perspective insists that we are, in the most profound way, "not our own": we belong, from the cells of our bodies to the finest creations of our minds, to the intricate, ever-changing cosmos. We both depend on that web of life for our own continued existence and in a special way we are responsible for it, for we *alone know* that life is interrelated and we *alone know* how to destroy it. It is an awesome—and unsettling—thought.

As we near the close of the twentieth century we have become increasingly conscious of the fragility of our world. We have also become aware that the anthropocentrism that characterizes much of the Judeo-Christian tradition has often fed a sensibility insensitive to our proper place in the universe.[2] The ecological crisis, epitomized in the possibility of a nuclear holocaust, has brought home to many the need for a new mode of consciousness on the part of human beings, for what Rosemary Ruether calls a "conversion" to the earth, a cosmocentric sensibility (Ruether, 89).[3]

What does all this mean for theology, especially for a theology of nature? Theology, I believe, has special responsibility for the symbols, images, the language, used for expressing the relationship between God and the world in every age. The sciences are also concerned with interpreting reality—the universe or universes, if you will—although cosmology means different things to scientists than it does to theologians. Nonetheless, here is a meeting place, a place of common interest, to scientists and theologians. David Tracy and Nicholas Lash have called recently for a "collaborative" relationship between science and theology in order to "help establish plausible 'mutually critical correlations' not only to interpret the world but to help change it" (Tracy and Lash, 91).[4] They note that relations between science and theology are not only those posed by a recognition of analogies between the two areas on methodological issues but, more pressingly, by a common concern with the cosmos. Thus, a focus on the cosmos with the intent both to understand it better—and to orient our praxis within it more appropriately—is one collaborative effort for science and theology in our time.

While cosmology may mean several different things, the theologian's contribution is concerned with "accounts of the world as God's creation," and, within that broad compass, one specific enterprise especially needed in our time involves "imaginative perceptions of how the world seems and where we stand in it" (Tracy and Lash, vii).[5] In other words, I propose that one theological task is an experimental one with metaphors and models for the relationship between God and the world that will help bring about a theocentric, life-centered, cosmocentric sensibility in place of our anthropocentric one.

This exercise would take place at the juncture between a theology of nature and a theocentric or life-centered ethic. That is, an analysis in some detail of one model of the God/world relationship—that of the world or universe as God's body—would mediate between concepts and praxis, between a theoretical and a practical orientation.

As we begin this task we must keep in mind some criteria for any theology of nature pertinent to the closing years of the twentieth century. First, it must be informed by and commensurate with contemporary scientific accounts of what nature is. Second, it needs to see human life as profoundly interrelated with all other forms of life, refusing the traditional absolute separation of human beings from other creatures as well as of God from the world. Third, it will be a kind of theology that is creation-centered, in contrast to the almost total concern with redemption in some Christian theologies. It will be a theology that focuses, in the broadest and deepest sense, on the incarnational presence of God in the world. Finally, it will acknowledge and press the interconnectedness of peace, justice, and ecological issues, aware that there can be no peace or justice unless the fabric of our ecosystem is intact. What this means, I believe, is that for the first time in the history of the human race, we see the necessity of thinking responsibly and deeply about *everything that is*. That is a tall order, but once the scales fall from the eyes and one understands the profound relationships between issues of peace and war, justice to the oppressed, and concern for our home—the earth—there is no possibility of going back to piecemeal thinking. In other words, a theology of nature must be holistic.

One task that needs to be done within this overarching assignment is to *imagine* in some detail and depth the relationship between God and the world in a way not only consonant with these criteria, but in a fashion that would help it to come alive in people's minds and hearts. Human behavior appears to be profoundly influenced by the imagistic, symbolical, narrative powers of human reflection. How would we, for instance, act differently if we imagined the world to be the body of God rather than considering it to be, as the tradition has, the realm of the Almighty King? That question is the basic one I want to consider in this paper.

The kind of theology I will be engaged in here, by no means the only kind, could be called heuristic theology; in analogy with some similar activities in the sciences, it "plays" with possibilities in order to find out, to discover, new fruitful ways to interpret the universe.[6] In the case of an heuristic theology focused on cosmology, the discovery would be oriented toward "remythologizing" creation as dependent upon God. More specifically, I propose as a modest contribution to the contemporary understanding of a theological cosmology for our time an elaboration of the model of the world as God's body, both as a critique of and substitute for the dominant model of the world as the realm of God the king.

The following, therefore, will be a "case study," with a theological model for reenvisioning the relationship between God and the universe. Before turning to this study, however, we will make some preliminary comments on the method employed in this kind of theology as well as on metaphors and models, their character and status.

IMAGINATION AND THEOLOGY

Christian faith is, it seems to me, most basically a claim that the universe is neither indifferent nor malevolent, but that there is a power (and a personal power at that) that is on the side of life and its fulfillment. Moreover, the Christian believes that we have some clues for fleshing out this claim in the life, death, and appearances of Jesus of Nazareth. Nevertheless, each generation must venture, through an analysis of what fulfillment could and must mean for its own time, the best way to express that claim. A critical dimension of this expression is the imaginative picture, the metaphors and models, that underlie the conceptual systems of theology. One cannot hope to interpret Christian faith for one's own time if one remains indifferent to the basic images that are the lifeblood of interpretation and that greatly influence people's perceptions and behavior.[7]

Many of the major models for the relationship between God and the world in the Judeo-Christian tradition are ones that emphasize the transcendence of God and the distance between God and the world: God as king with the world as his realm, God as potter who creates the cosmos by molding it, God as speaker who with a word brings the world to be out of nothing. One has to ask whether these models are adequate ones for our time, our ecological, nuclear age, in which the radical interdependence and interrelationship of all forms of life must be underscored. Quite apart from that crisis, however, responsible theology ought to be done in the context of contemporary science and were it to take that context seriously, models underscoring the closeness, not the distance, of God and the world would emerge. A. R. Peacocke makes this point well when he says,

There is increasing awareness not only among Christian theologians, but even more among ordinary believers that, if God is in fact the all-encompassing Reality that Christian faith proclaims, then that Reality is to be experienced in and through our actual lives as biological organisms who are persons, part of nature and living in society (Peacocke, 16-17).

For a number of reasons, therefore, experimentation with models underscoring the intimacy of God and creation may be in order and it is this task, with one model, that I will undertake. I have characterized the theological method operative here as heuristic and concerned with metaphors and models. Let us look briefly at these matters. Heuristic theology is distinct from theology as hermeneutics or as construction but has similarities with both.[8] The *Shorter Oxford English Dictionary* defines *heuristic* adjectivally as "serving to find out" and, when employed as a noun related to learning, as "a system of education under which pupils are trained to find out for themselves." Thus heuristic theology will be one that experiments and tests, that thinks in an as-if fashion, that imagines possibilities that are novel, that dares to think differently. It will not accept solely on the basis of authority but will search for what it finds convincing and persuasive; it will not, however, be fantasy or mere play but will assume that there is something to find out and that if some imagined possibilities fail, others may succeed. The mention of failure and success, and of the persuasive and the convincing, indicates that although I wish to distinguish heuristic theology from both hermeneutical and constructive theology, it bears similarities to both.

If the characteristic mark of hermeneutical theology is its interpretive stance, especially in regard to texts—both the classic text of the Judeo-Christian tradition (the Hebrew Scriptures and the New Testament) and the exemplary theologies that build on the classic text—then heuristic theology is also interpretive, for it claims that its successful unconventional metaphors are not only in continuity with the paradigmatic events and their significance expressed in this classic text but are also appropriate expressions of these matters for the present time. Heuristic theology, though not bound to the images and concepts in scripture, is constrained to show that its proposed models are an appropriate, persuasive expression of Christian faith for our time. Hence, while heuristic theology is not limited to interpreting texts, it is concerned with the same "matter" as the classic texts, namely, the salvific power of God.[9]

If, on the other hand, the distinctive mark of constructive theology is that it does not rely principally on classical sources but attempts its articulation of the concepts of God, world, and human being with the help of a variety of sources, including material from the natural, physical, and social sciences as well as from philosophy, literature, and the arts, then heuristic theology is also constructive in that it claims that a valid understanding of God and world for a particular time is an imaginative construal built up from a variety of sources, many of them outside religious traditions. Like theology as construction, theology as heuristics supports the assertion that our concept of God is precisely that—*our concept* of God—and not God. Yet, while heuristic theology has some similarities to constructive theology, it has a distinctive emphasis: it will be more experimental, imagistic, and pluralistic.

Its experimental character means it is a kind of theology well suited for times of uncertainty and change, when systematic, comprehensive construction seems inappropriate if not impossible. It could be called "free theology,"[10] for it must be willing to play with possibilities and, as a consequence, not take itself too seriously, accepting its tentative, relative, partial, and hypothetical character.

Its imagistic character means it stands as a corrective to the bias of much constructive theology toward conceptual clarity, often at the price of imagistic richness.[11] Although it would be insufficient to rest in new images and to refuse to spell out conceptually their implications in as comprehensive a way as possible, the more critical task is to propose what Dennis Nineham calls a "lively imaginative picture" of the way God and the world as we know it are related (Nineham, 201-2). It is no coincidence that most religious traditions turn to personal and public human relationships to serve as metaphors and models of the relationship between God and the world: God as father, mother, lover, friend, king, lord, governor. These metaphors give a precision and persuasive power to the construct of God that concepts alone cannot. Because religions, including Christianity, are not incidentally imagistic but centrally and necessarily so, theology must also be an affair of the imagination.

To say that heuristic theology is pluralistic is to insist that since no metaphor or model refers properly or directly to God, many are necessary. All are inappropriate, partial, and inadequate; the most that can be said is that some aspect or aspects of the God-world relationship are illuminated by this or that model in a fashion relevant to a particular time and place. Models of God are not definitions of God but likely accounts of experiences of relating to God with the help of relationships we know and understand. If one accepts that metaphors (and all language about God) are principally adverbial, having to do with how we relate to God rather than defining the nature of God, then no metaphors or models can be reified, petrified, or expanded so as to exclude all others. One can, for instance, include many possibilities: We can envision relating to God as to a father and a mother, to a healer and a liberator, to the sun and a mountain. As definitions of God, these possibilities are mutually exclusive; as models expressing experiences of relating to God, they are mutually enriching.

In summary, the theology I am proposing is a kind of heuristic construction that in focusing on the imaginative construal of the God-world relationship, attempts to remythologize Christian faith through metaphors and models appropriate for our time.

What, however, is the character and status of the metaphors and models that are the central concern of heuristic theology? A metaphor is a word or phrase used *in*appropriately.[12] It belongs in one context but is being used in another: the arm of the chair, war as a chess game, God the father. From Aristotle until recently, metaphor was seen mainly as a poetic device to embellish or decorate. Increasingly, however, the idea of metaphor as unsubstitutable is winning acceptance; what a metaphor expresses cannot be said directly or apart from it, for if it could, one would have said it directly. Here, metaphor is a strategy of desperation, not decoration; it is an attempt to say something about the unfamiliar in terms of the familiar, an attempt to speak about what we do not know in terms of what we do know.

Metaphor always has the character of *is* and *is not*: an assertion is made but as a likely account rather than a definition.[13] The point that metaphor underscores is that in certain matters there can be no direct description. It used to be the case that poetry and religion were thought to be distinctive in their reliance on metaphor, but more recently the use of metaphors and models in the natural and social sciences has widened the scope of metaphorical thinking considerably and linked science and theology methodologically in ways inconceivable twenty years ago.[14]

The difference between a metaphor and a model can be expressed in a number of ways, but most simply, a model is a metaphor with "staying power," that is, a model is a metaphor that has gained sufficient stability and scope so as to present a pattern for relatively comprehensive and coherent explanation.[15] The metaphor of God the father is an excellent example of this. In becoming a model, it has engendered wide-ranging interpretation of the relationship between God and human beings; if God is seen as father, human beings become children, sin can be seen as rebellious behavior, and redemption can be thought of as restoration to the status of favored offspring.

It should be evident that a theology that describes itself as metaphorical is a theology at risk. Jacques Derrida, in defining metaphor, writes, "if metaphor, which is mimesis trying its chance, mimesis at risk, may always fail to attain truth, this is because it has to reckon with a definite absence" (Derrida, 42). As Derrida puts it, metaphor lies somewhere between "nonsense" and "truth," and a theology based on metaphor will be open to the charge that it is closer to the first than the second. This is, I believe, a risk that theology in our time must be willing to run. Theology has usually had a high stake in truth, so high that it has refused all play of the imagination: through creedal control and the formulations of orthodoxy, it has refused all attempts at new metaphors "trying their chance." But a heuristic theology insists that new metaphors and models be given a chance, be tried out as likely accounts of the God-world relationship, be allowed to make a case for themselves. A heuristic theology is, therefore, destabilizing. Since no language about God is adequate and all of it is improper, new metaphors are not necessarily less inadequate or improper than old ones. All are in the same situation and no authority—not scriptural status, liturgical longevity, or ecclesiastical fiat—can decree that some types of language, or some images, refer literally to God while others do not. None do. Hence, the criteria for preferring some to others must be other than authority, however defined.

We come, then, finally, to the issue of the status of language about God. R. W. Hepburn has posed it directly:

The question which should be of the greatest concern to the theologian is . . . whether or not the circle of myth, metaphor, and symbol is a closed one: and if closed then in what way propositions about God manage to refer (Hepburn, 23).

The "truth" of a construal of the God-world relationship is a mixture of belief (Ricoeur calls it a "wager"), pragmatic criteria, and what Philip Wheelwright terms a "shy ontological claim," or, as in Mary Hesse's striking remark, "God is more like gravitation than embarrassment" (Arbib and Hesse, 5). Belief in God is not taken to be purely a social construct. At least this is what a critical realist would claim. Thus, metaphors and models of God are understood to be discovered as well as created, to relate to God's reality not in the sense of being literally in correspondence with it, but as versions or hypotheses of it that the community (in this case, the church) accepts as relatively adequate.[16] Hence, models of God are not simply heuristic fictions; the critical realist does not accept the Feuerbachian critique that language about God is nothing but human projection. On the other hand, any particular metaphor or model is not the only, appropriate, true one.

How does one come to accept a model as true? We live *within* the model, testing our wager by its consequences. These consequences are both theoretical and practical. An adequate model will be illuminating, fruitful, have relatively comprehensive explanatory ability, be relatively consistent, be able to deal with anomalies, and so on. This largely, though not totally, functional, pragmatic view of truth stresses heavily the implications of certain models for the quality of human and nonhuman life. A praxis orientation does not deny the possibility of the "shy ontological claim," but it does acknowledge both the mystery of God and the importance of truth as practical wisdom. Thus it acknowledges with the apophatic tradition that we really do not *know* the inner being of divine reality; the hints and clues we have of the way things are, whether we call them religious experiences, revelation, or whatever, are too fragile, too little (and often too negative) for heavy metaphysical claims. Rather, in the tradition of Aristotle, truth means constructing the good life for the *polis*, though for our time this must mean for the cosmos. A "true" model of God will be one that is a powerful, persuasive construal of God as being on the side of life and its fulfillment in our time.[17]

GOD AND THE WORLD

We turn now to consider models for the relationship between God and the world. The dominant model has been monarchical; the classical picture employs royalist, triumphalist metaphors, depicting God as king, lord, and patriarch, who rules over and cares for the world and human beings. Ian Barbour, theologian and philosopher of science, says of this model:

The *monarchical model* of God as King was developed systematically, both in Jewish thought (God as Lord and King of the Universe), in medieval Christian thought (with its emphasis on divine omnipotence), and in the Reformation (especially in Calvin's insistence on God's sovereignty). In the portrayal of God's relation to the world, the dominant western historical model has been that of the absolute monarch ruling over his kingdom (Barbour, 156).[18]

This imaginative picture is so prevalent in mainstream Christianity that it is often not recognized as a picture. It is a powerful imaginative picture and a very dangerous one. As Gordon Kaufman points out in *Theology for a Nuclear Age*, divine sovereignty is the issue with which theologians in the nuclear age must deal. In its cruder versions, God is the king who fights on the side of his chosen ones to bring their enemies down; in more refined versions God is the father who will not let his children suffer. The first view supports militarism; the second supports escapism. As Kaufman states, two groups of American Christians currently rely on these images of God in their responses to the nuclear situation: one group claims that if a nuclear holocaust comes, it will be God's will—the Armageddon—and America should arm itself to fight the devil's agent, Communist Russia; the other passively relies on the all-powerful father to take care of the situation. Is divine sovereignty the appropriate imagery for our time? It may have been for some ages, but in *our* time, when the interdependence of all life and our special responsibility for it needs to be emphasized, is it *for ours*?

As Kaufman points out, the monarchical model results in a pattern of "asymmetrical dualism" between God and the world, in which God and the world are only distantly related and all power, either as domination or benevolence, is on God's side (Kaufman, 39). It supports conceiving of God as a being existing somewhere apart from the world and ruling it externally either directly through divine intervention or indirectly through controlling the wills of his subjects. It creates feelings of awe in the hearts of loyal subjects and thus supports the "godness" of God, but these feelings are balanced by others of abject fear and humiliation: in this picture, God can be God only if we are nothing.

Very briefly, let me summarize a few major problems with this model as an imaginative framework for understanding God's saving love as an inclusive one of fulfillment for all of creation. In the monarchical model, God is distant from the world, relates only to the human world, and controls that world through domination and benevolence. On the first point: the relationship of a king to his subjects is necessarily a distant one for royalty is "untouchable." It is the distance, the difference, the otherness of God, that is underscored with this imagery. God as king is in his kingdom—which is not of this earth—and we remain in another place, far from his dwelling. In this picture God is worldless and the world is Godless: the world is empty of God's presence. Whatever one does for the world is not finally important in this model, for its ruler does not inhabit it as his primary residence, and his subjects are well advised not to become too enamored of it either.

Although these comments may at first seem like a caricature rather than a fair description of the classical Western monarchical model, they are the direct implications of its imagery. If metaphors matter, then one must take them seriously at the level at which they function, that is, at the level of the imaginative picture of God and the world they project. And one of the direct implications is distance and at best only external involvement. To be sure, kings want their subjects to be loyal and their realms peaceful, but that does not mean internal, intrinsic involvement. Kings do not have to, and usually do not, love their subjects or realms; at most, one hopes they will be benevolent.

But such benevolence extends only to human subjects: in the monarchical model there is no concern for the cosmos, for the nonhuman world. Here is our second objection to this model. It is simply blank in terms of what lies outside the human sphere. As a political model focused on governing human beings, it leaves out most of reality. One could say at this point that, as with all models, it has limitations and needs to be balanced by other models. Such a comment does not address the seriousness of the monarchical model's power, for as the dominant Western model, it has not allowed competing models to arise. The tendency, rather, has been to draw other models into its orbit, as is evident with the model of God as father. This model could have gone in the direction of parent (and that is clearly its New Testament course), with associations of nurture, care, guidance, and responsibility, but under the powerful influence of the monarchical model, the parent becomes the patriarch, and patriarchs act more like kings than like fathers: They rule their children and they demand obedience.

The monarchical model is not only highly anthropocentric, but it supports a kind of anthropocentricism characterized by dualistic hierarchies. We not only imagine God in our image, but those images we use for imaging God also become standards for human behavior. Dualistic, triumphalistic thinking fuels many forms of oppression.[19] While the monarchical model may not be responsible alone for hierarchical dualism, it has supported it: the dualisms of male/female, spirit/nature, human/nonhuman, Christian/ non-Christian, rich/poor, white/colored, and so forth. The hierarchical, dualistic pattern is so widespread in Western thought that it is often not perceived to be a pattern, but is felt to be simply the way things are. It appears natural to many that whites, males, the rich, and Christians are superior to other human beings, and that human beings are more valuable in all respects than other forms of life.

We come, then, to the third criticism of the monarchical model: God rules either through domination or benevolence, thus undercutting human responsibility for the world. It is simplistic to blame the Judeo-Christian tradition for the ecological crisis, as some have done, on the grounds that

Genesis instructs human beings to have dominion over nature; nonetheless, the imagery of sovereignty supports attitudes of control and use toward the nonhuman world.[20] Although the might of the natural world when unleashed is fearsome, as is evident in earthquakes, tornadoes, and volcanic eruptions, the power balance has shifted from nature to us, and an essential aspect of the new sensibility is to recognize and accept this. Nature can and does destroy many, but it is not in the position to destroy all, as we can. Extinction of species by nature is in a different dimension from extinction by design, which only we can bring about. This chilling thought adds a new importance to the images we use to characterize our relationship to others and to the nonhuman world. If we are capable of extinguishing ourselves and most, if not all, other life, metaphors that support attitudes of distance from, and domination of, other human beings and nonhuman life must be recognized as dangerous. No matter how ancient a metaphorical tradition may be and regardless of its credentials in scripture, liturgy, and creedal statements, it still must be discarded if it threatens the continuation of life itself. If the heart of the Christian gospel is the salvific power of God, triumphalist metaphors cannot express that reality *in our time*, whatever their appropriateness may have been in the past.

And this is so even if God's power is seen as benevolence rather than domination. For if God's rule is understood benevolently, it will be assumed that all is well—that the world will be cared for with no help from us. The king as dominating sovereign encourages attitudes of militarism and destruction; the king as benevolent patriarch encourages attitudes of passivity and escape from responsibility.[21] The monarchical model is dangerous in our time. It encourages a sense of distance from the world; it attends only to the human dimension of the world; and it supports attitudes of either domination of the world or passivity toward it. As an alternative model I suggest considering the world as God's body.

In what ways would we think of the relationship between God and the world were we to experiment with the metaphor of the universe as God's body, God's palpable presence in all space and time? If the entire universe is expressive of God's very being—*the* incarnation, if you will—do we not have the beginnings of an imaginative picture of the relationship between God and the world peculiarly appropriate as a context for interpreting the salvific love of God *for our time*? If what is needed in our ecological, nuclear age is an imaginative vision of the relationship between God and the world that underscores their interdependence and mutuality, empowering a sensibility of care and responsibility toward all life, how would it help to see the world as the body of God?

This image, radical as it may seem (in light of the dominant metaphor of a king to his realm) for imagining the relationship between God and the world, is a very old one with roots in Stoicism and elliptically in the Hebrew Scriptures. The notion has tantalized many, including Tertullian and Irenaeus, and though it received little assistance from either Platonism or Aristotelianism because of their denigration of matter and the body (and hence did not enter the mainstream of either Augustinian or Thomistic theology), it surfaced powerfully in Hegel as well as in twentieth-century process theologies.[22] The mystical tradition within Christianity has carried the notion implicitly, even though the metaphor of body may not appear: "The world is charged with the grandeur of God" (Gerard Manley Hopkins, 27). "There is communion with God, and a communion with the earth, and a communion with God through the earth" (Teilhard 1968a, 14).

As we begin this experiment with the model of the world as God's body, we must once again recall that a metaphor or model is not a description. We are trying to think in an as-if fashion about the God-world relationship, because we have no other way of thinking about it. No metaphor fits in all ways, and some are more nonsense than sense. The king-realm kind of thinking about the God-world relationship sounds like sense because we are used to it, but reflection shows that in our world it is nonsense. For a metaphor to be acceptable, it need not, cannot, apply in all ways; if it did, it would be a description. The metaphor of the world as God's body has the opposite problem to the metaphor of the world as the king's realm; if the latter puts too great a distance between God and the world, the former verges on too great a proximity. Since neither metaphor fits exactly, we have to ask which one is better in our time and to qualify it with other metaphors and models. Is it better to accept an imaginative picture of God as the distant ruler controlling his realm through external and benevolent power or one of God so intimately related to the world that the world can be imagined as God's body? Which is better in terms of our and the world's preservation and fulfillment? Which is better in terms of coherence, comprehensibility, and illumination? Which is better in terms of expressing the Christian understanding of the relationship between God and the world? All these criteria are relevant, for a metaphor that is all or mostly nonsense has tried and failed.

Therefore, a heuristic, metaphorical theology, though hospitable initially to nonsense, is constrained as well to search for sense. Christians should, given their tradition, be inclined to find sense in body language, not only because of the resurrection of the body but also because of the bread and wine of the eucharist as the body and blood of Christ, and the church as the body with Christ as its head. Christians have a surprisingly "bodily" tradition. Nonetheless, there is a difference between the traditional uses of body and seeing the world as God's body: when the world is viewed as God's body, that body includes more than just Christians, and more than just human beings. It is possible to speculate that if Christianity had begun in a culture less dualistic and antiphysical than that of the first-century Mediterranean world, it might have been willing, given the more holistic anthropology and theology of its Hebraic roots, to extend its body metaphor to God.[23] At any rate, in view of the contemporary holistic understanding of personhood, in which embodiment is the *sine qua non*, the thought of an embodied divine person is not more incredible than that of a disembodied one; in fact, it is less so. In a dualistic culture where mind and body, spirit and flesh, are separable, a disembodied, personal God is more credible, but not in ours. This is only to suggest that the idea of God's embodiment—the idea as such, quite apart from particulars—should not be seen as nonsense; it is less nonsense than the idea of a disembodied personal God.

We are imagining the world to be God's body. The body of God, then, would be nothing less than all that is—the universe or universes and everything they contain of which cosmologists speak. The body of God, as theologians would say, is creation, understood as God's self-expression; it is formed in God's own reality, bodied forth in the eons of evolutionary time, and supplied with the means to nurture and sustain billions of different forms of life. *We* give life only to others of our own species, but God gives life to *all* that is, all species of life and all forms of matter. In a monotheistic, panentheistic theology, if one is to understand God in some sense as physical and not just spiritual, then the entire "body" of the universe is "in" God and is God's visible self-expression. This body, albeit a strange one if we take ours as the model, is nothing less than all that exists.

Would God, then, be reduced to the world or the universe? The metaphor does come far closer to pantheism than the king-realm model, which verges on deism, but it does not identify God totally with the world any more than we identify ourselves totally with our bodies. Other animals may be said to be bodies that have spirits; we may be said to be spirits that possess bodies.[24] This is not to introduce a new dualism but only to recognize that, although our bodies are expressions of us both unconsciously and consciously, we can reflect about them and distance ourselves from them. The very fact that we can speak about our bodies is evidence that we are not totally one with them. On this model God is not reduced to the world if the world is God's body. Without the use of personal, agential metaphors, however, including among others God as mother, father, healer, lover, friend, judge, and liberator, the metaphor of the world as God's body would be pantheistic, for the body would be all there were.[25] Nonetheless, the model is most precisely designated as panentheistic; that is, it is a view of the God-world relationship in which all things have their origins in God and nothing exists outside God, though this does not mean that God is reduced to these things.[26]

Nevertheless, though God is not reduced to the world, the metaphor of the world as God's body puts God "at risk." If we follow out the implications of the metaphor, we see that God becomes dependent through being bodily in a way that a totally invisible, distant God would never be. Just as we care about our bodies, are made vulnerable by them, and must attend to their well-being, God will be liable to bodily contingencies. The world as God's body may be poorly cared for, ravaged, and as we are becoming well-aware, essentially destroyed, in spite of God's own loving attention to it, because of one creature, ourselves, who can choose or not choose to join with God in conscious care of the world. Presumably, were our tiny corner of this body destroyed, another could be formed; hence, God need not be seen to be as dependent on us or on any particular body as we are on our bodies. But in the metaphor of the universe as the self-expression of God — God's incarnation — the notions of vulnerability, shared responsibility, and risk are inevitable. This is a markedly different basic understanding of the God-world relationship than in the monarch-realm metaphor, for it emphasizes God's willingness to suffer for and with the world, even to the point of personal risk. The world as God's body, then, may be seen as a way to remythologize the inclusive, suffering love of the cross of Jesus of Nazareth. In both instances God is at risk in human hands: just as once upon a time in a bygone mythology human beings killed their God in the body of a man, so now we once again have that power, but in a mythology more appropriate to our time; we would kill our God in the body of the world. Could we actually do this? To believe in the resurrection means we could not. God is not in our power to destroy, but the incarnate God is at risk; we have been given central responsibility to care for God's body, our world.

If God, though at risk and dependent on others, is not reduced to the world in the metaphor of the world as God's body, what more can we say about the meaning of this model? How does God know the world, act in it, and love it? How does one speak of evil in this metaphor? In the monarchical model, God knows the world externally, acts on it either by direct intervention or indirectly through human subjects, and loves it benevolently, in a charitable way. God's knowledge, action, and love are markedly different in the metaphor of the world as God's body. God knows the world immediately just as we know our bodies immediately. God could be said to be in touch with all parts of the world through interior understanding. Moreover, this knowledge is empathetic, intimate, sympathetic knowledge, closer to feeling than to rationality.[27] It is knowledge "by acquaintance"; it is not "information about." Just as we are internally related to our bodies, so God is internally related to all that is — the most radically relational Thou. God relates sympathetically to the world, just as we relate sympathetically to our bodies. This implies, of course, an immediacy and concern in God's knowledge of the world impossible in the king-realm model.

Moreover, it implies that the action of God in the world is similarly interior and caring. If the entire universe, all that is and has been, is God's body, then God acts in and through the incredibly complex physical and historical-cultural evolutionary process that began eons ago.[28] This does not mean that God is reduced to the evolutionary process, for God remains as the agent, the self, whose intentions are expressed in the universe. Nevertheless, the manner in which these intentions are expressed is internal and, by implication, providential — that is, reflective of a "caring" relationship. God does not, as in the royal model, intervene in the natural or historical process *deus ex machina* fashion, nor does God feel merely charitable toward the world. The suggestion, however, that God cares about the world as one cares about one's own body, that is, with a high degree of sympathic concern, does not imply that all is well or the future assured, for with the body metaphor, God is at risk. It does suggest, however, that to trust in a God whose body is the world is to trust in a God who cares profoundly about the world.

Furthermore, the model of the world as God's body suggests that God loves bodies: in loving the world, God loves a body. Such a notion is a sharp challenge to the long antibody, antiphysical, antimatter tradition within Christianity. This tradition has repressed healthy sexuality, oppressed women as sexual tempters, and defined Christian redemption in spiritualistic ways, thus denying that basic social and economic needs of embodied beings are relevant to salvation. To say that God loves bodies is to redress the balance toward a more holistic understanding of fulfillment. It is to say that bodies are worth loving, sexually and otherwise, that passionate love as well as attention to the needs of bodily existence are part of fulfillment. It is to say further that the basic necessities of bodily existence — adequate food and shelter, for example — are central aspects of God's love for all bodily creatures and therefore should be central concerns for us, God's co-workers. In a holistic sensibility there can be no spirit/body split: if neither we nor God is disembodied, then denigration of the body, the physical, and matter should end. Such a split makes no sense in our world: spirit and body or matter are on a continuum, for matter is not inanimate substance but throbs of energy, essentially in continuity with spirit. To love bodies, then, is to love not what is opposed to spirit but what is one with it — which the model of the world as God's body fully expresses.

The immanence of God in the world implied in our metaphor raises the question of God's involvement with evil. Is God responsible for evil, both natural and humanly willed evil? The pictures of the king and his realm and of God and the world as God's body obviously suggest very different replies to these enormously difficult and complex questions. In the monarchical construct, God is implicitly in contest with evil powers, either as victorious king, who crushes them or as sacrificial servant, who (momentarily) assumes a worldly mien in order to free his subjects from evil's control. The implication of ontological dualism, of opposing good and evil powers, is the price paid for separating God from evil, and it is a high price indeed, for it suggests that the place of evil is the world (and ourselves) and that to escape evil's clutches, we need to free ourselves from "the world, the flesh, and the devil." In this construct God is not responsible for evil, but neither does God identify with the suffering caused by evil.

That identification does occur in the metaphor of the world as God's body. The evil in the world, all kinds of evil, occurs in and to God as well as to us and the rest of creation. Evil is not a power over against God; in a sense, it is God's "responsibility," part of God's being, if you will. A monistic, panentheistic position cannot avoid this conclusion.[29] In a physical, biological, historico-cultural evolutionary process as complex as the universe, much that is evil from various perspectives will occur, and if one sees this process as God's self-expression, then God is involved in evil. But the other side of this is that God is also involved, profoundly, palpably, personally involved, in suffering, in the suffering caused by evil. The evil occurs in and to God's body; the pain that those parts of creation affected by evil feel God also feels and feels bodily. All pain to all creatures is felt immediately and bodily by God: one does not suffer alone. In this sense God's suffering on the cross was not for a mere few hours, as in the old mythology, but it is present and permanent. As the body of the world, God is forever "nailed to the cross," for as this body suffers, so God suffers.[30]

Is this to suggest that God is helpless in relation to evil and that God knows no joy? No, for the way of the cross, the way of inclusive, radical love, is a kind of power, though a very different kind from kingly might. It does imply, however, that unlike God the king, the God who suffers with the world cannot wipe out evil; evil is not only part of the process but its power also depends on us, God's partners in the way of inclusive, radical love. And what holds for suffering can be said of joy as well. Wherever in the universe there is new life, ecstasy, tranquility, and fulfillment, God experiences these pleasures and rejoices with each creature in its joy.

When we turn to our side of this picture of the world as God's body, we have to ask whether we are reduced to being mere parts of the body. What is our freedom? How is sin understood here? How would we behave in this model? The model did not fit God's side in every way, and it does not fit ours in every way either. It seems especially problematic at the point of our individuality and freedom. At least in the king-realm model, human beings appear to have some freedom since they are controlled only externally, not internally. The problem emerges because of the nature of bodies. If we are parts of God's body—if the model is totally organic—are we not totally immersed, along with all other creatures, in the evolutionary process, with no transcendence or freedom? It appears, however, at least to us, that we are a special part. We think of ourselves as *imago dei*, as not only possessing bodies but being agents. We view ourselves as embodied spirits in the larger body of the world which influences us and which we influence. That is, we are the part molded on the model: self:body::God:world. We are agents, and God possesses a body: both sides of the model pertain to both God and ourselves. This implies that we are not mere submerged parts of the body of God but related to God as to another Thou. The presence of God to us in and through God's body is the experience of encounter, not of submersion. For the saving love of God to be present to human beings it would have to be so in a way different from how it is present to other aspects of the body of the world—in a way in keeping with the peculiar kind of creatures we are, namely, creatures with a special kind of freedom, able to participate self-consciously (as well as be influenced unconsciously) in an evolutionary process. This gives us a special status and a special responsibility: We are the ones like God; we are selves that possess bodies, and that is our glory. It is also our responsibility, for we alone can choose to become partners with God in care of the world; we alone can—like God—love, heal, befriend, and liberate the world, the body, that God has made available to us as both the divine presence and our home.

Our special status and responsibility, however, are not limited to consciousness of our own personal bodies, or even of the human world, but extend to all embodied reality, for we are that part of the cosmos where the cosmos itself has come to consciousness. If we become extinct, then the cosmos will lose its human, although presumably not its divine, consciousness. As Jonathan Schell remarks, "In extinction a darkness falls over the world not because the lights have gone out but because the eyes that behold the light have been closed" (Schell, 128).[31]

It is obvious, then, what sin is in this metaphor of the world as God's body: it is refusal to be part of the body, the special part we are as *imago dei*. In contrast to the king-realm model, where sin is against *God*, here it is against the world. To sin is not to refuse loyalty to the king, but to refuse to take responsibility for nurturing, loving, and befriending the body and all its parts. Sin is the refusal to realize one's radical interdependence with all that lives; it is the desire to set oneself apart from all others as not needing them or being needed by them. Sin is the refusal to be the eyes, the consciousness, of the cosmos.

What this experiment with the world as God's body comes to, finally, is an awareness, both chilling and breathtaking, that we, as worldly, bodily beings, are in God's presence. We do not have to go to some special place— a church, for instance—or to another world, to find God, for God is present with us here and now. We have a basis for a revived sacramentalism, that is, a perception of the divine as visible, as present, palpably present in the world. But it is a kind of sacramentalism that is painfully conscious of the world's vulnerability, its preciousness, its uniqueness. The beauty of the world and its ability to sustain the vast multitude of species it supports is not there for the taking. The world is a body that must be carefully tended, that must be nurtured, protected, guided, loved, and befriended both as valuable in itself—for like us, it is an expression of God—and as necessary to the continuation of life. We meet the world as a Thou, as the body of God where God is present to us always in all times and in all places. In the metaphor of the world as God's body the resurrection is remythologized as a worldly, present, inclusive event—the offering of the world, God's body, to all: "This is my body." As is true of all bodies, however, this body, in its beauty and precariousness, is vulnerable and at risk—it will delight the eye only if we care for it; it will nourish us only if we nurture it. Needless to say, then, were this metaphor to enter our consciousness as thoroughly as the royal, triumphalist one has entered, it would result in a different way of being in the world. There would be no way we could any longer see God as worldless or the world as Godless. Nor could we expect God to take care of everything, either through domination or through benevolence.

We see through pictures. We do not see directly. The pictures of a king and his realm and of the world as God's body are ways of speaking, ways of imagining the God-world relationship. The one pictures a vast distance between God and the world; the other imagines them as intrinsically related. At the close of day one asks which distortion (assuming that all pictures are false in some respects) is better by asking what attitudes each encourages. This is not the first question to ask, but it may well be the last. The monarchical model encourages attitudes of militarism, dualism, and escapism; it condones control through violence and oppression; it has nothing to say about the nonhuman world. The model of the world as God's body encourages holistic attitudes of responsibility for and care of the vulnerable and oppressed; it is nonhierarchical and acts through persuasion and attraction; it has a great deal to say about the body and nature. Both are pictures. Which distortion is more true to the world in which we live and to the good news of Christianity?

It may be, of course, that neither picture is appropriate to our time and to Christian faith; if so, others should be proposed. Our profound need for a powerful, attractive, imaginative picture of the way God is related to our world demands that we not only deconstruct but reconstruct our metaphors, letting the ones that seem promising try their chance.

The model of the universe as God's body is admittedly an immanental one, significant in part because it redresses the heavily transcendent imagery for God in the Judeo-Christian tradition. But it also suggests, in its own way, a model of transcendence—what one might call cosmocentric transcendence—that is awe-inspiring. The common "creation story" emerging from the fields of astrophysics, biology, and scientific cosmology makes small any myth of creation from the various religious traditions: some ten billion or so years ago the universe began from a big bang exploding the "matter," which was infinitesimally small and infinitely dense, outward to create the untold number of galaxies of which our tiny planet is but one blip on the screen. From this beginning came all that followed, so everything that is is related, woven into a seamless network, with life gradually emerging after billions of years on this planet (and perhaps on others) and resulting in the incredibly complex, intricate universe we see today.[32] To think of God as the creator and continuing creator/sustainer of this massive, breathtaking cosmic fact dwarfs all our traditional images of divine transcendence—whether political or metaphysical. And yet, to think of the transcendence of God this way would not contradict the immanental body image. Rather, the two would come together in a cosmocentric, immanental model of transcendence: God the creator of the evolving, incredibly vast and complex universe understood as the divine "body."

What I am suggesting is that we learn to think differently about what the saving love of God must mean in our time if it is to be really *for our time*, addressing the question of the possible end of existence raised by ecological deterioration and nuclear escalation—and that we do this by thinking in *different images*. The one I have suggested is just that: *one image*—many others are needed. We must be careful, very careful, of the imagistic glasses through which we interpret God and the world. As Erich Heller, the German philosopher and literary critic, said: "Be careful how you interpret the world. It is like that."

Some treatments attempting to raise consciousness on the ecological, nuclear situation paint a picture of nuclear winter or the extent of death and destruction that will occur after such an event. But it is even more telling in terms of our perception of the world, of how wondrous it is and how much we do in fact care for it, to think small. Almost anything will do—sheep on the English hills, a child's first steps, the smell of rain on a spring day, whatever, as long as it is some particular, cherished aspect of the world—and then dwell on its specialness, its distinctiveness, its value, until the pain of contemplating its permanent loss, not just to you or me, but to all for all time, becomes unbearable. This is a form of prayer for the world as the body of God that we, as lovers and friends of the world, are summoned to practice. This prayer, while not the only one in an ecological, nuclear age, is a necessary and permanent one. It is a form of meditation to help us think differently about the world, to enable us to work together with God to save our beleaguered planet, our beautiful, vulnerable earth, our blue and green marble in a universe of silent rock and fire.

NOTES

1. This paper is based in part on material from my book, *Models of God: Theology for an Ecological, Nuclear Age*. In that work I experiment with the models of God as mother/creator, lover/redeemer, friend/sustainer of the world understood as God's body. The present essay is written in two tracks: the central argument, which appears as the text, and the scholarly discussion, especially as regards issues pertinent to the Annecy meeting, which appears as the endnotes.

2. Present-day concern among theologians with anthropocentrism or homocentrism is wide-spread. James M. Gustafson, in the first volume of *Ethics from a Theocentric Perspective*, states the concern succinctly with his pithy remark that while human beings are the *measurers* of all things, they are not the *measure* of all things (Gustafson, 82). Our anthropocentrism can, he believes, be overcome only by a profound acknowledgment of the sovereignty of God, a consent to divine governance that sets limits to human life and in which we "relate to all things in a manner appropriate to their relations to God" (p. 113). Only then will human beings, he says, "confront their awesome possibilities and their inexorable limitations" (pp. 16-17). Stephen Toulmin echoes these sentiments in an elegant statement on the cosmos understood on the model of our "home": "We can do our best to build up a conception of the 'overall scheme of things' which draws as heavily as it can on the results of scientific study, informed by a genuine piety in all its attitudes toward creatures of other kinds: a piety that goes beyond the consideration of their usefulness to Humanity as instructions for the fulfillment of human ends. That is an

alternative within which human beings can both *feel*, and also *be*, at home. For to be at home in the world of nature does not just mean finding out how to utilize nature economically and efficiently—home is not a hotel! It means making sense out of the relations that human beings and other living things have toward the overall patterns of nature in ways that give us some sense of their proper relations to one another, to ourselves, and to the whole" (Toulmin, 272). Sigurd Daecke finds anthropocentrism to be deeply embedded in Protestant theologies of creation reaching back to Luther ("I believe that God has created me") and Calvin (nature is the stage for salvation history) and finding a twentieth-century home in the humanistic individualism of Bultmann as well as the Christocentrism of Barth ("the reality of creation is known in Jesus Christ") (see Daecke). In a somewhat different vein, Tracy and Lash, while agreeing that the anthropic principle is untenable in science, find a certain kind of anthropocentrism appropriate in theology: (1) human beings are both products of and interpreters of the evolutionary process; (2) human beings are responsible for much of our world's ills: "if we are the 'center' of anything, we are the center of 'sin,' of the self-assertive disruption and unraveling of the process of things, at least on our small planet" (Tracy and Lash, 280).

3. James M. Gustafson and WCC materials appear to prefer the phrases "theocentric" and "life-centered" to "cosmocentric" (see Gustafson, vol. I, esp. pp. 87-113). Each phrase highlights a somewhat different focus on a set of interrelated entities: God, life, and the total environment that both supports and includes life. It is helpful, I believe, to use all three in a variety of contexts; if only one is chosen, the intrinsic interrelations are forgotten.

4. Tracy and Lash contrast the collaborative model with two others, described as confrontational and concordist, neither of which is appropriate for our time. In a similar fashion Ernan McMullin asks for "consonance" between scientific and theological views. The theologian "should aim at some sort of coherence of world-view, a coherence to which science and theology, and indeed many other sorts of human construction like history, politics, and literature, must contribute" (McMullin, 52). It is in this spirit that the present essay is written. However, those of us concerned to find such relationships between distinct fields should heed the cautious word of Cambridge physicist Sir Brian Pippard when he says that each field thrives by virtue of its own methods and not by aping those of others: "The fabric of knowledge has not been woven as a seamless robe but pieced together like a patchwork quilt, and we are still in the position of being able to appreciate the design in individual pieces much more clearly than the way they are put together" (Pippard, 95-96).

5. Tracy and Lash define cosmology in a variety of ways. "The term can refer to theological accounts of the world as God's creation; or to philosophical reflection on the categories of space and time; or to observational and theoretical study of the structure and evolution of the physical universe; or, finally, to 'world views': unified imaginative perceptions of how the world seems and where we stand in it" (Tracy and Lash, vii). Peacocke finds a similarity of intention in religious and scientific cosmologies: "Both attempt to take into account as much of the 'data' of the observed universe as possible and both use criteria of simplicity, comprehensiveness, elegance, and plausibility. ... Both direct themselves to the 'way things are' not only by developing cosmogonies, accounts of the origin of the universe, but also in relation to nearer-at-hand experience of biological and inorganic nature"

(Peacocke, 31). The *intention* of my modest effort with the model of the world as God's body falls within these parameters.

6. Many philosophers of science claim that science is also an imaginative activity. Max Black insists that the exercise of the imagination provides a common ground between science and the humanities, "for science, like the humanities, like literature, is an affair of the imagination" (Black, 243). Mary Hesse suggests that "art" or "play" characterizes some aspects of scientific problem-solving: "A great deal of scientific theorizing, especially in fundamental physics and cosmology, is not too distant from the creation of science fiction, which might indeed be said to be speculative theory without the full rigor of experimental control" (Hesse, 50). See also my *Metaphorical Theology: Models of God in Religious Language*, chapter 3, for a treatment of the role of the imagination in science and theology.

7. Dennis Nineham writes that it is "at the level of the *imagination* that contemporary Christianity is most weak." He goes on to say that people "find it hard to believe in God because they do not have available to them any lively imaginative picture of the way God and the world as they know it are related. What they need most is a story, a picture, a myth, that will capture their imagination, while meshing in with the rest of their sensibility in the way that messianic terms linked with the sensibility of first-century Jews, or Nicene symbolism with the sensibility of philosophically-minded fourth-century Greeks" (Nineham, 42).

8. An outstanding example of theology as hermeneutics is the work of David Tracy, especially *The Analogical Imagination: Christian Theology and the Culture of Pluralism*. A fine illustration of theology as construction is the work of Gordon D. Kaufman, especially *The Theological Imagination: Constructing the Concept of God*.

9. How that power is understood involves specifying the material norm of Christian faith. It involves risking an interpretation of what, most basically, Christian faith is about. My interpretation is similar to that of the so-called liberation theologies. Each of these theologies, from the standpoint of race, gender, class, or another basic human distinction, claims that the Christian gospel is opposed to oppression of some by others, opposed to hierarchies and dualisms, opposed to the domination of the weak by the powerful. This reading is understood to be commensurate with the paradigmatic story of the life, message, and death of Jesus of Nazareth, who in his parables, his table fellowship, and his death offered a surprising invitation to *all*, especially to the outcast and the oppressed. It is a destabilizing, inclusive, nonhierarchical vision of Christian faith, the claim that the gospel of Christianity is a new creation for *all* of creation—a life of freedom and fulfillment for all. As Nicholas Lash has said in a variety of contexts, the story as told must be "a different version of the same story, not a different story" (Lash, 30, 44).

10. Robert P. Scharlemann uses this phrase to describe the kind of theology that constructs theological models, and he sees it as an alternative to other kinds of theology, confessional, metaphysical, biblicistic, religious thought. "It is free theology in the sense that it can make use of any of these materials—confessional, metaphysical, biblical, religious, and secular—without being bound to them" (Scharlemann, 82-83).

11. The relationship between image and concept that I support is articulated by Paul Ricoeur, whose well-known phrase "the symbol gives rise to thought" is balanced by an equal emphasis on thought's need to return to its rich base in symbol.

12. There are probably as many definitions of metaphor as there are metaphoricians and one hesitates to contemplate how many of the latter there may be. In

1978 Wayne Booth, commenting on the explicit discussions of metaphor having "multiplied astronomically in the past fifty years," claimed that he had extrapolated with his pocket calculator to the year 2039 and determined "at that point there will be more students of metaphor than people" (Booth, 47). With that sobering introduction, I am grateful to Janet Martin Soskice for her straight-forward, uncomplicated definition of metaphor: "Metaphor is a figure of speech in which one entity or state of affairs is spoken of in terms which are seen as being appropriate to another" (Soskice, 96).

13. My position here is very close to that of Ricoeur, as found in *The Rule of Metaphor* and elsewhere.

14. The conversation between science and theology on the matter of metaphors and models is a long and interesting one, with the Annecy conference as one of its results. I am especially indebted to the work of Ian Barbour, Mary Hesse, Frederick Ferre, E. H. Hutten, Rom Harre, Max Black, and N. R. Hanson, among others, for their interpretations of this conversation. For my modest contribution to it, see *Metaphorical Theology*, chapters 3 and 4.

15. I find Ian Barbour's definition of theoretical models in science serves as well in theology: "theoretical models are novel mental constructions. They originate in a combination of analogy to the familiar and creative imagination in creating the new. They are open-ended, extensible, and suggestive of new hypotheses . . . such models are taken seriously but not literally. They are neither pictures of reality nor useful fictions; they are partial and inadequate ways of imagining what is not observable" (Barbour, 47-48).

16. This perspective acknowledges with Nelson Goodman that, as Ernest Gombrich insists, "there is no innocent eye. The eye comes always ancient to its work. . . . Nothing is seen nakedly or naked" (Goodman, 7-8). This means, of course, that we are always dealing in interpretations of reality (the reality of God or anything else); hence, there are no descriptions but only readings. Some readings, however, are more privileged than others and this judgment will be made by the relevant community. New readings are offered in place of conventional or accepted ones, not with the view that they necessarily correspond more adequately to the reality in question *in toto*, but that they are a discovery/creation of some aspect of that reality overlooked in other readings, or one especially pertinent to the times, etc.

17. The heavily pragmatic view of truth suggested here is similar to that of some liberation theologians and rests on an understanding of praxis not simply as action *vs.* theory, but as a kind of reflection, one guided by practical experience. Praxis is positively, "the realization that humans cannot rely on any ahistorical, universal truths to guide life" (Chopp, 36). It assumes that human life is fundamentally practical; hence, knowledge is not most basically the correspondence of some understanding of reality with "reality-as-it-is," but it is a continual process of analysis, explanation, conversation, and application with both theoretical and practical aspects. This understanding is not new; Aristotle's view of life in the *polis* as understood and constructed is similar: such knowledge is grounded in concrete history within the norms, values, and hopes of the community. Likewise, Augustine's *Confessions* is not a theoretical treatise on the nature of God, but a history, his own concrete, experiential history, of God acting in his life. On the present scene we see a clear turn toward pragmatism in the work of Richard Rorty, Michel Foucault, Richard Bernstein, and others. While I would not identify my position with the extremes of pragmatism, it is, nonetheless, a healthy reminder that religious truth,

whatever may be the case with other kinds of truth, involves issues of value, of consequences, of the quality of lived existence.

18. Edward Farley and Peter C. Hodgson agree: "The Christian movement never abandoned the royal metaphor of God and God's relation to the world. The logic of sovereignty, which presumes that God employs whatever means are necessary to ensure the successful accomplishment of the divine will, eventually pervaded the total criteriology of Christendom" (Farley and Hodgson, 68).

19. Many theologians have criticized the monarchical model as oppressive. Dorothee Soelle claims that authoritarian religion that images God as dominating power lay behind the "obedience" of Nazism and thus behind the Jewish Holocaust. John B. Cobb, Jr., and David R. Griffin view the classic Western God as "the Cosmic Moralist," whose main attribute is power over all creatures rather than responsive love that could lead to the fulfillment of all creatures. Jürgen Moltmann objects to the "monarchical monotheism" of Christianity, which supports hierarchalism and individualism, and insists instead that a social, Trinitarian doctrine of God is needed. Edward Farley claims that the royal metaphors for God have fueled the notion of "salvation history" and its "logic of triumph" (Farley 1982).

20. See the well-known essay by Lynn White which makes this accusation in its strongest form. See also a refutation of White's argument in Peacocke, pp. 275ff.

21. There is, however, another metaphorical tradition of benevolence that moves in a more positive direction: God as gardener, caretaker, and hence preserver of the world and its life. Here benevolence is not distant goodwill, as in the royal metaphor, but intimate nurture. Gardeners and caretakers "touch" the earth and the life they care for with the goal of creating conditions in which life other than their own can grow and prosper. Such benevolence promotes human responsibility, not escapism and passivity, and hence these metaphors are helpful ones in our time. For further analysis, see Phyllis Trible, pp. 85ff.

22. For a treatment of some of these theological traditions, see Grace Jantzen, chapter 3. The metaphor is widespread, especially in its form as an analogy—self:body::God:world—particularly among process theologians, as a way of overcoming the externality of God's knowledge of and activity in the world. Theologians of nature, who take the evolutionary reality of the world seriously, also find it attractive as a noninterventionist way of speaking of God's agency in history and nature. See, for example, Claude Stewart's *Nature in Grace*. Even among more traditional theologies, the embodiment of God is receiving attention. Grace Jantzen's position, for example, is that, given the contemporary holistic understanding of personhood, an embodied personal God is more credible than a disembodied one and is commensurate with traditional attributes of God.

23. See Jantzen's fine study on the dualistic, antimatter context of early Christian theology (Jantzen, chap. 3).

24. John Cobb makes this point and adds that total identification with our bodies becomes impossible when they are sick, maimed, aging, enslaved, or dying. We are not our bodies at such times (Cobb).

25. At first glance, there might appear to be tension between the model of the world as God's body and the models of God as mother, lover, and friend. Is the relationship narcissistic? Is it monistic? I firmly support Jay McDaniel's view of "dialogical panentheism" *vs.* "emanationist panentheism," the former being consonant with the model of the world or universe as God's body (McDaniel, 87). I find the kind of relationality implied in the model of the world as God's body *less*

narcissistic than some understandings of orthodox Trinitarianism, in which God's "other" is God's own self, with divine relationality seen in terms of the relations among the persons of the immanent Trinity. This solipsistic view is epitomized in C. S. Lewis's statement that God is "at home in the land of the Trinity," and, entirely self-sufficient and needing nothing, "loves into existence totally superfluous creatures" (Lewis, 176). One might also ask about the "source" of God's body, the world: How can someone be the mother of their own body? One must recall what this "body" is: it is nothing less than all that is—the universe or universes of which the cosmologists speak. The body of God, then, is creation, understood as God's self-expression; it is formed in God's own reality (although not thereby identical with it), bodied forth in the eons of evolutionary time. What could this body be except God's *own* creation? Could some other creator have made it—if so, then *that* creator would be God. God could be said to be the mother of all reality, for God is the source of all that is. As Julian of Norwich writes of God as mother: "We owe our being to him [sic] and this is the essence of motherhood" (Julian of Norwich, chap. 60). The seeming incoherence here, I think, comes from the fact that our bodies are given to us, as are all other aspects of our existence. But as the creator of all that is, God is necessarily the source, the mother, of her own body.

26. Paul Tillich's definition of pantheism is close to Karl Rahner's and Herbert Vorgrimler's definition of panentheism: "Pantheism is the doctrine that God is the substance or essence of all things, not the meaningless assertion that God is the totality of all things" (Tillich, 324); and "This form of pantheism does not intend simply to identify the world and God monistically (God = the 'all') but intends, instead, to conceive of the 'all' of the world 'in' God as God's inner modification and appearance, even if God is not exhausted by the 'all' " (Rahner and Vorgrimler, 275).

27. Most theologians who employ the analogy of self:body::God:world speak in these terms about God's knowledge of the world. Since God is internally related to the world, divine knowledge is an immediate, sympathetic awareness (see, e.g., Hartshorne, "Philosophical and Religious Uses of 'God' " in *Process Theology: Basic Writings*, edited by Ewert Cousins, page 109; also see Schubert Ogden, "The Reality of God," p. 123 of the same volume and Jantzen 1984, 81ff.).

28. To understand the action of God as interior to the entire evolutionary process does not mean that some events, aspects, and dimensions cannot be more important than others. See, for example, the analysis of "act" of God by Gordon Kaufman, in which he distinguishes between "master" act (the entire evolutionary process) and "subordinate" acts such as Jesus' march to the cross as an essential constituent of the master act (Kaufman 1979, 140ff.).

29. This position is not unlike that of Boehme, Schelling, and Tillich that in some sense evil has its origin in God. In an evolutionary perspective, however, the issue of evil is so complex that to say that evil has its origin in God means something very different from what saying this means in nonevolutionary theologians such as the above.

30. The suffering of God as a way of dealing with evil of various sorts is a major topic with a wide variety of theologians, ranging from Jürgen Moltmann and Arthur Peacocke to Ian Barbour and most process theologians. In these discussions, the suffering God participates in the pain of the universe as it gropes to survive and produce new forms. It is obvious that not all species, let alone all individuals in any species, survive and flourish—for a variety of reasons. In this kind of theodicy

Gethesemane, the cross, and the resurrection are important foci for understanding the depths of God's love, who, in creating an unimaginatively complex matrix of matter eventuating finally in persons able to *choose* to go against God's intentions, nonetheless grieves for and suffers with this beloved creation, both in the pain its natural course brings all its creatures and in the evil that its human creatures inflict upon it. I find this discussion rich and powerful; nonetheless, I would raise a caveat concerning what it tends to underplay—human sin and responsibility. By locating the discussion of evil in the context of the entire cosmic complex, one may overlook the particular powerful role that human beings increasingly play in bringing evil to their own species and to other species as well. Teilhard de Chardin in his *Divine Milieu* says that our lives have an active and a passive phase: in the first phase we must work with all our heart, mind, and soul to help bring about the great evolutionary project, while in the second phase we must accept the deterioration and death that always come (Teilhard 1968b). By stressing the suffering of God—the passive side—one may fail to underscore the peculiar position of human beings in the universe as the active agents who can choose or not choose to side with God as co-workers, co-creators. At the close of the twentieth century, with ecological deterioration accelerating and the nuclear threat ever with us, we need to feel not acceptance but the challenge to join forces *on the side of life*, for while we, like all creatures, are ultimately part of a universe that is brutal and may well end, we have, while we live, a part to play different from that of any other creature: we are responsible agents who can join with our loving parent to help our own and other species to survive and flourish. This means, of course, engaging in difficult and complex decisions of justice and care, as we seek to determine the economic, social, political, and cultural rights of individuals in our own species and as we pay attention to the rights of the silent, nonvoting majority which is made up of all the other species. But complexity is not the main problem, for creatures who can go to the moon, manage multinational corporations, and build nuclear arsenals have the ability to do considerably better than they do on justice and ecological issues. The main problem is the perversion of the human heart, which is turned in upon itself, as Augustine said, rather than being open to the other beings as well as to the Source of all being. In sum, divine suffering for the cosmos (including each sparrow that falls) must not obscure human responsibility for a tiny corner of it—our earth.

31. I am indebted to Rosemary Radford Ruether for the import of this paragraph.

32. Brian Swimme, physicist and ecologist, writes in the following way of this awesome, cosmic fact: "Humans and yeast are kin. They organize themselves chemically and biologically in nearly indistinguishable patterns of intelligent activity. They speak the same genetic language. All things whether living or not are descendents of the supernova explosion. All that exists shapes the same energy erupting into the universe as the primeval fireball. No tribal myth, no matter how wild, ever imagined a more profound relationship connecting all things in an internal way right from the beginning. All thinking must begin with this cosmic genetical relatedness" (quoted in *Cross Currents* [Summer/Fall 1987]: 222).

WORKS CITED

Arbib, Michael, and Mary Hesse. *The Construction of Reality.* Cambridge: Cambridge University Press, 1986.

Barbour, Ian. *Myths, Models and Paradigms: A Comparative Study in Science and Religion*. New York: Harper & Row, 1974.

Black, Max. *Models and Metaphors*. Ithaca, NY: Cornell University Press, 1962.

Booth, Wayne. "Metaphor as Rhetoric: The Problem of Evaluation." In *On Metaphor*. Ed. Sheldon Sacks. Chicago: University of Chicago Press, 1978.

Chopp, Rebecca. *The Praxis of Suffering: An Interpretation of Liberation and Political Theologies*. Maryknoll, NY: Orbis Books, 1986.

Cobb, John. "Feminism and Process Thought." In *Feminism and Process Thought*. Ed. Sheila Greene Daveney. New York: Edwin Mellen Press, 1981.

Cobb, John B., and David R. Griffin. *Process Theology: An Introductory Exposition*. Philadelphia: Westminster Press, 1976.

Daecke, Sigurd. "Profane and Sacramental Views of Nature." In *The Sciences and Theology in the Twentieth Century*. Ed. A.R. Peacocke. Notre Dame, IN: University of Notre Dame Press, 1986.

Derrida, Jacques. "White Mythology: Metaphor in the Text of Philosophy." In *New Literary History* 6 (1974):5-73.

Farley, Edward. *Ecclesial Reflection: An Anatomy of Theological Method*. Philadelphia: Fortress Press, 1982.

Farley, Edward, and Peter C. Hodgson. "Scripture and Tradition." In *Christian Theology: An Introduction to Its Traditions and Tasks*, rev. ed. Ed. Peter C. Hodgson and Robert H. King. Philadelphia: Fortress Press, 1985.

Goodman, Nelson. *Languages of Art: An Approach to a Theory of Symbols*. Indianapolis: Bobbs-Merrill, 1968.

Gustafson, James M. *Ethics from a Theocentric Perspective*. Chicago: University of Chicago Press, 1981.

Hartshorne, Charles. "Philosophical and Religious Uses of 'God.' " In *Process Theology: Basic Writings*. Ed. Ewert H. Cousins. New York: Newman Press, 1977.

Hepburn, R. W. "Demythologizing and the Problem of Validity." In *New Essays in Philosophical Theology*. Eds. Antony Flew and Alasdair MacIntyre. London: SCM Press, 1955.

Hesse, Mary. "Cosmology as Myth." In *Cosmology and Theology*. Ed. David Tracy and Nicholas Lash. Edinburgh and New York: T. & T. Clark and Seabury Press, 1983.

Hopkins, Gerard Manley. *Poems and Prose of Gerard Manley Hopkins*. London: Penguin Books, 1953.

Jantzen, Grace. *God's World, God's Body*. Philadelphia: Westminster Press, 1984.

Julian of Norwich. *Showings*. Trans. Edmund Colledge and James Walsh. New York: Paulist Press, 1978.

Kaufman, Gordon. *God the Problem*. Cambridge: Harvard University Press, 1979.

———. *The Theological Imagination: Constructing the Concept of God*. Philadelphia: Westminster Press, 1981.

———. *Theology for a Nuclear Age*. Philadelphia: Westminster Press, 1985.

Lash, Nicholas. *Theology on the Road to Emmaus*. London: SCM Press, 1986.

Lewis, C. S. *The Four Loves*. New York: Harcourt, Brace & Co., 1960.

McDaniel, Jay. "God and Pelicans." In *Church and Society, Report and Background Papers*. Meeting of the Working Group. Glion, Switzerland: World Council of Churches, 1987.

McFague, Sallie. *Metaphorical Theology: Models of God in Religious Language*. Philadelphia: Fortress Press, 1982.

————. *Models of God: Theology for an Ecological, Nuclear Age*. Philadelphia: Fortress Press, 1987.

McMullin, Ernan. "How Should Cosmology Relate to Theology?" In *The Sciences and Theology in the Twentieth Century*. Ed. Arthur Peacocke. Notre Dame, IN: University of Notre Dame Press, 1982.

Moltmann, Jürgen. *The Trinity and the Kingdom of God*. San Francisco: Harper and Row, 1981.

Nineham, Dennis. *The Myth of God Incarnate*. Ed. John Hick. Philadelphia: Westminster Press, 1977.

Peacocke, Arthur. *Creation and the World of Science*. Oxford: Clarendon Press, 1979.

Pippard, Sir Brian. "Instability and Chaos: Physical Models of Everyday Life." In *Interdisciplinary Science Reviews* (1982): 91-102.

Rahner, Karl, and Herbert Vorgrimler. *Kleines theologishches Wortenbuchen*. Freiberg: Herder & Herder, 1961.

Ricoeur, Paul. "Biblical Hermeneutics," *Semeia* 4 (1975):29-145.

————. *The Rule of Metaphor: Multi-disciplinary Studies of the Creation of Meaning in Language*. Study 8. Trans. Robert Czerny. Toronto: University of Toronto Press, 1977.

Ruether, Rosemary. *Sexism and God-Talk: Toward a Feminist Theology*. Boston: Beacon Press, 1983.

Scharlemann, Robert P. "Theological Models and Their Construction." In *Journal of Religion* 53 (1973): 65-82.

Schell, Jonathan. *The Fate of the Earth*. New York: Avon Books, 1982.

Soelle, Dorothee. *The Strength of the Weak: Toward a Christian Feminist Identity*. Trans. Robert and Rita Kimber. Philadelphia: Westminster Press, 1984.

Soskice, Janet Martin. *Metaphor and Religious Language*. Oxford: Clarendon Press, 1985.

Stevens, Wallace. *Opus Posthumous*. Ed. S.F. Morris. New York: Alfred A. Knopf, 1957.

Stewart, Claude. *Nature in Grace: A Study in the Theology of Nature*. Macon, GA: Mercer University Press, 1983.

Teilhard de Chardin, Pierre (a). *Writings in Time of War*. Trans. Rene Hague. London: William Collins, 1968.

———— (b). *Divine Milieu*. New York: Harper and Row, 1968.

Tillich, Paul. *Systematic Theology*. Vol. 1. Chicago: University of Chicago Press, 1963.

Toulmin, Stephen. *The Return to Cosmology: Postmodern Science and the Theology of Nature*. Berkeley: University of California Press, 1982.

Tracy, David. *The Analogical Imagination: Christian Theology and the Culture of Pluralism*. New York: Crossroad; London: SCM Press, 1981.

Tracy, David, and Nicholas Lash, eds. *Cosmology and Theology*. Edinburgh and New York: T. & T. Clark and Seabury Press, 1983.

Trible, Phyllis. *God and the Rhetoric of Sexuality*. Philadelphia: Fortress Press, 1978.

White, Lynn. "The Historical Roots of Our Ecologic Crisis." In *Ecology and Religion in History*. Ed. David and Eileen Spring. New York: Harper & Row, 1974.

15

Revisioning God and the Self: Lessons from Buddhism

Jay B. McDaniel

As Christians take the next step in liberation thinking, recognizing that the very theme of liberation needs to be extended to the whole of life, two shifts in thought and action are needed. First, we need to develop an ethic that attunes us to the value and moral considerability of all life, not human life alone. We need to adopt a life-centered ethic. Second, we need to develop a way of understanding God that shows God to be concerned with and intimately connected to the whole of life, not human life alone. We need to place our trust in a life-centered God.

In an age in which we have become increasingly aware of other faiths and religious traditions in our own backyards and in other parts of the world, we cannot develop our life-centered ethics and our life-centered understandings of God in isolation. Rather we must do so in dialogue with other faiths, for many of those faiths have something quite important to add to our own perceptions. The next step in liberation thinking involves

In 1983 the Sixth Assembly of the World Council of Churches at Vancouver invited all churches to engage in a process of mutual commitment to justice, peace, and respect for the integrity of creation. Though the phrase *integrity of creation* was clearly intended to encourage ecological responsibility and a concern for the well-being of life, its exact definition remained unclear. Subsequent consultations sponsored by the World Council were charged with working out more precise definitions. McDaniel, a member of the Working Area of the Church and Society Sub-unit of WCC, wrote two papers for WCC consultations, one of which was on the conceptual foundations of a life-centered ethic, and the other on a life-centered understanding of God. Both now appear in his *Of God and Pelicans: A Theology of Reverence for Life*. This essay builds upon those papers by showing the relevance of a dialogue with other religions—in this instance a dialogue with Zen Buddhism—to a deepening of Christian ecological consciousness.

a move, not only beyond anthropocentrism, but also beyond religious exclusivism.

In this essay I have two distinct but related aims. The first is to outline the life-centered ethic and life-centered understanding of God that I believe most appropriate for the next step of liberation thinking. The second is to show how Buddhism, particularly the Zen school of Mahayana Buddhism, can contribute to an understanding of that ethic and that way of thinking about God.

To achieve these aims the essay is divided into three sections. In the first I discuss what it can mean for Christians truly to respect the integrity of creation. Here I adumbrate aspects of a life-centered ethic. In the second and third sections I explain two proposals for Christian self-understanding that originate from a dialogue with Buddhism and that have direct relevance for the adoption of life-centered ethic and belief in a life-centered God. Put simply, the ideas are: (1) that the world of "rocks and trees, hills and rivers"—to use a Zen phrase—is immanent within, though not exhausted by, each and every human self, and (2) that this world, and indeed the universe in its entirety, is also immanent within, though not exhausted by, God.

RESPECT FOR THE INTEGRITY OF CREATION

What does it mean to respect the integrity of creation? Recall the question the lawyer asked Jesus: "And who is my neighbor?" (Lk 10:29).

Our neighbors are those with whose destinies we identify, recognizing that their well-being is inseparable from our own. Influenced by liberation theologies, we rightly recognize that all humans, particularly the poor, are our neighbors. Of course, we ought not impose our respective cultures on others, nor should we impose our religious orientations. Indeed, we ought to often let others alone and thus respect their integrity. But we ought to do so out of care rather than indifference. This means that we ought to perceive all other humans as our sisters and brothers. Corporately and individually our failures to approximate this ideal are widespread and obvious.

Even if we did better approximate this ideal, however, we might not be attending to all our neighbors. The lyrics in a popular Christian hymn from Malawi remind us that our neighbors are not only other people "black and white, rich and poor," but also "animals and trees, mountains and grass, and all creatures on earth."[1] Many of us who live in urban, industrial settings forget that we are members of a larger community of life, that we share with other creatures a common evolutionary heritage, that we depend on them for our sustenance, and that the earth is their home as well as our own. Unless we feel the effects of environmental damage directly, as do so many of the poor, or unless we are enriched by cultural perspectives that are explicitly biocentric rather than anthropocentric, as are many influenced by African, Asian, and Native American traditions, we tend to disregard nature in our social analyses and in our concept of full community. We forget that the vast majority of our neighbors are plants and fellow animals.

Such disregard, which is by no means the monopoly of Christians, has its consequences. As contemporary societies plunder the earth's forests, contaminate its air, pollute its waterways, overuse its soil, deplete its mineral resources, empty its ozone layer, and overpopulate its habitats, we are undermining the very foundations upon which we depend. From such degradation future human generations will undoubtedly suffer, as are present generations. Furthermore, at the same time that we undermine our own future, we are threatening or destroying the habitats of other species at rates unparalleled in natural history. Conservationist Norman Meyers estimates that the earth is now losing one species a day through habitat destruction, which is about four hundred times the natural rate of evolution, and that by the turn of the century we may be driving 130 species into extinction daily (Meyers, 155). To the five to ten million species of plants and animals on our planet, most humans are by no means good neighbors.

Nor are we good neighbors to the hundreds of millions of individual animals we subject to direct manipulation. Animal welfare activists remind us that hundreds of millions of animals are used each year as tools for questionable research in science and as victims of inhumane treatment in industry, including food industries that rear and slaughter animals for meat. Many of these animals suffer severe pain and debilitating bondage, yet they share with us the very qualities—the will to live and the capacity to suffer— that, as possessed by fellow humans, rightly elicit our moral regard (Regan). If humans deserve our moral regard by virtue of their possession of these qualities, would not other animals deserve similar consideration? Animal welfare advocates answer in the affirmative. Here, too, we are quite brutal neighbors.

Of course, many humans cannot afford to be good neighbors. Over two billion people rely on wood for household fuel, for example, and the supply for seventy percent of them is insecure. Their hope is that they can get three to four sticks a day in order to have minimum fuel for cooking or heating. When they cut trees faster than the timber stock can replenish itself, they do so "out of tragic compulsion" (Meyers, 114). Others, I among them, have greater choice in the matter. As members of dominant social classes we have the luxury to change our behavior patterns and to work toward more just social orders so that others, too, can live more lightly on the earth. We also have the responsibility to relinquish much of our power and privilege. Christians need to work for social orders that enable all humans to live in what the World Council calls justice, peace, and respect for the integrity of creation.

In its thematization at the 1983 Vancouver Assembly, the phrase *integrity of creation* was clear in general implication but lacking in exact definition.[2] In meetings of the Church and Society Working Committee, the phrase has come to name the *intrinsic value* that each and every living being has in and for itself as a creature loved by God, and the *instrumental value* that living beings can have for one another and for God as instances of an evolutionary and web-like creation. In its theological context the phrase "integrity of creation" refers to both kinds of value simultaneously. It is "the intrinsic and instrumental value of every living organism in its relation to its environment and to God" (Birch 1988, 192).

Respect for the integrity of creation requires ecological sensitivity and life-centeredness. To be ecologically sensitive is to be knowledgeable about, and respectful of, the beauty and dynamic equilibria of ecosystems, particularly those upon which one has an impact and of which one is a part. It is also to recognize that all entities — from protons through living cells to animals and galaxies — are formed by their relations to their environments. To be life-centered is to be especially attuned to the value of living beings amid one's ecological sensitivity, cognizant of their value in and for themselves, for one another, and for God. To recognize the value of living beings in and for themselves, their intrinsic value, is not to deny their relationality; rather it is to recognize that, amid their dependence on their environments, they are concerned with their own survival and well-being. Their lives are of value to themselves, and ought concomitantly to be of value to us. Respect for the integrity of creation entails the recognition that all living beings, humans and nonhumans alike, are neighbors.

To be sure, the very process of living inevitably involves the taking of life and the violation of other creatures' interests. As Whitehead put it, life is robbery. Hence the practice of a life-centered ethic requires judgment concerning whom to rob, when to rob, and how to rob, complemented by a desire to minimize our robbery. This in turn requires the recognition of gradations of intrinsic value and the weighing up of intrinsic value with instrumental value. In distinguishing gradations of intrinsic value, I recommend the following guideline: The greater a living organism's capacity for sentience, exemplified in part by the complexity of its nervous system, the greater its intrinsic value, and hence the greater the seriousness with which we must respect its individual interests.

This means that trivial human pleasures and comforts must indeed be sacrificed for the sake of another animal's well-being, or for that of a group of animals. For example, if the safety of a vaccine to combat hepatitis B virus, which is rarely fatal, must be tested on chimps, whose numbers are dwindling, and if in so doing many of the fifty thousand chimps who remain in the wild may be killed or captured for vaccine makers' colonies, it is best that humans "find some other way of solving its problem that is not to the detriment of the threatened population" (Birch and Cobb, 161). The costs to the animals are not worth the benefits to humans.

Any concern for individual animals under human domestication must itself be complemented by a concern for animals in the wild and for plants, particularly since plants play such important roles in supporting life on earth. Cognizant of the value both of human life and of wildlife, those who adopt a life-centered ethic will act so as to maximize the quality, not the quantity, of human life, making a preferential option for the poor and attempting to exercise this option with minimum abuse of individual animals under human domestication and with minimum impact on wildlife and habitats (Birch and Cobb, 173). Our aim will be to allow as many forms of life as possible to flourish in their intrinsic and instrumental value.

The adoption of a life-centered ethic can itself be energizing. Conversion beyond anthropocentrism need not be experienced as the addition of another series of issues to an already burdened stockpile of concerns, or as a dispersal of already limited moral energies (Moran). Rather it can be enjoyed as an enrichment of the Christian life and a way of drawing closer to God. Often the very practices that serve human life can complement, if not also serve, other living beings (Birch and Cobb, 174-75, 234-331; Callicott 1988). Moreover, our moral energies can themselves be nourished by sharing in that reverence for life which, so I have argued elsewhere, is characteristic of God's own consciousness (McDaniel 1989a, 1989b).

It helps, of course, if we have theologies that encourage reverence for life. As we seek to adopt life-centered perspectives, we are often disappointed when we turn to classical theologies for help. Many ignore flora and fauna altogether, focusing instead on the relations of humans to one another and to God, or they treat animals and plants primarily as tools to be managed in a stewardly way for the sake of human well-being. The latter approach is certainly preferable to the former. With its emphasis on stewardship it allows us to affirm that the nonhuman world ought to be used in an ecologically responsible manner for the benefit of all humans. But it does not go far enough. It fails to recognize that other living beings have value apart from their usefulness to human beings and that they are loved by God for their own sakes. To view the earth and its creatures *only* as resources for human use is to be decidedly anthropocentric.

It is for this reason that the World Council of Church's emphasis on respect for the integrity of creation is so important. With this emphasis the World Council explicitly invites Christians throughout the world to begin developing nonanthropocentric, life-centered forms of Christian understanding. The need is not for a single theology of life to which all Christians subscribe, but rather for many different theologies of life, each of which encourages a reverence for life relevant to the perspectives of member churches.

There are at least three fruitful approaches to the development of such theologies, all of which are being taken today, and all of which are advocated by the World Council. One way is to explore underemphasized traditions from the Bible and from the Western and Orthodox theological heritages. With this in mind Christians rightly turn to biblical authors who go beyond stewardship to stress a just treatment of animals; to Orthodox traditions with their emphases on a sacramental understanding of nature; and to classical, Western writers such as Irenaeus, the later Augustine,

Francis of Assisi, and the Rhineland mystics who stress the value of creation as a whole. In the latter regard, H. Paul Santmire whose study of the history of Western attitudes toward nature is one of the best available, provides perspective when he writes: "The theological tradition of the West is neither ecologically bankrupt, as some of its popular and scholarly critics have maintained and as numbers of its own theologians have assumed, nor replete with immediately accessible, albeit long-forgotten ecological riches hidden everywhere in its deeper vaults, as some contemporary Christians, who are profoundly troubled by the environmental crises and other related concerns, might wistfully hope to find" (Santmire, 5). Rather, the Western tradition is ambiguous, with elements both promising and unpromising. The task is to extract those elements that are promising and acknowledge those elements that are unpromising.

A second way is to learn from contemporary theological perspectives that are explicitly life-centered and that represent emerging directions of Christian thought. These perspectives include feminist theologies, African theologies, Native American theologies, Asian theologies, and process theologies. Some of these draw from non-Western cultural and religious traditions that are abundant with ecological insights; others, such as feminist theologies, draw from experiential sources that heretofore have been neglected in the dominant male-controlled theological traditions; and still others, such as process theology, draw from contemporary philosophical points of view that are explicitly ecological and cosmological in orientation. Inasmuch as Christianity itself is an ongoing historical movement, developmental and pluralistic at the outset, these new perspectives can be welcomed as possible advances in Christian self-understanding.

A third way is to internalize new insights gained from a dialogue with other faiths and ideologies. My aim in the following sections is to illustrate this third approach by discussing two proposals for Christian self-understanding that emerge from a dialogue with Buddhism. I speak of the ideas to be discussed as proposals rather than truths because in my view ideas that emerge out of a dialogue with other faiths and ideologies appropriately function, not as absolute truths to which all thinking Christians have an obligation to assent, but rather as experimental suggestions—lures for thought and feeling—that are fittingly evaluated by different Christian communities relative to needs and contexts. A buddhized Christianity may indeed be relevant to some Christians, given their situations, but not to others. My view is that the ideas that follow are relevant at least to privileged and powerful Christians, precisely as an antidote to their privilege and power.

But why Buddhism? At least two reasons. First, because it is has important resources for helping advance ecological awareness among Christians, particularly with its stress on the relational character of all existence. Second, because Buddhists are found throughout the world as potential dialogue partners for Christians. With over six percent of the world's pop-

ulation, the world's Buddhist population now includes approximately four-
teen thousand people in Africa, five hundred thousand in Latin America,
seventeen thousand in Oceania, three hundred fifty thousand in the Soviet
Union, two hundred thousand in Europe, and two hundred thousand in
North America, as well as several hundred million in South and East Asia
(Encyclopedia Britannica, 1987).[3]

Heretofore, of course, Buddhists have been most visible to Christian
theologians from Asia. Asian theologians such as Wesley Ariarajah, Tissa
Balasuriya, Kosuke Koyama, Lynn de Silva, and Aloysius Pieris have found
a dialogue with Buddhism both necessary and valuable for their own reflections on Christian faith. Pieris speaks for many Asian theologians when he
says that Christian theology must be "baptized by immersion" in the waters
of Asian spirituality for its own renewal (quoted in Ariarajah, 4). Today,
however, many non-Asian theologians, too, are in dialogue with Buddhists.
Small but growing numbers of Christian theologians in Europe and North
America have begun to meet regularly with Buddhists to foster mutual
understanding and growth, one result of which is the recently established
international Society for Buddhist-Christian Studies.[4] In addition, following
the lead of the late Trappist monk, Thomas Merton, many Roman Catholic
monastics have begun to use meditative practices as an adjunct to their
own spiritual disciplines (Walker).

However, despite the presence of Buddhism throughout the world and
the influences of Buddhism on Christian theologians and monastics, few
Christian theologians interested in developing ecological theologies have
drawn from Buddhist sources. This is particularly strange since it has so
often been assumed, both by advocates of Eastern (South and East Asian)
perspectives and by environmentalists and philosophers in the West, that
Eastern religions are much more resourceful for ecological sensitivity than
are Judaism, Christianity, and Islam. Huston Smith, who is former professor
of philosophy at MIT and noted interpreter of Eastern religions in the
United States, speaks for many when he says that while "the West oppo-
sitioned herself to nature," Asia "retained a deep, unquestioning confi-
dence in nature, appreciative of it, receptive to it" (quoted in Callicott
1987a, 122).

Still, Smith's generalization is questionable, and this for two reasons.
First, generalizations concerning Eastern religions are themselves problematic. There are considerable differences among the Eastern religions themselves, particularly between those originating in India (Hinduism and
Jainism) and those originating in the Far East (Taoism, Confucianism, and
Shintoism). Buddhism is unique in this regard inasmuch as it has been
influenced both by Indian and by Far Eastern ways of thinking. In any case,
some Western environmentalist philosophers have found the religions
shaped by Chinese and Japanese cultures to be more ecologically helpful
than the varieties of metaphysical monism, such as Advaita Vedanta, which
have emerged in Indian cultures.[5]

Second, like Christianity, individual Eastern religions are often ambiguous. They contain strands of thinking that are resourceful for a life-centered ethic and strands that are not. Sometimes a single idea can cut in both directions. For example, the idea of reincarnation as found in Hinduism, Jainism, and Buddhism can both encourage and discourage the protection of an individual animal from victimization in scientific experimentation. It can encourage such protection inasmuch as the animal is seen as having perhaps been a close and dear relative, and yet it can also discourage such protection inasmuch as the animal can be seen as sacrificing itself for the sake of a better birth in the future, leading ultimately to an escape from rebirth altogether (Bowker, 6). Given the ambiguities within individual Eastern religions and the differences between them, it is very difficult to judge whether, collectively, they are or are not better than Judaism, Christianity, and Islam at respecting the integrity of creation. Nor is it clear why this judgment is needed.

What is clear is that Christians have something to learn from Eastern religions. In an age that is ecologically endangered, but that is also rich in possibilities for interreligious dialogue, there is no need to assume that all divine guidance has been limited to historical Christianity. We appropriately celebrate rather than deny the presence of potentially helpful ideas in other religions, whether those ideas are confirmations of truths already contained in Christianity, or whether they offer something new and heretofore unrecognized by Christianity. As a recent report from the World Council puts it, other traditions "can enrich our understanding and, at times, help us to reformulate our views" (Niles, 12). Illustrative of this fact is the way a study of Buddhism can enrich our understanding of the human self and God.

RESOURCES FROM BUDDHISM FOR THINKING ABOUT THE SELF

An adage from the *Panchatantra*, a fifth-century collection of tales from India, reads: "For the sake of one's self, the world may be sacrificed." There is much truth in the saying, at least if we think of the self as a self-enclosed substance isolated within the body and cut off from the world by the boundaries of the skin. Given this perspective, the interests of the world outside the body and the self inside the body are quite distinct. When we act egotistically, it would follow that we are choosing the interests of our inner, self-enclosed selves over those of the outer world. We are sacrificing the world for the sake of the self.

But how accurate is this way of thinking about the self? Are our selves *really* enclosed within our bodies and isolated from the world by the boundaries of our skin? For almost two and a half centuries, Buddhists have insisted not. With their doctrine of *anatta*, or no-self, they have proposed that the self-encapsulated ego is a fiction, one that induces suffering and greed. Recently many environmental philosophers in the West have come to agree.[6] One of the most influential among them is J. Baird Callicott, professor of philosophy and natural resources at the University of Wisconsin, author of numerous influential works on environmental ethics and foremost interpreter of the pioneer of Western environmental philosophy, Aldo Leopold. We do well to see the relevance of the denial of an atomized self for an environmentalist like Callicott and then see how Buddhism supports and enriches his claim.

From the Atomized Self to the Ecological Self

To think of the self as a self-enclosed substance cut off from the world by the skin is to think atomistically. In such thinking the self is conceived as an independent, invisible atom residing within the body: a ghost within a machine. Callicott argues that atomistic conceptualities of the self are ontologically inaccurate, and that they lead us wrongly to suppose the central problem of moral philosophy is whether we should manage or overcome the inclinations of isolated egos. In fact, suggests Callicott, we have no isolated egos to be managed or overcome (Callicott 1986).

This is not to say that we do not act egotistically. It is obvious to most of us, including Callicott, that we do. Moreover, as feminist theologians point out, the disparagement of egotism in male-controlled Christian theology, and in Western philosophy as well, can itself be problematic. If the word *egotism* includes positive self-regard and creative self-determination, and if—being female, or poor, or a person of color—we have been denied opportunities for such self-regard and self-determination, we may act egotistically for good reasons. But feminist theologians point out that such egotism does not stem from an isolated ego. Rather it issues from a creative, relational self. If we think of the self relationally, so feminists propose, we can be both self-affirming and world-affirming (Keller, 155-215). It is the relationality of the self that Callicott wants to affirm.

To think of the self relationally is to think of its very existence as affected or constituted by the world external to the body, that is, by other humans, by plants and other animals, by the earth, and by the sky. If we adopt a relational view of the self, so Callicott avers, our aggression toward nature can be reduced, not through management or overcoming, but rather through insight. Understanding that our selves and the rest of nature cannot be sharply separated, we recognize that the interests of our selves and those of the biotic communities of which we are a part are often inseparable. In cooperating with nature, we serve our selves.

Callicott illustrates what he means by a "relational self" in two ways. First, he shows that our bodies, which are the physical part of who we are as psychophysical organisms, have their existence and identity in dependence on, and relation to, our environments. Our bodies are not external to the world; they are the world itself, coagulations of natural substances and processes. Because environing gases and other materials flow in and out of our bodies all the time, we are ever-changing concretions of the earth's materials (Callicott 1986, 314). We are not cut off from the natural world, we are manifestations of that world.

Second, he argues that our states of awareness, which are the psychic part of who we are as psychophysical organisms, have their existence and identity in dependence on, and relation to, our environments. Making the point in evolutionary terms Callicott reminds us that "the very structure of one's psyche and rational faculties are formed through adaptive interaction with the ecological organization of nature." The "more primitive elements of animal consciousness—palpable hunger and thirst, fear and rage, pleasure and pain—are as clearly evolutionary adaptations to an ever more elaborate ecosystem as fur and feathers, toes and digits, eyes and ears." He then suggests, following Paul Shepard, that conceptual thought itself, which we might be tempted to treat as separate from nature, "evolved as the taxonomical array of animals and plants was mapped by the emergent consciousness of primate hunter-gatherers" (Callicott 1986, 314-15).

It is with an affirmation of relational selfhood of the sort Callicott proposes that Christians have much to learn from Buddhism. Of course, most biblical understandings of human life suggest a relational understanding of human life. From the perspective of most biblical authors, a person has his or her identity in relation to, not independent from, other people, the earth, fellow creatures, and God. Nevertheless, influenced by more atomistic modes of thinking inherited from the Greeks, many Christians came to think of the self as a soul isolated from the body and cut off from the world by the boundaries of the skin, an immortal substance in a perishable body. It is this way of thinking that Buddhism helps us to overcome. Of particular relevance is the Buddhist doctrine of no-self and its corresponding affirmation in Zen, the doctrine of the true self.

No-Self

The doctrine of *anatta*, or no-self, is one of the earliest and most pervasive of Buddhist ideas. Put simply, the doctrine says that we have no permanent or independent selves. When we wrongly believe that we possess such selves, so Buddhists say, we generally cling to these fictions at the expense of our own well-being and that of others. Living our lives in terms of an illusion, we cause ourselves and others to suffer.

This is not to say that we are ourselves an illusion. Buddhists recognize that we exist, though not in the way we imagine if we think in terms of permanent substances. They say that our lives are a series of experiences extending from birth (and perhaps before) to death (and perhaps after). Be it an instance of waking, sleeping, eating, crying, loving, hating, or dying, each experience is itself "a little birth and a little death." At any given moment we *are* the "little birth and little death" that we are doing or undergoing, including as it does conscious and subconscious memories of the past and future.[7] There is no separate person locked within the body to whom the experience belongs, no separate owner or possessor of the flow of experience. There is only the flow itself.[8]

Considered in itself, of course, there is nothing particularly ecological about the view that humans are sequences of experiences. After all, each experience in a life-stream could be conceived atomistically as a self-enclosed monad. But this is not the case in Buddhism. Most schools of Buddhist thought envision experiences themselves as relational: that is, as originating in dependence on other realities. They call this relationality *pratitya-samutpada*, or dependent origination. Thus the Buddhist doctrine of no-self implies not simply that that there is no enduring substance underlying or overriding the flow of life-experiences, but also that each life-experience is intimately connected to, and dependent on, other realities. It is with this emphasis on relationality or connectedness that the Buddhist analysis of experience points in a direction similar to Callicott and other environmental philosophers.

But relationality itself can be conceived in at least two ways. In the first place, it can be conceived as causal dependence: that is, the dependence of one entity on preceeding entities or states of affairs. Billiard balls in motion can be conceived as connected in this sense, as when one billiard ball strikes another, and the latter's motion is thereby dependent on the former's impact. So can psychic states, as when one feeling is said to exist because it has been conditioned by preceding states of awareness. Many early Buddhist texts are detailed catalogues of the latter kind of conditioning. Connectedness as causal dependence also seems to be what Callicott has in mind when he says that our states of consciousness are formed through adaptive interaction with the ecological organization of nature (Callicott 1986). It is not that nature is immanent within our awareness, but rather that natural realities have conditioned the content and existence of our awareness. As evolutionary adaptations to ecological circumstances, our states of awareness are causally dependent on those circumstances.

The second way of conceiving connectedness is more radical and can be found in the Zen school of Mahayana Buddhism. Here connectedness is conceived not only as the causal dependence of one entity or state of affairs on others, but as the actual immanence of those other entities in the very constitution of the entity at issue. An example here would be the way in which organelles are part of the very constitution of a living cell. Not only is the cell as a whole causally dependent on those organelles, the organelles are part of what the cell is. Similarly, according to various interpreters of Zen Buddhism, other realities are part of the very constitution of a living person. Indeed, for many Buddhists each entity is part of the very constitution of every other entity. In this sense, reality is profoundly and radically ecological. Zen finds this ecological principle instantiated in the very nature of the true self.

The True Self

Of course, it may seem strange for a religion noted for its rejection of self simultaneously to affirm a true self. Not all schools of Buddhism make this affirmation. In Zen, however, the true self is affirmed as the everyday mind that remains after the reality of no-self has been understood.[9] Thomas Kasulis, whose *Zen Action/Zen Person* is an excellent discussion of Zen approaches to the self, explains that the true self is not something different from immediate experience; rather it is immediate experience itself. It is whatever a person is doing or undergoing in the present, as lived from the inside (Kasulis 1981).

In order to explain the Zen perspective, Kasulis recounts the following story about the ninth century master Lin-chi or (in Japanese) Rinzai. While giving a talk to a group of monks, Rinzai said:

> In this clump of raw flesh there is a true person of no status contin- ually entering and exiting your sense organs. Those of you who have not yet authenticated this fact, look! Look! (Kasulis, 51).

At this point a monk came forward and asked, "What sort of thing is this person of no status?" Rinzai came down from his seat, took hold of the monk, and said to him, "Speak! Speak!" The monk hesitated, thinking the matter over, at which point Rinzai released him, saying, "The true person of no status, what a dried-up manure-stick he is," and then returned to his chamber.

One point of this story is that the monk thought his true self was a thing or substance external to his own experience, an entity that could be objec- tified and then analyzed. Rinzai recognized that the monk's true self was none other than his immediate experience at that moment, confronted as it was with the challenge of responding to Rinzai's order to "Speak! Speak!" Rinzai's hope was that the monk would directly and immediately express his experience, in its depth and breadth, by uttering a creative word or performing a creative act. Obviously, the monk failed.

The fact that Rinzai hoped for a creative response is itself exemplary of the fact that, in Zen, the true self includes volition as well as awareness. In its volitional aspect, immediate experience is an act of decision, an act of cutting off certain possibilities for response to an immediate situation in the process of actualizing others. The agent of this decision is not different from the decision itself; the decider is the deciding. In Zen, as Kasulis explains, there "is something more than mere determinacy from the past, there is also the present moment working in its own creative way" (p. 139). An immediate experience actually "structures itself" from within its own prereflective depths (p. 140). In our essence, so Zen suggests, we are this act of self-structuring.

But we are also, and simultaneously, an act of *pratitya-samutpada*, or dependent origination, and this in the radical sense identified above. For our self-structuring is itself always a response to the very objects we experience, whatever they are. It is a way of integrating their influence. Moreover, the objects we experience are within our experience, and hence within us. This means that, inasmuch as we are consciously or subconsciously aware of earth and its creatures, they actually enter into our very constitution, forming its objective content. As was said of one Zen master, "the rocks, the river, everything he could see, all this was his true self" (Bancroft, 29).

In Callicott's discussion of the human body noted earlier, he too points toward this more radical sense of connectedness. He indicates that our bodies are actually composed of the earth's materials and of environmental gases, and that in this sense the earth is part of us. Zen extends the point in a direction with which Callicott would be sympathetic. Notice that the true self includes mental states as well as bodily sensations. Mental states involve processes of perceptual awareness, such as seeing, hearing, and smelling. For the Zen Buddhist, such perceptual processes actually include the world within themselves. When we see trees, the trees are actually immanent within, though not exhausted by, the act of seeing; when we hear flowing water, the water is actually immanent within, though not exhausted by, the act of hearing; when we smell a flower, the flower is actually immanent within, though not exhausted by, the act of smelling. Not only are our bodies made of the earth, our subjective perceptions, too, are composed of the earth. It is as if our true selves extend outward beyond our bodies to include rocks and rivers within themselves. As Kasulis puts it in alluding to the objects of his own experience: "These are not merely things in my experience; they are my experience. My self does not relate to these things; my self is these things" (Kasulis, 90).

If appropriated by Christians, this understanding of the true self has important implications for a Christian understanding of neighborly love. It suggests that neighborly love is an expression of, rather than an exception to, the very structure of our experience. Just as what happens in our bodies is part of us, so what happens in the world is part of us. We love our neighbors as ourselves because we realize that, even as they retain their own autonomy, our neighbors *are* ourselves. This does not mean that our neighbors are reduced to our awareness of them. Zen Buddhists generally reject such forms of idealism, insisting instead that the world forms the self, not vice versa (Nishitani, 139; Kasulis, 89-91). But it does mean that, as we feel the presence of our neighbors, they are actually present within us as constituents of our own lives. As the Church and Society sub-unit of the World Council would emphasize, our immanent neighbors are both human and nonhuman. They are other people, particularly the poor, and they are also other animals and plants, rocks and trees, hills and rivers. They are whoever and whatever we experience and are affected by in any way: consciously or unconsciously, directly or indirectly, vividly or vaguely.

Even if we do not perceive them as neighbors and identify with their destinies, they *are* our neighbors, because, in experiencing them, our destinies are connected to theirs.

Relevance to Christianity

In order to see how Buddhist notions of no-self and the true self can enter into Christian self-understanding, the proposals of John B. Cobb, Jr., are noteworthy (Cobb 1975, 203-20; cf. Cobb 1982). As a process theologian Cobb argues that the appropriation of insights from other religions can be authentically Christian, inasmuch as Christianity is itself an ongoing process capable of creative transformation through openness to other Ways. He finds Buddhism particularly helpful as a stimulus for Western Christians, because it can help us to overcome that isolated individualism by which so many have become trapped, and thus better to approximate that perfection of love toward which all are called. As Cobb puts it, those of us in the West can benefit from trying to understand and internalize the truth of the doctrine of *anatta*, thereby freeing ourselves from "attachment to individualized personal existence as a final good" (Cobb 1975, 220).

By "personal existence" Cobb means a certain way of experiencing. In the life of a given individual, a way of experiencing is a result of both habit, itself conditioned by social and historical circumstances, and choice. It is a way in which an immediate experience in a given life-stream "structures itself," to use Kasulis's phrase, in response to its experiential data. Personal existence is not the only way immediate experience can structure itself; rather it is one among many possible ways. Amid the way of personal existence, we identify with and cling to past and future experiences in our own life-stream, accentuating our own continuity over time, but often at the expense of also identifying with other people and the rest of the world. We think of ourselves as "who I have been" and "who I might be," and we think of everything else as "not-I," though not necessarily without its own value. If we are shaped by a theistic heritage, our aim is to live out this way of experiencing in faithfulness to God and with respect for others.

From Cobb's perspective personal existence has value. Historically it has yielded a rich sense of individuality and ethical responsibility. But he believes that it has also had its costs in personal misery and aggression, and that it is in some tension with biblical emphases on the self as constituted by relations to a community. This is because, amid personal existence, other-interest and self-interest are dichotomized. The call to love others is therefore experienced "either as a remote and hardly relevant ideal, a burdensome and guilt-producing law, or as a supernatural gift" (Cobb 1975, 108). To better realize our own Christian ideals for love of neighbor, says Cobb, a new "postpersonal" way of experiencing is needed, encouraged by an encounter with Buddhism. Postpersonal experiencing is not a return to prepersonal modes of existence, nor is it a sheer annihilation of personal existence. Rather it is a passing beyond personal existence while retaining its achievement. It is an extension to others, both human and nonhuman, of that empathetic identification we normally feel toward our own personal pasts and futures. In so doing, we learn to feel the presence of others, nonhuman and human, as part of who and what we are. Cobb believes that Buddhism can help move Christians in this postpersonal direction. In his words: "Perhaps the encounter with the transpersonal existence of the Buddhist, the recognition of the serenity and strength it embodies, the experience of Buddhist meditation, and the study of Buddhist philosophy will give us the courage to venture into that kind of radical love which can carry us into a postpersonal form of Christian existence" (Cobb 1975, 220).

Foretastes of Postpersonal Experiencing

· If proposals such as Cobb's are to be effective, it is helpful if we can find in our own lives certain foretastes of postpersonal experiencing. Many of us already know something of postpersonal experiencing, particularly in relation to loved ones. Intuitively we feel the presence of family members and friends as part of us even though they are external to our bodies. What happens to them happens to us. Indeed, many of us feel this sense of solidarity with other people beyond the sphere of family members and friends, sometimes in demonic ways and sometimes constructive ways. Something of this broadened sense of connectedness must have been part of Paul's sense that he and other Christians were "members of one another" as united in "one body" of Christ (Rom 12:5).

What is important about Zen for Christians interested in respecting the integrity of creation is that it suggests that we can feel this solidarity with the earth as well, with rocks and trees, hills and rivers. Even this may not be foreign to our experience. Consider the following personal account from Callicott. Having grown up roaming the banks of the Mississippi River, he returned to its banks.

As I gazed at the brown silt-choked waters absorbing a black plume of industrial and municipal sewage from Memphis and followed bits of some unknown beige froth floating continually down from Cincinnati, Louisville, or St. Louis, I experienced a palpable pain. It was not distinctly located in any of my extremities, nor was it like a headache or nausea. Still, it was very real. I had no plans to swim in the river, no need to drink from it, no intention of buying real estate on its shores. My narrowly personal interests were not affected, and yet *somehow I was personally injured. It occurred to me then, in a flash of self-discovery, that the river was part of me* (Callicott 1986, 315-16; emphasis mine).

The Zen analysis of the true self would suggest that Callicott's feeling was indeed a flash of self-discovery, that the river was in fact part of his true self. No doubt many of us have these sorts of feelings with various aspects of the natural world by which we are shaped. Our feelings of solidarity with the earth may be joyful or, as Callicott's example makes clear, painful. For Christians this sharing of the earth's degradation can be understood as a sharing of Christ's suffering. As Freda Rajotte puts it, "for some of us it is exactly in the desolation of the Murora atoll, the toxic and choking gasses of Cubatao, the dead river Rhine, the devastation of Kyshtym, the cloud of Bhopal, the death of Hiroshima, that the suffering and crucifixion of Christ confront us, convict us and challenge us to commitment" (Rajotte 1987, 186). From Zen we learn that if Christ's suffering is indeed to be found in the despoliation of the earth, then his suffering, too, is part of our true selves. Not only are we part of his body, his body, or at least his suffering, is part of us.

Even if we do have foretastes of postpersonal experiencing, however, such feelings are oftentimes fleeting. All too easily we slip back into a way of experiencing that is disconnected from the world. Here Zen encourages us to consider three further proposals. The first is that a knowledge of the world as part of the self is continually at work in us at a prereflective level, even if we are not consciously aware of this fact. The second is that through the practice of meditation, or *zazen* we can experientially uncover, or be released into, this prereflective awareness. And the third is that this pre-reflective knowledge can then become a quality of our everyday experience such that, even when interacting in ordinary ways with the world, we can continually be aware of our "non-dual" relation to the world. The Rinzai tradition of Zen stresses that the third stage comes only after a sudden awakening in the *satori* experience, whereas the Soto tradition says that no such experience is necessary. In any case, both emphasize that our feelings of deep connectedness with the world need not come and go. They can be part of our everyday mind.

The contemporary Zen philosopher Keiji Nishitani describes this pre-reflective awareness in discussing a saying of the Japanese poet, Basho. In describing how he composed his poetry, Basho wrote:

> From the pine tree
> Learn of the pine tree,
> And from the bamboo
> of the bamboo.

Nishitani notes that Basho is not here speaking of detached observation or scientific study. Rather Basho "means for us to enter into the mode of being where the pine tree is the pine tree itself, and the bamboo is the bamboo itself, and from there to look at the pine tree and bamboo" (Nish-itani, 128). Indeed, says Nishitani, the Japanese word for "learn" (*narau*) carries with it "the sense of 'taking after' something, of making an effort to stand essentially in the same mode of beings as the thing one wishes to learn about" (p. 128). To learn from the pine tree or from the bamboo in a conscious way is to make effective a kind of "nonobjective knowing" that has been implicit in our experience throughout, and that is central to our true identity (p. 163).

Kasulis adds that this prereflective knowledge is itself a form of compassion. "For Zen," he writes, "compassion and intuitive wisdom are the same" (Kasulis, 98). In his view, not only do we already know the world as part of our self, we already care for it. In the depths of our prereflective experience, he believes, there is already at work a kind of sympathy for the world that is clouded over and neglected, but never entirely lost. A similar view is found in various forms of Christian mysticism and also in process theology. If valid, this view rightly gives Christians and others hope that respect for the integrity of creation is less alien to human life, and more attainable, than circumstances have often led us to believe.

But *is* the view valid? Zen Buddhists would insist that its validity must be tested through meditation. To discover the depths of our true self and its capacities for wisdom and compassion, they say, it is important that on a regular basis we intentionally release ourselves from the vicissitudes of reflective awareness, descending into that domain of pure alertness which characterizes *zazen*. Of course the purposeful cultivation of psychic states has often been viewed with suspicion by Protestants. It is no accident that most of the Christians experimenting with various forms of Buddhist meditation have been Roman Catholic and Orthodox, not Protestant.

Indeed, Protestants have sometimes had good reasons for being suspicious of meditation. Such cultivation easily becomes an end in itself, an absolutization of psychic states at the expense of social action and at the expense of the risk and insecurity that accompany authentic faith in God. For different reasons, most Zen Buddhists are also leery of such absolutization. They believe that it obstructs a full realization of the Zen life. That life, they say, is an everyday life, centered in the here and now, capable of experiencing the entire range of human emotions, all the while devoid of a spectator self, and all the while connected to the world as part of the true self. The practice of *zazen* must be understood in this broader context. Meditation is an expression of, and a contribution to, the art of living in the world.

Perhaps Protestants, too, can experiment with Zen meditation in this broader context. After all, most Protestants realize that we cannot simply think our way into respect for the integrity of creation. Reflection must be complemented by worship and prayer, action and service. Zen suggests that we add *zazen* to this list of complements to reflection. If *zazen* can enrich our own capacities to respect rocks and trees, hills and rivers, and to see that they are part of our true selves, the suggestion seems well worth a try.

RESOURCES FROM BUDDHISM FOR THINKING ABOUT GOD

There is still another reason why *zazen* or a study of Zen philosophy might be helpful. If, as Zennists claim, such endeavors lead us to learn something about the fundamental nature of our own experience, they might also lead us to learn something about the fundamental nature of God's experience. At least this is the case if we assume that God too "experiences," and that the structure of God's experience is something like our own.

While arguable, these assumptions are reasonable for Christians to make. Following biblical metaphors, God is imaged by most Christians as a cosmic Self who responds to worldly happenings in various ways, and who, in so doing, takes those happenings into account, or experiences them in some way. If we are among the Christians who think this way, we necessarily imagine divine experiences as structurally similar to, though perhaps much more wise and compassionate than, our own experiences; otherwise there is no meaning to our idea that God experiences. Thus, we must presuppose some kind of ontological continuity between the structure of our experience and that of God's. This is not to say that we fully understand the mystery of God. We do not. Still, as soon as we address "God" in prayer or use the word *God* in thought, we inevitably image God in one way or another. For this reason it is important that we choose our images carefully, albeit with tentativeness and humility. The idea of God as an experiencing Self is one such image. And here Zen can help. It can stimulate us to imagine the divine Self in new, more ecological ways. At least this is the line of thought I develop in the remainder of this chapter.

Though stimulated by an encounter with Zen, the speculations that follow go well beyond the perspective of Zen, though not necessarily beyond those of other, more theistic schools of Buddhism such as the Pure Land traditions. For at least two reasons Zennists, along with other nontheistic Buddhists, do not speak of God. The first concerns the nature of the "ultimate," to which Zen and other schools of Buddhism point, and from which Zen experience originates. Zennists rightly recognize that when Christians and other theists speak of God, more often than not we mean a cosmic Self, a personal Being, by whom the world is loved and lured toward wholeness. By contrast, the ultimate to which Zen and other schools of Buddhism point is not a Self among selves, not even a cosmic Self. Rather it is the immediacy of experience itself, understood as the ultimate reality of each and every self. Keiji Nishitani and other members of the Kyoto School of Japanese Zen philosophy speak of this ultimate as Emptiness. By Emptiness they do not mean an underlying One into which selves are absorbed; nor do they mean a sheer privation of being. Rather they mean the very root, what Nishitani calls the very "home-ground," of a self's existence (Nishitani, 151-52). This home-ground is named Emptiness because it is empty of static being even as it is full of becoming, empty of self-existence even as it is full of relationality, empty of an external creator even as it is full of creativity. Emptiness is the immediacy of whatever we are doing or undergoing. One cannot worship this immediacy, or love it, or be guided by it, or pray to it. One can only realize one's identity with it, and then, as Rinzai insisted of the monk, express it in novel and creative ways. Zennists do not speak of God, in part because they sense that the word *God* does not name this immediacy.

To this point some Christians might respond that when Christians speak of God, we are not really speaking of a Self among selves, but rather the ultimate reality of each and every self. God, these Christians might say, is actually Emptiness, the sheer immediacy of experience, and Emptiness is God. While this response to Zen might appeal to some of a mystical orientation, it would miss what is most important to the vast majority of Christians past and present. For most Christians God is indeed a Self among selves, a supreme Consciousness to whom one prays, by whom one is loved, and through whom individuals and communities find the courage, often despite odds to the contrary, to seek the fullness of life. For Christians who address God as a Thou, it would be false to suggest that Emptiness is just another name for God, or vice versa. A better approach is to agree that the word *God* has more often than not pointed to a cosmic Self by whom the world is guided and loved, and to explore the possibility that God as thus understood is an instance of the very Emptiness to which Buddhism points. If we look for parallels in Buddhism, God would not be the Emptiness of which all sentient beings are instances; rather God would be a cosmic Bodhisattva—like "Amida" of whom Pure Land Buddhists speak—who "vows to save all sentient beings," and who is himself a supremely sentient Being.

However, even if Zen Buddhists recognized the existence of a cosmic Bodhisattva, as do their Pure Land fellow travellers, there is a second reason why Zennists might not speak of God. The word *God* is a Christian word, and often when Christians use it, we refer, not to a relational Bodhisattva who adapts to each situation, but rather to a changeless and independent Consciousness who saves only Christians and who is cut off from the world by the boundaries of divine transcendence. In the latter respect God is the very kind of self—in this instance a cosmic Self—that the doctrine of *anatta* denies. The Zen enlightenment experience is a revelation of the full relationality of all that exists, and hence of the nonexistence of any such selves, human or divine. If theism implies belief in a self-encapsulated divine Being, many Buddhists, even Pure Land Buddhists, are atheists.

By this definition, however, many contemporary Christian theologians too are atheists. For different reasons and in different contexts Christians throughout the world have been rejecting atomistic ways of thinking about God. For the most part, they have not been responding to challenges from Buddhism. In the North American context they have been responding to the inadequacies of the atomistic theologies for what Sallie McFague calls our "ecological, nuclear age." As McFague points out, an atomized God is a "monarchical" deity who is imaged as a divine King separate from, and standing over, his earthly realm. In our time, argues McFague, it will not do to think of God as a sovereign power to be "worshiped and glorified as the sole power in the universe," even if divine power is conceived as providential and loving (McFague, 16). The monarchical model "encourages attitudes of militarism, dualism, and escapism; it condones control through violence and oppression; it has nothing to say about the nonhuman world" (p. 78). What is needed, she says, is a way of thinking about God that enables Christians to accept responsibility for protecting life, and that provides us with images of shared power, not dominating power. What is needed, she seems to say, is a God who is less like a benevolent dictator and more like a cosmic Bodhisattva.

In search of alternatives McFague offers imagery that well serves the World Council's interests in peace, justice, and respect for the integrity of creation. She suggests that we try envisioning God as Mother, Lover, and Friend, and that we try imagining God's relationship to the world as analogous to that of a self to its body. It is with the latter suggestion that I think Zen Buddhism has something to offer McFague and, accordingly, all Christians who find it helpful to imagine the world as God's body. First, let us look briefly at how, given the discussion of the self in the previous section, it would be true to say "the world is my body," and then show how the Zen way of thinking might help us imagine the world as God's body, too.

The World Is My Body

One whose perspective is inspired by Zen can rightly say "the world is my body." Here the word *world* refers to that which is external to a person's body: rocks, trees, hills, rivers, plants, people, other animals, stars, galaxies. To say that the world *is* my body is to say that I, as identical with my immediate experience, am related to my body and to the world in a similar way. The world is external to my body, but immanent within my self.

At the outset, however, it is very important to recognize two kinds of relation between self and world that would *not* obtain in a Zen context or in a buddhized Christian context. The first is that of *control*. If the metaphor that "the world is my body" suggests that we have, or ought to have, the same control over the world that we have over our bodies, then the metaphor is misleading. From a Zen perspective and from a Christian perspective we do not and ought not control the world in the same way that we control our bodies. Amid our self-structuring dependent origination, which in Zen is the very nature of the true self, we ought to respect as much as possible the capacities of others, both nonhuman and human, to originate dependently in their own self-structuring ways. Rinzai did not force the monk to express his true self; he enticed him to do so and to do so creatively.

The second kind of relation that would not obtain is that of *self-expression*. If the metaphor that "the world is my body" suggests that we have, or ought to have, the world as a medium for personal self-expression in the same way that we have our bodies as such media, then the metaphor itself is again misleading. We do not, and ought not, treat the world as a theater for personal self-expression. Rather we ought to respect the intrinsic value of living beings in and for themselves. The 14th Dalai Lama, exiled leader of Tibetan Buddhism, captures the spirit of such respect in explaining the Buddhist approach to life. Suggesting that we ought to extend our care to all living creatures, he points to the fact that animals ought to matter to us because they matter to themselves.

> Life is as dear to a mute creature as it is to a man. Even the lowliest insect strives for protection against dangers that threaten its life. Just as each one of us wants happiness and fears pain, just as each one of us wants to live and not to die, so do all other creatures (quoted in Chapple, 226).

Note that the Dalai Lama does not say that we ought to respect animals because they are useful to us, or because they are concoctions of our egos, or because they are extensions of our bodies. Rather, we appreciate them because they have needs and interests of their own, as do we. If the metaphor "the world is my body" prevents respect for creatures on their own terms, for their own sakes, then again it is dangerous.

What kind of relation *would* carry the metaphor? It is that of *subjective composition*.

To say that "the world is my body" is to say that the world forms me in the same way that my body forms part of the content of my immediate subjective experience. As a true self identical with my lived experience, I am composed of the world in the same sense that, when I have a stomach-ache, my immediate experience is formed by the ache in my stomach. Just as I feel the presence of an ache in my stomach, and the ache thereby becomes part of me, so when I feel the presence of rocks, trees, hills, and rivers, they too become part of me. Subjectively, the rocks and rivers that I experience are no less part of me than an ache in my abdomen or a pleasure to my palate. In *this* sense, and not in the sense of control or self-expression, the world is my body.

The World Is God's Body

I suggest that it is also in *this* sense, and not in the others, that it can be appropriate to speak of the world as God's body. Let us note first why the other two senses are inappropriate.

First, consider control. If in saying that the world is God's body, we mean that God controls the world in the same way that we control our bodies, then we have the same moral problems with God that we have with humans who rely on coercive power. A God who acts coercively would lack moral respect for human freedom. More importantly, the image of divine control presents insuperable problems for theodicy, and this not only in relation to human history but also in relation to the history of nature. Much of the history of biological life is built on opportunism; and, as evidenced in predator-prey relations, this opportunism is cruel, at least from the point of view of the victims. If the history of nature is a result of unilateral, divine control, then God's love must be questioned, for the history of life on earth does not readily attest to the existence of an all-controlling and all-loving God. If God is all-controlling, God is not all-loving.

In order to avoid this implication, one theological option is to suppose that God is indeed all-loving, but that God is not all-controlling, at least if the latter implies the power to *unilaterally* control worldly events. Elsewhere I have explained this alternative as "relational panentheism" (McDaniel 1989a, 26-27). It might also be called ecological panentheism, for it emphasizes that God and worldly creatures structure themselves in relation to, and the mutual formation of, one another. From the perspective of an ecological or relational panentheism, God is by no means powerless. Indeed, God is the most enlivening and ubiquitous power in the universe. In faith, we can live by God's presence. Yet, as the cross of Jesus can suggest, the presence of God is, and always has been, invitational rather than coercive, a pull from ahead to which creatures may or may not respond, rather than a push from behind by which they are inevitably compelled. Just as the cells in our bodies have creative powers that can contravene our own aims, so, from a relational perspective, the cells in God's body, including us, have powers that can contravene divine aims. If the metaphor "the world is God's body" suggests the contrary, it highlights divine power at the expense of divine love.[10]

Second, consider the implications of conceiving the world as God's personal self-expression. Whether or not this position is objectionable depends on what is meant by self-expression. Often such language is understood substantially and monistically. It conveys the image of a divine One, from whose very substance the world emerges as a manifestation, appearance, or emanation. In contrast to relational panentheism, it expresses what I have called "emanationist panentheism" (McDaniel 1989a, 26-27). Not only does a perspective of this sort raise questions for theodicy, it also cuts against a recognition of the intrinsic value of individual organisms. For when monistic thinking of this sort prevails, individual organisms are not really appreciated for their own sakes and on their own terms. Rather they are appreciated only in reference to their origin and emanator, God. The individual animal being taken to slaughter may be defended because it is an expression of God, and this attitude is beneficial to the animal. But the attitude does not go far enough. As the Dalai Lama suggests, truly to appreciate an organism in its intrinsic value is to recognize that it is important on its own terms and for its own sake, regardless of what metaphysical substances it may or may not express, and regardless of its ultimate origins, divine or otherwise.

Here, too, relational panentheism is helpful. Rather than saying that God loves the world because it expresses the divine essence, the relational panentheist can say that God, like a divine Lover or Friend, loves the world because the world is lovable (McFague, 130-36). This need not contravene the idea that God in some way creates the world, though it will suggest that God creates "out of chaos" from a beginningless past rather than creating "out of nothing" from a finite past (McDaniel 1989a, 36-37). Nor need it contravene the self-body analogy. Just as the cells in our body have lives of their own even as they contribute to, and are part of, our lives, so, from this perspective, the cells in God's body can have lives of their own, even as they contribute to, and are part of, God's life. God loves, and is enriched by, each cell on its own terms and for its own sake. No less than the Dalai Lama, the divine Self is attuned to the intrinsic value of living beings.

To expand this more relational way of saying the world is God's body, Zen can be helpful. Recall that from a Zen perspective the idea that the world is my body does not mean that the world emerges from my subjective ego; rather it means that the world composes my own immediate experience, my own true self. This does not reduce "rocks and trees, hills and rivers" to mere projections of my subjectivity, nor does it mean that I am incapable of a creative response to the world. But it does mean that my subjective awareness is constituted by worldly realities in the same way that it is constituted by sensations in my body. Analogously, the idea that the world is God's body need not suggest that the world is an expression of the divine essence. Rather, it can mean that the world, in its creativity and intrinsic value, composes God's immediate experience, God's own true self. This would not imply that the earth and its living creatures are mere projections of God, or that God lacks creativity in God's own right. But it would mean that God's subjectivity is constituted by the earth and its creatures in a way similar to that in which our lives are constituted by sensations in our bodies. Just as aches in our stomachs are part of who and what we are, even though they are not emanations of our intentions, so aches in the world are part of who and what God is, even though they are not emanations of divine essence. As the body of God, the world is part of God, but it is not reduced to God.

Interestingly, the metaphor that the earth and its creatures are God's body might even be more true for God than it is for us. Our subjective experience is very much mediated by our physical bodies. When we say "the world is my body," we are being metaphorical. We mean that the world is *like* our bodies in some respects, even as it is unlike our bodies in others. By contrast, the cosmic Self, which presumably is everywhere at once, would not have a physical body. As all-inclusive, the closest thing God would have to a body would be the world itself. The earth and its creatures, plus the heavens and their celestial bodies, would be present to God more directly than they are present to us. Almost literally, the world would *be* God's body.

Understood in this Zen-influenced way, the metaphor of the world as God's body can contribute considerably to Christian efforts to respect the integrity of creation. It suggests that the whole of nature is part of the divine self; it shows how the exploitation of nature impoverishes the very richness of divine experience; it encourages a respect for the intrinsic value of individual organisms; and, in saying that God loves the world as a self loves a body, it suggests that embodiedness itself is a good to be cherished rather than an evil to be avoided (McFague, 74). And yet, because it is relational rather than emanationist, it accomplishes these ends without reducing God to the world or the world to God.

Still, there are two possible objections to this way of thinking. The first is that it denies divine transcendence, and the second is that it violates traditional intuitions that God is personal. In closing let me respond to each objection, and in so doing further elaborate the way in which a Christian encounter with Buddhism can stimulate thought concerning a theology of creation.

Traditionally, language concerning divine transcendence has often meant at least two things. First, it has meant that God has something like thoughts, feelings, and intentions of God's own, which are distinguishable from worldly thoughts, feelings, and intentions. If we take our self-body analogy from Buddhism, there is nothing in what has been said above that contradicts this idea. Even though the monks to whom Rinzai was speaking were part of Rinzai's very body, the Zen master nevertheless had thoughts, feelings, and intentions of his own, which were distinguishable from those of his audience. Rinzai hoped that the individual monk he enjoined to "speak!" would respond creatively, and he was frustrated when the one monk did not. Hope and frustration were themselves coalescences of thought, feeling, and intention. They were aspects of Rinzai's experience, and only indirectly of the monk's.

Analogously, even though the world might be understood as the body of God, God might nevertheless have thoughts, feelings, and intentions that are distinguishable from those of worldly creatures. Of course, we do not really know what divine thoughts, feelings, and intentions are like. Perhaps, as process theologians suggest, they are instances of "prehending" or "taking into account" experiential data from a subjective point of view. As such they would be instances of, rather than exceptions to, the very kind of experiential activity that occurs in all living things and, so process thinkers speculate, in all existents, even subatomic events. But this is not the place to present arguments for pan-experientialism (Griffin). My point here is that there is nothing in the self-body metaphor that precludes divine subjectivity. A true self, even if divine, will consist both of the content of experience and the subjective acts of prehending, or taking that content into account. In something of the same way Rinzai took into account the monks with hope and frustration, so God might take into account the world with wisdom and compassion. In that wisdom and compassion would lie God's transcendence.

If we are influenced by Buddhism, however, we are provoked further to imagine that God, even if embodying a transcendent subjectivity, exemplifies *anatta*. This would mean at least two things. First, it would mean that God is identical with divine experience. In order to press the point, let us imagine God in personal terms: either as a caring Father or perhaps better in our time, as a strong and compassionate Mother, since father imagery can so often bring with it associations of patriarchal domination. In her transcendence, so the doctrine of *anatta* would suggest in the first instance, the Mother of the world would not *have* wisdom and compassion, as if she were one thing and her subjective states another. Rather she would *be* her wisdom and compassion. She, like us, would have no self apart from her experience. Second, the doctrine would suggest that God's subjective transcendence is fluid and adaptive rather than solid and unchanging. As situations in the world change, so would the subjective forms of God change. Her wisdom and compassion would remain constant, but the particular forms they would take would be relative to the requirements of the situation. Sometimes it might be wise for her to be firm, at other times tender; sometimes it might be compassionate for Her to be judgmental, at other times tolerant. In her flexibility she would exemplify what Buddhists call *upaya*, skillful ways of responding to situations at hand. This means that, as illustrative of *anatta*, Her transcendence would be a *relational transcendence*: an ever-changing and ever-adaptive act of freely responding to new situations in the interests of life's fullness.

Mention of divine responsiveness to the world takes us to a second meaning of divine transcendence. Often biblical language concerning divine transcendence has implied, not simply that God is partially constituted by subjective feelings of her own, but that God has the power to exercise an effective influence in the world, particularly in times of crisis and particularly by offering new and hopeful possibilities for responding to such crises. This is the understanding of divine transcendence that is most meaningful for people in oppressed situations. At issue here is not transcendent subjectivity, it is transcendent power.

I believe that an emphasis on transcendent power is also compatible with a Zen-influenced understanding of the world as God's body. Just as Rinzai shook the monk, so Christians influenced by Zen can say, God shakes the world. For reasons noted above, however, it is important to emphasize that divine shaking is invitational rather than coercive. The lure of God can be experienced as a prod, a spur, a prompt, and a challenge, but it cannot be experienced as an *irresistible* force. Though it may be a source of new and unanticipated possibilities for life's fullness, we must ourselves actualize the possibilities derived from it. As a beckoning toward justice, peace, and respect for the integrity of creation, God requires our response for a fulfillment of her aims.

In an ecological, nuclear age, so McFague reminds us, it is in our interests to align ourselves with the aims of God, for God herself is on the side of life. Furthermore, as the World Council would emphasize, she is on the side of the poor. This means that God's transcendent power is a lure within the hearts of the poor to seek the fullness of life for themselves and others, and a lure within the hearts of the privileged and powerful to identify with the aspirations of the poor, thereby relinquishing our power and privilege. Just as God's transcendent subjectivity is adaptive to each situation, from a buddhized Christian perspective, God's transcendent power is adaptive to each situation. The divine Mother beckons the leper to have hope, and she beckons the rich young ruler to sell his possessions and give to the poor.

Of course, such personal imagery raises the second objection mentioned earlier. If we conceive the world as God's body, can we legitimately speak of God as Mother, Lover, or Friend? If so, do we inevitably adopt an anthropocentrism that cuts against our desire to affirm the integrity of creation? Here as well, an internalization of Buddhist sensibilities can help.

The relevance of personal imagery to God partly hinges on our concept of person. The word *person* here means an individual human being as he or she assumes a role or guise in relation to others. Persons are fathers and mothers, teachers and students, friends and lovers, saints and prophets, and so on. Defined as such, persons may or may not exemplify what earlier we called the "personal" way of experiencing. In any case, as these examples suggest and as Zen and other schools of Buddhism lead us to recognize, we rightly think of persons relationally (Kasulis, 132). Persons do not first exist and then enter into relations with others; rather, they emerge out of relations with others as outcomes of the contextual self-structuring of immediate experience. Inasmuch as the contextual self-structuring of immediate experience is the true self, it is true to say that the person becomes from the self. As selves, we *become* mothers, lovers, and friends in contexts appropriate to such becoming. As someone needs our care, we become a mother; as someone elicits our passion, we become a lover; as someone shares with us a life, we become a friend. In the beginning was our self— that is, the immediacy of our experience—from which emerged, in response to the needs of others, those persons we have become and are becoming.

Analogously, if we think of God in personal terms, an encounter with Buddhism invites us to speculate that God's personal qualities, too, emerge in relation to, rather than independence from, the needs of creatures. Amid the self-structuring of the divine experience, God, too, might become a mother for those who need divine parenting, a friend for those who need divine friendship, and a lover for those who need divine intimacy. Indeed, God might become different Persons for us at different stages in our lives; or a plurality of Persons. Globally, God may have become many different

Persons for many different people. To say that God becomes a Person of one sort or another is to say that the divine True Self feels each of us according to our deepest needs, empathetically bestows affection upon us in accordance with those needs, and lures us as that Person might. It is not as if divine Persons are mere masks of God; they are who and what the divine True Self actually becomes, for us.

Such speculation presupposes, of course, that there is something in the depths of divine self-structuring that is empathetic and that yearns to meet needs. Pure Land Buddhists might call this something the primordial Vow of Amida; feminists and process thinkers might call it the primordial Eros of the universe; and more traditional Christians might call it Grace. In any case, if the presupposition that God is fundamentally empathetic is not itself too anthropocentric, and I think it not, it offers a way of both affirming divine personality and of transcending anthropocentrism. It invites us to imagine that the cosmic Self feels each cell in its body in terms appropriate to that cell, and then responds by luring that cell toward that kind of fulfillment relevant to its needs and its context. Inasmuch as many humans need a personal God, the cosmic Self feels us, and responds to us, in a personal way. But the cosmic Self would also appreciate other creatures on their terms and in ways appropriate to them. God would identify with the subjective sensations and aspirations of diatoms, rattlesnakes, beetles, and "all things counter, original, spare, strange" (Gerard Manley Hopkins, "Pied Beauty"). From this perspective, God would not be a cosmic Person who relates first and foremost to people and who also, in some less important way, also relates to nonhuman organisms. Rather, God would be a cosmic Self who relates to nonhuman organisms on their own terms and for their own sakes, and who also, in relation to people, becomes that Person or those Persons whom we need.

Of course, there is often a drastic difference between what we need and what we want. Oftentimes those of us who are privileged and powerful *want* a God who sanctions our own complicity in unjust social orders or our exploitation of other forms of life. We want a God who is white and male, or who loves only humans. Yet, like the rich young ruler, we *need* a God, both for ourselves and for others, who impels us to change our ways. We need a God whose care requires that we share our goods with our sisters and brothers, whose erotic passion invites us to transcend our fear of embodiedness, and whose companionable spirit encourages us to be friends of the earth. Perhaps, as McFague suggests, we need a God who is a mother, lover, and friend. Cognizant of this possibility, we must ourselves evaluate and rank different images of God, as does McFague in criticizing monarchical images and offering alternatives. As a working principle, perhaps the World Council of Churches offers a guideline. We might assume that those images that, to the best of our judgment, serve the interests of justice, peace, and respect for the integrity of creation reveal something of God; and that those images that serve the ideologies of injustice, violence, and ecological degradation distort God. In making these judgments, we must be cognizant of our own finitude, our own inability fully to understand the divine mystery. And we must allow ourselves to be influenced and shaped by the poor and victimized, human and nonhuman, whose cries can unmask our ideologies. Inasmuch as we hear these cries, we may realize that the omni-adaptive God, while not a servant to our wants, is a complement to our needs, particularly our need for full community with those whom we have heretofore victimized. Such, I believe, is a christological norm for evaluating divine images.

But of course speculations concerning divine images, much less the ranking of such images, take us far beyond what many Buddhists would affirm. Such thinking certainly takes us beyond the austere, nonspeculative simplicity of Zen. But perhaps it does not take us far beyond Christianity. As Christians we are part of a dynamic tradition capable of growth and change. We are pilgrims in an historical adventure that is partly propelled by the vitality of our own imaginations. The adventure was partly launched, but not finished, by Jesus, who showed us "the way of radical identification with all others" (McFague, 53). To be Christian today is to follow this way and imagine God according to its spirit. It is to identify with all other people, particularly the poor, such that we feel their destinies as inseparable from our own. It is also to identify with rocks and trees, hills and rivers; with experimental mice and slaughtered cows; with a depleted ozone layer and shrinking forests. In this chapter I have tried to show how an encounter with Buddhism can encourage this kind of identification. It can stimulate us to imagine that the world is our body and that, even more directly, it is God's.

NOTES

1. The hymn was taught to me by Harvey Sindima, author of *Community of Life: Foundations for Religious and Political Transformation* (Cambridge University Press, forthcoming). As translated by Sindima, the lyrics are:
Jesu, Jesu
Fill us with your love
Show us how to serve
The neighbors we have from you.
Neighbors are rich people and poor
Neighbors are black people and white
Neighbors are nearby and far away.
This is the way we should love
This is the way we should live
This is the way we should serve the world.
Neighbors are animals and trees
Neighbors are mountains and grass
Neighbors are all creatures on earth.
2. So, for that matter, are the words peace and justice. Here, following Birch

and Cobb, I use the word *peace* to refer to the absence of violence and the absence of the threat of nuclear war. I use the word *justice* to refer to *economic equity* (in which basic needs for food, clothing, shelter, health care, and meaningful employment are availed to all), *political participation* (in which people are allowed to participate in the decisions by which their lives are affected), and *personal liberties* (such as the freedom to dissent, travel freely, adopt a religious or philosophical orientation of one's own) (Birch and Cobb).

3. There is a third reason why I focus on Buddhism. I have some experience with it, having studied and taught it to undergraduate students for ten years, and having practiced Buddhist meditation periodically, most meaningfully under the guidance of a Zen Buddhist master from Japan for whom I served as a language instructor for one year. It is largely by virtue of his influence that I have focused on Zen in my own study and teaching, and that I emphasize Zen in this essay.

4. For information write to the Society for Buddhist-Christian Studies, Graduate Theological Union, 2400 Bridge Road, Berkeley, CA 94709 USA.

5. "In classical Indian thought," so Callicott maintains, "all things are one because all things are phenomenal and ultimately illusory manifestations or expressions of *Brahman*." The experience of nature's unity is "homogeneous and oceanic." In contemporary environmental thinking, by contrast, "no undifferentiated Being mysteriously 'manifests' itself." Rather nature is viewed as "a structured, differentiated whole" in which all things are intimately connected with one another, and in which "the multiplicity of particles and living organisms" is retained (Callicott 1986, 312).

6. Environmental philosophy is a growing subdiscipline within Western philosophy, characterized by the assumption that traditional Western metaphysics and moral theory are inadequate to the solution of environmental problems and that in our age alternative, ecological world views and axiologies are needed.

7. The sense of continuity over time, which is characteristic of much but not all of my experience, is a function of memory. In that present experience, with which I am identical, past experiences are remembered as "who I was" and future experiences are anticipated as "who I will be." But the one doing the remembering is always in the present. After he remembers, he will himself perish, to become part of the "who I was" for successor experiences.

8. From a Buddhist point of view the flow of experience constituting a lifetime is exemplary of the very nature of reality. Reality itself is more like a verb than a noun—a process empty of reifiable being yet full of unreifiable becoming.

9. The phrase *true self* is shorthand for other terms that appear in traditional Zen literature, such as *true person of no status* and *original face*.

10. This is a fundamental weakness of Grace Jantzen's perspective in *God's World, God's Body*. Jantzen's work is philosophically astute in its exploration of the self-body metaphor for God. Yet she argues that "God has complete control over all parts of his body all the time" (Jantzen, 89). In so doing, as she recognizes, the reality of evil remains a serious problem.

WORKS CITED

Ariarajah, S. Wesley. "Religious Plurality and Its Challenge to Christian Theology." *World Faiths Insight* 19 (1988): 2-15.

Bancroft, Anne. *Zen: Direct Pointing to Reality*. New York: Thames and Hudson, 1979.

Birch, Charles. "The Scientific Environmental Crisis: Where the Churches Stand?" *The Ecumenical Review* 40 (1988): 185-93.

Birch, Charles, and John B. Cobb, Jr. *The Liberation of Life: From Cell to Community*. Cambridge: Cambridge University Press, 1981.

Bowker, John. *Animal Sacrifices: Religious Perspectives on the Use of Animals in Science*. Ed. Tom Regan. Philadelphia: Temple University Press, 1986. Introduction.

Callicott, J. Baird. "The Metaphysical Implications of Ecology." *Environmental Ethics* 8, no. 4 (1986): 301-16.

———(a). "Conceptual Resources for Environmental Ethics in Asian Traditions of Thought: A Propaedeutic." *Philosophy East and West* 37, no. 2 (1987): 115-30.

———(b). *Companion to a Sand County Almanac*. Madison: University of Wisconsin Press, 1987.

———. "Marx Meets Muir: Toward a Synthesis of the Progressive Political and Ecological Visions." Co-authored with Frances Moore Lappe. *Tikkun*, 2, no. 4 (1988): 16-21.

Chapple, Christopher. "Noninjury to Animals: Jaina and Buddhist Perspectives." *Animal Sacrifices: Religious Perspectives on the Use of Animals in Science*. Ed. Tom Regan. Philadelphia: Temple University Press, 1986.

Cobb, John B. *Christ in a Pluralistic Age*. Philadelphia: Westminster Press, 1975.

———. *Beyond Dialogue: Toward a Mutual Transformation of Christianity and Buddhism*. Philadelphia: Fortress Press, 1982.

Griffin, David Ray. "Of Minds and Molecules: Postmodern Medicine in a Psychosomatic Universe." In *The Reenchantment of Science: Postmodern Proposals*. New York: State University of New York Press, 1988.

Jantzen, Grace. *God's World, God's Body*. Philadelphia: Westminster Press, 1984.

Kasulis, Thomas. *Zen Action/Zen Person*. Honolulu: The University Press of Hawaii, 1981.

Keller, Katherine. *From a Broken Web: Separation, Sexism, and Self*. Boston: Beacon Press, 1986.

McDaniel, Jay (a). *Of God and Pelicans: A Theology of Reverence for Life*. Louisville: Westminster/John Knox Press, 1989.

———(b). *Earth, Sky, Gods, and Mortals: Developing an Ecological Spirituality*. Mystic, Connecticut: Twenty-Third Publications, 1989.

McFague, Sallie. *Models of God: Theology for a Nuclear Ecological Age*. Philadelphia: Fortress Press, 1987.

Meyers, Norman. *Gaia: An Atlas of Planet Management*. Garden City, New York: Anchor Books, 1984.

Moran, Gabriel. "Dominion over the Earth." *Commonweal*, vol. 114, 21 (1988): 697-701.

Niles, Preman, ed. "Integrity of Creation: An Ecumenical Discussion." *Report from JPIC Consultation at Granvollen, Norway, February 25 to March 3, 1988*. Distributed by World Council of Churches.

Nishitani, Keiji. *Religion and Nothingness*. Trans. Jan Van Bragt. Berkeley: University of California Press, 1982.

Rajotte, Freda. "The Silence of the Churches on the Environmental Crisis." *Church and Society: Report and Background Papers of the Working Group.* Glion, Switzerland: World Council of Churches Press, 1987, pp. 183-93.

Regan, Tom. *The Case for Animal Rights.* Berkeley: University of California Press, 1983.

Santmire, H. Paul. *The Travail of Nature: The Ambiguous Promise of Christian Theology.* Philadelphia: Fortress Press, 1985.

Walker, Susan. *Speaking of Silence: Christians and Buddhists on the Contemplative Way.* New York: Paulist Press, 1987.

PART 5

New Directions
for the Church

Earlier sections of this book have shown that various types of Christian ecological theology are possible, all of which can contribute to a liberation of life.

Clearly, however, such theologies can only be effective if applied by churches and ecclesial organizations.

Besides advancing the possibilities of ecological theologies even further, the following essay offers concrete suggestions for implementation in churches.

Afterword

The Role of Theology of Nature
in the Church

John B. Cobb, Jr.

In general, academic theology spends too much time asking formal questions about the nature and method of theology and too little in actually doing the work of theology. We learn more about what theology is by thinking theologically than by standing back, objectifying it, and asking what it is.

It is more important to think theologically about nature than to ask questions about that enterprise.

Nevertheless, there is also a place for this secondary activity of reflection about what is going on and about what should be going on. This is because the main problem now is not so much a lack of good ideas as the way this whole discussion is viewed by the larger church. There it appears, at best, as a side issue of legitimate interest to specialists, at worst, as a distraction from the truly urgent priorities. The response is not, therefore, serious debate of the alternative doctrines of nature that the discussion embodies but a not altogether benign neglect. I want to understand why this is the case and what can be done in response to it.

Many of the authors in this book propose new ways of imaging human relations to nature, the earth, and nonhuman animals. Some self-consciously propose a new, life-centered theology of nature and a life-centered ethic. What is the role of such a theology of nature in the life of the church? Is it simply a restatement of already existing doctrines of creation? In the following essay John Cobb—who in his own work has been responsible for inspiring many theologians around the world, including several authors in this volume, to develop more ecologically inclusive visions—addresses these questions. Cobb recognizes that the current need in Christianity may not be for still more excellent ideas, but rather for the actual adoption of already-developed ideas by existing church communities. Why has such adoption not yet occurred, and how might it occur? Here Cobb offers his own suggestions.

I understand by *theology* self-conscious Christian reflection about important matters. The suffering of animals is an important matter. The interconnectedness of all the elements making up the biosphere is an important matter. The deterioration of the chemical cycles on which all life depends is an important matter. How best to understand the relationship of human activities to all these features of the natural world is an important matter. And there are many other important matters that can be grouped together under the heading of *the integrity of creation* or *a theology of nature*. But I find an equally important matter to be the church's difficulty in appreciating the importance of these matters. It is this to which I will be directing my attention. I think of this, therefore, not only as the kind of secondary activity I have described above, a thinking *about* theology instead of thinking about the topics with which theology properly deals, but also as itself a theological enterprise.

Theology as I have defined it can never be a *purely* private enterprise. Since reflection is theological only as it is self-consciously Christian, and since to be Christian is to be part of a large historical movement and living community, theological reflection is always in part corporate. Nevertheless, there is an important place for reflection that pioneers new areas of thinking without regard for whether this new thinking will give direction to the wider movement. A major concern of the Christian as Christian is to find truth, and this often leads to sharp divergence from dominant ideas and inherited opinions. On the other hand, there is also an important place for reflection that is geared to expressing the emerging consensus within the church, the sort of reflection that goes into the making of creeds and confessions. Between these there is a place for reflection that seeks ways of influencing the church, guiding its response to changing conditions and situations. This is badly needed now. How can ideas that have arisen at the private pioneering end of the spectrum be brought into fruitful relation to the pre-existing consensus of the church?

Such a question is often, even usually, interpreted in a way that is very far from my intention. The ideas that have been attained, in this case the new reflection about the natural world, are treated as a commodity, and the question is understood to be one of marketing. To market these ideas one turns to experts in communication who identify target audiences and package the ideas so as to reach them.

That, too, may have its place, but my concern is quite different. I am asking theologically about the relation of the ideas that seem now to constitute at least the beginning of a theology of nature to the ideas by which the church is accustomed to living. At present this relationship, or lack of relationship, is an important matter.

To answer this question drives us further back to reflect on what has been going on in Christian theology in recent decades. The theme of this discussion, the theology of nature, is suggestive here. We have had theologies of liberation, of women's experience, of Judaism, of culture, of religion, of the body, of worship, of humor, of play, of work, of institutions, of the church, of the world, and so on, and so on. Now we are adding one of nature. We cannot understand the church's response to a theology of nature apart from this multiplication of "theologies of." What is going on in this new language?

One way of understanding this language would be to suppose that this is simply a new way of speaking of "doctrines of." We could understand a theology of liberation as a doctrine of liberation, namely, as what the church teaches about liberation. Similarly we could understand a theology of women's experience as what the church teaches about women's experience. But to say this is to make immediately evident its inadequacy to what these theologies have been about. A theology of liberation is not asking what the church has said and now should say about liberation. It is arguing that all that the church says about all topics should be rethought from the perspective of the centrality to its mission of the liberation of the oppressed. It is a proposal about how to do *all* theology. A theology of women's experience may not make *quite* so radical a claim. It may call only for the equal validity of a theology expressive of women's experience with the inherited theology expressive of man's experience. But it is likely to ask for a profound rethinking of the latter also. In any case it is something profoundly different from what would be traditionally understood by a doctrine of women's experience. The latter would inevitably have been an interpretation of women's experience from man's point of view!

Some of the other examples could be more easily interpreted as using the term *theology* where once the church would have spoken of doctrine. A theology of institutions hardly exists, but the call for it *may* be only a call for the church to think seriously about institutions. Theologies of play and of the body could be understood as the church's teaching on these topics, although in fact they tend to call for some shift in Christian thinking as a whole based on attention to what can be learned as one takes play or the body seriously.

Those of us interested in a theology of nature need to clarify what we are doing on this spectrum. One possibility is that we are simply using this current language to speak of the importance of the church's developing its doctrine of nature more fully and in ways appropriate to our new understanding of the relation between human beings and the natural world. But most of us, I think, want more than that. We are not trying only to spell out what traditional theology implies about nature. Instead, we want to see the whole of theology influenced and reconceived in light of what we are learning about nature. This makes "the theology of nature" something different from "the doctrine of creation."

But if that is what we want, we need to recognize that we are engaged in claiming a place for an additional "theology of" in a time when the church as a whole is reacting against the multiplication of competing theologies of this sort. We can, of course, dismiss this trend as simply reactionary in the bad sense, and we would have much justification for doing so. Those who do not want to deal with the issues raised by liberationists and women are trying to close the door upon them. Many are simply tired and confused by the endless demands for change and want the church to be an island of confident changelessness in the sea of secular confusion. For them the old-time religion is the answer. Such reaction must be taken seriously but not normatively.

On the other hand, there are real problems with the multiplication of "theologies of." At least in appearance they are all in conflict with one another. Even if their relation is not strictly conflictual, to whatever extent they are calls to reorganize all theology from a particular perspective, they are necessarily in tension with one another. Some people can live in such tension and find it fruitful, but many find it bewildering, and the church as a whole, even when it has goodwill toward the many claims placed upon it, becomes confused about its mission. The multiplication of "theologies of" has been a valuable stage in the church's thinking, but something more is needed. Unless the vitality and creativity that has been expressed in the "theologies of" make a further breakthrough, the church will revert to the doctrinal approach to theology. It will learn something from what liberationists, women, and others have said, but it will incorporate only what can be assimilated into the mainstream of a relatively unchanged tradition. If that is the church's destiny, it would be better for us to drop talk of a theology of nature and simply reflect together on how we can contribute to the enrichment of the church's doctrine of creation.

I hope, however, that we can do better. If the "theologies of" become "doctrines of," I fear that the church as a whole will not be freed from its basic alliance with the dominant bourgeois class, its patriarchalism, its suspicion of the body, its individualism, or its anthropocentrism. Slightly improved doctrines about the oppressed, about women, about the body, about community, or about the whole of creation will not change the church much. In many, many respects the church will continue to be part of the problem rather than the bearer of good news. Can we envision a more promising scenario?

I think we can. Up until now the major challenge to business as usual and the old-time religion has been from liberation theology. I should, more properly, speak of liberation theologies. I refer to black theology, Latin American liberation theology, Minjung theology, and other theologies emergent in the third world. They do not speak with one voice, but there has been sufficient coherence in their message that they have constituted a shared challenge to established ways of thinking and acting. For a while it seemed that, at least in the ecumenical movement and at leadership levels in a number of churches and denominations, they might carry the day. Now, however, the tide has turned. Liberation theologies remain an important factor in the church scene, but they are being contained by more "moderate" voices. They are being treated as offering to the church one theme alongside other themes to which it needs attend. In short, there is danger that liberation theology will become a doctrine of liberation in a general theology that is not itself liberated.

There is, however, some positive possibility in this changed situation. When the liberation theologies thought that by a united front among themselves they could carry the day, they tended to give short shrift to other "theologies of." They were not very interested in feminism, not very sensitive to Christian anti-Judaism, not much interested in culture or in primal and Eastern religions, not particularly concerned about the repression of the body, and so forth. Certainly they were not much concerned about nature. The tendency was to see most of these "theologies of" as expressing the interests of discontented bourgeois and as irrelevant to the truly pressing problem of liberating the oppressed. But as time passed, and as the unlikelihood of single-handed lasting victory has become apparent, the mood has changed. There is more willingness to listen to other concerns and to take them seriously as legitimate needs rather than to dismiss them as establishment fads. This opens the door to networking and mutual support among the advocates of the "theologies of."

If instead of a babble of competing voices, the advocates of the "theologies of" were heard in the church as making a coherent claim for a shift of direction, of thought and action, the chance for real change would be greatly enhanced. But the obstacles are still enormous. There are real tensions and conflicts among the various "theologies of" as they are now formulated. These generate oppositions that are fed by often unjustified mutual suspicions. Sometimes in retreat people guard their turf all the more intensely, even fanatically. Defenders of one "theology of" do not want to have to deal with the ridicule or anger directed to others; so they make clear their distance from the others. If there is unity underlying the various "theologies of," that is not clear to most of their advocates. What at an earlier stage could be regarded as fruitful tension now appears as destructive fragmentation. Can anything be done to reverse this slide into self-destruction of what has been a redemptive expression of Christian vitality in the past two decades? I believe there are possibilities. I propose two.

My first proposal is inspired by the Theology of the Americas Conferences sponsored by the Maryknoll Fathers in the '70s. Participants noted that there were three vigorous movements of persons determined to speak with their own voice in a church that in the past had not heard them. These movements were among blacks in the United States, among peasants and workers in Latin America, and among women in the United States. They noticed also that there were profound suspicions among them, but they believed that there was a commonality deeper than the differences. They gathered representatives of the three movements. These aired their mutual suspicions honestly and with passion. The Latin Americans were convinced that class differences were primary; the blacks, that the deepest issues were those of race; and the women, that all other problems flowed first and foremost from patriarchy. These divergences did not disappear during the course of the series of conferences. But each group genuinely heard the others. By the end, most of the participants acknowledged that all three issues were important. Real changes occurred within each, and in addition, a recognition of common interests emerged that has, to some degree, withstood the struggles of the ensuing period. At the very least, it is harder to play these groups off against each other than it would have been had the Theology of the Americas Conferences not occurred.

It is obvious that issues of creation or nature did not play much role at the Theology of the Americas Conferences. Indeed, many other issues were neglected that are important to other "theologies of." Hence the emerging solidarity from those conferences left a great deal out, and what was left out has become more obviously important to the church in the subsequent period.

My proposal is that it is now time to bring together representatives of a wider range of "theologies of." Obviously, I am assuming that representatives of the theology of nature would be an important part of such a meeting. I believe the theology of nature has a particular and peculiarly important role to play in bringing out the deeper shared concerns on many (even all) of the "theologies of." I see this special relation in three ways.

First, all of the other "theologies of" are anthropocentric. This statement needs some qualification in that several of them are open to the natural world in ways that our dominant modern tradition has not been. Nevertheless, in all cases the starting point is in the human realm. Discussions among representatives of these traditions, even if individual members occasionally raise questions about anthropocentrism, will not thematize this issue. Representatives of the theology of nature are crucial for setting the discussion of human problems in the wider context.

Second, it is my observation that advocates of the theology of nature are appreciatively open to other "theologies of" in a way that these others are often not open to one another and certainly not to the theology of nature. There is a logic to this difference. The natural world cannot exclude the human world. The reverse is not the case. Indeed, those who have tried to include the natural world within the human world have in fact excluded much of what is most important. They are inevitably suspicious of those who raise these issues that they have excluded. Further, the more inclusive approach opens one to hearing many different voices and special interests, whereas those who begin with particular aspects of the human problem sometimes find the raising of other aspects of the human problems distracting.

By pointing out this greater openness on the part of theologians of nature I do not mean to say that we already include all the others and can do the job by ourselves. This is far from the case. What the "theologies of" have shown again and again is that those most deeply immersed in a situation have insights and understanding that more detached observers can never gain on their own. The study of women by men, even by sympathetic men, would never have gone below the surface of women's experience. What we have learned from women as they explored their own experience could have been learned in no other way. Only those who have immersed themselves passionately in the study of Christian anti-Judaism could have become conscious of how deeply it pervades our tradition and our continuing practice. There is an enormous difference between what white sociologists and social ethicists told us about the black experience and what we learned when blacks forced us to listen to their own voices. Part of what we must most fear in the current reaction against "theologies of" is that the leadership of the church will once again try to speak for all rather than hear the many voices in their own integrity and wisdom. Theologians of nature certainly do not want to fall into that trap!

Third, theologians of nature can provide the context in which voice can be given to parts of creation that have been almost wholly excluded from the Christian discussion. I refer to nonhuman animals. Obviously, we cannot have porpoises or guinea pigs as direct participants. But this does not constitute a decisive obstacle. In the inner theological discussion we have listened to the voices of those Christians who have immersed themselves in the study of Christian anti-Judaism. Of course, we have also had dialogues with Jews as well, and these have been important. But Christians who speak as Christians about what Christian teaching has done to Jews represent Jews in these discussions in their own distinctive and highly effective ways. Animals can similarly be represented by human beings who have devoted themselves to studying how animals suffer at human hands and how Christian teaching has supported and encouraged their torture. This is a voice that no other "theology of" will introduce, and even theologians of nature will fail to do so effectively except as they consciously introduce spokespersons.

Whether a conference or a few conferences would succeed in bringing a new synthesis out of the multiplicity of voices cannot be predicted. It could not happen until a great deal of mutual suspicion and anger had been aired. Perhaps it would all end in mutual recriminations. But I am convinced that in and through the diversity there is a common spirit, a deeper underlying passion—I would call it a passion for life—that could come to expression. I also believe that a common faith in Christ has the potentiality to open us up to one another in such a way that genuine hearing occurs. Hence I am hopeful that should such a strategy be adopted, the results would be positive. If they were, then the emergent theology could compete on a more equal basis with traditional ones, and the insights and convictions now gathered under the heading of a theology of nature could penetrate more deeply into the life of the church.

The second approach I recommend is one that does not require major conferences. It is a move toward formulating a theology informed by the theology of nature but expressing itself in central categories of traditional theology and displaying its relevance to the whole range of Christian issues. This move is implicit in the call for a theocentric theology. Yet the need is to go beyond displaying that theocentric thinking gives a role to the whole of the natural world and articulating what that role is. Probably I can explain what I have in mind better by giving a concrete proposal as an example than by talking about what it would be like. The rest of this section is a probe in that direction.

In discussing the "theologies of" I described a tension between the tendency to particularity and the tendency to make universal claims. It is the acknowledgment of particularity that makes it possible to think of a creative synthesis emerging from their vigorous and honest interactions. But it is also possible to move from any one "theology of" to formulations that make the universal features of the claims more apparent. This has happened especially among Latin American liberation theologians, who have worked out the full gamut of Christian doctrines in a way that can lay claim to being a continuation and transformation of the whole tradition. Something like this can also be done from the side of the theology of nature, and, as I have indicated, I believe this is the most promising starting point in the "theologies of" because, in principle at least, it is the most inclusive. What then is the form that a theology must take in order to be able to lay claim to being Christian theology as such rather than a "theology of"?

Some suppose that in order to be Christian theology as such, a position must be somehow neutral as among all competing voices. This is, of course, absurd. Any student of ideology can show that all Christian theologies in the past have expressed the experience and interests of some Christians rather than others. One of the things we have learned from the "theologies of" is that it is better to be honest and open about this than to pretend to oneself or others that one has found a neutral starting point. This needs to be said especially against the pretensions of academic theology.

Nevertheless, the inevitability of cultural and historical conditioning, if not of class, racial, or gender interest, does not prevent there being a difference between what can claim to be Christian theology as such and a "theology of." A "theology of" can become Christian theology as such only if it takes its starting point in the reaffirmation of what it takes to be central features of the tradition. For Protestants, these will almost necessarily be found in the Bible.

We are hopefully free from the illusion that there can be a "biblical theology" in the sense that all the themes and ideas present in the Bible can be brought to a harmonious unity, which can then be reaffirmed as true Christian theology. Rather, the Bible reflects a historical movement spread over many centuries, facing many different situations, and responding in quite diverse ways. Its unity is much more the unity of a socio-historical movement than of a coherent system of teachings. Different parts of the biblical record take on relevance and importance as the church faces different situations.

Healthy Christian theology is always written in view of the real situation of the time, whether the issues it addresses are social, cultural, or more purely intellectual. In one sense it is always "theology of." But instead of allowing a particular analysis of one contemporary problem to dominate its approach, it can return to its sources, inevitably influenced by present experience, and listen to them again. The difference is one of degree, but that *is* the difference between Christian theology as such and "theologies of." The difference, even if only one of degree, is nevertheless real.

Let me illustrate with my own experience. When I look to the Bible for the purpose of developing a theology of nature, I turn to the early chapters of Genesis, the story of Noah, some of the Psalms, some of Jesus' teachings, John 1, and Romans 8. I then want to see what has been said in subsequent theology about some topics that have usually been peripheral to the discussion. On the other hand, when I think about the theological task as such, I turn directly to many other passages. My question is shaped by my perception that the greatest problem for responding healthily to a wide range of issues, many of which are directly relevant to nature, is now the heritage of the Enlightenment. The Enlightenment fastened upon our minds anthropocentrism, dualism, and individualism. Modern thought has worked out with great consistency the implications of the view that each entity, including each person, is basically a self-contained being related to others only externally. This applies to the relations among human beings, the relations of human beings to the rest of the world, and the relations between God and the world, if these are allowed at all. The relations among the academic disciplines and the whole way we have been conditioned to see the world are also consistent consequences of the teaching of the Enlightenment. I personally have been particularly disturbed by the way this modern vision leads economists (and policy makers) to see the economic enterprise as a self-contained feature of reality such that what happens in the physical world is not relevant to its theory or practice. I am also troubled by the extent to which theology has allowed itself to be defined as one academic discipline among others with its distinctive subject matter and method, related only externally to other disciplines. This has rendered academic theology virtually irrelevant to the pressing needs of our time.

I can see that there are roots of this atomism in the biblical tradition, but I am also convinced that they do not dominate it. Quite the contrary. Hence I want to claim the biblical heritage as a source of authority against what has happened to the modern world, including academic theology and much of the life of the church. I think this is a legitimate theological enterprise in the mainstream of church theology. In carrying out this enterprise all the passages I mentioned above in connection with a theology of nature are relevant, but they do not stand out for me as the most important ones. I turn instead to the apostle Paul. I find in him an ecstatic vision of what philosophically I call internal relations. For Paul the Spirit and Christ are within us and we are in Christ. This mutual immanence is not rhetorical carelessness but central to his articulation of Christian experience. Furthermore, at least those of us who are Christian are members one of another, as well as joint members of the Body of Christ. Although the imagery goes further in Paul than elsewhere in the Bible, it is by no means discontinuous with much that is said throughout. If we ask whether the Bible is better understood by a hermeneutic of external relations alone or by one that allows for internal relations as well, I, for one, have no doubt that the latter answer is correct. I think this could be argued in a hundred ways, but this is not the place for that.

To me it seems that the central image of the mutual immanence of God and the world and even of people in one another is Christ. Hence I prefer Christocentrism to theocentrism. The word *God*, even in Paul, suggests a greater degree of separation or over-againstness. This has been so accented in much of Christian history and modern culture that talk of God is often very alienating. I have certainly not given it up, and I often call myself theocentric. But at least as we speak with one another within the church, I prefer to say Christocentric.

I trust you do not misunderstand me. By Christocentric I do not mean Jesus-centric, although the human-historical Jesus too has a central place. There may be times when one could substitute Jesus for Christ in Paul's language and make sense, but that is by no means always the case. We are not "in" the human historical Jesus in the way we are "in" Christ. We cannot read the later Trinitarian doctrine back into Paul; nevertheless, for us to affirm with Paul that we are in Christ and Christ is in us *is* the affirmation that we are in God and God is in us. There is no objective difference between theocentrism and Christocentrism. I prefer Christocentrism because the rhetoric of the church about Christ has kept the sense of God's incarnate presence in us and in the world in a way that language about God does not insure.

Few after Paul maintained the vivid sense of mutual immanence that pervades his writing. Greek language and habits of mind worked against it. Nevertheless, there were central Christian teachings that simply could not be articulated without it. One was the doctrine of the incarnation. In Antioch that was understood in terms of the divine indwelling in Jesus. But it was in Alexandria that, according to Alfred North Whitehead, the struggle with the central Christian mysteries of Trinity and incarnation led the theologians to the one great metaphysical advance since Plato—the doctrine of the immanence of one entity in another.

The struggle continued in later centuries. The tendency of Catholic theology was to image grace in a way that suggests external relations between God and the recipient. Protestantism in many ways carried individualism further than Catholicism had. Nevertheless, at this point its Biblicism helped. Grace could not be viewed as something external to God and externally added to the human recipient. Grace came to be understood as the living and effective presence of the Holy Spirit in the believer.

Nowhere in Christian history has the understanding of indwelling, of mutual immanence, or of internal relations been understood clearly enough or carried far enough. Even Paul did not generalize it fully. He was so preoccupied with the relation of Christ and the believer that we cannot say whether Christ is in all things or all things are in Christ. For strong affirmation that all things are created and cohere in Christ and that Christ is in all things we must turn to Colossians. Further, I do not know where to find any clear statement that all things are members one of another. Still, in this general vision there is the basis for a powerful Christian protest against the habits of mind that have dominated us since the Enlightenment. If Christians could come to see that we cannot understand the saving work of God within us, the incarnation of God in the world, the presence of the Holy Spirit, or the character of the Christian life apart from a doctrine of mutual indwelling that is irreconcilable with atomistic individualism and all its works, we could have powerful leverage to liberate us from oppressive canalizations of thought and practice.

I hope it is clear that, at least in my own perception, I am not falsifying the central message of the Bible or even exaggerating the importance within it of this motif. I am not searching the Bible to find a message that I can use for purposes that are not really dictated by the Bible. I believe that Christian thought has suffered immensely from its inability to grasp and articulate the depth of mutual indwelling that Paul, and other biblical writers, experienced and affirmed. I believe we see that impoverishment more clearly today because its consequences and their destructiveness are so manifest. I believe it is authentically Christian thinking to single this out for special focus and to imply it in the fresh application of the relations between God and the world, among human beings, and between human beings and other creatures.

One reason for the suspicion against which I am arguing is that I have made no secret of the great influence on me of Whitehead's philosophy. This arouses the suspicion that I am using theology to support philosophical ideas rather than the other way around. But these alternatives do not apply. On the issue of internal relations, so central to his philosophy, Whitehead understood himself to be adopting an insight from Christian theology and generalizing it. I have adopted its generalized form, learning this from Whitehead himself. Certainly this has in turn affected the way I read the Bible. This seems to me a normal and healthy expression of the development of Christian thought.

I describe this personal situation because it points to another of those barriers erected in modern times that I would like to see come down. This is the barrier between theology and philosophy. It is now thought that each has its own proper province and that no confusion should be allowed. The result has been bad for theology and worse for philosophy. Philosophy has withdrawn from the discussion of most important matters. Only at its fringes, where a few brave souls talk about environmental issues or animal rights, does it enter the public arena. Theology, on the other hand, has truncated its capacity to deal with those important issues it does raise by giving the appearance of authoritarianism or special pleading rather than participating from its own resources in free and open discussion. Neither contributes much to the human need for an inclusive vision within which to understand the many divergent strands of life and thought.

This whole approach of reifying separate disciplines that are then allowed to impinge on each other only externally is but one expression of the atomism from which Christian faith should set us free. When we think self-consciously as Christians we should be free to think as clearly and as vigorously, as openly and as honestly, as it is humanly possible to think. Whether our help comes from those who are called scientists, or those who are called philosophers, or those who are called Hindus, is a quite secondary consideration. It is as important to liberate theology to pursue saving truth wherever it can be found as to liberate particular groups of people from oppression.

If a vision of this sort becomes central to Christian theology as such, then there will be no further need for a theology of nature. It will suffice to have a doctrine of creation. A theology of nature is needed when the guiding images at the center of theology as such are not informed by what needs to be learned in reflection on nature. If the theology of nature has informed the center, it can then allow itself to be shaped by that center as a doctrine that flows from that center. If, for example, our reflection on other animals takes place in the context of the conviction that Christ is in them and they are in Christ, that we and they are members one of the other, and that together we build up the body of Christ, it would no longer be possible to turn our backs upon their suffering with indifference. It is, to repeat, because current formulations of Christian theology in general do not picture our relations to animals in any such way that we need the corrective of a theology of nature.

The question would remain whether a Christocentric theology of this sort could render unnecessary the other "theologies of." The answer, I think, is yes and no. No, in that no general formulation would take the place of hearing the special insights that come from those who suffer in varied ways and who are pressed by suffering to reexamine much that others take for granted. Yes, in that such a theology would affirm precisely the need of each to hear the other and to be transformed through what one hears. That process of transformation would affect the center as well. The meaning of "Christ" cannot remain the same after the impact of black theology or of the recognition of how often and how easily Christocentrism has been used to evoke and justify the persecution of the Jews. But such a center would provide a way of hearing the many voices in which their tendency to exclude one another would be overcome and they could be more fully incorporated into the ongoing creation and transformation of theology as such.

Appendix

Liberating Life: A Report to the World Council of Churches

INTRODUCTION: THE HISTORICAL CONTEXT

The theme of the 1991 General Assembly at Canberra is "Come Holy Spirit, Renew the Whole Creation." There are many ways in which creation needs renewal. It needs renewal from the debilitating poverty, repression, and violence under which hundreds of millions of people now suffer. It needs renewal from the shrinking of its forests, the loss of its topsoil, the pollution of its atmosphere, and the contamination of its waters. It needs renewal from the abuse of individual animals in factory farms and scientific

This report was produced at a consultation sponsored by the World Council of Churches held at Annecy, France, in September 1988. Fourteen theologians attended, representing different theological traditions and coming from different parts of the world. As is apparent from the introduction to the report, liberation theologies and non-Western theologies played a prominent role in discussion. All participants, including those from North America and Europe, came to realize that the theme of liberation can itself be a promising stimulus toward modes of Christian thought that free people, the earth, and other creatures from various forms of exploitations.

The report was composed by the participants after their papers, written for the consultation, had themselves been discussed. Some of the papers in this volume (Birch, Cobb, Daly, Haught, McDaniel, McFague, Noh, Regan) were presented originally at the consultation and subsequently modified for this anthology. Others were written independently of the consultation and do not necessarily agree with the conclusions of the Annecy report.

The Annecy report is not an official report *of* the World Council of Churches. Rather it is a report *to* the World Council of Churches *by* people brought together by the World Council for the purpose of deliberating upon the integrity of creation. The members of the consultation felt that the report should not be altered in any significant way before being considered before the appropriate bodies of the World Council (except by Charles Birch and Jay McDaniel for this volume). Charles Birch and Jay McDaniel have added a few additional paragraphs and sentences to the original as originally submitted to the World Council, though for the most part the report is precisely as produced at Annecy. The additional material is bracketed.[1]

laboratories. It needs renewal from war and the threat of nuclear war. This renewal depends on us as empowered by God, the Holy Spirit, who works in and through the whole creation.

Indeed, life, in all its forms, cries out for liberation, for freedom. People across the earth are fighting for liberation from the pain of oppression due to poverty, gender, race, handicapping conditions, and many other causes. Liberation needs to be extended to animals, plants, and to the very earth itself, which sustains all life. Thus "the liberation of life," which is the theme for this report, extends the worldwide plea for peace and justice to all creatures, whom we humans need in order to exist, but of equal importance, who are valuable in and for themselves and to God.

Exploitation of People and Destruction of Other Forms of Life Are Inseparable.

Consider South Africa. In 1988 the Afrikaner minority celebrated the 150th anniversary of the white man's "trek" into "the North," which was described in the Piet Relief Manifesto as "a beautiful country teeming with game" of every kind. In fact it was a beautiful country, where grass grew as tall as humans and silver streams cascaded down to the oceans on either side. In spite of internecine conflict, humans lived together in community with nature, and children innocently played with crystals later identified as precious diamonds. The indigenous people felt the presence of what they called *Modimo*, the Source and Presence of life, which penetrates through plants, humans and other animals, dark caverns and tall mountains. With "industrialization" and "development" this land has now been divided and fenced into farms, and its surface scarred and scratched to make a few people rich and powerful. It has been disemboweled at points and left agape in a quest for minerals, coal, gold, diamonds, and uranium for nuclear power. For sport alone, animals are hunted as trophies and some species have been rendered extinct. In less than two centuries a land of pristine splendor has become a repository of human heartlessness, a victim of "progress" and "civilization." As if this were not enough, this relentless onslaught has spilled over to human beings themselves. By means of Land Acts, native reserves were created and then developed into tribal homelands, human movement restricted by influx control, homes and family life disrupted to serve the interests of industry and commerce.

Or consider Korea. For four thousand years the Korean peninsula and the island just south of it, Cheju, had been a homogenous community of people united with the land. People spoke of their home as "the land of morning calm." In 1910 the Japanese colonized Korea, after which Korean women were recruited into the military, then forced to be prostitutes. Over two hundred thousand women died of sexual abuse. Then, immediately after the liberation from Japanese rule in 1945, the United States and the Soviet Union divided the peninsula. The Korean people were not consulted.

Family members were separated against their will, and eighty thousand of the three hundred thousand Cheju islanders who protested the division of the peninsula were killed by Korean soldiers under the Far East command of the United States. Most of the victims were male. Now the island is famous for three things, strong winds, volcanic rocks, and its many women. Indeed, Cheju has become a center of international sex tourism. There are houses of prostitution with three to five hundred women in each. Meanwhile, polluting industries have been exported to the southern parts of the peninsula. Not only the land, air, and water have been harmed. Not long ago tens of thousands of people mourned the death of a fifteen-year-old boy who died of toxic poisoning as a result of working for only six months in a mercury-producing factory. A once united land has become a land of violence, division, and exploitation.

In each of these and myriad other situations, integral communities of people, animals, plants, and land have been neglected and destroyed. [This is not to say that the communities existed in a state of perfection prior to the arrival of foreign powers. They did not. As with all communities, they were mixtures of good and evil. It is to say, however, that the good they had achieved—in terms of satisfying relations between humans, between humans and other animals, and between humans and the earth—has been dramatically disrupted by the arrival of foreign powers, bringing with them science, technology, and nonindigenous concepts of "development."

Increasingly we realize that "development" promoted by advances in science and technology has been a two-edged sword. It has freed human life from much superstition and has opened a Pandora's box of goods and services to enrich life. But with these obvious benefits have come setbacks and destruction. With every passing day the potential of science and technology for bringing swift and widespread benefits to humanity is matched by its potential for ever swifter and more widespread damage and destruction to life and the environment.]

In many cases in the past the foreign powers offering "development" came from the West. They were accompanied by inadequate Christian perspectives—what Korean Minjung theologians call "division theologies"—which themselves become a source of community disintegration. The disintegration of these communities as a result of this assault by foreign powers, sometimes with the collaboration of indigenous elites, has had tragic consequences.

What characterizes a "division theology"? In its neglect and disdain for living communities, it has at least two features. The first is an arrogant approach to nature. The land and its creatures are objectified as mere tools for human use. The value of plants, animals, and land in their own right—as expressions of the Source and dynamic Presence of life itself, called *Modimo* by some Africans, and *Hanulnim* in Korea—is forgotten. Moreover, those who see nonhuman life in this way also often see human life in a similar manner. People become objects. The second feature of "division theology" is that it is male-centered. This way of thinking subordinates nature to human exploitation, the poor and destitute to the privileged and powerful, and women to control by men.

In response to the massive destruction of all forms of life, a theology that serves the liberation of life is needed. Such a theology must offer a view of creation that moves beyond arrogant anthropocentrism and promotes respect for communities of life in their diversity and connectedness to God. Moreover, the needed theology should welcome contributions from many voices, from those who have been heard, and especially from those who have not. Finally, and perhaps paradoxically, this new theological vision must promise to liberate those who, often unwittingly, are parties to oppression. Just as it liberates the victimized, humans and other living beings, a theology for the liberation of life can liberate people of privilege and power from their complacency and isolation. A theology that so serves the liberation of life is a theology of justice, peace, and respect for the integrity of creation.

A THEOLOGY FOR THE LIBERATION OF LIFE

As just said, the current destruction of living communities demands conversion to new thinking and commitment, a theology for the liberation of life. Informed by the biblical witness, the insights of science, and our experience of the interdependence of life, this theology needs to address the brokenness of our world and its intricate web of life with a new statement of the healing words of Christian faith.

The Biblical Witness

Christian visions of the world and of salvation are profoundly shaped by the biblical story of creation. For many generations in the West, this story was read primarily in human-centered terms; human beings were created in the image of God, commanded to be fruitful and multiply, given dominion over the rest of creation, only to disobey God and fall. This one-sided interpretation led to reading the remainder of the Bible as the story of human salvation alone. It also supported exploitative attitudes and practices in relation to the remainder of creation and the destruction of the habitat of many species.

As the disastrous consequences of this exploitation, both for the rest of creation and for humanity as a whole, have become manifest, Christians have reread the creation story. We have found that it locates the story of humanity in a much wider context, as a cosmic one. Before and apart from the creation of human beings, God sees that the animals are good. When humanity is added creation as a whole is very good. The command to human beings to be fruitful and to multiply does not nullify the identical command to animals. The image of God with its associated dominion is not for exploitation of animals but for responsible care. The plants that are good in themselves are given to both animals and human beings for their food. This is the integrity of creation in its ideal form.

According to the biblical stories, human sin disrupts this integral creation. As a consequence, there emerges competition and war between farmers and pastoralists. Injustice and strife proceed so far that God repents having created the world. Nevertheless, God saves the Noah family from the deluge, and at God's command this human family exercises its rightful dominion in saving all animal species from a watery death. When the waters recede God makes a covenant with the animals. From this vision of creation and human sin there follows a longing for inclusive salvation. The whole creation praises God, but this whole creation also groans in travail. As human sin has caused the subjection of all creation to futility, so the liberation of all life can come about only through the liberation of humanity from its bondage to Mammon.

The ideas expressed in the creation and Noah stories and the consequent vision of universal salvation have profound relevance today. All creatures have value in themselves as well as for one another and for God. Each, therefore, claims respect from human beings. The whole creation in all its rich complexity has a special value that is diminished when forests are turned into grasslands and grasslands are turned into deserts. The Noah story highlights God's concern for the preservation of species.

From these stories we acquire a distinctive understanding of "the integrity of creation." *The value of all creatures in and for themselves, for one another, and for God, and their interconnectedness in a diverse whole that has unique value for God, together constitute the integrity of creation.*

As human beings who participate in this creation we have a unique responsibility to respect its integrity, but in fact we have violated it in many ways. Indeed, our violence against one another and against the rest of creation threatens the continuation of life on the planet. It is now our opportunity and our duty, by God's grace, to be restored to peace and justice both in our relations to one another and in our relations with the rest of creation. As long as human beings order their lives to short-sighted economic gain or increased wealth, there will be no end to violence, oppression, or to the exploitation of the other creatures. Only a society ordered to the regeneration of the earth will attain peace and justice. Only in such a world is the integrity of creation respected and achieved.

Within the message of Jesus we find a profound deepening of the importance of our treatment of one another and especially of the weak and oppressed. "Truly, I say to you as you did it to one of the least of these my brothers and sisters, you did it to me" (Mt 25:40). Primarily this refers to our treatment of human beings, but on the lips of the Jesus who speaks of God's care for the grass of the field and the fallen sparrow, these too are included among "the least of these." In the hunger of millions of children, in the loneliness and humiliation of the homeless, in the wretchedness of the raped, in the suffering of the tortured, and also in the pain of myriads of animals used for human gain without regard to their own worth, Christ is crucified anew (Eph 1:10).

The Contributions of Science

The contributions of the sciences are also an essential part of a theology for the liberation of life. When they avoid the assumptions of scientism and materialism, they open up the mystery of the cosmos in a most impressive way. Indeed, while in one sense science diminishes the area of the unknown, in another sense it leads us deeper into incomprehensible mystery. Recent discoveries in physics, biology, and other sciences tell us the story of an evolving universe that needs to be put side by side with our religious narrative. According to recent astrophysics, the universe originated in an event known as the Big Bang. During the first few moments of our world's infancy its fundamental pre-atomic physical features acquired numerical values that would eventually allow for the origin and evolution of living, sentient, and thinking beings. The stellar production of elements that make up cells and organisms required a universe of sufficient breadth and temporal duration to make life possible. The specific physical properties, the immense size, and the age of the universe are intimately related to the existence of life.

The biological theory of evolution with its ingredients of chance and struggle for existence requires a deeper understanding of divine power. God is not a magician but one who lovingly invites the created world to participate in the unfolding of the cosmic story. Evolutionary thinking compels us to acknowledge more explicitly than ever before the continuity of the whole network of life with the universe as such. The evolutionary cosmic epic contributes to a deeper understanding of the universe as our origin and our home. We are made of the same stuff as the stars. Our existence is deeply embedded in the existence of the universe itself.

Of course, there are senses in which human life is unique. Our unique qualities lie, not in an ontological discontinuity between us and the rest of nature, but rather in the remarkable degrees to which we can realize certain evolutionary capacities. We humans are unique in the range of our sensibilities, in our degree of freedom, in our capacities to understand the world, and in our control of the world through cultural evolution. These capacities are themselves developments out of, rather than apart from, the evolutionary process.

As these remarks concerning evolution suggest, an ongoing dialogue between science and theology is indispensable for addressing environmental issues. Such a conversation will help science to understand its task in the service of the whole creation. And it will also enable theology to remain in contact with the real world and thus be faithful to the earth. The world of the sciences, including the social sciences, is of special significance for demonstrating the intricate interrelatedness and interdependence of the biosphere, human community, and the cosmic totality. Without constant attention to the latest developments in the sciences, Christian theology will become irrelevant to those who strive to preserve peace, justice, and the integrity of creation. For theology to do less than come to terms with our present scientific understanding, for it to accept outmoded assumptions about reality from a different time, seems blatantly wrong-headed, even allowing for the qualification that science is an evolving and fallible enterprise.

Imaging the New Sensibility

A contemporary reading of Scripture suggests an interrelatedness of all creatures within the earth and with God. Likewise, the story of the universe emerging from the sciences indicates that all that exists is part of everything else. How should Christians image this sensibility when speaking of God and of world? Whenever human beings attempt to speak about God, we do so in the language of our own time, our various cultures, and from familiar and important relationships. In biblical times, this language was of God as king and lord, but also of God as creator, father, mother, healer, and liberator. As we think about the way to express the relationship of God to the world in our time, we realize that metaphors such as king and lord limit God's activity to the human sphere; moreover, these metaphors suggest that God is external to the world and distant from it.

The creation narrative of our time, the awesome story of the beginning of the universe some ten billion years ago, evolving into our incredibly complex and intricate cosmos in which "everything that is" is interrelated, suggests the need for different symbolic language. Instead of a king relating to his realm, we picture God as the creator who "bodies forth" all that is, who creates not as a potter or an artist does, but more as a mother. That is to say, the universe, including our earth and all its creatures and plants, "lives and moves and has its being" in God (cf. Acts 17:28), though God is beyond and more than the universe. Organic images seem most appropriate for expressing both the immanence of God in and to the entire creation as well as God's transcendence of it. In the light of the incarnation, the whole universe appears to us as God's "body." Just as we transcend our bodies, so also the divine spirit transcends the body of the universe. And, just as we are affected by what happens to our body, so also God is affected by what happens in the world. The sufferings and joys of people and other creatures are shared by God.

When we express the relationship between God and the world (or universe) in organic images, several things become clearer. First, all of us, humans and other living creatures, live together within this body—we are part of each other and can in no way exist separately. Second, unlike the king-realm image which is hierarchical and dualistic and encourages human beings to adopt similar postures toward other members of their own species as well as toward other species, the organic symbolism underscores the inherent worth of all the different parts of the body, different species as well as individuals within those species. Third, while the body metaphor has been used since the time of Paul to express Christ, the Church (1 Corinthians 12:12-26), extending it to the cosmos (we are all members of the body of God, the universe) places us in intimate relations with all our fellow human beings as well as with all other forms of life. We not only empathize with all who are oppressed and suffer—victims of war and injustice, both humans and other living creatures—but we also feel responsibility for helping to bring about peace and justice to the suffering members of God's "body." God's glory and God's closeness are expressed in this image. We stand in awe of the One upon whom this universe depends, whether we view it through a telescope in which its vastness enthralls and terrifies us or through a microscope in which the intricate patterns of the veins of a leaf amaze us. And at a molecular level of life, the complex and beautiful structure of the DNA molecule that can exist in an indefinite variety of forms gives us a sense of awe and wonder. We also, each of us, are part of this universe, this body, in which God is present to us. We feel God's presence here in our world as we touch one another, love and serve one another, that is, all the others that make up the fabric of existence.

Our scripture speaks of the cosmic Christ (Colossians 1), the presence of God in the cosmos, God's embodiment, God's "incarnation." In this image of divine embodiment, we have a helpful way of talking about creation that is biblical, consonant with contemporary science, and experientially illuminating. The universe, everything that is, each and every living thing and the ecosystem that supports all things, is bound together, intrinsically and inextricably, with its creator. Within this bond, the oppression of life is common history, the liberation of life is our common responsibility and our common hope.

AN ETHIC FOR THE LIBERATION OF LIFE

An ethic for the liberation of life calls for seeing the whole of creation in its integrity and therefore demands respect of every creature. Human respect for fellow creatures properly emphasizes individual members of the human community itself. Peace among nations and justice both within and between them are crucial. But this human community is part of a larger community of creatures whose health is essential for the well-being of human beings. An ethic for the liberation of life involves concern for this larger community not only because of its importance to human beings but also for the sake of its other members.

An ethic for the liberation of life would involve treating all of these topics in detail. Fortunately, the issues of peace and justice have been treated throughout the history of the World Council of Churches and vigorous discussion is continuing. Accordingly, section 1 is a brief statement pointing toward this larger discussion. Section 2 is a slightly longer statement building on earlier discussions of a sustainable society. Section 3 notes very briefly the special importance of drastically reducing the extinction of species caused by human actions. These three sections are not unrelated. When any of these levels of the discussion is pressed, the others appear. Although reflection about peace and justice begins with human relations, relations with other creatures are extricably involved. The health of the ecosystem is essential for animals and human beings alike, and violence against ecosystems involves the oppression of human beings and the decimation of species. The need to preserve species is for the sake of the creatures themselves and at the same time for the sake of human purposes.

Section 4 is somewhat different. It does not discuss the benefit to human beings of right treatment of animals. Indeed, it implies that even when respect for animals does not coincide with human benefit it is still required of Christians. Perhaps it is partly for this reason that this topic has been ignored by the World Council of Churches and by most of its member churches up to now. To bring this neglect to focused attention, this section is more extensive. It rejects anthropocentrism by affirming the integrity of creation with peculiar vividness. The themes that unite this fourth section to the others are two: first, that the integrity of creation requires human beings to abandon domination and exploitation as a style of relating both to one another and to the rest of creation, and, second, that respect for the integrity of creation calls upon us to expand our conviviality, that we live with other creatures in peace and justice.

Peace and Justice

Much of the discussion of peace and justice has dealt with their interrelatedness: There is no peace without justice, no justice without peace. This means that the mere absence of war between the superpowers, essential as that is, is not peace, and that an egalitarianism enforced by violence is not justice. An ethic for the liberation of life expands on these familiar ideas. For there is no true peace when the wider community of life is violated, and there is no justice when its animal members are not respected.

The quest for peace between nations aims to end the enormous expenditures and preparations especially for war by the superpowers and their allies. These expenditures not only add to the threat of military destruction but also rob the earth of resources that could be used to meet pressing human needs and contribute to global pollution. In the United States the endless preparation for war gives grossly unjust power to the military-industrial-university complex. Even unaligned nations are drawn into arms races that distort their economies. The emphasis on arms often leads to military dominance of their governments and the oppression of their people.

Respect for the Integrity of the Ecological Community

The integrity of the ecological community is threatened when plants and animals are used exclusively as objects without due consideration for the long-term sustainability of the ecological community.

With the exception of minerals and petro-chemical products, modern civilization depends entirely upon products from four ecological systems: croplands, pastures, forests, and fisheries. Yet in most if not all countries today, each of these ecological systems shows symptoms of being over-stressed. In the case of forests and fisheries, the stress is so great that global production itself is declining.

Below are some selected examples of ecological communities that are under threat. They are a few of any number of examples that might be chosen. In each of these examples ecological communities are used for food and other products. There is a conflict between the present self-interest of some people, the present public interests of many people, the interests of posterity, and the interests, present and future, of nonhuman nature itself. No one of these interests can become dominant without another suffering.

[The conception of the sustainable community is one that is helpful here. It envisions a management of ecological communities such that they continue to exist indefinitely into the future. This does not necessarily mean that they persist without change, but that such changes as do occur are within the limits that permit sustainability of the community as a whole. The sorts of changes in the Sahel regions of Africa in the last decade, for example, were such as to result in desertification and irreversible destruction of the ecological community that had persisted for numerous biological generations. These sorts of changes are unsustainable; what is needed are modes of human interaction with the rest of nature that are sustainable.]

Modern Agriculture — Croplands and Grasslands. Agricultural practices over the millennia have often proved unsustainable. Whole civilizations have collapsed when they exhausted the soils that supported them. Half the land that was available when farming began is now unstable. The pace at which desertification proceeds has greatly accelerated with capital-intensive agriculture in the past fifty years as much sustainable family farming has been replaced by corporate agriculture. This has driven millions of people off the land and into urban slums especially in the United States and in many third world countries. The laborers who replace the family farmers often suffer from the chemicals that also cause the soil to deteriorate. Nations formerly capable of feeding themselves are now dependent upon imported food. For example, in parts of Brazil, mono-cultures of sugar cane have replaced the staple crops of rice and beans that formerly contributed to a staple diet.

One major cause of the unsustainability of modern agriculture, which is chemically intensive, energy intensive and mono-cultural, is the deterioration of soil structures. This in turn is caused by the intensive use of chemical fertilizers and pesticides, which deplete the soil of microorganisms that normally maintain soil structure. Another cause is rising water tables in irrigation areas with consequent salination of the soil. When the plants no longer cover the soil from these and other causes, wind often blows away much of the top soil. The violence of much industrialized agriculture to the life-support system is at the same time violence against the poor. It violates the integrity of creation.

Forestry. Tropical rain forests are now disappearing at the rate of one football field every second, mostly in Latin America and South East Asia. These forests sustain the greatest diversity of plants and animals known in any terrestrial habitat. The destruction of habitats is the main cause of extinction on earth today. Hence the destruction of rain forests is the main cause of the extinction of species in our own time. When the forests are cleared, soil erosion sets in and in many places the soil becomes useless. In other places attempts are made to replace the forest with farms, often with disastrous results. The chances of the forests returning are remote. So when the rain forest is gone, it is gone forever. The tragedy of the ecological community is paralleled time and time again by human tragedy. This is particularly so when the forests have been the home and livelihood of indigenous peoples. As in unsustainable agriculture, we find unsustainability of the ecological community due to human interference by one group of people leads to misery and tragedy for others.

Marine Communities. Much could be said about disrespect for the integrity of marine communities. A few examples will have to suffice. The major oceanic fisheries around the world have declining yields (for example, the anchovy fisheries off the coast of Peru and a number of fisheries in the North Atlantic). Two main causes of these declines seem to be over-fishing and pollution. In both cases we have good guidelines for preventing such interferences with the natural communities so that they may be sustained. But the implementation of such practices seem to be exceedingly difficult. Very often the people who suffer most are the poor who are dependent upon such fish as they can catch or buy cheaply. The greed and mismanagement of the few leads to the suffering of the many.

The recent deaths of seals in the North Sea and Baltic Sea illustrate a trail of interconnections that lead to ecological disaster. It seems that toxic wastes in the sea, resulting from industrial pollution, may cause an immune deficiency in the seals. This renders them susceptible to a virus or viruses to which they are normally immune. In a healthy environment seals do not succumb to such viruses. A greater respect for the health of their environment might well have avoided the death of the seals.

Experience tells us that if we look after nature, nature looks after us. That is a prudential reason for not turning ecologically sustainable communities into unsustainable ones. But an ethic for the liberation of life goes only part of the way if it ends there. It should be extended to the well-being of individual organisms. This is the subject of section 4.

The Maintenance of Biological Diversity

Throughout the history of life numerous species have become extinct. Human activity from early times has increased the rate of extinction. With the vast growth of human population and economic activity in this century the rate of extinction has accelerated.

There are many reasons to be concerned. Much of potential value to human beings is lost. Innumerable creatures that should be respected are being destroyed instead. The rich diversity of plant and animal life which, according to Genesis, God saw to be, in community with human beings, "very good," is being simplified. The life of God is impoverished.

Although attention is often focused on efforts to protect some endangered species, such as the California condor, by quite artificial means, the major cause of extinction is destruction of habitat. In general, habitat has been wilderness, and the human pressure on wilderness has greatly reduced it on every continent. The lessening of this pressure is a matter of moral urgency. Instead of viewing wilderness as empty or undeveloped, we must learn to see it as full of life, often far richer and more diverse than what we call "occupied" or "developed" land. Wilderness is usually able to sustain a vast diversity of life for tens of thousands of years, whereas "development" often leads to great reduction of this diversity and sometimes to the inability to sustain even that for extended periods. The attitude of conquest should give way to reverence toward the integrity of these parts of creation.

Respect for Individual Animals

The biblical and theological messages about the value of animals speak with one voice: Animals do not exist for the sake of the unbridled pursuit of human avarice and greed. And yet the increasingly powerful transnational corporations prefer that people not know, or not care, about the pain and death literally billions of animals are made to suffer every year in the name of corporate mass-production and consumer over-consumption. Some examples follow.

Cosmetics and Household Products. Many areas of the world have an abundance of toothpastes, colognes, after-shaves, deodorants, perfumes, powders, blushes, detergents, oven and window cleaners, furniture and floor polishes, and other cosmetics and household products. This is well-known. What is not well-known is that these items routinely are tested on animals in a variety of painful ways, including acute eye-irritance tests as well as so-called "lethal dose" tests, in which animals are force-fed a deodorant or floor polish, for example, until a specific number die. When we purchase the products of the major cosmetic and household products' corporations, we support massive animal pain and death—all of which is unnecessary. For there are alternatives. Attractive cosmetics and effective household products that are both safe and economical, that have *not* been tested on animals, already exist and are available, and others would be if enough consumers demanded them.

Fashion. Mass-production and over-consumption encourage ignorance and indifference in the name of fashion. Nowhere is this more evident than in the case of fur products (coats, capes, gloves, and the like). Fur-bearing animals trapped in the wild inevitably suffer slow, agonizing deaths, while those raised on "modern" fur-farms live in unnatural conditions that severely limit their ability to move, groom, form social units, and engage in other patterns of behavior that are natural to their kind. When we purchase the products of commercial furriers, we support massive animal pain and death—all of which is unnecessary. For there are alternatives. Many attractive coats, capes, gloves, and the like, which are not directly linked to the commercial exploitation of animals, already exist and are available, and others would be if enough consumers demanded them.

Food. Increasingly, the family farm is being replaced by national and often multi-national interests, business ventures void of any roots in the land or bonds to the animals they raise. The goal of mass-production is to raise the largest number of animals in the shortest time with the least investment. The "good shepherd" has given way to the corporate factory.

Corporate animal agriculture relies on what are called "close-confinement" or "intensive rearing" methods. The animals are taken off the land and raised permanently indoors. There is no sunlight, no fresh air, often not even room enough to turn around. In many cases six to eight laying hens are packed in a wire-mesh metal cage three-quarters of the size of a page of daily newspaper. For up to five years, many breeding sows are confined to stalls barely larger than their bodies. Veal calves (typically male calves born to dairy herds) routinely are taken from their mothers at birth and raised in permanent isolation. Increasingly even dairy cattle are being taken off the land and raised indoors.

Because of the massive numbers of farm animals raised for slaughter (upwards of 4 billion annually, just in the United States), huge amounts of grains are used as feed. More than 90 percent of the oats, corn, rye, barley, and sorghum crops grown in the United States, for example, are fed to animals, and this use of food is enormously wasteful. Every pound of complete protein produced by beef cattle requires eight to nine pounds of complete vegetable protein, while every pound of complete protein supplied by hogs requires four to five pounds of complete vegetable protein. When more protein is being used to produce less, it is no exaggeration to say that we have a protein production system running in reverse.

On the corporate factory that is today's animal farm, virtually every natural form of behavior is thwarted, from preening and dust bathing in chickens to nursing and gamboling in veal calves. When we purchase the products of corporate factory farming, we support massive animal deprivation and death—all of which is unnecessary. For alternatives exist. People can choose to purchase the products of the remaining small-scale family farms or explore a dietary life-style free from all direct commercial connections with the suffering death of animals.

Entertainment. Many different animals are used for commercial purposes in entertainment. The forms of entertainment include circuses, stage and aquatic shows, rodeos, bullfights, and organized cock and dog fights. In whatever form, the animals are treated as mere means to human ends. Sometimes (as in the case of bull and bronco busting in rodeos) the animals are caused more than incidental pain. Sometimes (in the case of the housing and transportation of circus and other "performing" animals) the animals are subjected to severe and often protracted deprivation. Sometimes (as in the case of animals who perform "tricks" in stage and aquatic shows) the animals are rewarded for their ability to mimic human behavior (for example, by balancing themselves on balls or jumping through hoops). And sometimes (as in the case of bull, cock, and dog fights) some of the animals are killed and all are made to endure acute suffering.

When we patronize these forms of entertainment, we support those commercial interests that reduce the value of animals to the status of the purely instrumental, often at the cost of great pain (and sometimes even death) for the animals themselves—and all of this is unnecessary. For alternatives exist. We do not have to train, exploit, outwit, or outmuscle animals, or to support those who make a profit from doing so, in order to take pleasure in their presence or their beauty. Benign forms of recreation involving animals exist. For some people this may involve photography, scuba, and other forms of ocean diving, or the viewing of any one of the thousands of films about wildlife. For all people this can involve becoming attentive to and appreciative of many forms of animal life that live in community with us, wherever we live.

Education. A traditional rite-of-passage for children and adolescents in the affluent world is compulsory dissection of animals. Those students who resist or refuse for reasons of conscience routinely are ridiculed or punished for their moral sensitivity. Often they stand alone, abandoned even by their parents, ostracized by their peers. And yet this exercise in scholastic coercion is totally unnecessary. For alternatives exist. These include detailed drawings of animal anatomy and physiology, state-of-the art videos of relevant dissections, and even computer programs that enable students to "dissect" a frog, for example, on a screen rather than dissect a once living organism. When we support an educational system that callously punishes young people for being concerned about the integrity and value of animals, we tacitly support not only the unnecessary pain and death of countless numbers of animals but also the moral damage done to our children.

The examples given above are only that: examples. There are many other ways in which people fail to show minimal respect for animals as creatures of God. These include instances of wasteful, needlessly duplicative, and poorly executed scientific use of animals, the "sport" of hunting, and the killing of members of rare and endangered species, such as the African elephant and the black rhino. Like the previous examples, these further ones have a common denominator: A creature having intrinsic value is reduced to one having only instrumental value—as an object of mere scientific curiosity, a trophy, or a source of illegal profit.

The ethic of the liberation of life is a call to Christian action. In particular, how animals are treated is not "someone else's worry," it is a matter of our individual and collective responsibility. Christians are called to act respectfully towards "these, the least of our brothers and sisters." This is not a simple question of kindness, however laudable that virtue is. *It is an issue of strict justice.* In all our dealings with animals, whether direct or indirect, the ethic for the liberation of life requires that *we render unto animals what they are due, as creatures with an independent integrity and value.* Precisely because they cannot speak for themselves or act purposively to free themselves from the shackles of their enslavement, the Christian duty to speak and act for them is the greater, not the lesser.

In facing this new challenge—this challenge to liberate all life, the animals included—Christians should aspire to two ideals:

1. Seek knowledge.
2. Act justly.

The first ideal enjoins us to break the habit of ignorance when it comes to how animals are being treated. It bids us to ferret out truth, to make the invisible visible, to make the obscure clear. The second ideal bids us to make our own life a living expression of justice towards God's creation, to bring peace to our own lives even as we work to bring peace to the world. Indeed, we are unlikely to succeed in doing the latter if we fail in doing the former. There is little hope, that is, that we can change the world if we cannot even change ourselves: in the choice of the cosmetics and household products we use, the clothes we wear, the food we eat, and the entertainment we patronize. The ethic for the liberation of life begins at home.

Much else remains to be considered. Laws and institutions that permit or encourage the oppression of animals need to be identified and changed. The truth about the ways animals are oppressed needs to be made known, beginning in the church itself. Our children need to be sustained in their natural empathy with and compassion for animals, and this means that certain traditional practices in their education, including in particular compulsory dissection, will have to be altered. Clearly, the struggle to liberate life is not for the faint of heart.

Yet just as clearly it is a struggle no thoughtful Christian can avoid. When St. Paul says that "the whole creation has been groaning in travail together until now," he speaks to our time and our circumstances. For the animals have been groaning, though we have heard them not. We hear them now. They cry for justice. We cannot fail to answer.

CONCLUSION

The theme of this report is "the liberation of life." Increasingly during this century Christians have come to understand the gospel, the Good News, in terms of freedom, both freedom *from* oppression and freedom *for* life with God and others. Too often, however, this freedom has been limited to human beings, excluding most other creatures as well as the earth. This freedom *cannot* be so limited because if we destroy other species and the ecosystem, human beings cannot live. This freedom *should not* be so limited because other creatures, both species and individuals, deserve to live in and for themselves and for God. Therefore, we call on Christians as well as other people of good will to work toward the liberation of life, *all* life.

RECOMMENDATIONS

1. There is a real need to bring together persons of diverse emphasis and perspective from Latin American liberation theologies, feminist theologies, black theologies, ecological theologies, Minjung theologies, and African theology, those committed to animal rights, those struggling to free Christianity from its anti-Jewish tendencies and those involved in dialogue with persons of other living faiths.

The aim would be to go beyond the still somewhat fragmentary and divisive works of such thinkers to a consensual theological statement that would not be a specialized theology geared to particular issues, but a fresh statement of the heart of Christian faith for the whole community of believers.

We therefore request JPIC ("Justice, Peace, and Integrity of Creation") to organize such a meeting for the further development of Christian theology that expresses the convictions of persons concerned for justice, peace, and the integrity of creation.

2. We recommend that JPIC and the sub-unit on Church and Society of the World Council of Churches co-sponsor a series of conferences designed to envision in concrete terms what social, economic, agricultural, and industrial structures and practices would make possible ecologically sustainable modes of development and progress which take account of human respect for the integrity of creation, peace, and justice. Such conferences should include persons representing points of view similar to those identified in

recommendation 1. Those willing to think in new categories from such areas as political theory, sociology, anthropology, economics, agriculture, climatology, and oceanography should also be included.

3. We commend the sub-unit on Church and Society for its work in bringing together theologians and scientists for informative and critical dialogue. In the light of our description of the role of the sciences in the theology for the liberation of life, we recommend that these conferences continue.

4. In view of the ecologically unsustainable practices of modern agriculture and forestry we recommend to JPIC that these issues be priorities on the agenda of JPIC.

5. Seminary education is woefully lacking in basic courses in ecology and/ or perspectives in science and religion. It is certainly not necessary for divinity students to have in-depth understanding of scientific procedures. What is imperative is a basic, even minimal, perspective of how contemporary science depicts reality. Many men and women preparing for the ordained ministry hold a Newtonian, individualistic, substantialist view of reality. It is this understanding that they attempt to correlate with Christian faith, resulting in an individualistic, otherworldly theology of salvation. We recommend to the sub-units of Theology and Education of the World Council of Churches that member churches of the WCC counsel their seminaries to require coursework in the contemporary scientific "picture" of reality, a picture that underscores the interdependence and interrelatedness of all reality. Such a view could profoundly influence how church leaders preach and teach in regard to the relationship of human beings to the environment.

6. In view of the widespread maltreatment of animals throughout the world and in view of the intrinsic value of individual animals to themselves and to God we recommend that Church and Society take appropriate steps to: (a) encourage the churches and their members to acquire knowledge about how animals are being treated and in what ways this treatment departs from respect for the intrinsic value to themselves and of animals as creatures of God and how abuses could be minimized through legislation and other means; (b) encourage members of the Christian community to act according to such guidelines as the following:

    i. Avoid cosmetics and household products that have been cruelly tested on animals. Instead, buy cruelty-free items.

    ii. Avoid clothing and other aspects of fashion that have a history of cruelty to animals, products of the fur industry in particular. Instead, purchase clothes that are cruelty-free.

    iii. Avoid meat and animal products that have been produced on factory farms. Instead, purchase meats and animal products from sources where animals have been treated with respect, or abstain from these products altogether.

    iv. Avoid patronizing forms of entertainment that treat animals as mere means to human ends. Instead, seek benign forms of entertainment, ones that nurture a sense of the wonder of God's creation and reawaken that duty of conviviality we can discharge by living respectfully in community with all life, the animals included.

7. We recommend that Church and Society encourage the member churches of the World Council of Churches to involve Christians in environmental causes and to cooperate with organizations which defend ecological communities at regional and parish levels.

8. We recommend that Church and Society sponsor a series of courses for church leaders on the emergent theme of our consultation: the liberation of life. In such courses church leaders from different parts of the world, selected by a subcommittee of the sub-unit in consultation with any additional sponsors, could be introduced to the environmental crises of our time, to problems of animal abuse, and to theological perspectives emerging out of the JPIC process, such as those proposed in this report, which encourage a constructive response to such issues.

A NOTE ON THE REPORT

1. The report has received considerable worldwide attention, not least because it represents one of the strongest statements ever produced by a Christian ecumenical body on respect for animals. While the participation at the Annecy Consultation felt the issue of animal rights is an important topic on which, unfortunately, the church has been all too silent for centuries, they did not feel this the only important issue addressed in the document. Equally important, from the point of view of the participants, is the report's emphasis on linking concerns for ecological sustainability with concerns for social justice; on moving beyond oppressive understandings of God; on recognizing the deleterious effects of exclusively Western understandings of development on the peoples of Asia, Africa, Latin America, and Oceania; on recognizing the importance of science for contemporary Christian thought; and on recognizing biblical resources for affirming what the World Council has called the integrity of creation.

One important feature of the report is that it attempts to offer a biblically rooted, succinct definition of that phrase — *the integrity of creation.* According to the report: *The value of all creatures in and for themselves, for one another, and for God, and their interconnectedness in a diverse whole that has unique value for God, together constitute the integrity of creation.* The participants at Annecy thought that this definition invites Christians to recognize the ultimate inseparability, at least from God's point of view, of concerns for ecological sustainability, social justice, and animal protection. In any case the editors of this book hope that this report will stimulate constituent members of the World Council of Churches, as well as readers in general, to formulate their own positions on these important issues.

Authors

JOHN AUSTIN BAKER has been Bishop of Salisbury in England since 1982. He is Emeritus Fellow of Corpus Christi College (Oxford) and author of *The Foolishness of God* and *The Whole Family of God*. From 1980-82 he was Chair of the Church of England Board of Social Responsibility; and from 1983-86 he was a member of the Standing Commission of Faith and Order of the World Council of Churches.

THOMAS BERRY, cultural historian, scholar, and Passionist priest, is founder and director of the Riverdale Center for Religious Research in New York City. He has taught at the Institute for Asian Studies at Seton Hall University, the Center for Asian Studies at St. John's University, Columbia University, Drew University, and the University of San Diego, and was professor of the history of religions at Fordham University. Influenced by Teilhard de Chardin, Berry is a pioneer in ecological theology. His "Riverdale Papers," obtained through the Riverdale Center, have had a wide impact on many seeking connections between religious self-understanding and the modern evolutionary paradigm. His most recent book in ecological theology, published by Sierra Club, is *Dream of the Earth*.

CHARLES BIRCH is a biologist and graduate of the Universities of Melbourne and Adelaide, Australia. A fellow of the Australian Academy of Science, he is retired Challis Professor of Biology and head of the School of Biological Sciences in the University of Sydney. Among his publications are *Nature and God* and, with John Cobb, *The Liberation of Life: From Cell to Community*.

JOHN B. COBB, JR. is Ingraham Professor of Theology, the School of Theology at Claremont (California) and Director of The Center for Process Studies in Claremont. Among his publications are *Is It Too Late?: A Theology of Ecology*; *Process Theology as Political Theology*; *For the Common Good: Redirecting the Economy Toward Community, the Environment, and a Sustainable Future*; and, with Charles Birch, *The Liberation of Life: From Cell to Community*.

LOIS K. DALY is a recent graduate of Chicago Divinity School who worked with James Gustafson. Her Ph.D. dissertation was on the theologies of Karl Barth and Albert Schweitzer, though her recent interests have developed in the areas of Latin American liberation theologies and feminist theologies. She is assistant professor of religious studies at Siena College (New York) and director of the Reinhold Niebuhr Institute of Religion and Culture. She is particularly interested in extending the claims of feminist theologians that feminist theology is itself an ecological form of North American liberation theology.

WILLIAM EAKIN is editorial consultant for the Marshall T. Steel Center for the Study of Religion and Philosophy. He is coordinator of a Liberation Theology Dialogue Group of the Buddhist-Christian Society. He received M.A. degrees in philosophy from Baylor University and the University of California at Davis, and he was the 1989 president of the Arkansas Philological Association. His publications include the introductory essay for the book *Thomas Reid's Lectures on Natural Theology* and numerous articles and book chapters in epistemology, literature, and spirituality.

WESLEY GRANBERG-MICHAELSON has been the director of the sub-unit on Church and Society of the World Council of Churches since 1989. Prior to that he was president of the New Creation Institute in Missoula, Montana. He is the author of *A Worldly Spirituality: A Call to Care for the Earth* and editor of *Ecology and Life: Accepting Our Environmental Responsibility* and *Tending the Garden: Essays on the Gospel and the Earth*.

PAULOS MAR GREGORIOS is Metropolitan of Delhi of the Indian Orthodox Church and former president of the World Council of Churches. He chaired the World Council Conference on Faith, Science, and the Future (at MIT in 1979) and is the author of several books, including *The Human Presence: An Orthodox View of Nature*, in which he addresses environmental problems from an Orthodox perspective.

JOHN HABGOOD is Archbishop of York of the Anglican Church. Also trained as a chemist, he is the author of numerous articles and several books on relations between religion and science. He is the moderator of the sub-unit on Church and Society of the World Council of Churches, in which context he has contributed considerably to its recent reflections on environmental ethics, AIDS, biotechnology, and nuclear power.

JOHN F. HAUGHT, who received the Ph.D. from Catholic University, is professor of theology at Georgetown University. He has written extensively on religion and science. His books include *The Revelation of God in History*; *What is God?*, *The Cosmic Adventure*, *Nature and Purpose*, and *Religion and Self-Acceptance*.

INGEMAR HEDSTRÖM was born in Silbodal, Sweden. He graduated from the theological seminary in Lidingö, Sweden, in 1971, studied sociology at the University of Stockholm in 1971-72, and received his licentiate in biology, chemistry, and geography at the University of Uppsala, Sweden, in 1981. He received a M.Sc. in natural sciences from Uppsala in 1982, where he studied tropical ecology and entomology. He was ordained as a pastor of the Mission Covenant Church of Sweden in 1972. Since 1983 he has been a member of the investigative team of the Departamento Ecuménico de Investigaciones (DEI) and professor at the School of Biology at the University of Costa Rica. His books include: *Born to be Free: Trafficking in Endangered Species in Costa Rica and Ecuador*; *The Gift of the Poor to the Rich: Nonviolent Struggle in Latin America*; *Will the Swallows Return: The Reintegration of Creation from Latin American Perspective*; and *We Are Part of a Great Balance: The Ecological Crisis in Central America*.

JAY B. McDANIEL is director of the Marshall T. Steel Center for the Study of Religion and Philosophy and associate professor of Religion at Hendrix College (Arkansas). He is on the board of directors of the Meadowcreek Project, Inc., a nonprofit research facility and environmental education organization in Arkansas; and he is the author of *Of God and Pelicans: A Theology of Reverence for Life* and *Earth, Sky, Gods, and Mortals: Developing an Ecological Theology*.

SALLIE McFAGUE is the author of numerous articles and several books, including *Metaphorical Theology* and the recent *Models of God: Theology in an Ecological,*

Nuclear Age. McFague is Carpenter Professor of Theology at Vanderbilt Divinity School in Nashville, Tennessee.

JONG-SUN NOH has taught at Yonsei University, Soonjun University, and Korea Christian Academy in Seoul. He studied at Yonsei University, Harvard Divinity School, Yale Divinity School, and Union Theological Seminary in New York. Among his publications are *Social Ethics and Christianity, First World Theology and Third World Critique*, and *Religion and Just Revolution*.

TOM REGAN is professor of philosophy at North Carolina State University, where he has twice been named Outstanding Teacher and in 1977 was selected Alumni Distinguished Professor. He has written or helped to edit ten books, including *The Case for Animal Rights* and *All that Dwell Therein*.

HARVEY SINDIMA, a Presbyterian minister, was born and raised in Malawi. He graduated from the Church of Central Africa Presbyterian Theological Seminary in Blantyre, Malawi, and did postgraduate work at the University of Edinburgh, Scotland, and at the Interdenominational Theological Center in Atlanta. His Ph.D. in religion and society is from Princeton Theological Seminary. He is author of *Community of Life: Foundations for Religious and Political Transformation* (forthcoming) and *Drums of Freedom: African Theology* (forthcoming).